GETTYSBURG
TO
GREAT SALT LAKE

George R. Maxwell in uniform,
probably shortly after enlistment.
*Photograph courtesy of Maxwell Fisher Turner,
Elizabeth Jane Cunard Carey, and Bruce Turner Cunard II.*

GETTYSBURG TO GREAT SALT LAKE

George R. Maxwell,
Civil War Hero and Federal Marshal
among the Mormons

by
JOHN GARY MAXWELL

John Gary Maxwell (signature)

THE ARTHUR H. CLARK COMPANY

An imprint of the University of Oklahoma Press

Norman, Oklahoma

2010

Library of Congress Cataloging-in-Publication Data
Maxwell, John Gary, 1933–
   Gettysburg to Great Salt Lake : George R. Maxwell, Civil War hero
and federal marshal among the Mormons / by John Gary Maxwell.
      p. cm.
   Includes bibliographical references and index.
   ISBN 978-0-87062-388-2 (hardcover : alk. paper)
   1. Maxwell, George R., 1842–1889. 2. United States marshals—Utah—Biog-
raphy. 3. Frontier and pioneer life—Utah. 4. Mormons—Utah—History—
19th century. 5. United States—History—Civil War, 1861–1865—Biography.
6. Michigan—History—Civil War, 1861–1865—Biography. 7. United
States. Army. Michigan Cavalry Regiment, 1st (1861–1866) 8. Soldiers—
Michigan—Biography. 9. Utah—Biography. I. Title.
   F826.M28M396 2010
   973.7092—dc22
   [B]

2009032946

The paper in this book meets the guidelines for permanence and durability of
the Committee on Production Guidelines for Book Longevity
of the Council on Library Resources, Inc. ∞

1 2 3 4 5 6 7 8 9 10

To Cheryl—

without you,
this would never be

Contents

Acknowledgments 11
Abbreviations 15

Introduction: The Flight of the Eagle 19

Part One. 1842 to 1869

1 Origins of a Hero 31
2 The Thunderbolt of Sheridan 47
3 Return with Your Shield or on It 71

Part Two. 1869 to 1892

4 Turning West amid the Hostiles 87
5 The Disputants in the Theologic War 109
6 Register of Land 117
7 Indispensable Opposition 147
8 Ann Eliza's Next Best Friend 173
9 Devils and Angels 189
10 Mountain Meadows, John Doyle Lee, and Marshal Maxwell 207
11 Marshal Maxwell's Muddle 233
12 Health, Battles, and Tragedy 257
13 A Time of Lengthening Shadows 283
14 Stricken Eagle 307
15 Lance of Iron, Wings of Stone 331

Bibliography 347
Index 369

Illustrations

George R. Maxwell in uniform . . . . . . *frontispiece*

Emma Elizabeth Maxwell 40

Campus Martius Square, Detroit, Michigan 53

Civil War–era patient ward, Armory Square Hospital . . . 78

Drawing of George R. Maxwell after leg amputation . . . 79

Union officers who survived amputations, including Maxwell, 1865 81

Custer Medal replica 84

Emma Belle Turner Maxwell 89

Gen. George R. Maxwell in Utah 127

Mary Ann Sprague Maxwell 185

Judge Boreman, John D. Lee's lawyers, and Marshal Maxwell at Lee's first trial 206

Utah Territorial Penitentiary, circa 1870 237

Matthew B. Burgher 238

Grand Army of the Republic party invitation 295

George R. Maxwell tombstone, Salt Lake City . . . 302

Inscriptions on George R. Maxwell tombstone . . . 302

Custer Medal carving, Gettysburg National Monument . . 303

James H. Kidd 309

Caricature of Brigham Young, Daniel H. Wells, and Hosea Stout 319

Acknowledgments

The amateur is vital.
Paul M. Edwards

NOTHING ACCUMULATED IN FORTY YEARS AS AN ACADEMIC surgeon, instructing young men and women in the science and art of surgery, qualified me to attempt a biographical history. This was a clean jump into a new field, for I did not come to the pleasures of reading and writing history as one experienced, educated in the field, or recognized as a historian. Yet I have been warmly welcomed by many to the collegiality, the earnest community of those men and women who are so educated and recognized. I have much to learn of this discipline, but my nescience allows me certain advantages. It grants me freedom to make my own assessments of the intellectual honesty and integrity brought to the study of this contentious period of Utah and United States history. Trusting friendships have formed from this base.

I am indebted to several historians of western America and Utah Territory. Will Bagley, David L. Bigler, Ardis E. Parshall, William P. MacKinnon, Floyd O'Neil, and Walter Jones have helped in the birth of this work through their constructive review, their encouragement, their honest criticism, and their kind nature. They have welcomed me to the Utah Westerners, the Utah State Historical Society, and the Mormon History Association. They shared insights, led me to references and primary source material, and introduced me to other historians whose memories, skills, and publications have aided me immensely. I am indebted to Ronald O. Barney, senior archivist, LDS Church Archives, Family and Church History Department, and Robert A. Clark of the Arthur H. Clark Company, who were willing to look beyond my inexperience and whose enthusiasm and constructive editorial suggestions have resulted in an improved manuscript. Copy editor Rosemary Wetherold's perspective and skills, applied with patience and meticulous attention to detail, have resulted in an undeniably improved work; I gratefully acknowledge her contributions.

Recognition and thanks for their contributions to the history and background of the Maxwell, Hawley, Heritage, Custer, and Christiancy families in Monroe County, Michigan, must go to Doris Blessing, archivist and secretary of the Genealogical Society of Monroe County; Carl Katafiasz, head of Reference Services at the Ellis Reference and Information Center in Monroe; and Chris Kull of the Monroe County Historical Museum. Rosina Tammany, archivist at the Eastern Michigan University Archives in Ypsilanti, Michigan, provided important information about the Michigan State Normal School and its antebellum students. Frankie Langton and her daughter Scarlet introduced me to the Maxwell family's old homesite and farmland and gave me an original 1837 red brick artifact from the original Reuben Maxwell home, no longer standing, in Ash, Monroe County, Michigan.

The material dealing with the historical details of the Civil War was capably scrutinized and improved by the criticism and advice of Civil War historian John R. Krohn, Jr., MD, a licensed battlefield guide at Gettysburg National Military Park, Gettysburg, Pennsylvania, and Chris Calkins, chief of interpretation at Petersburg National Battlefield, Petersburg, Virginia. Careful editorial criticism and advice were provided by Donald G. Johnson, MD, MA (History), MPH, Department of History, University of North Carolina at Wilmington.

Special thanks are due to Bruce Turner Cunard II, Elizabeth Jane Cunard Carey, Maxwell Fisher Turner, and the extended family who are descendants of Emma Elizabeth Maxwell Turner, the sister of the man who is the subject of this work. Now residing in New England, mostly in Connecticut and Massachusetts, these Turner relatives have provided encouragement by sharing what few original letters and authentic photographs remain. This family, with several ancestors having served in the Revolutionary War, the Civil War, and World War I, continues its record of patriotic military service in the footsteps of the long-gone cavalryman George R. Maxwell.

Friends and the curious ask why, if little prepared for the task, I would attempt to traverse the cactus-spike landscape of a historiography and biography that interdigitates the controversial, intractable dichotomy of the Mormon and non-Mormon conflict in Utah Territory. Why attempt writing of an early non-Mormon hero whose biography, no matter how assiduously the aim of objectivity and honesty is sought, is almost guaranteed to offend one side or both? The knee-jerk reflex response is that the man deserved to be remembered and honored. A more articulate response has been difficult to put to paper. Social scientist and historian Paul M. Edwards has touched on part of the answer: "In history as in no other discipline the amateur is vital. For it is the interest, the love of the past, the willingness to become half lost in the imagination of previous days that is the historian's first tool."[1]

My more complete and most honest answer is that it has enabled me, in a journey from elsewhere, to follow my own god home.[2] It has been a fulfilling release from my own relative ignorance of the bowdlerized history-beneath-the-surface of my own ancestors, on whose shoulders I now stand with a far deeper appreciation of their lives. My exploration of the cultural history of Utah, the South, and the Civil War, and of the racial, religious, ethical, and social conflicts that constitute the core issues of our history, has rekindled and elevated my patriotism and pride in this nation.

---

[1] Edwards, "Irony of Mormon History," 409.
[2] Paraphrased from the poem "A Ritual to Read to Each Other," by William Stafford, cited in Chisholm, *Following the Wrong God Home*, 2003.

Abbreviations

BYC   Brigham Young Collection, LDS Church History
       Library and Archives, Salt Lake City
DN   *Deseret News*
JH   *Journal History of the Church of Jesus Christ of Latter-*
       day Saints
LDS   Latter-day Saints
OR   Robert Nicholson Scott and Henry Martyn Lazelle,
       The War of the Rebellion: A Compilation of the Official
       Records of the Union and Confederate Armies, 4 ser.,
       70 vols. (Washington, D.C.: Government Printing
       Office, 1880–1901)
RG 60 General Records of the Department of Justice,
       Record Group 60, National Archives, Washington,
       D.C.
SLH   *Salt Lake Herald*
SLT   *Salt Lake Tribune*

GETTYSBURG
TO
GREAT SALT LAKE

Introduction: The Flight of the Eagle

So the struck eagle, stretch'd upon the plain,
No more through rolling clouds to soar again,
View'd his own feather on the fatal dart,
And wing'd the shaft that quiver'd in his heart.
  Lord George Gordon Noel Byron

THE YEAR WAS 1875. THE SUN ROSE INTO A CLOUDLESS SKY ON the Sunday morning of the Fourth of July in the small mining town of Alta, Utah Territory. Even in midsummer, the mountains' night chill did not lift until the sun had warmed the gray granite peaks encircling the tight bowl of a small valley at 9,100 feet above sea level.

If any of the silver miners, merchants, saloon keepers, livery men, "soiled doves," or hangers-on harbored any intention of sleeping late on this holiday, it was only because they had forgotten what had become the widely practiced custom of zealous patriots and Civil War veterans. They greeted the sunrise of this special day by making noise, shooting rifles and revolvers. They had no cannons, but dynamite sticks and small kegs of black powder would be at hand in a mining town. Anything that would explode and be noisy would suffice, as the celebrants warmed to the prospect of making July Fourth begin very early and continue far into the night.

The previous day, the special excursion trains chugged uphill, while wagon teams labored the eight miles of Little Cottonwood Canyon, on the final steep and most demanding leg of their twenty-six-mile trek from Salt Lake City on the valley floor. The loads of military men and federal officeholders, and their ladies, together with other non-Mormon citizens of the city, were housed in "pleasant quarters" to which evergreens and flowers had been tastefully added. The Stars and Stripes floated from many housetops on poles erected especially to display them.[1]

The celebration of this national holiday in Utah was unique, different from that in all other states and territories, because here it was divided into two camps based almost solely on religious orientation. With the holiday falling on Sunday, the Mormons would move their recognition of the day to Monday. Even that day would see no public celebration; the Mormons' activities down in the valley would be subdued and restrained, lacking the enthusiasm that would attend their own celebration on July Twenty-fourth, when they honored the arrival of the first Mormon settlers on that date in 1847. The Mormons' newspaper, the *Deseret News*, instructed the Saints, "The coming fourth of July will not be celebrated by any special demonstration in this city, further than making Monday, the 5th a general holiday among all classes. . . . [E]verybody will observe the day in a manner to suit himself . . . in rejuvenating festivities."[2] In contrast, the July Fourth celebration by the "Gentiles," as non-Mormons were labeled in local parlance, generated the same display of citizens' patriotism and national pride that it did in New York or Massachusetts or Michigan.

At noon, white popcorn clouds began forming over the Wasatch mountain range. Echoes from hammer on anvil and from gunpowder explosions again pealed the message of the arrival of the ninety-ninth anniversary of the "day dear to the hearts of all true Americans."[3] Reverend Josiah Welch, of Salt Lake City's only Presbyterian church, began the program with a patriotic prayer that "breathed the spirit of piety and love of country." With sonorous voice, John McDonald read the Declaration of Independence. The parade of 2,500 people through narrow Alta streets went as planned; lawyer Frank Tilford of Salt Lake City was the orator of the day, Judge William Gill Mills of the city of

---

[1] "The Fourth," *Salt Lake Tribune* (hereafter "*SLT*"), July 7, 1875, 4, col. 2.

[2] "General Holiday," *Deseret News* (hereafter "*DN*"), July 2, 1875, 3, col. 2; "The Fourth," 2, col. 2.

[3] "The Fourth," 4, col. 2.

Alta rendered patriotic poems, and then George Washington Bostwick introduced the pending release of the eagle, the "proud bird of the mountain," with "a few generous and appropriate remarks."[4]

Gen. George R. Maxwell, a thirty-two-year-old Civil War veteran, was aided up the steps of the rudely constructed platform built to hold the visiting dignitaries and speakers. His wooden leg was as much an impediment as an aid in the climb. The bald eagle that Maxwell had purchased in Salt Lake City from Dr. C. W. Higgins specifically for this holiday was perched on a pedestal at the side of the lectern, a canvas hood covering its head and the sun glistening on its iridescent brown-black feathers.[5] Maxwell had found the bird languishing in a cage in the Mormon merchant's store, where it had gone unsold for many weeks. No sooner had Maxwell seen the bird than he purchased it, formulating a plan for its display. This would be the day most appropriate to free this symbol of the U.S. government to soar into the sky, high above the people who despised the federal presence among them. No place would be more appropriate to release the eagle than from the boomtown of Alta, after Mormon leaders had worked for years to prevent the establishment of mining within their agrarian-based economy.[6] Maxwell, the U.S. marshal, together with Frederic E. Lockley, editor of the anti-Mormon *Salt Lake Tribune*, organized the details of the plan. From ore taken from Alta's most fecund mine, the Emma, they had jewelers fashion a pure silver amulet that was now attached to the leg of the immense bird. In the metal were carved the words that Maxwell read to the crowd:

> The Salt Lake Tribune Eagle,
> July 4, 1875,
> From the Chain Gang of Zion
> to the Free Air of Alta.[7]

A roll of the drums and the sounding of the bugles led to the moment when Maxwell would release the bird. Hood removed, flung into the

---

[4] Ibid.

[5] "City Jottings," *SLT*, June 25, 1875, 4, col. 2.

[6] The first mining claim in Alta was staked in 1865. By 1872 the town had nearly eight thousand seasonal residents, but by 1875 the population had decreased. The Emma mine became world famous for huge finds of gold, silver, and lead, whose yield from 1871 to 1880 exceeded $13 million. Sadler, "Impact of Mining."

[7] "The American Eagle," *SLT*, July 4, 1875, 4, col. 3; "The Fourth," 4, col. 3.

air, the bird strained to remain aloft, to catch a draft that would propel it upward. But the bird was weak, unable to fly, and fell in a tumble of feathers amid the crowd. Some of the men, embarrassed, stared at their shoes and laughed softly, while several of the women sniffled and dabbed hankies to their now moist eyes. Disappointment reigned over all, for the federal eagle had not conquered: "Long confinement . . . on the chain-gang of Zion had deprived the monarch of the air of the use of its wings."[8]

In retrospect, this incident with the eagle might seem portentous. Wounded in the Civil War, General Maxwell had come to Utah Territory in 1869 with orders to enforce federal law among the Mormons. Twenty years later, his eulogy in the *Salt Lake Tribune* would allude to this episode at Alta as symbolic, describing him as a stricken federal eagle who, as a non-Mormon outsider and physically impaired, had been doubly disadvantaged during his long tenure in Utah.[9]

Maxwell's ancestral roots were in southeastern Michigan and the Finger Lakes area of upstate New York, near Palmyra and Fayette, where coincidentally the Church of Jesus Christ of Latter-day Saints had its origins. This Maxwell family traces back to Revolutionary War soldiers in Massachusetts and, before that, perhaps to New Hampshire. Their earliest lineage is lost among the thousands of undocumented Maxwell men who immigrated to the North American continent from Scotland, Ireland, and England. No male descendants of the line are known to have survived from whom DNA testing could give scientific proof that the subject of this biography and its author are not connected by a common bloodline. Favoritism in interpretation does not become a proper historian, but any lapse by the author toward partiality cannot be attributed to ties of direct kinship.

Very few of Maxwell's personal papers or letters survive. There is no war diary, no family treasure chest, and sparse are the memorabilia of this soldier that attest to details. Most of his life story must be reconstructed

---

[8] "The American Eagle," 4.

[9] Frederic E. Lockley, Sr., also a Civil War veteran, may be the author of the editorial note published in the *Salt Lake Tribune* at Maxwell's death. He was a journalist and editor of Cleveland, Ohio, and Leavenworth, Kansas, newspapers before coming to Utah in 1873. Lockley sat as the editor of the *Salt Lake Tribune* from that time until he sold his interest in the paper in 1880. He subsequently lived in Frisco, Utah; Butte, Montana; Arkansas City, Kansas; and Salem, Oregon. Rankin, "Sweet Delusion"; Charles E. Rankin, "Type and Stereotype: Frederick E. Lockley, Pioneer Journalist," in Ritchie and Hutton, *Frontier and Region*, 72–76.

from other sources, and most of those sources that deal with Utah are unmistakably pro-Mormon or anti-Mormon in bias.

It is known that as a patriotic teenager Maxwell left college and his father's farmland to join the Union forces to fight against slavery and secession. By age twenty-two, he had become a general in one of the Civil War's most renowned groups, the Michigan Cavalry Brigade. He was an authentic American hero, selected for special reward by his role model and flamboyant commander, Brig. Gen. George Armstrong Custer. In the opinion of many, the Michigan Cavalry Brigade was the finest mounted unit of volunteer cavalry to serve the Union during the Civil War. Its men were the first among the Yankees to discredit the idea of the supremacy of the South's mounted troops. They bravely fought the famed cavalry legions of Confederate general James Ewell Brown "J. E. B." Stuart in Virginia, brought them to a standstill in Pennsylvania, and prevented Stuart's men from turning the flank on Union general George Gordon Meade and attacking the rear of his Army of the Potomac in the Battle of Gettysburg on July 3, 1863.[10] It was the Michigan Cavalry that turned the Battle of Five Forks, Virginia, into the "Waterloo of the Confederacy" on April 1, 1865.

Maxwell's courageous battle exploits over the four years of the war won him a reputation as a "Thunderbolt of Sheridan" and the prestigious Custer Medal, reserved for only a small number of the Michigan Brigade's most deserving officers. Wounded for the eighth time at Five Forks, Virginia, in the war's last major battle, he survived to become engaged in the stubbornly fought mismatch in the Territory of Utah.

The decades-long struggle between the Mormons seeking statehood and the non-Mormons opposing statehood for Utah Territory pitted Mormon men, claiming to rule under God's direct instruction, against the forces of the American republic and the people appointed to its service, such as Maxwell. He was twenty-seven years old when President Ulysses Grant, his former commander, appointed him as the Register of Land for Utah Territory in 1869. In 1873 Grant named Maxwell to be the lone U.S. marshal for the territory. Maxwell was never welcomed into the bosom of the majority in Utah. His twenty years there coincided precisely with an extremely contentious era in the history of the Mormon people, as they colonized three hundred settlements in a

[10] Wittenberg and Husby, *Under Custer's Command*, xiii.

mammoth segment of the western American continent, all the while embracing theocracy and polygamy.

It deserves great emphasis that the Mormon experience of the years 1861 to 1865 had been totally different from that of the rest of America. For most Americans, the period was one of consuming struggle, a prolonged earthquake of destruction. Affecting millions, death and sorrow came on an unprecedented scale, touching almost every family, North and South. For Mormons it was a time of separation and disengagement, observing the catastrophic events they believed were shortly to usher in the millennium. With a sense of validation and satisfaction they watched what they considered God's vengeance loosed on America's citizens for the unpardonable sin of having murdered their founding prophet and failing to accept God's one and only restored church. Beyond polygamy, beyond theocracy, beyond a peculiar theology, the unbridgeable obstacle of this unshared war experience prevented understanding and communication and further deepened the estrangement of the Mormon people and the Civil War veterans among them.

Many times wounded, George R. Maxwell came in pain to Utah Territory, with only one leg, one functional arm, one normal hand, and scar-frozen shoulder joints. He did not come to Utah paternalistically leading a family constellation of the zealous converts who were gathering in the western heartland of the Mormons. He came widowed, with none of his family from Michigan. No friends were waiting to greet the train or to welcome him in Salt Lake City. The circumstances and purposes that brought him 1,500 miles from his family ties in Michigan were a puzzle to be investigated and interpreted. He did not seem to belong in Utah, and indeed, as his life proved, he did not.

As early as the 1857–58 Utah War, when the U.S. Army and its camp followers entered the territory, but certainly by the time of the non-Mormon influx following completion of the transcontinental railroad in 1869 until the granting of statehood in 1896, Utah Territory was divided into two unequal camps. It was a place of deeply felt personal conflict, of irreconcilable moral and ethical differences, of rhetoric and bravado. Neither the Mormons nor the non-Mormons gave public evidence of any doubt about the primacy, the rightness, of their respective positions. Diplomatic restraint was uncommon, and compromise nearly nonexistent; courtesy and even civility were often forgotten. Creative insults to individuals, groups, and institutions were elevated by both Mormons and non-Mormons to oratorical and journalistic art forms. The line separating a war of words from open physical violence—whether originating from either side within Utah or from the federal government—was often dangerously thin.

The Church of Jesus Christ of Latter-day Saints—the Mormon church—of Ohio, Missouri, Illinois, and the Utah territorial era was strikingly different from the present-day church. In that early era, the Mormon church had recently restored Truth as an all-embracing ideology; a monarch who answered only to God; a single political party; surveillance, strict rules, and harsh punishments for nonconformists; secret societies and secret agents; a standing army; and a view to world dominion.[11] Unified by years of persecution, the church was a closed, male-dominated, communal society based on an almost exclusively agrarian economy. Polygamy had grown to become a cardinal tenet in its theology and an essential sacrament for men and women to find glory in heaven's highest tiers. Unity of the ecclesiastical and the secular was its Kingdom of God on earth. Preparations were being made for the millennium, which the leadership assured its members was not far distant. A theocratic oligarchy recusant to federal law was its government.

In contrast, most of the men who had been granted federal appointments to Utah by President Ulysses S. Grant, including Maxwell, were non-Mormon veterans of the War of Attempted Secession—known in the Northern states as the War of Rebellion and to Southerners as the War of Northern Aggression. But the conflict in Utah—from 1857 to the time when polygamy was allegedly relinquished in 1890, to statehood in 1896—was not fought with rifle, saber, cannon, or grapeshot. This was a war of belief and words, of man's law against God's law. The battlegrounds were not the lands of the Shenandoah, but as historian David Bigler has explained, "since divine rule encompasses all human institutions, emptying them of purpose, the struggle was waged on all fronts."[12] The fighting took place in the political arena, in courtrooms, in the U.S. Congress, in the pulpits of Utah and those of diverse Protestant

---

[11] Obert Clark Tanner, Utah professor of philosophy and Salt Lake City philanthropist, left this reflection regarding capitalization of the word "Truth": "Now I am quite certain that truth is spelled with a small t, there are many truth possibilities." Tanner, *One Man's Journey*, 135.

[12] Bigler, "Aiken Party Executions," 459.

religious groups in the Northern states. Skirmishes took place in the pages of books and newspapers, on the Chautauqua Circuit, and in the court of popular opinion. It was as uncompromising and relentless a contest as the Civil War had been; this war was fought without quarter, with damage and casualties on both sides, and it too created its own heroes. Its more than fifty years constituted the longest campaign of overt civil disobedience in American history.[13]

Of the sixteen U.S. marshals who served the people of Utah from 1850 to its statehood in 1896, George R. Maxwell was the ninth.[14] Only the first, Joseph Leland Heywood, was a Mormon. He was, more notably, a four-wife polygamist Mormon. Therefore, he was "one of them," accepted, respected, and understood by the people of the territory he served.[15] In contrast, Maxwell and all of the other U.S. marshals to Utah were outsiders, aliens, "Gentiles." To a varying degree, all of the U.S. marshals were at odds with the Mormon people. Fusion of the Mormons' religious and governmental leadership, and the practice of taking multiple wives, both sacred principles and practices to the early Mormons, became anathema to non-Mormon federal officers appointed to live among them while attempting to enact and enforce federal law.

The patriotic credo of the cavalry officer that Maxwell had learned from serving under General Custer and Maj. Gen. Philip Henry Sheridan—that "the post of danger is the post of honor"—sustained him in service to his nation. Though his uncommon Civil War sacrifice was

---

[13] Hardy, *Doing the Works of Abraham*, 13, 392. Mormon civil disobedience over polygamy was alleged, and commonly thought, to have ended in 1890, but it did not. Neither was it ended by the 1904–1907 Senate investigation of polygamy precipitated by the election of Reed Smoot, a monogamous Mormon, as Utah's senator. Secret plural marriages continued to be performed by church leaders at least until 1910. K. Flake, *Politics of American Religious Identity*, 238; Hardy, *Solemn Covenant*, 328–29.

[14] Brown, "United States Marshals," 213. Two local Mormon territorial marshals served their people before the appointments of U.S. marshals began in 1850. John Van Cott was appointed October 1847, and Horace S. Eldredge was appointed marshal of the Great Salt Lake Valley by the High Council of the LDS church on February 24, 1849. Morgan, "The State of Deseret," 69, 77. Non-Mormon Benjamin Franklin Ficklin served briefly as an interim U.S. marshal in 1857–58, during the contentious period of the Utah War. MacKinnon, *At Sword's Point*, 36; MacKinnon, "'Lonely Bones,'" 158.

[15] Even though he was a respected Mormon elder, Heywood experienced the same financial difficulties and severely tangled financial accounts that beset the many non-Mormon U.S. marshals who followed him. He was abruptly dismissed by President Franklin Pierce for brawling with a clerk in Washington, D.C., while attempting to settle his troubles by bribery. MacKinnon, *At Sword's Point*, 56.

not honored in Utah, he nevertheless became an unexpected and unappreciated contributor to Utah's long-delayed statehood. Indeed, the Mormon faithful might find it ironic that Maxwell's criticisms helped indirectly to bring internal change within the structure and practices of the Mormon church. Statehood in 1896—and enhanced acceptance of that religious institution and the Mormon people, far beyond their early regional, cultural, and ecclesiastical boundaries—followed.

Although the unique story of the Mormon people, their religion, and their settlement of the West has been told by many, it deserves telling in a different voice, for we have not been given even a partial account from the small numbers of the non-Mormon men like George R. Maxwell who came to Utah at the call of the federal government. To be understood more completely, this period must also be seen through the eyes of one of the non-Mormon minority. Historian Stuart McConnell reminds us of the relatively recent emphasis on the responsibility of the historian to examine the past from many perspectives: "there are many versions of the past, all potentially true from somebody's point of view, and . . . the imposition of a master narrative is little more than an arrogation of power on the part of the historian."[16]

Maxwell was not the lone man whose singular efforts were pivotal in shaping the events of Utah's path to statehood. He and many other fellow government appointees, although minor figures when judged individually, have been inequitably relegated to judgments that they were merely noxious or irrelevant within the larger picture of the "master narrative" of immense Mormon accomplishment.[17] Maxwell deserves a fresh look, an objective appraisal, before his contributions are dismissed and he is relegated to undeserved anonymity.

This biography is therefore divided into two parts. The first focuses on Maxwell's first twenty-two years and aims to describe and honor an unrecognized Civil War hero. His remaining twenty-some years, set within a fresh historiography, provide a different, contrasting view, through his eyes as a non-Mormon Civil War veteran, of an extremely troubled time in Utah's past.

---

[16] Stuart McConnell, "Epilogue: The Geography of Memory," in Fahs and Waugh, *Memory of the Civil War*, 264. McConnell recognizes the inherent danger of "versions of the past" that do not meet the standard set by qualified, professional historians.

[17] Much of the narrative of immense accomplishment by the Mormons can be found in the mammoth bibliography in Allen and Leonard, *Story of the Latter-day Saints*.

PART ONE
1842 *to* 1869

I

Origins of a Hero

When tillage begins, other arts follow.
The farmers . . . are the founders of . . . civilization.
Daniel Webster,
"Remarks on the Agriculture of England"

GEORGE R. MAXWELL'S FOREFATHERS WERE NEW ENGLAND farmers, respected men and women, not famous but locally distinguished. His long-lived great-grandfather, Thompson Maxwell, was born in 1742 in Bedford, Middlesex County, Massachusetts, and devoted more than fifteen years of his life in volunteer military service in three major wars. He first served in the French and Indian War at the Battle of Ticonderoga in 1758, remaining with the military until 1763. He returned to service during the Revolutionary War, participating in the battles at Bunker Hill, Three Rivers, Trenton, and Princeton, among many others. Wounded first at Bennington and again at Saratoga, he was a captain in the First New Hampshire Regiment by 1780. In 1806 Thompson Maxwell, by then a widower, migrated into Ohio, where he remarried in Butler County in 1807.[1] By 1808 he returned to an early Northwest Territory settlement on land that would become Michigan. Thompson Maxwell received 128 acres on the south bank of the Raisin River, in one of the ribbon parcels granted to the white

---

[1] Thompson Maxwell married Sibyl Daniel Wyman in 1763, Mary Little in 1807, and widow Eleanor Hickox in 1823.

settlers by a local group of Potawatomi tribal chiefs.[2] Most of the non-Indian landholders along the Raisin were men of French origin who had followed Francois Navarre, the first white man to arrive in the area and, in 1785, the first to be granted land from the Indians. Thompson Maxwell was seventy years old when he again volunteered in the War of 1812. He served at the Battle of Brown's Town, was taken prisoner at Detroit, took part in the battles of Fort George and La Colle Mill, was taken prisoner a second time near Fort Erie and incarcerated at Quebec, finally returning to the United States in 1815.[3] He died in 1832, at age ninety, and was buried in Wallaceville Cemetery, near present-day Dearborn, Michigan. Thompson Maxwell had been dead three years when his grandson, Reuben Maxwell, son of George Maxwell and father of George R. Maxwell, arrived in Monroe County, Michigan.

George Maxwell was born in 1774, also in Middlesex County, Massachusetts. Here George Maxwell and wife, Betsy (née Whitney), lived and their eight children were born. In 1814 George and Betsy moved the family, which included two sons, Cyrus and Reuben, to a new farm in Eaton, Madison County, New York, an area slightly east of the idyllic Finger Lakes region of the state. Eaton was near the eastern segment of the cities comprising the east-west Seneca Turnpike that connected the communities of Auburn, Canandaigua, and other upper New York cities to those in the west. Reuben Maxwell, the youngest of George Maxwell's eight children, was two years old when the family migrated to this fertile land.

The Maxwell siblings grew up during a time of profound change in upstate New York, brought about by the construction of the water superhighway of the Erie Canal. In 1817, when construction of the canal began, the area relied on a one-crop economy, supplying the coastal markets of Massachusetts, Connecticut, and New York with massive quantities of wheat. Despite malaria, political disputes, and technical

---

[2] The "ribbon" parcel farm system allowed each landholder access to the river by providing a small footage on the riverfront, as one end of a long, narrow strip extending away from the river, sometimes going deep into the forest. Hutchinson and Hutchinson, *Monroe*, 7–18.

[3] Thompson Maxwell was granted a government pension in 1818. U.S. National Archives (hereafter "NA"), Full Pension File (NATF 85A), S 3483 and 7148; "Revolutionary Pensioners on the Roll of Michigan under the law of March 18th, 1818 from the passage thereof to this day with the rank they served and the Lines in which they served," in *The Pension List of 1820* (Washington, D.C.: Gales and Seaton; LOC 91-73094), 663.

obstacles, the canal was completed in 1825.[4] This engineering feat created a narrow, shallow thread of navigable water 360 miles long, uniting New York City's harbor with upper New York State and with cities on the banks of Lake Erie. New York City thereby became the Atlantic seaport of the Midwest. Brobdingnagian economic change and stimulation took place as the Erie Canal led to booming wealth, new industries, societal change, heightened materialism, and a new middle class. Cities mothered by the canal became the most rapidly growing urban areas in the entire nation, with centers of culture and learning developing. It was to this atmosphere of rapid economic growth and cultural change that Cyrus and Reuben Maxwell, as well as the nearby family of Joseph Smith, were exposed.

ORIGIN OF THE LATTER-DAY SAINTS CHURCH

Living in Eaton, the Maxwell family was a scant eighty-five miles from the city of Palmyra, New York, the principal local market center. The Erie canal was finished to Palmyra in 1822, and it was to this growing city that a man named Joseph Smith, Sr., had moved his wife and nine children from their Vermont farm in the winter of 1816–17, to better provide for them. Born of this common surname, the third son of this family, Joseph Smith, Jr., would become the founder of an unusual religion that would grow into a worldwide church claiming more than thirteen million members.

It was near Palmyra that Joseph Smith, Jr., announced that he had received golden plates surrendered from the ground by an angel named Moroni. From ancient engravings inscribed on the plates, Smith alleged that he had transcribed a holy book, which was given the title *Book of Mormon*. This work describes a group of pre-Babylonian Jews from the area near Jerusalem who crossed the desert and the ocean to reach the Americas, to become the original inhabitants of the Western Hemisphere. Here, the *Book of Mormon* claims, they became the ancestors of the Indians of the North and South American continents. This transcribed record of Christ's followers in America became the basic, unique religious scripture of the church that Smith founded in Fayette, New York,

---

[4] Death from disease and mishaps was common, and the Erie Canal was "lined with the bones" of its Irish laborers. Dwyer, "Irish in the Building of the Intermountain West," 224.

in 1830, now known as the Church of Jesus Christ of Latter-day Saints, commonly called the Mormon church.[5] Five thousand copies of the *Book of Mormon* were printed by Egbert B. Grandin, publisher of the local newspaper, the *Wayne Sentinel*, and the books were first offered for sale March 26, 1830, in bookshops and the Erie Canal stores of Palmyra.

The publication of the *Book of Mormon* made Joseph Smith a minor national figure; his new religion received a great deal of publicity, almost uniformly negative, throughout upper New York State.[6] Biographer Richard Bushman writes that three Rochester newspapers had "substantial comments" and "elevated Joseph from an obscure money digger of local fame to full-blown religious imposter."[7] The reviews of the *Book of Mormon* by Rochester newspapers were severe in their criticism. The *Anti-Masonic Enquirer* described it as "a jumble of unintelligent absurdities."[8] The *Rochester Daily Advertiser* asserted: "A viler imposition was never practiced. It is an evidence of fraud, blasphemy, and credulity, shocking both to Christians and moralists."[9] And the *Palmyra Freeman* was equally harsh: "The greatest piece of superstition that has come within our knowledge now occupies the attention of a few individuals of this quarter."[10] Bushman observes that the editors of the various newspapers "drew on two vocabularies to discredit Smith": "Words like 'enthusiasm' or 'fanaticism' were used for false religions, but predominantly they called him a charlatan, a word for conspirators in treasure seeking schemes."[11] In the nearby canal town of Port Byron, Brigham Young, a man who would later succeed Joseph Smith and become the second president of the Mormon church, described this abundant publicity as the origin of his first knowledge of the existence of the book.[12]

Given the attention created by the publication of the *Book of Mormon*, or "Golden Bible," it is likely that members of the George Maxwell family would have discussed Smith and his new religion over their

---

[5] *The Book of Mormon*, *The Doctrine and Covenants*, and *The Pearl of Great Price* comprise the basic trilogy of religious scripture of the Church of Jesus Christ of Latter-day Saints. Mormons believe these three works supplement the King James Version of the Bible.

[6] Richard Bushman deals in detail with the difficulties Smith had with the publication of the *Book of Mormon*. Bushman, *Rough Stone Rolling*, 80–83.   [7] Ibid., 81.

[8] Linn, *Story of the Mormons*, 47.   [9] Brodie, *No Man Knows My History*, 82.

[10] Bushman, *Beginnings of Mormonism*, 111.   [11] Bushman, *Rough Stone Rolling*, 83.

[12] Brigham Young also lived in several small villages within seventy miles from the Maxwell family in Eaton, New York. At this time Young was a skilled carpenter, painter, and glazier and worked for a period constructing boats for the canal. Bringhurst, *Brigham Young*, 6–20.

dinner table in Eaton. Many of the early subscribers to Smith's message were devout Methodists, as was the George Maxwell family, but any discussion of it that may have taken place in the Maxwell household appears to have had little impact. Despite geographic proximity, there is no evidence that this family was touched by the flames of revivalism that burned over the region, or that any of them had interest in the sect championed by the charismatic Joseph Smith, Jr.

WESTWARD TO NEW LANDS

Despite the opportunities for profitable ventures that the Erie Canal may have brought, Reuben Maxwell, twenty-three years of age and unmarried, decided to move from Madison County, New York, to Michigan Territory, the very area that had earlier attracted his grand-father Thompson Maxwell. Following the western flow of commerce, Reuben crossed the 240 miles of Lake Erie to an area on its western shore.[13] Reuben, accompanied by his brother Cyrus, six years his elder, left Madison County in the spring of 1834, as soon as the ice thawed and traffic resumed on the Erie Canal. They passed through the port of Buffalo, a city transformed with the number of emigrants arriving by way of the canal. Boats arrived hourly, filled with goods, furniture, and motley human freight. Passengers combed the streets to purchase neces-sities, to satisfy curiosity, or to ask about distant locations. Days that saw a thousand boats come and go on the canal were not uncommon.[14]

Cyrus Maxwell initially settled in Cuyahoga County, Ohio, where three of his children were born, but in 1845 he and his family rejoined Reuben in Monroe County, Michigan. The two owned land less than a mile from one another in Ash Township. Here they worked their farms and raised their families.[15] The land in southern Michigan was flat, first-rate farming country with rich soil, plenty of water, and thick

---

[13] The economic expansion was also experienced on the western end of the Erie Canal. Newspa-per editor Edward Dimick Ellis wrote: "It is to the canal alone that Michigan owes her pres-ent rapid increase of population and gradual advancement in wealth." "Sketches of the Erie Canal with Hints to Persons Emigrating to the Country Bordering on Lake Erie," *Michigan Sentinel*, June 10, 1826.

[14] Quotation from *Genesee Farmer*, cited in the *Rochester Daily Advertiser*, June 9, 1832.

[15] From three wives, Cyrus Maxwell was the father of six children. He remained in Monroe County, Michigan, where he died in 1879. Betsy Maxwell remained in Madison County, New York, where she married David Morre, a farmer, with whom she had three children.

forests. Early settlers of the River Raisin drainage found it full of black bass, sturgeon, whitefish, as well as ducks, geese, and swans. Muskrat, beaver, mink, otter, and deer were abundant. By this time many of the Potawatomis had been moved to reservations or had drifted westward. Reuben wrote that when he arrived in Ash Township, it was primitive, with no roads, no schools, no churches; it took two days to travel the twelve miles to the gristmill at either Monroe or Dundee.

The River Raisin was so named before 1785 by French fur trappers for the abundance of grapes that grew along its banks. The village, a mile upstream from its junction with Lake Erie, was appropriately called Frenchtown. Following President James Monroe's visit in 1817 it was renamed in his honor. By 1837, when Michigan was granted statehood and two years after Reuben Maxwell arrived, Monroe County had begun to prosper. Its more than ten thousand inhabitants supported a mill for flour and one for wool, an iron foundry, a tannery, three banks, six churches, and two printing offices.[16]

THREE MOTHERS

Reuben Maxwell continued working his forty acres and raised a brick home in Ash about 1837. In January 1839, at age twenty-seven, he married fifteen-year-old Mary Elizabeth Heritage, who had recently immigrated from England. On their undulating green, rich farmland on Little Swan Creek, George R. Maxwell was Reuben's firstborn on September 16, 1842. It was perhaps prescient that the site of George R. Maxwell's origin had been a tragic battleground. The 1813 Battle of the River Raisin was the "single most deadly battle for the United States during the [1812] war," with several hundred troops killed or taken prisoner.[17] Near the Huron and Raisin rivers a group of sixty-five surrendered American troops from Kentucky, left as prisoners by the victorious British as they withdrew to Detroit, were massacred by the Wyandotte chief Roundhead.[18]

By the time of George R. Maxwell's birth, Reuben had two barns, one with a second story. There was a large crib for animal feed, a modest

[16] Frost, *General Custer's Libbie*, 13–16.
[17] Hutchinson, *Monroe*, 7.
[18] "Remember the River Raisin!" became the battle cry of the remainder of that war. Ibid., 20–21.

pioneer cabin, and a small shed on the property, located two hundred yards southeast from the Chicago–Canada South railroad tracks that ran diagonally through the county. Alfalfa, corn, oats, and wheat were his cash crops, and hogs, sheep, and cattle were for the family's use.

After George R. Maxwell, two other children were born to Mary Elizabeth Heritage and Reuben Maxwell: William B., in 1843, and Emma Elizabeth, in 1846. It was to this sister, Emma, that George R. Maxwell developed a close, lifelong attachment. When Mary Elizabeth died in 1849, at age twenty-five, Reuben promptly remarried, as was customary. His choice was Mary E. Harrison, who, like his first wife, was an English immigrant. This union resulted in a daughter, Sarah Rosetta, born in 1852.

George and his siblings likely were schooled until 1856 at home by their stepmother. George was also schooled in the nearby city of Monroe, twelve miles to the south. James Edward Keegan, one of Maxwell's contemporaries, recalled their days in Mrs. Keiser's Juvenile School, where their teacher was "a good, motherly woman, and maintained good government so that the children learned many things besides those that were gleaned from their books.[19] Next, Keegan and Maxwell attended a well-known school conducted by Miss Ada Crumps, followed by district schools taught by Miss Dussenberry and Mr. Stewart. Keegan switched to the Union School at Sixth and Washington streets when it was completed and attended night school under Mr. John Davies. Keegan noted: "I knew personally all the young men of Monroe who enlisted, [including] George Maxwell, the daredevil cavalryman, who took for his model Kilpatrick, the great Michigan cavalryman who fought with Custer, and reached a lieutenant-colonel's commission [*sic*]. Maxwell had some of Custer's qualities as a fearless soldier and . . . [his] great personal bravery."[20]

George's home life following the death of his biological mother appears to have been troubled. About 1856, Reuben and Mary Harrison were divorced, and Mary, with three-year-old Sarah Rosetta, moved to the city of Monroe, where she remarried.[21]

---

[19] Bulkley, "Biography of James Edward Keegan," 1:790–91.
[20] Ibid.
[21] Mary Harrison Maxwell married Frank Williams, a carpenter. Sarah Rosetta Maxwell married but had no children.

Reuben Maxwell again promptly remarried, this time to Emeline Hawley, a native of New York. This marriage was long-lasting, and six children, all sons, were added to the family: Edwin Cark in 1859, Frank Elmer in 1861, Charles E. in 1864, Wallace "Willis" Grant in 1865, Daniel in 1868, and Horton Jerome "Auty" Maxwell in 1876. Over time Reuben's farm prospered as well; by 1857 it had increased to 200 acres, and by 1876 it was 280 acres.

AWAY AT SCHOOL

In the early 1860s, George R. Maxwell attended the Michigan State Normal School. Founded in Ypsilanti in 1849 and located on Huron Bluff in Washtenaw County, slightly southwest of Ann Arbor and Dearborn, the school was the first teachers college founded west of the Allegheny Mountains and the first normal school established outside the original thirteen colonies. Its founders envisioned it as a school to educate teachers for the public school system, but many students who enrolled were aiming higher, and the institution made steady progress toward academic excellence, eventually becoming Eastern Michigan University.[22] Adonijah Strong Welch, professor of Greek and Latin, was the Normal School's first principal and a man whose own career was colorful and extraordinary.[23] Maxwell became the earnest student of Professor Welch in the fall of 1860 and spring and summer of 1861. He attended Term Sixteen, from October 1860 to March 1861, passing grammar, spelling, and physical geography with a grade of B, and arithmetic with a C. During Term Seventeen, from March to July 1861, he passed algebra by examination and was excused early to join the war.[24] His letter to his sister, Emma, opens a window to the mundane events of his student life there:

[22] Colburn, *Story of Ypsilanti*, 140.

[23] Adonijah Strong Welch, born 1821 in Connecticut, graduated from the University of Michigan in 1846, went west in the 1849 California gold rush, served in the Civil War, was elected to the U.S. Senate from Florida, and became the first president of Iowa State Agricultural College. *Biographical Directory of the United States Congress*, http:/bioguide.congress.gov/scripts/biodisplay.pl?index=W000261.

[24] Caleb John Klinger, archivist and graduate student, and Rosina Tammany, archivist, Eastern Michigan University Archives, Ypsilanti, pers. comm., June 2007.

Ypsilanti   Oct 26 1860

Dear Sister Emma,

    I . . . will not lose this opportunity of sending you a line and want you should be shure and write me that long letter that you promised to write me several weeks ago. I have been very busy today. This forenoon I was at a meeting of the Ashaflora Cultural Society and this afternoon the Normal National Ball Club players against the Seminary Club and I am so tired that I could lay down with a good heart. . . . I have got to make bread so while I am waiting I will write some little of the news. . . . Tell Father that all of his fears that I would lay abed until something serious happened (no matter what) that I get up about 4 o'clock every morning but Saturday and Sunday. Well, we eat breakfast and [———] the dishes and set down to study until school time and then [———] for school and stay there from 8 to 12½ o'clock with a short recess. . . . Lo says that you are getting savering of your paper ain't you. Well now for the arrangements. Well, if you want to distinguish your self just Whisper once and then you will sit on the rostrum all day and if you want to distinguish your self still, why just whisper the second time and you will have a permanent seat in the armed chair all Winter they say but I guess they would not have him in the way that long. Well from all absent or tardy once, you have to get an excuse from Prof Welsh and he says the won't excuse any more. . . . Lo joined the Sunday school today and I am going to join the bible class. We are going to move to Morrow when the team comes to fetch Cy up. We have got two rooms way up in the third story of a store where we will be obliged if any of our friends will condescend to visit us. Am going to learn like a house a fire here. Just write and tell me who is going to teach school there this Winter and so on and etc. . . . Give my love to Frank and [———] to my sister Emma Elizabeth Maxwell. . . .

George Maxwell[25]

"Lo" was fellow student Edward Bigelow, who would soon serve in Company C, Fifth Michigan Infantry, and "Cy" appears to have been Cyrus F. Whelan, who would serve with the Ninth Kansas Cavalry under Maj. Gen. James Gillpatrick Blunt. Frank was Frank Hawley, the younger sibling of his stepmother and a man who would be at Maxwell's side throughout the war. Also attending the Normal School before the war was James Harvey Kidd, later of the Sixth Michigan

---

[25] George R. Maxwell to his sister, from family papers supplied by Bruce Turner Cunard II of Connecticut. No attempt has been made to correct grammar or spelling.

Emma Elizabeth Maxwell,
the sister with whom George R.
Maxwell formed an eduring bond.
Courtesy of Maxwell Fisher Turner,
Elizabeth Jane Cunard Carey, and
Bruce Turner Cunard II.

Cavalry and part of the Michigan Cavalry Brigade. Kidd was destined to rise, as Maxwell did, to brevet brigadier general; the two would be together in many battles during the war, and Kidd would become a prolific writer, recording the pursuits of the Michigan cavalrymen.[26]

Leaving Monroe to attend school in Ypsilanti, then abandoning his college education by dropping out to enlist, George missed the births of his half-siblings except the first one. Neither did he know them well after the war, for he returned to Michigan infrequently, briefly, and for other reasons.

---

[26] Klinger and Tammany, pers. comm., June 2007.

INFLUENTIAL FAMILIES:
THE CUSTERS AND THE CHRISTIANCYS

Two Monroe County families came to be very important in the life of George R. Maxwell in the Civil War and in his Utah battles against plural marriage and theocracy. The first was that of George Armstrong Custer. Later to be admired as General Custer, he was born December 5, 1839, in New Rumley, Ohio, a hamlet slightly south of the Michigan state line.[27] Custer spent much of his childhood in the city of Monroe and was schooled there while living with his married half-sister, Lydia Ann Kirkpatrick Reed. Custer, like Maxwell, was not born into money, position, or high society, and he also started life as a farm boy. As a struggling schoolteacher in Ohio in 1857, Custer had the good fortune to be granted appointment to the United States Military Academy at West Point. He ranked last in his 1861 graduating class, and many of those classmates who stood above him went on to become the military leaders for both sides in the Civil War.[28]

While on leave during the Civil War in 1864, Custer married Elizabeth Bacon, a woman of beauty, charm, and intelligence, born and raised in a prominent family of Monroe. Affectionately known as Libbie, she was the daughter of Daniel Bacon, distinguished Monroe bank president, circuit court judge, and Michigan state senator—a man very well connected politically. Following their marriage Libbie Bacon Custer became a skillful booster of her husband's professional career. Her charms and attractions were quickly noted by people of influence she came to know while living in the beehive activity of Washington, D.C. U.S. senator Zachariah Chandler of Michigan (later to be secretary of the interior), U.S. representative F. William Kellogg of Michigan, Admiral David Farragut, Presidents Lincoln and Grant, Speaker of the House and later Vice President Schuyler Colfax, and a bevy of Union generals were among those she knew from dances, theatrical performances, meetings in the hotel, or official visits. Comments on her beauty and bearing, and praise for her husband's accomplishments,

---

[27] Ownership of land near New Rumley was the object of a bloodless "war" between the states of Michigan and Ohio, resulting in the area's being ceded to Ohio.

[28] Custer was known to be respectfully cordial to all his former West Point mates and was said to personally greet any of these officers, Union or captured Confederate, and offer whatever assistance he was able.

came frequently from these men. Although indirect, George R. Maxwell's ties to Custer, and also to Chandler, Grant, and Colfax would become very valuable in his war career and afterward.

The second important tie was to the senior member of the Christiancy family, Isaac Peckham Christiancy, who compiled a distinguished and accomplished record following his arrival in Monroe County from Fulton County in upper New York. A lawyer, he served as Monroe County's prosecuting attorney, a member of the Michigan state senate from 1850 to 1852, and then as a Michigan Supreme Court justice. He was owner and editor of the county newspaper, the *Monroe Commercial*, a visitor for the U.S. Military Academy, a U.S. senator for Michigan, and finally an ambassador to Peru.[29] Christiancy knew Custer after the latter's graduation from West Point and was very well acquainted with both Daniel Bacon and daughter Libbie before her marriage to Custer. Christiancy would be counted among the honored guests at the wedding of George Armstrong Custer and Elizabeth Bacon.

Adamantly opposed to slavery, Christiancy left the Democratic Party and helped organize the Republican Party in Michigan. In 1861, when the events in South Carolina ignited the nation, he gave a rousing, patriotic oration in the Monroe town square, urging Michigan men to volunteer. Although fifty years of age, he himself served for a time in 1863 with the Third Michigan Cavalry. Three of his sons served in Michigan units, as did George R. Maxwell and his younger brother William B. Maxwell.

Isaac P. Christiancy was undeniably a patriot, but he was also a realist and, as a concerned father, sought a safe assignment for his son Henry Clay Christiancy and made sure that Henry and his brother did not serve in the same unit. George Armstrong Custer assisted Isaac Christiancy, with letters to Gen. Andrew Atkinson Humphreys and Gen. Daniel Adams Butterfield requesting Henry's placement. The efforts were productive, for Henry C. Christiancy, after starting in the First Michigan Infantry in 1861, was reassigned to the relative safety of the position of aide-de-camp in the headquarters of General Humphreys, where he served from November 1862 to September 1864, and was present at the battles of Fredericksburg and Gettysburg.

---

[29] Biographies, Michigan Supreme Court Historical Society, www.micourthistory.org/bios.php?id=33.

Christiancy's second son, James Isaac Christiancy, posed a different and more difficult problem. With a weakness for alcohol and bawdy houses, James had become the family's heartache, the trial of his father's life. Isaac Christiancy asked Custer to place James on his personal staff, to do all he could to reform him, and to keep him under his watchful eye. In July 1863 Custer replied in a letter: "If [James] . . . was willing to accept a position on my staff as aide de camp I would be glad to have him with me. If he could procure the leave and come here I can obtain authority from Gen. Meade to retain him."[30] James Christiancy joined Custer's staff, but true to his rebellious nature, avoiding combat was not a privilege that he accepted. Rather, he put himself in the gunsights of the Confederates, voluntarily leading a battle line and suffering serious wounds at Haw's Shop in July 1864. His thumb was amputated, and his thigh and hip were torn up by a Confederate rifle ball.[31] Libbie Custer, finding James in a Washington hospital that she considered unsatisfactory, moved him to her own quarters in the city, where she cared for him and aided his recovery while constantly urging him to abstinence and the responsibilities of marriage and adulthood.

Isaac Christiancy's professional life brought him influence and political power, and later, when Custer was seeking the command of the Seventh Michigan Cavalry, many letters went back and forth from Custer to Christiancy. Christiancy gained support from Michigan governor Austin Blair for the position Custer sought. On his visits to Washington, the senior Christiancy often socialized with Libbie Custer, and whether out of truth or ego, she reported Christiancy's flirtatious advances in letters to her husband.[32]

Historians point out that, when in the field, Custer did not often establish close friendships among officers of the line.[33] Despite this propensity, there were undoubtedly many opportunities that brought together some combination of the officers Maxwell and Custer and the Christiancy brothers. Henry Christiancy's war diary makes note of

---

[30] George Armstrong Custer to Judge Isaac Christiancy, July 26, 1863, Henry Clay Christiancy Diary, 1862–64, 27.

[31] In 1892 James Christiancy was awarded the Medal of Honor for his Civil War service. He died on December 18, 1899, and was buried in Arlington National Cemetery.

[32] Libbie Custer's writings describe Christiancy as flirtatious with the women of Washington society. Merington, *Custer Story*, 122–23.

[33] Phipps, *"Come On, You Wolverines!"* 16.

seeing his brother, Jim, frequently throughout 1863, spending time with him in the down moments of the war. Maxwell knew of the reputation of the Christiancy family and surely foresaw that influential contacts among the Christiancys and the Custers could be useful if he survived the war. Indeed, these associations benefitted Maxwell in his post-war federal appointment and in being able to work directly with the senior Christiancy in the late 1870s. Isaac P. Christiancy by this time had become an influential Michigan senator, and Maxwell worked from Utah and in Washington to gain his sponsorship and support of numerous Senate and congressional bills, all addressing a solution to various features of the "Mormon question" in the Utah Territory.[34]

MAXWELL's ALTER EGO

Rapidly ascending the army ranks during the Civil War, Custer came to command the cavalry unit in which Maxwell served as an officer. Maxwell took Custer as his role model, adopted the same leadership skills, and developed the same ability as Custer to have men follow his lead. Like Custer, he seemingly ignored personal risk of death and injury.

In the popular mind and press, the name of Gen. George Armstrong Custer is most commonly associated with his post–Civil War service in the West, with killing Indians on the Washita River and, most notably, with the carnage at the Little Big Horn, where he and his men of the Seventh Cavalry were annihilated by waves of Lakota warriors on June 25, 1876. This focus on what many Custer historians insist was an event totally uncharacteristic of his usual skill as a military leader deprives him of credit due for his role as one of the most successful cavalry leaders of the Civil War from either the Union or Confederate ranks. Comments of praise made about Custer can easily be found in abundance throughout Civil War historical literature. For example, Congressman Kellogg described him as "one of the best, if not the very best cavalry officer anywhere in the service": "Under his command the Michigan

---

[34] Other men from Michigan who served in federal positions in Utah Territory include Obed Franklin Strickland, associate court justice, and Philip H. Emerson, who replaced Strickland. There were also attorneys Orlando W. Powers, Sumner Howard, and Gen. Henry Andrew Morrow, commander at Camp Douglas, and the First Michigan surgeon Amos K. Smith. It was Isaac P. Christiancy who pushed the nomination of Philip Taylor Van Zile as U.S. attorney for Utah's Third Judicial District in 1878.

Brigade has achieved a reputation and secured for itself frequent and honorable mention in the history of war. Their devotion to their lion-hearted leader is almost idolatrous and they never once failed to follow him."[35] Biographer Gregory J. W. Urwin defines the unique attribute of personal leadership that in his opinion Custer, more than any other Civil War Union leader, seemed to possess:

> He saw war as a grand game, an exhilarating test . . . to be won by the fit and the quick-witted. . . . Custer's great achievement was his ability to instill this lethal spirit . . . into his willing Wolverines and Red Ties. It was no easy feat to get half-grown boys and callow young men, most of them decent, Bible-bred Christians, to kill with evangelistic fervor—to go rushing through shot and shell with a shout, to keep cheering as they thrust their sabers into human beings, disfiguring their limbs and faces and spilling their warm guts onto the rich soil of Pennsylvania or Virginia—and to still cheer as they themselves were maimed or blown out of existence.[36]

No war journal written by George R. Maxwell has been found that records how he came to be like Custer, possessed of sangfroid, an apparently fearless, aggressive cavalryman. Perhaps these were internal, inherent talents, but more likely he learned them from the master models, his various cavalry commanders. Lawrence A. Frost, a Custer historian, observes that what marked these men as different and effective leaders was their penchant for forgoing safety in the rear, which would have forced them to direct by messenger and rely on the observations of subordinates: "Sheridan, Pleasonton, Phil Kearny, Kilpatrick and Custer, were firmly of the opinion that a cavalry fight could best be won by being in front of the line, [constantly] in motion with their eyes on the adversary. Each had won often enough to attest to the technique."[37] Frost's list of such cavalry leaders could well include George R. Maxwell.

Defining experiences that Maxwell may have had with these five cavalrymen are impossible to dissect out of the argot of military reports. It is understandable that once he was engaged in battle, the press of decision and action would obscure any sign of fear, but what of the quiet moments of introspection, of reflection while in the forests of Virginia's

[35] Congressman F. William Kellogg, letter to the editor, *Detroit Advertiser and Tribune*, October 11, 1864.

[36] Urwin, *Custer Victorious*, 280.

[37] Frost, *General Custer's Libbie*, 128–29.

wilderness, or while waiting in front of the entrenched Confederates at
the Opequon River in the Shenandoah, or anticipating the day at Gettysburg? Whatever his emotions, his actions never hinted of hesitation
or delay in following his orders.

In his early years Maxwell had also gained many skills that served
him well in wartime. He had hunted deer, ducks, geese, and muskrats in
the lands surrounding the River Raisin and farmed alongside his father
near Little Swan Creek. By his own words, we know that Maxwell also
spent time "as a sailor," likely on vessels trafficking to Detroit, Toledo,
Sandusky, Cleveland—ports between Monroe and Buffalo. And as his
career would soon attest, he was a skilled horseman and excelled with
rifle, carbine, pistol, and saber. The shift from the farmland to a career
that would span becoming a Civil War hero and a hero of a different
combat in Utah Territory began when George R. Maxwell was among
the first of the many zealous, patriotic citizens to volunteer for Civil
War service in the frenetically organizing Union units of Michigan.

2

The Thunderbolt of Sheridan

Only a fool or a fraud sentimentalizes the merciless reality of war.
U.S. senator John McCain, remarks at
Los Angeles World Affairs Council, March 26, 2008

GEORGE R. MAXWELL SERVED AS A UNION VOLUNTEER FROM near the beginning of the Civil War to eight days short of Gen. Robert E. Lee's capitulation in Virginia at Appomattox Court House. A brave and aggressive cavalryman, Maxwell was dedicated to serving until victory was earned.

Did he rush to enlist, as did many of the callow young men, naively seeking adventure, who were wanting to be "off to see the elephant"? This phrase morphed through various colloquial meanings: to experience and see all there is to see; to have gone to the big city starry-eyed and returned in disappointment; to have experienced the journey in search of California gold. The use of the phrase came to be used in reference to experiencing army life and combat in the Civil War.[1] Most people in America in 1861 had never seen an elephant. With unusual animals and exciting events, the circus broke the humdrum of antebellum rural life. Seeing elephants and the animals of the circus was a time of fun and diversion. But it was inexperienced farm boys who

---

[1] Another example of the phrase "see the elephant" as meaning a disparity between naive expectation and reality can be found in the exclamation of a discouraged California gold-rush miner who lamented that he had "seen the elephant and eaten his ears . . . [and] now he was going home to his wife." Reid, *Policing the Elephant*, 1.

envisioned any war, but especially this war, in such terms. Once they saw this beast, their innocence was brutally gone; they were forever changed.

Would Maxwell have enlisted out of patriotism, a deep belief that the Union must be preserved, or out of revulsion over immoral slavery? Was there need to express rebellion, to escape the difficulties of home or the drudgery of farm life? Would he have been thought a coward if he resisted the wave of patriotism that washed over his home county? Did the private's salary of thirteen dollars a month constitute an attraction? Did he hope to emulate the military deeds of his forefathers?

Certainly the citizens of Monroe and Ypsilanti were strong opponents of slavery. Both cities were well-known stations offering a haven in the journey to freedom, in what was inaccurately but euphemistically called the Underground Railroad. For slaves fleeing from the Southern states through Tennessee and Kentucky and across the Ohio River, it was no easy ride on a cushioned train seat.[2] With help from former slaves and abolitionists, runaways walked hundreds of miles, mostly at night, to safe houses marked by a hitching-post lantern, following the North Star to their freedom. Michigan's citizens were brimming with patriotism; enthusiasm for enlisting in support of the Union was epidemic. No county in the entire Union States had a higher number of volunteers, proportionately, than did Monroe County, Michigan.[3] In Maxwell's own family, all of the five eligible men served creditably as Union volunteers.[4] In addition to his younger brother, William B., who served in the First Michigan Cavalry, two of his cousins, sons of his uncle Cyrus, served in the western front with the Ninth Michigan Infantry: twenty-two-year-old Cyrus Wesley Maxwell and twenty-nine-year-old Reuben D. Maxwell. Reuben Lewis Heritage, a first cousin on his mother's side, served in the Eleventh Michigan Infantry. All but William B. Maxwell survived the war. Cyrus and Reuben returned to farming the fields bordering Little Swan Creek.

---

[2] Bordewich, *Bound for Canaan*, 189–96.

[3] Hutchinson, *Monroe*, 8.

[4] Patriotism continues to thrive in Monroe County, where many fly the American flag and drape banisters and porches with bunting year-round. Photographs of heroes from every war abound in libraries, courthouses, and public buildings. A small American flag is frequently renewed on the grave of each Monroe veteran who died in service.

PATRIOTISM AND ENLISTMENT

Forty days after the Confederate firing on Fort Sumter, Michigan Supreme Court justice Isaac Peckham Christiancy spoke to a large gathering in the Courthouse Square in Monroe. Mixed with descriptions of Southern men as arrogant brutes who embraced the immorality of slavery while huffing their superiority over Northern men, Christiancy spoke stirring words of patriotism:

> Shall we plead guilty to . . . cowardice . . . ? Never, never, never, while our Northern heart continues to beat. . . .
>
> The first shot fired at Fort Sumter . . . has produced a moral earthquake. 20,000,000 people have sprung to their feet . . . and resolved that treason shall be extinguished in blood. . . . [A]ll are equally resolved on victory or death and contending only who shall be foremost in the fight, feeling that the post of danger is the post of honor. . . . If I had a son . . . who would refuse or evade the call of his country, I would disavow him— and I pity the dastardly soul of that man who, in a time like this, would not rather fall himself or have his sons fall gloriously fighting for his country to dragging out an inglorious existence at home.[5]

Justice Christiancy's admonitions led many men to immediately come forward. Another patriotic rally, among the many held, was that at Michigan State Normal School in Ypsilanti, where Professor Ezra Mead Foote exhorted his young male students with song: "We are coming, Father Abraham, three hundred thousand more."[6] When Maxwell registered at the Normal School for the 1861 summer courses, he told his father that he planned to serve. His father tried to dissuade him, but George dropped the second term. Thus, it was not his father but Professor Welch who witnessed Maxwell's volunteer papers as he worked to form a company. He signed on at Trenton, Michigan, on August 15, 1861, four months after Union forces at Fort Sumter fell to the Confederate bombardment in Charleston Harbor, and three weeks following the Union's jolting July 21 defeat at the First Battle of Bull Run, near Manassas, Virginia.

A month short of nineteen years old, Maxwell was of medium build, weighing 160 pounds, and had dark curly hair. At six feet one inch, he

---

[5] Isaac Peckham Christiancy Papers, 1830–74, reel 1.
[6] E. R. Isbell and Donald W. Disbrow, "The Michigan State Normal School and the Civil War," in Bald, Peckham, and Williams, *Michigan Institutions*, 87.

stood tall against many of the men of his time. Most of the young men at Michigan State Normal were formed into the Seventeenth Michigan Infantry, but Maxwell chose a cavalry unit. He entered as a corporal in Company K, First Michigan Cavalry. Maxwell's choice not to follow his classmates into an infantry unit was unsurprising. Proportional to its population, Michigan would supply more mounted volunteers than any other state in the Union. As historian Edward Longacre notes, "Men who fancied themselves cavalry material appeared to be especially active in Michigan; . . . because Michigan had only recently been carved out of the wilderness . . . , transportation by horseback was as much a way of life there as it was below the Mason-Dixon line."[7]

If Maxwell, his friends Edward Bigelow and Cyrus F. Whelan, and most of his classmates at Michigan State Normal, were anticipating a short, glorious, and romantic war and a quick return to their former life, the Union defeat at Manassas brought them up short, just as it did the rest of the North. None anticipated dying, but as Maxwell would later learn, twenty-seven of the untested raw recruits of the Seventeenth Michigan Infantry died in September 1862 at the Battle of South Mountain. Many were still boys when they charged the rock wall at Fox's Gap and found themselves suddenly in a nightmare of hand-to-hand, close-quarters combat with units of North Carolina infantry. Both Bigelow and Whelan, as well as many of Maxwell's Normal School classmates, died while serving the Union.[8] Bigelow succumbed to disease in Virginia in February 1862. Whelan was wounded five times and died in Little Rock, Arkansas.[9]

Serving by Maxwell's side in the First Michigan Cavalry throughout the war was a close friend and relative by marriage, Francis "Frank" Robert Hawley, the younger brother of his father's third wife. Maxwell's junior by only eight months, Hawley entered Union service on the same day and in the same city as Maxwell. Initially assigned as a private of Company B, First Michigan Cavalry, Hawley requested a discharge on December 21, 1863, so that he could reenlist as a veteran into Maxwell's Company K. To war's end they were together; they shared the eagerly awaited letters from family and friends in Monroe

---

[7] Longacre, *Custer and His Wolverines*, 17–18.
[8] Isbell and Disbrow, "Michigan State Normal School," 92.
[9] Putnam, *History of the Michigan State Normal School*, 282, 294.

and looked after each other's safety in battle. Hawley rose in rank to sergeant, survived the war, and afterward traveled west with the Michigan Veteran Cavalry to serve in the Powder River campaign against the Plains Indians.[10]

The descriptive term "First" would come to have more than one meaning, as the First Michigan Cavalry shortly gained a reputation for tenacious bravery. It became the elite veteran of the cavalry corps, to which all other Michigan and Union units would be an understudy. Cavalryman James Kidd of the Sixth Michigan described the unit as "one of the savviest and most tenacious regiments of horse." Especially formidable in saber charge, its men were regarded second to none when under fire: "When the First Michigan could not stand before a storm of bullets, no other regiment in the cavalry corps need try."[11]

Within days of enlistment Maxwell was moved to the training field on the outskirts of Detroit, formerly the Hamtramck race track. Conditions at Camp Lyon were primitive; initially the volunteers had no bedding. Shortly, they were issued uniforms of light blue jersey pants, with a double-lined seat; dark blue, single-breasted jackets trimmed with yellow piping; high-crowned hats with the numeral *1* above crossed sabers of silver; and knee-high black boots. Rudimentary drilling, dismounted training, and care of their animals and equipment occupied their time.

The First Michigan Cavalry was mustered into service on September 13, 1861. Maxwell's nineteenth birthday had come and gone by the time the various Michigan units received their colors, on September 28 in the Campus Martius Square in Detroit. They formed in front of the H. R. Andrews Rail Road Hotel, the Odd Fellows Hall, McLodeon Manufacturing, and Marcus Stevens Furniture House and were looked upon by a throng gathered in their finery, the ladies protected from the sun by parasols. The following day they boarded a train bound for the nation's capital, where they were lodged at Camp Rucker, alongside the Potomac River, a site providing even less comfort than had Camp Lyon. Maxwell's letter to his brother William told their circumstances:

---

[10] Hawley was discharged March 25, 1866, with the First Michigan Veteran Cavalry while serving in Utah Territory. Longacre, *Custer and His Wolverines*, 283–89. Returning to Michigan, he married and had three children. At the time of his death, on January 10, 1926, in Ash, he was one of the few surviving members of the Perry Baker Post of the Grand Army of the Republic. Obituary, *Carleton Messenger*, January 16, 1926.

[11] Kidd, *Personal Recollections of a Cavalryman*, 9–10.

We are not more than 80 or a hundred yards from the capital. . . . [T]he first few nights we did not have it very comfortable as we had no straw . . . we had to sleep on the ground. . . . [T]he ground was wet and we caught cold but are getting tough and can stand almost anything. . . . [W]e have not got our horses yet and we have not had any drill since we left Detroit.[12]

In late October, a thousand horses arrived, and the men were issued their weapons. Each received a .44-caliber, Colt Army revolver, a saber, and a .52-caliber, single-shot Sharps carbine.[13] In a letter from Camp Rucker, Maxwell had these words for his sister, Emma:

We are going to VA soon. . . . I have got to be perfectly indifferent, a mere machine. . . . [W]e had a disastrous defeat near Leesburg and another grand blunder . . . at Bull Run. Any common soldier might has told them better than to place themselves between a powerful foe and an impassable river with but one old scow. . . . I got a little black mare . . . call her Millie—gave her to Frank and got a large chestnut—call him Bounder . . . or Son of Thunder. This forenoon I galloped after the officers and went to drill but did not join them but went down to a flying artillery camp and was practicing. . . . [W]e have a great deal of sickness in camp. Frank is not very well but will be all straight in a few days. Cy is well and saucy. . . . Gen Scott has resigned and gone to Europe and McClellan takes his place.[14]

It was December, when the First Michigan was again relocated, this time marching through Georgetown, up Pennsylvania Avenue, and across the Potomac, sixty miles into the Maryland countryside, where the men set up camp on Worman's farm. They would remain there for two months, until ordered to the not yet green fields of the Shenandoah Valley.

The infantryman fantasized the cavalryman as leading a glamorous, easier life. Not so, according to historian Stephen Starr: "In no time at

---

[12] George R. Maxwell to William Maxwell in Michigan, date illegible, in possession of Bruce Turner Cunard II.

[13] The seven-shot, repeating Spencer was not available until January 1863. At the Battle of Gettysburg the 770 troopers of the Fifth Michigan Cavalry were the only regiment with the seven-shot Sharps. The First Michigan was still equipped with the Sharps single-shot. The .54-caliber Burnside carbines were first issued sometime in 1861, and at Gettysburg the Seventh Michigan was armed with them. Phipps, *"Come On, You Wolverines!"* 13–15.

[14] George R. Maxwell to Emma Elizabeth Maxwell in Michigan, November 1861, in possession of Bruce Turner Cunard II. It is unclear whether "Cy" is Cyrus Whelan, from college, or cousin Cyrus Maxwell. Neither was known to serve with the Michigan Cavalry at this time.

Campus Martius Square, Detroit,
where Michigan units were given their send-off to the war.
Courtesy of the Burton Historical Collection, Detroit Public Library.

all the glamor evaporated. In its place came a life of hardship . . . compounded of exposure, filth, an unspeakable diet, medical care primitive even by the standards of the day, disease, disability and death."[15] Not always riding a beautiful, smooth-coated stallion, its head held high, a metal scabbard flashing in the sunlight, he was, at times, mounted on a plodding animal foraged from conquered fields. If the government horse supply faltered, Union officers resorted to purchasing animals with their own money. Each cavalryman was his own stable hand, fed and brushed his horse, and, as the only veterinarian available, treated his animal for whatever ailment presented, be it saddle sores or foot rot.

[15] Starr, *Union Cavalry*, 1:xi–xii.

Over the course of the war, the cavalryman evolved to became not only the eyes of the army but the indispensable tool of multiple uses, the "Swiss Army knife" of the Union military forces. The cavalryman was expected to fight mounted or as a foot soldier, to scout enemy positions, and to carry dispatches and messages. He was to appraise the geography for its battle advantages, forage for food for men and animals, protect the flanks of the moving army, destroy enemy supply depots, oppose the enemy cavalry, and even act as a military policeman. Among the Confederates, Gen. Robert E. Lee also relied heavily on a cavalryman, Maj. Gen. James Ewell Brown "J. E. B." Stuart, to be his eyes, returning with vital information on the identity, location, and strength of Union forces. Cavalry being quick and mobile, able to hit hard and be gone before an infantry could be dug in and its heavy cannons positioned, was an evolving concept in the science of warfare.

That cavalry should be used in innovative ways was the product of the thoughts of Confederate officers like Gen. J. E. B. Stuart and Union officers such as Maj. Gen. Philip Henry Sheridan, Maj. Gen. Alfred Pleasanton, and General Custer. Considered radical, such changes were opposed by older, conservative line officers who thought of cavalry only as secondary to the primary role of infantry and artillery. To the older officers, cavalry were desirable, not essential. As the war rolled on and Sheridan's tactics increasingly resulted in winning, Maxwell and his fellow First Michigan cavalrymen had to master the evolving fighting skills.[16] Each man had to control his animal in noise and chaos, and to judge its stamina. Each officer had to recognize when exhaustion of the unit's mounts dictated retreat rather than charge. He must execute various maneuvers with rifle, pistol, and sword, all while on horseback, jumping obstacles and maneuvering to avoid the enemy. He must dismount and fight on foot in all terrain, in all weather, and be able to quickly remount to fight in the most adverse contingencies. Had Maxwell and his troops not mastered these skills, battles such as the Wilderness and Five Forks would surely have uncovered their deficiency and lessened the likelihood of their survival.

---

[16] In his memoirs, Sheridan contrasts the views of older officers with his own view that cavalry should take a primary role. Sheridan, *Personal Memoirs*, 1:354–57.

MANY TIMES WOUNDED

George R. Maxwell received multiple wounds during the course of the war. Both knees and both shoulders were hit by missiles. He sustained a saber wound to the groin, a gunshot wound to the left forearm just below the elbow, and partial amputations of several fingers of the left hand. One can almost create a map of the war, using the dates and places where he sustained battle injuries.

By the spring of 1862 the First Michigan Cavalry was in the Shenandoah Valley, fighting the forces of Gen. Thomas Jonathan "Stonewall" Jackson at Winchester and Front Royal as Jackson attempted to resupply Richmond. In April 1862, Maxwell was fighting Confederate forces as they retreated over a bridge on the Shenandoah River at a stronghold called Mount Jackson. To halt pursuing First Michigan Cavalry troops, the Confederates set fire to the only remaining bridge over the rain-swollen river. Two companies of First Ohio Infantry attempted to storm the burning wooden bridge, only to be stopped by flames and intense Confederate fire. Edward Longacre describes Maxwell's role:

> At a critical moment the [Union] detachment found itself leaderless; stepping in to fill the void, Corporal George R. Maxwell of Company K ordered his comrades to dismount at river's edge, scoop up water in their high crown hats, and douse the flames. Thanks to cover fire from the Ohioans, which forced the nearest Confederates to hug the earth, Maxwell's unit saved the bridge. Looking on from the rear, now Brigadier General Kimball praised the "splendid dash" and "gallant charge" that had salvaged the [Union] pursuit. His commendation, seconded by Col. Brodhead, would mean sergeant stripes for Maxwell. The promotion would set a . . . meteoric course: he would end the war as a lieutenant colonel and regimental commander with the brevet rank of colonel [*sic*] for gallantry in action.[17]

Now a first lieutenant, Maxwell was in several July 1862 skirmishes that preceded the humiliating August defeat in the Second Battle of Bull Run, when he narrowly escaped death. Unit reports of the First Michigan note that Lieutenant Maxwell was "taken prisoner at Bull Run" on August 30, the last day of that battle. With his letter to his

---

[17] Longacre, *Custer and His Wolverines*, 51–52.

sister, Emma, written on December 1, 1862, he enclosed a button from his own tunic that had been deformed by a ball that nearly took his life at Bull Run. He wrote that "if the piece had come one inch closer . . . I would be kicking out of my hole as thousands are now doing on that field," but he made no mention of his capture in this letter's accounting.[18] He also sent her a coin purse, formerly owned by a Union soldier and retaken when he captured a Confederate captain and 80 men. In December, Maxwell was present when 250 men of the Second Pennsylvania Cavalry inadvertently engaged what they soon discovered was an 8,000-man force of General Stuart's cavalry raiders at Selectman's Ford on the Occoquan River. A large number of Pennsylvanians were cut off; four successive Union rallies had failed. According to Capt. Charles Chauncey's understated report, Lieutenant Maxwell and his the First Michigan men "rendered efficient service": "Under his [Maxwell's] direction, a heavy fire was poured into the advance of the rebels, and they were driven back, thus giving [the Pennsylvanians] an opportunity to cross in safety. . . . Maxwell . . . headed the men most nobly, and for a time kept the enemy at bay."[19]

A gunshot wound to Maxwell's right shoulder is recorded at the Battle of Brentsville, Virginia, on New Year's Eve of 1862, when he was one of only three survivors of a seven-man patrol. Captured by twenty men of Gen. Wade Hampton's South Carolina Cavalry Legion, Maxwell, Pvt. Matthew B. Burgher, and their third unnamed companion were fortunate to be rescued the next day by members of First Massachusetts Cavalry under command of Maj. Samuel E. Chamberlain. Maxwell apparently formed a strong bond with Burgher, a fellow Michigan volunteer, and later the two shared a close professional association in Utah Territory, where Maxwell appointed him as the prison warden.[20]

---

[18] George R. Maxwell to Emma Maxwell, December 1, 1862, in possession of Bruce Turner Cunard II.

[19] Report of Charles Chauncey, Captain, Detached Second Pennsylvania Cavalry, December 31, 1862, in Scott and Lazelle, *The War of the Rebellion: A Compilation of the Official Records of the Union and Confederate Armies* (hereafter "*OR*"), ser. I, vol. 21, part 1: 710. Other *OR* reports give the date of this encounter as December 28, 1862.

[20] *OR* I, 21:750–51. Pvt. Matthew B. Burgher, of Decatur and Odessa, Michigan, served with Company M of the First Michigan Cavalry. Wounded twice, he was promoted to first lieutenant and later served in the Eighth and the Eleventh Michigan Cavalry and as aide-de-camp on the staff of Bvt. Maj. Gen. A. C. Gillem. Promoted to captain in the Ninth Michigan Cavalry, he received a gunshot wound of the lung in the Battle of Stone's River, ultimately resulting in his retirement.

On recovery leave for thirty days for his shoulder wound acquired at Brentsville, Maxwell went home to Michigan in January 1863. While there, he traveled to the township of Flat Rock, where he became a master Mason at Hiram Lodge 110.[21] On his return from leave, he was sent to Washington, D.C., where his unit was part of the defense perimeter of the city. As the spring offensive opened, he was present at the Battle of Kelly's Ford, near Culpeper, Virginia, and the April and May 1863 battle in the woods south of the Rapidan River, in Virginia. This Battle of Chancellorsville is described by other names; however, by any name it was a disaster for the Union. With a force of 133,000 troops, Maj. Gen. Joseph Hooker of the Army of the Potomac was defeated by the 50,000 men of Gen. Robert E. Lee's Army of Northern Virginia. In seven days, from April 30 to May 6, Union forces suffered losses of more than 16,000 men killed, wounded, or missing, and the Confederate forces, 13,000. The battleground was strewn with hastily buried bodies. Here Maxwell suffered his second wound. Details are lost, but it appears he sustained a gunshot injury to a shoulder or clavicle.

Streaming into Culpeper County, Virginia, after their victory at Chancellorsville, most of the Confederate cavalry under General Stuart were camped near Brandy Station on the foggy morning of June 9, 1863. Ten thousand Union cavalry under Brig. Gen. Alfred Pleasonton crossed the Rappahannock to collide with 10,000 Confederates in what proved to be the largest and greatest cavalry-only battle on the North American continent. After twelve hours of raging combat, Confederate brigadier general William H. Fitzhugh "Rooney" Lee arrived with fresh men and horses, and the Union troops retreated back across the river. Each side experienced about a thousand casualties, among them the late-arriving General Lee, who sustained a serious wound of the thigh. Although Civil War historians declare there was no clear winner, this encounter unequivocally established the skill and bravery of Union cavalrymen as equal to those of South's mounted forces. Within thirty days, Union cavalry against Confederate cavalry would be severely tested again, this time in a formerly quiet Pennsylvania hamlet.

---

[21] Maxwell was suspended from the Masonic lodge in Michigan in 1877 for nonpayment of dues, presumably because he had been in Utah since 1869. A search of the records of the Masons' library in Salt Lake City gives no indication of his lodge participation while in Utah. Dues and other membership expenses, as well as costs for required livery conveyances, are the likely explanation of his inactivity among the Masons in Utah.

"Greatest" Battle

By late June 1863, the soldiers of the Army of Northern Virginia, commanded by military tactician Gen. Robert E. Lee, were in high spirits, buoyed by victories at Fredericksburg in December 1862 and Chancellorsville in May 1863. Their advance into Maryland, the border state that had wavered on secession, and into Pennsylvania brought an opportunity not only for further military victories but also for weakening the resolve of the Northern public to continue a war so costly in lives and dollars. A war of attrition carried to their own soil might aid Pennsylvania Democrats in their efforts to sway President Lincoln to end the war.[22]

To this point, Union superiority of numbers of men and war materials had not brought the victories expected. Now the soldiers of the Union army could be motivated not only by the issues of slavery and preservation of union but also by the prospect that they would be liberators, driving Confederate invaders off Union soil. Maj. Gen. George G. Meade had very recently been given command of the Army of the Potomac, and he had a core of determined veterans like George R. Maxwell in the ranks, who volunteered to remain on duty for the duration, in a quest for total military victory and unconditional surrender.[23]

Now approaching was the battle of two maneuvering armies in and around the small borough of Gettysburg, in Adams County, Pennsylvania. Many historians who interpret the events of the Civil War emphatically declare that the Battle of Gettysburg on July 1–3, 1863, was the "greatest" battle of that war and the greatest ever fought in the Western Hemisphere. A total of 160,000 soldiers were engaged, and more than 50,000 of them would be killed, wounded, captured, or go missing.

The Confederate forces had struck across Virginia, crossed the Potomac, and pushed into Maryland and Pennsylvania; they were positioned in a arc-shaped line west and north of Gettysburg. Lee brought three corps under the leadership of Lieutenant Generals James Longstreet, Richard Stoddert Ewell, and Ambrose Powell Hill, together with the cavalry division of J. E. B. Stuart. By the second day, Meade's forces were formed in a shorter, parallel, arc-shaped line inside the larger Confederate line.

---

[22] Some historians contend that General Lee came north for a raid on Philadelphia, believing that Northern factions would then bargain for the war's end. Rejuvenating his troops in the rich farmlands of Maryland and Pennsylvania was also a consideration.

[23] General Meade had replaced Maj. Gen. Joseph Hooker on June 28, 1863. On the third day of this new command he was directing the Battle of Gettysburg.

One of the Union cavalrymen, Brig. Gen. John Buford, a West Point graduate, appraised the topography and advised General Meade regarding the positioning of his Union forces around Gettysburg, and it was Buford's cavalry that opened the Battle of Gettysburg on July 1. His troops were pitted against a much larger infantry body approaching from the west, commanded by Confederate major general Henry Heth.[24] Fighting dismounted on McPherson Ridge, Buford's cavalrymen were outnumbered at least three to two by the Confederate infantry, but Buford's men were able to slow Heth's advance until Union major general John F. Reynolds arrived with the first division of his corps, the Iron Brigade commanded by Brig. Gen. Solomon Meredith and the Second Brigade commanded by Brig. Gen. Lysander Cutler.[25] By the end of July 1, Union forces, thanks in large part to Buford's cavalry, had taken the high ground of Cemetery Ridge and the area southward on the ridge nearly to the two promontories known as Big and Little Round Top. While these two armies did battle in and around Gettysburg and west of Cemetery Ridge, 5,000 to 6,000 Confederate cavalry under the command of Gen. J. E. B. Stuart were east of Gettysburg, trying to make contact with the body of Lee's army.[26]

On July 2 the Confederate army, positioned in a shepherd's-crook arc west, north, and east of the Union's lines, unfolded en echelon attacks by parts of General Longstreet's and General Hill's corps, directed on the Union forces located toward the southern end of Cemetery Ridge and at Devil's Den, the Peach Orchard, and the Wheatfield. From late afternoon to darkness, the boulder-strewn wheat field changed hands at least seven times, with an estimated 7,000 casualties in an area not larger than a football field. At the southern end, at Little Round Top, Col. Joshua Lawrence Chamberlain and his Twentieth Maine Infantry held the line. Their ammunition nearly exhausted, they repulsed the advancing Confederates with a bayonet charge that saved the day. On the northern end of the forces, three hours of fierce Confederate assaults by General

---

[24] Trowbridge, "Operation of the Cavalry," 3. Details of troop strength are from Busey and Martin, *Regimental Strengths and Losses*, 206.

[25] Coddington, *The Gettysburg Campaign*, 575. Trowbridge, "Operation of the Cavalry," 3. General Reynolds was killed on McPherson Ridge, probably by a sniper, as he was directing his troops.

[26] On June 30, Stuart fought against units of the Union cavalry near Hanover, Pennsylvania, fourteen miles east of Gettysburg. Stuart continued north to Carlisle, finally reaching Gettysburg on July 2.

Ewell's Second Corps gave them the lower half of Culp's Hill on the eastern slope of Cemetery Hill. Meanwhile, Maxwell and the Michigan Cavalry Brigade spent the night of July 2 in the saddle, arriving at the village of Two Taverns, about five miles south and east of Gettysburg, in time for only a very short interval of rest on the bare ground.[27]

By day three, Confederate major general Stuart's cavalry forces were attempting to flank the Union troops and attack them from the northeast, at their rear, on Meade's back side. Meade was on the high ground of Cemetery Ridge and focused west on the Confederate infantry on Seminary and Warfield ridges. Analysts suggest that Lee hoped to achieve a pincer movement, with the cavalry under Stuart attacking from the northeast while the infantry under Longstreet and Maj. Gen. George Edward Pickett came from the southwest, moving together to cut the federal lines in half.

Opposing General Stuart's 5,000 to 6,000 thousand were 2,800 Union cavalry, including George R. Maxwell and the men of the Michigan Brigade, led by the twenty-three-year-old, newly minted "Boy General," Brig. Gen. George Armstrong Custer. Early on the morning of July 3 the Union cavalry forces moved from Two Taverns to a point on the farm fields near the intersection of the Hanover Road and Low Dutch Road, now called the East Cavalry Field.[28] By eleven that morning Captain Maxwell and his men had established a lengthy, very thin picket line along the small creek called Little's Run.[29] As Stuart's men advanced, they were met and stopped, first by the Fifth Michigan with its seven-shot Sharps carbines and then by the Seventh Michigan Cavalry. Seeing his advance stalled, Stuart sent the riders of the First North Carolina and others of the brigade commanded by Gen. Wade Hampton. Stuart also ordered into action his "Invincibles," the men of the First Virginia Cavalry, under Gen. Fitzhugh Lee. Stuart later reported, "This hand to hand contest involved nearly all of my command," and Hampton added, "I went forward to extricate the 1st NC and Jefferson Davis' legion, and . . . I saw my whole brigade . . . charging."[30] Gen. Luther S. Trowbridge noted in his recounting, "On the Union side, to meet this new danger, reliance was mainly on the 1st

[27] Letter of Lt. George G. Briggs, March 26, 1888, in Ladd and Ladd, *Bachelder Papers*, 1256.
[28] Ibid., 1253–54.
[29] Trowbridge, "Operation of the Cavalry," map depicting location of military units, 17.

Michigan. The odds against them were great, but that regiment had established a reputation for desperate fighting."[31] The Third Pennsylvania Cavalry, led by Capt. William E. Miller and aided by seventy men of the First New Jersey Cavalry, charged at the advancing Confederate left flank, helping to split portions of the attacking force.[32]

Lt. William Brooke Rawle, also serving with Miller in the Third Pennsylvania Cavalry, described what he had observed:

> Everyone saw at once that unless this, the grandest attack of all, were checked, the fate of the day would be decided against the Army of the Potomac. They were Stuart's last reserves, and his last resource. If the Baltimore Pike was to be reached, and havoc created in our rear, the important moment had arrived. . . . Then Gen. Gregg rode over to the 1st Michigan Regiment . . . and gave them the word to charge. . . . Custer dashed up . . . and placed himself at its head.[33]

As the order was given for sabers to be drawn and the column to advance, Custer, who was at its head, picked up speed. Some of the men in the front rows hesitated, and Custer waved his finely tempered steel saber and shouted the words that propelled them forward, words that have become legend: "Come on, you Wolverines!"[34] Pennsylvania's Miller described the scene: "The First Michigan rushed forward with a fierce yell, and the enemy horsemen raced into each other with a crash one participant likened to 'falling timber.' So violent was the collision that many horses were turned end over end and crushed their riders beneath them. As fierce, hand to hand fighting ensued, Union forces closed in from the flanks and ripped through Stuart's column from both sides."[35] Lend an ear to the sounds heard by the fighters: "The clashing of sabers, pistols firing, demands for surrender and cries of combatants

---

[30] Letter of Captain Amasa E. Matthews, January 11, 1887, in Ladd and Ladd, *Bachelder Papers*, 1494.

[31] Trowbridge, "Operation of the Cavalry," 14.

[32] Capt. William E. Miller, Carlisle, Pa., to Gen. John B. McIntosh, June 8, 1878, in Ladd and Ladd, *Bachelder Papers*, 651–54. Miller was awarded the Medal of Honor and, when he died in 1919, was buried at Gettysburg.

[33] William Brooke Rawle, "Gregg's Cavalry in the Gettysburg Campaign," in Cavanaugh, *Military Essays and Recollections*, 163.

[34] Phipps, *"Come On, You Wolverines!"* 42–44. One saber of Custer's was so well-crafted that it could be bent nearly double. On its blade, engraved in Latin, is the motto: "Do not draw me without cause, do not sheath me without honor." Swanson, *G. A. Custer*, 16.

[35] Miller to McIntosh, June 8, 1878.

now filled the air. [36] Now visualize the men of the First Michigan as they "chopped and blasted their way through the wall of gray as though determined to win the day's struggle singlehandedly."[37]

One survivor of the Michigan Brigade at Gettysburg left his personal record of the details of the several units that made up the brigade. Samuel Harris, first lieutenant of the Fifth Michigan Cavalry, recounted in detail the actions of his unit and of Maxwell's, the Michigan First Cavalry:

> It was at this time that General Custer called on . . . the First Mich-igan[, who] struck the rebels on their left flank, about in the middle and actually went clear through them, cutting them in two parts. The sabre was all they used. Many a rebel was knocked over, horse and all by being struck with the horses of the First, and many more were killed and wounded by the sabre.
>
> The First Michigan boys striking the rebs in the left flank, crowded them up in a heap, so much so that the rebs could hardly do anything but try to defend themselves. . . . Although the rebs outnumbered the First four to one, yet they were completely beaten. . . . Without a doubt this was the most gallant cavalry charge made during the war. . . . [I]t was absolutely necessary to break that charge. . . . If the rebels could have destroyed them, our army would have been compelled to retreat.[38]

General Trowbridge later gave this summation of the two cavalry forces having faced one another: "While other troops performed their full duty, and deserve their full measure of credit, the fact still remains that the brunt of the fighting fell on Custer's brigade, and to that brigade chiefly belongs the credit of winning the fight."[39] The First Michigan Cavalry met the opposing cavalry and drove two Confederate brigades from the field, turning defeat into victory for the Union forces and assuring there would not be a pincer move against the Union forces on Cemetery Ridge.

Lee began his July 3 attack on Cemetery Ridge near noon with an intense artillery barrage, but unknown to his artillerymen—and to Lee—was that they were firing faulty ordinance, with 90 percent

---

[36] Longacre, *Cavalry at Gettysburg*, 238.   [37] Ibid.

[38] This text conforms to the handwritten record. Samuel Harris, 1st Lieut. Co. A, 5th Michigan Cavalry, "The Michigan Brigade of Cavalry at the Battle of Gettysburg," in *Civil War Unit Histories*, part 4, 9–16.

[39] Trowbridge, "Operation of the Cavalry," 17. Brig. Gen. David McMurtrie Gregg commanded the Second Division of the Cavalry Corps of Maj. Gen. Alfred Pleasanton at the Battle of Gettysburg.

of their shells not exploding. Their targets obscured by smoke, Lee's observers could not see that their barrage had done insufficient damage. As a result, Confederates charged across three-quarters of a mile of open ground against General Meade's pre-sighted artillery, and his well-prepared and little-damaged infantry troops atop Cemetery Ridge. Meade's guns had about fifteen feet of elevation above the open fields into which they were firing. In what became a disastrous encounter many Southern infantry units were virtually annihilated, literally shredded into pieces by intense Union artillery and rifle fire. A 100 percent loss was sustained by University of Mississippi students who made up the University Grays of the Eleventh Mississippi Infantry. The Color Company of the Thirty-eighth North Carolina Infantry, and Company F of the Twenty-sixth North Carolina Infantry, also lost 100 percent.[40] Many Confederate soldiers simply disappeared, their bodies so torn apart that identification of their fragments was not possible. Flesh, blood, and bodies dissolved into "a dense cloud of . . . arms, heads, blankets, guns and knapsacks."[41] An estimated 7,500 Confederate soldiers were lost during the massive infantry charge led by several Confederate generals, including Pickett, J. Johnston Pettigrew, and Isaac R. Trimble; the failure of the charge sealed the battle at Gettysburg, and it is now infamously labeled as "Pickett's Charge." Although he did not personally witness the battle, Col. Joshua Lawrence Chamberlain, an educated college professor, left his articulate description of it:

> Ploughed through by booming shot; torn by ragged bursts of shell; riddled by blasts of whistling canister; straight ahead to the guns hidden in their own smoke; straight on to the red, scorching flame of the muzzles, the giant grains of cannon-powder beating, burning, sizzling into the cheek; then upon them!—pistol to rifle shot, saber to bayonet, musket-butt to handspike and rammer; the brief frenzy of passion; the wild "hurrah"; then the sudden, unearthly silence; the ghastly scene; the shadow of death.[42]

Maxwell lost portions of several fingers from a saber wound to his left hand during the cavalry battle at Gettysburg. Although his wound was comparatively minor, the carnage he witnessed was staggering. In three days the Union lost more than 23,000 killed, wounded, captured,

---

[40] Stewart, *Pickett's Charge*, x.   [41] R. Alexander, *Five Forks*, 50.
[42] Chamberlain, *Passing of the Armies*, 146.

or missing. Confederate losses were said to total 28,000 soldiers. The description of the hospitals provides a different measure of the reality and severity of the battle:

> Virtually every house and barn in Gettysburg had been turned into an improvised hospital, where the haggard surgeons struggled to save the mangled wounded. Carpets and floors were awash in gore, walls were spattered with blood, and piles of amputated limbs were heaped outside the open windows. . . . [T]he Gettysburg court house was . . . overflowing with casualties, lying on the bare floor, covered with blood, and dirt and vermin, entirely naked having perhaps only a newspaper to protect their festering wounds from the flies.[43]

While poet Walt Whitman's words describe the scene he observed in the field shortly after the Battle of Chancellorsville in May 1863, they could just as accurately apply to the aftermath at Gettysburg in July. The numbers of wounded overwhelmed even the ability of improvised hospitals to house them, and these wounded, Union and Confederate, both lay unhoused in open fields:

> The groans and screams—the odor of blood, mixed with the fresh scent of the night, the grass, the trees—that slaughter-house! O well is it their mothers, their sisters cannot see them—cannot conceive, and never conceiv'd, these things. One man is shot by a shell, both in the arm and leg, both are amputated—there lie the rejected members. Some have their legs blown off—some bullets through the breast—some indescribably horrid wounds in the face or head, all mutilated, sickening, torn, gouged out—some in the abdomen—some mere boys—many rebels, badly hurt—they take their regular turns with the rest, just the same as any—the surgeons use them just the same.[44]

Lee retreated. The Union did not fully press its advantage, for it was already a Pyrrhic victory. Meade's forces were badly depleted, strained to near breaking point by forced marches to arrive in time for deployment. And to them was left the burden of attending to the wounded and the dead: "an estimated six million pounds of human and animal carcasses lay strewn across the field in the summer heat, . . . with 22,000 wounded who remained alive but in desperate condition."[45]

---

[43] C. Clark and Editors, *Voices of the Civil War*, 142.

[44] Whitman, "Night Battle," 35.

[45] Faust, *This Republic of Suffering*, 69.

At the midnight raid that Custer's cavalry made upon the retreating Confederates as they went westward through the mountains at Monterey Pass, Pennsylvania, Maxwell was wounded for the fourth time. Torrential rain, lightning, thunder, intense darkness, and steep, narrow roads made the battle more nightmarish than usual. Maxwell took a minié ball in the back of the knee joint, but it missed the major artery. No operation was done, but he was placed on medical leave and returned to Monroe for recovery. His right knee was forever painful and never again fully functional.

Encounters of 1864

Maxwell spent January through March 1864 in Michigan, recruiting for Union volunteers, but in May the First Michigan returned to the location where the Battle of Chancellorsville had taken place almost exactly a year earlier.[46] He saw the residual of the two days of recent fighting in the woodland, where visibility had been measured in yards, where the conflict was "the equivalent of a knife fight inside a dark closet . . . an engagement fought and ultimately settled by the actions of small knots of determined men shooting, stabbing, punching and wrestling each other beyond the control of their clueless commanders."[47] Historian Richard Bak observes that "in the massive Virginia campaigns of 1864, Grant would suffer one hundred thousand casualties—a tremendous cost, but one that Grant and Lincoln knew Lee's dwindling army could not match."[48] Nearly 18,000 Union men of Maj. Gen. George G. Meade's Army of the Potomac were killed or wounded in the defeat. Lee's forces sustained 7,500 casualties. Many of these deaths, as well as terrible suffering, resulted as wildfires started in the dense growth by the explosions of shells and advanced through tall grass, and as pine trees exploded when the flames reached their tops.

Maxwell's role in the country along the Rapidan River in early May 1864 is described by Gen. James H. Kidd, one of the few officers of the Michigan Brigade who left a lengthy personal record:

---

[46] Historians designate the 1864 battle as that of the Wilderness to distinguish it from the 1863 Battle of Chancellorsville, which was fought in nearly the same location.

[47] Bak, *Distant Thunder*, 180.

[48] Ibid.

Pickets on the Brock pike, under Captain Maxwell, First Michigan, were driven in, and a large force of the enemy's cavalry appeared on my front. . . . Captain Maxwell, with one squadron of the First Michigan Cavalry, charged the enemy in front. The enemy, after contesting the ground obstinately, was driven from the field in great disorder, leaving his dead and many of his wounded upon the ground. We also captured a considerable number of prisoners, who informed us that we had been engaged with Fitzhugh Lee's division of Cavalry.[49]

May 11 marked the Battle of Yellow Tavern, in which thousands of cavalry under General Custer collided with similar elements of the Confederacy under General Stuart. Custer sent his most experienced unit, the First Michigan, to charge across a terrain obstructed by five fences and a narrow bridge:

At a signal, the First spurred toward the left flank of the battery, everyone screaming what Custer called "a yell which spread terror before them." Distracted by the cannon- and carbine-fire steadily raking their center and right, the enemy gunners were slow to swing their pieces toward the charging mass. This gave the First Michigan . . . time to gather irresistible momentum. The First was so quickly upon them that the gunners could not depress the barrels of their cannon enough to strike back. Half the battery quickly went under, gunners and teams falling beneath the sabers of the attackers.[50]

Two weeks later, in the predawn hours of May 27 the Union forces were preparing to cross the Pamunkey River at Hanovertown, Virginia, by laying a pontoon bridge: "Custer sent a body of the First Michigan, led by the resourceful Captain Maxwell, across the stream in a pontoon boat. Leaping ashore, Maxwell's team charged and routed the enemy, taking a half-dozen prisoners."[51] The next day, at Salem Church and Haw's Shop, Virginia, Custer's Fifth and Seventh Michigan Cavalry were being decimated from the crossfire sprayed by a brigade of South Carolina mounted infantry from their position among trees and behind a swamp.[52] At Custer's order, Maxwell and the men of the First and Sixth Michigan Cavalry were ordered to charge, dismounted, into this

---

[49] *OR*, I, 36, part 1: 816.
[50] Longacre, *Custer and His Wolverines*, 213.
[51] Ibid., 222.
[52] "Haw's Shop" refers to a large blacksmith's shop not far from Richmond.

maelstrom.[53] Custer's personal report tells the tale: "The men [moved] forward with a cheer, driving the enemy from his position in great confusion and compelling him to leave the ground strewn with his dead and wounded."[54]

Custer's losses were greater in this battle at the blacksmith's shop than in any other engagement of this Virginia campaign, and Maxwell was among those severely wounded. Maxwell felt the thud of the heavy lead ball that struck his left forearm, and he heard the fracturing of the radius and ulna bones as they splintered. Evacuated to the General Hospital in Georgetown, Maryland, he avoided amputation but required three operations, resulting in the removal of several inches of bone. He was left with a draining, infected wound and forearm disability that would continue for the remainder of his life.[55] Maxwell was now joined to the small cadre of Civil War officers of both sides who continued to fight with only one useful arm.[56]

It was in this battle that Lt. James Isaac Christiancy, Custer's personal aide, was wounded, losing the end of one thumb and sustaining a severe gunshot wound of the thigh and hip.[57] The lieutenant was hospitalized in Washington and then cared for by Libbie Custer in her private apartments. There is no record, however, but hopefully Mrs. Custer stopped by the hospital bed of George R. Maxwell to leave a word of encouragement or concern.

Maxwell was transferred to St. Mary's Hospital in Detroit, Michigan, for further recovery.[58] However, he was back in the saddle for duty by September 19, 1864, according to Custer's own report. Custer tells of the movements of his command as they were ordered to cross the

---

[53] Dismounting and fighting on foot was a standard tactic of the time. Every fourth man held the horses, so the led horses would be available for quick remount. This reduced the fighting force by one-fourth. Confederate cavalry also fought dismounted but lacked repeating weapons, unless they had been acquired by capture.

[54] *OR*, I, 36, part 1: 821.

[55] His three operations were performed by surgeon S. R. Wooster, of the Michigan Cavalry. Barnes, Otis, and Huntington, *Medical and Surgical History*, 10:945.

[56] Among these were Confederate major general John B. Hood, whose left arm, from Gettysburg, was flail, and three major generals on the Union side—Oliver O. Howard and George J. Stannard, both of whom had right arm amputations, and Philip Kearney ("Kearny the Magnificent"), who had lost an arm at Churubusco in the Mexican War.

[57] Urwin, *Custer Victorious*, 152.

[58] NA, Full Pension File for George R. Maxwell, NATF 85, WC 277-346, master no. 1182162 (hereafter "NA, Full Pension File for George R. Maxwell").

Opequon Creek in the Shenandoah Valley, where they were confronted by entrenched Confederate infantry on the far side of the water. Initially the Seventh Michigan and the Twenty-fifth New York Cavalry were ordered ahead under protective fire from Col. James Kidd's Sixth Michigan, from his position on the heights above. Maxwell was commanding two squadrons of the First Michigan, and Custer gives him due praise: "Lt. Col. Maxwell, one of the most dashing and intrepid officers of the service, ordered the charge, and under cover of the heavy fire poured in by the Sixth Michigan, gained a footing upon the opposite bank, capturing rifle pits and a considerable number of prisoners."[59] Once the First and Seventh Michigan were on the other side of the river, Custer ordered them to test the strength and number of the enemy: "Lt. Col. Maxwell, who headed the charging column, as was his custom, succeeded in piercing the enemy's line of infantry and reaching to within a few feet of their artillery. Overwhelming numbers alone forced him to relinquish the intent of their capture, and he retired after inflicting a severe loss upon the enemy."[60]

By the fall of 1864 a gulf separated the old-timers—the 1861 "veteran volunteers" like Maxwell who remained after their initial commitment of three years—from the draftees and the paid-for substitutes now filling the ranks of the expanding Union army. Maxwell set a standard of performance and dedication to task that was to be emulated by the healthy and whole newcomers. He had, from the time of his wounding at Haw's Shop, only limited use of his left forearm and hand, and he told his sister in October that his arm was "again to be operated upon."[61] He was not able to hoist either the eight-pound Spencer that had become, in the hands of the Wolverines, the feared scourge of the Confederates with its rapid and massive firepower, or even the single-shot, rapidly reloaded Sharps carbine. Not unlike the one-armed cavalry major general Philip

[59] OR, I, 43, part 1: 455; Carroll, *Custer in the Civil War*, 33–34.

[60] OR, I, 43, part 1: 455; Carroll, *Custer in the Civil War*, 33–34. Also called the Third Battle of Winchester, this was the bloodiest clash to take place in the Shenandoah Valley. More than 54,000 men were massed by General Sheridan and Lt. Gen. Jubal Early near the two-hundred-acre Huntsberry farm and the small river called the Opequon. Union losses were 5,000 and Confederate losses 3,000, resulting in the defeated Confederates' retreat to Winchester.

[61] George R. Maxwell to Emma Elizabeth Maxwell, October 3, 1864, in possession of Bruce Turner Cunard II.

Kearny, who held the reins in his teeth, Maxwell was forced to rely on face-to-face, close-quarters combat, with a cavalry saber held in his right hand and a revolver on his belt. He fought by asserting leadership, in person and up close.

This conduct in battle had merited Maxwell not only retention but promotion to lieutenant colonel. He acquired command of the First Michigan Cavalry in the fall of 1864 and was given twenty days' leave in January 1865. But by February and March, he led his unit into western Virginia from Camp Russell near Winchester. In an official report of events on February 19, 1865, Maxwell wrote:

> As the column got well under way the rear guard was charged by about fifty men of the Twelfth Virginia Cavalry of McCausland's command. . . . [T]he enemy suffered severely in this encounter, as they could not compete with our superior carbine. I halted my column, sent a part across Tom's Brook, and with 100 men of the First Michigan charged them and drove them back within one mile and a half of Edenburg.[62]

The Union troops continued their march south from Charlottesville toward Scottsville, on the sharp hairpin curve of the James River, where Maxwell and his men were ordered to the city of Palmyra, on the Rivanna River southeast of Charlottesville. They destroyed bridges, mills, manufacturing plants, canal locks, and Confederate stores of cotton, tobacco, and other subsistence. As they turned back toward Scottsville, they destroyed an iron furnace at Little Fort Valley, and Maxwell "executed efficiently the duty entrusted to him, destroying the Rivanna Bridge at Palmyra, together with one cotton mill, one flouring mill and immense amounts of wheat, flour, cotton, wool, marching the same night to Scottsville."[63]

In mid-March, Maxwell was leading the advance of the First Michigan Cavalry at Hanover Court House, where he and his men destroyed a commissary wagon and a railroad bridge at the North Anna River crossing near Oxford. Shortly thereafter he was cited by Brig. Gen. Thomas C. Devin and made brevet colonel for "conspicuous gallantry in action."[64]

---

[62] *OR*, I, 46, part 1: 460.
[63] Ibid.
[64] Brig. Gen. Thomas C. Devin to Capt. E. M. Baker, *OR*, I, 46, part 1: 1127.

DEATH OF BROTHER WILL

On March 14, 1865, on or near the day following George R. Maxwell's meritorious recognition and field promotion, his younger brother, William B. Maxwell, died of disease in the hospital at Harper's Ferry. William had entered the Union army as a volunteer on September 20, 1864, as a private in Company B of the First Michigan Cavalry. He was missing for a period that October, causing great concern in his family; George commandeered ten men to search the battle lines and woods, looking for evidence that William was wounded, dead, or taken prisoner. Maxwell wrote to his sister that he himself had narrowly escaped being taken prisoner on this endeavor.[65] Will had also merited a path of rapid advancement and had been promoted to second lieutenant on March 7, 1865, but his death had come only a week later. Like countless thousands who succumbed in this war, he was only twenty-one years of age. William's body was sent home and buried in the family plot in Ash, Monroe County, a stone's throw from the fields his father farmed.

For many soldiers on both sides, their religious faith and their belief that they were serving God sustained them in combat; however, by 1864–65 the battlefield experiences moved many away from such certainty. Gerald Linderman describes the change: "Gone was that untroubled confidence that faith would extend the mantle of God's sanctification over all their activity. It was indeed difficult to see God's hand in combat and to remain convinced that it was driving the war forward in order that good might ensue."[66] Brother Will's death and an accumulating uncertainty about God's place in this grisly war brought no discernible outward change in Maxwell's commitment. Yet a letter to his sister, Emma, in November 1863 suggests that even before his brother's death, he had concern about depression among his "boys" and some doubt about the afterlife reward for those whose last sacrifice had been death: "All of the boys of the 1st Michigan, those who are left, hardly any are sick while those who are dead, I guess are well off in heaven, I guess, at least I hope so."[67]

---

[65] George R. Maxwell to Emma Maxwell, October 3, 1864.
[66] Linderman, *Embattled Courage*, 257.
[67] George R. Maxwell, Strasburg, Va., to Emma Maxwell, November 14, 1863, in possession of Bruce Turner Cunard II.

3

Return with Your Shield or on It

*Courage is a perfect sensibility of the measure of danger,
and a mental willingness to endure it.*

Gen. William Tecumseh Sherman

ON MARCH 31, 1865, UNION FORCES WERE NEAR PETERSBURG, Virginia, where their giants, Generals Ulysses S. Grant and Philip Henry Sheridan, had two goals: to interrupt the South Side Railroad, and to draw the Confederates out of their entrenched fortifications defending Petersburg and Richmond. By midafternoon that day, the First Michigan Cavalry, including Maxwell's unit and others of Sheridan's cavalry, found themselves in a difficult, retreating battle along the Dinwiddie Court House Road. Colonel Maxwell, working under Brig. Gen. Peter Stagg, was fighting on the left of a line along Brooke's Road. Mounted at first, Maxwell and his men soon found it necessary to dismount, as they were forced backward by heavy fire from superior numbers of Gen. George Pickett's infantry and Confederate cavalry under Gen. Fitzhugh Lee. They narrowly missed being entrapped.[1]

Pickett's having superior force on this day was uncharacteristic, for by this time the Confederates were outnumbered ten to one and had little left except spirit.[2] Unfortunately for their cause, Pickett did not press his temporary advantage of numbers but withdrew at dusk toward the hastily built,

[1] Hewett, *Supplement to the Official Records*, part 1, *Reports*, 9:827.
[2] Foote, *Civil War: A Narrative; Five Forks to Appomattox*, 130–131; Urwin estimates that Pickett had five infantry brigades and a total of about nineteen thousand men. Urwin, *Custer Victorious*, 236.

low entrenchment along White Oak Road. Confederate supplies were very short at Five Forks and Dinwiddie; Pickett's troops had only small rations of dried corn. His men were still standing but were starving.[3]

At nightfall the cavalrymen under Custer camped slightly north of the Dinwiddie Court House. Those under Brigadier Generals Thomas C. Devin and Peter Stagg, with whom Maxwell was serving, camped south of the courthouse. General Sheridan remarked that this had been "one of the 'liveliest' days in his experience, fighting infantry and cavalry with cavalry only."[4] However, Gen. Robert E. Lee was not deceived by the success, for he knew his forces were still in grave danger. Lee sent a message to Pickett: "Hold Five Forks at all hazards . . . [to] prevent Union forces from striking the Southside [*sic*] Railroad."[5]

That evening, anticipating his counterattack for the next day, Maxwell did what he had done for a thousand or more evenings. Whatever time was needed was devoted to his mount, for he knew the condition of his horse could determine his survival. The animal was fed as well as conditions would allow, then given his nose bag of oats and wheat. Combed and groomed, fetlocks cleaned, shoes secured, the animal was hobbled to allow it to forage but not stray. The rugged McClellan saddle and single-reined bit were inspected. He cleaned and oiled his revolver and made sure that the blade of his light-cavalry saber was polished, razor-sharp, and sparingly oiled and that it met with the correct degree of resistance as it was pulled from its metal scabbard. In the days preceding, rain had been heavy and frequent, so he replaced his tools of war in wax-coated canvas.

Early on April 1, Fools' Day, he donned the relatively new officer's uniform, with its short waist, that Union cavalry units had been issued that spring. Not knowing it was for the last time, Maxwell strapped on the heavy, black leather cavalry belt, which bore a cross-draw holster for his .44-caliber Army Colt six-shot revolver. His right hand was strong, now accustomed to wielding the saber. On the front of the belt was attached a small leather pouch for fresh percussion caps, and at the back, a larger one for additional ammunition. On his left side, his saber

---

[3] Foote, *Civil War: A Narrative; Five Forks to Appomattox*, 217.
[4] Bearss and Calkins, *Battle of Five Forks*, 46.
[5] Lee and Grant were aware of the strategic importance of Five Forks. As Charles Coffin put it at the time, "To take Five Forks is to take all. . . . [I]f Lee lost that position, all was lost—Petersburg, Richmond, his army, the Confederacy." Coffin, "Late Scenes in Richmond."

was held angled over the hip by two leather straps attached to the waist belt. Though he was almost incapable of using it, a Sharps carbine hung at his right side, suspended from his left shoulder by a leather belt.

Custer was ordered out in the early morning to follow Pickett's forces that had retreated. He found them behind a line about a mile in length, constructed of wooden fence rails, logs, and earthen mounds, on White Oak Road at the junction of the Five Forks. Custer was instructed to hold what he had taken but not to advance.[6]

From their campsites, Devin, Stagg, and Maxwell were also ordered out early and were to retrace their path of action of the previous day, northwest on the Dinwiddie Court House Road in the direction of the Five Forks junction. The morning air was pleasingly cool. The terrain on either side of the road was a mix of a gently undulating tableland, small farmsteads, tangled thickets, shallow ravines, pinewoods, and bogs, all moist from recent rain. Yellow dandelions and daffodils, bird's-foot violets, and bluebells were beginning to bloom; wild crocuses were pushing up. There were a few white blossoms on the dogwoods, and many of the trees were budding their green leaves. The hot pink blossoms of the flowering mimosa trees that they had seen other summers in Virginia's forests had not yet erupted. For the farmer this was a time of promise, of planting, of early green and growth; for this cavalryman it was time for more blood on the fields. It was a beautiful Virginia spring morning for one's final battle.

Moving slowly, Custer confirmed the observations about the entrenched Confederate positions. His men kept a substantial fire into the line, content to keep the infantrymen busy in their positions behind mounds and railings. Not until about four thirty in the afternoon did they finally hear their signal to charge.[7] The massive noise was not from the discharge of cannons but from the concentrated firing of muskets by the twelve thousand men of the Union Fifth Corps, under Maj. Gen.

---

[6] Bearss and Calkins, *Battle of Five Forks*, 83–84.

[7] Because Gen. Philip Sheridan was incensed with Gen. Gouverneur K. Warren that the start of the engagement was delayed until late in the afternoon, Sheridan took the extraordinarily severe step of relieving Warren of his battlefield command. However, the delay had worked to a serendipitous Union advantage. Generals Pickett and Fitzhugh Lee were absent from their units, attending a shad bake hosted by General Rosser, serving fish caught in the Nottoway River. Officers bearing urgent messages to warn of the attack did not know the whereabouts of their superiors. By the time Pickett returned to his unit, half of his forces had been lost or captured. Foote, *Civil War*, 3:138.

Gouverneur K. Warren, as they attacked the North Carolina and South Carolina infantry and Gen. Thomas T. Munford's cavalry at the eastern end of the Confederate mass.[8] This confrontation would come to be another of the multitude of aptly named "bloody angles" in this grisly war. The small cavalry brigade of Brig. Gen. Ranald Slidell Mackenzie, north of the angle, was moving west to seal the Confederates inside it.[9]

Union colonel Charles L. Fitzhugh now ordered his Second Brigade cavalrymen dismounted, and under heavy fire they advanced through the woods across a branch of Chamberlain Bed toward the Confederate line on White Oak Road. War historian Andrew Humphreys describes what an observer would have seen: "The natty cavalrymen . . . swarmed through the pine thickets and dense undergrowth, looking as if they had been especially equipped for crawling through knotholes. Those who had magazine guns created a racket in those pine woods that sounded as if a couple of army corps had opened fire."[10]

The men of the First Michigan, remaining mounted, also crossed the creek to reinforce the assault. In several places they closed within twenty yards of the Confederate works, and in other spots they breached the defense line and took several prisoners.[11] However, they were shortly convinced that the Confederate position was yet too strong, and Devin ordered them to regroup in the woods. Custer's forces were on the far left side of the assault line. Maxwell found that his force had lost contact with the units of Colonel Fitzhugh, on his right, and informed Col. Alexander C. M. Pennington, Third New Jersey Cavalry, First Brigade, that he would ride his Michigan men parallel to the Confederate line, in order to contact the separated groups and seal any hole in their line of advancing cavalry forces. This maneuver would expose Maxwell and make him and the men of the First Michigan a particularly inviting target for Confederate fire.

Not only were the units of Devin and Stagg charging forward into the breastworks taking ferocious fire from infantry, but they were also targets for two Napoleon cannons and a three-inch rifled cannon placed

---

[8] General Warren did not have cannons in his attack; heavy rains in previous days made passage of these heavy pieces on muddy surfaces impractical.

[9] Bearss and Calkins, *Battle of Five Forks*, 91.

[10] Humphreys, *Virginia Campaign of '64–'65*, 350–51.

[11] This episode, in which Maxwell charged Confederate lines protectively enclosed by stacked railroad ties, may be the one that he later refers to as having merited his field promotion to brigadier general.

on the slightly higher ground of the Five Forks junction. Virginia Artillery colonel William Johnson Pegram had instructed his men, "Fire your canister low!"[12] Thomas Taylor Mumford described the scene that followed: "The roar of gallant Pegram's thunderous guns . . . gave volume to the tumultuous voice of battle. The earth trembled under the shocks . . . sulfurous smoke wreathed the trees in ghostly, trailing garments. The low sun showed faintly through the smoke-clouds like a pale moon."[13] Despite the heavy musket and cannon fire, the several cavalry units of General Sheridan, Maxwell's among them, pressed nearer to the entrenched Confederate line.

Following Sheridan's battle plan, Custer circled his men to the western end of the Confederate line, in concert with Mackenzie's cavalry and Warren's Fifth Corps closing on the eastern end. The Confederates were doubly flanked. Pickett's entire force of infantry and cavalry was caught in a massive pincer. The Confederates were thus routed in what historians have said was undoubtedly the "Waterloo of the Confederacy."[14]

The celebration on this April night was described by one of Grant's officers: "All but the imperturbable general-in-chief were on their feet giving vent to wild demonstrations of joy. . . . [T]here was a bewildering state of excitement, grasping of hands, tossing of hats, and slapping each other on the back. [The Battle of Five Forks] meant the beginning of the end. . . . It pointed to peace and home."[15]

---

[12] Smoothbore twelve-pound Napoleon cannons fired canister rounds. Canister was similar to present-day shotgun shells, but much larger in size. A round consisted of a metal cylinder filled with twenty-seven metal balls, each the size of a golf ball, that scattered in an expanding pattern into the oncoming enemy. Pegram's single rifled cannon was firing special Read-Broun shells, designed specifically for the longer-ranged, rifled weapons. Pegram ordered his gunners to aim low in order to avoid overshooting their targets. Chris Calkins, Five Forks, National Parks Service, pers. comm., May 2007. See also Bearss and Calkins, *Battle of Five Forks*, 106; Foote, *Civil War: A Narrative; Five Forks to Appomattox*, 140.

[13] Thomas Taylor Mumford, "Five Forks: The Waterloo of the Confederacy, or the Last Days of Fitz Lee's Cavalry Division," typescript (ca. 1908), MSS 5:1 M9237:1, Virginia Historical Society, Richmond, 29–30.

[14] Jeffry Wert observes that "Pickett . . . had 5 brigades of infantry, 3 divisions of cavalry, 10 cannon and roughly 10,000 men"; Wert, *Controversial Life*, 218. Not only Urwin, but other historians put the combined numbers of infantry and cavalry under Pickett at 19,000 men; e.g., Boatner, *Civil War Dictionary*, 282. Richard O'Connor estimates that Union casualties at Five Forks were 830 men, and Confederate losses 2,950. He also states that "Sheridan took 6,000 prisoners, 6 guns, [and] 13 battle flags"; O'Connor, *Sheridan, the Inevitable*, 254. Later restudy of Confederate losses at Five Forks puts the number of prisoners at 3,200 to 4,500; Calkins, "Battle of Five Forks."

[15] Calkins, "History and Tour Guide," 101.

George R. Maxwell did not participate in the night's celebration with his fellow officers, however. Near dusk, only minutes from the darkness that would halt firing on both sides, Maxwell was fighting with his one good arm, when suddenly his military career was brought to an abrupt end. He had just dismounted when he received his last, most serious, most disabling wound. It was as if he had been hit with a fence post swung by a strong Georgia farm boy. Knocking him to the ground, a conoidal minié ball had come from his right and entered his left knee on its inner side, shattering the bones of the joint. He could feel nothing of his foot, and movement of the knee was excruciatingly painful. Through the night he lay quietly on the moist loam pad of fallen leaves in the tangled woods, checked and rechecked the wound site, but bleeding remained modest. Before dawn, he was found by his close friend and relative Frank Hawley and taken to the nearby Gravelly Run Methodist Episcopal Church. With the ground and the roads still muddy from the heavy rains of the preceding days, they picked their way on horseback through the trees, a trooper at each side supporting him in the saddle. With each movement of his mount, white-hot pain shot upward in his injured leg.

The previous morning, Gravelly Run Church had been the marshaling site for the troops of General Warren's Fifth Corps. As darkness fell, the small church was transformed into a local field hospital for the wounded of both sides. George Townsend describes the scene he observed there: "I found . . . on its base floors the screaming wounded. Blood ran in little rills across the planks, and, human feet treading in them, had made indelible prints in every direction. . . . Federal and Confederate lay together. . . . [A]ll the while came in the dripping stretchers, to place in this golgotha new recruits for death and sorrow."[16]

Either refusing or not yet requiring an immediate amputation, Maxwell was moved from Gravelly Run Church to the Cavalry Corps Hospital at City Point, on the James River. Over the next thirteen days Maxwell's pain intensified, as the swelling and discoloration of his leg increased. His condition deteriorated, and unmistakable signs of infection appeared. On April 15 he was transferred by the hospital steamer *Connecticut* and admitted on April 16 to Armory Square Hospital in

---

[16] George Townsend, from his description at the church on observing the death of Union brevet brigadier general Frederick W. Winthrop of the Fifth Corps, in *New York World*, cited in Bearss and Calkins, *Battle of Five Forks*, 117–18. Shot through the lung, Winthrop died as he arrived at the improvised hospital.

Washington, D.C., where there was alleged to be "everything modern that could alleviate suffering."[17]

Maxwell was initially evaluated by acting assistant surgeon Charles Augustus Leale. On the evening of April 14, two days preceding Maxwell's admission, Dr. Leale had been the first physician to reach the side of President Abraham Lincoln when he was shot at Ford's Theater. Returning shortly to his duties at Armory Square immediately after Lincoln's death, Leale found Maxwell's case of great interest and made it the subject of a specific case report that was later published, complete with a drawing of a very thin, youthful-appearing George R. Maxwell and his healing stump.[18] Done with ether anesthesia, Maxwell's operation was reported in detail in the *Medical and Surgical History of the Civil War*:

> The left knee joint was opened, . . . a conoidal ball . . . was extracted. . . . He was very anaemic and in a generally unfavorable condition; . . . the knee joint was filled with pus, and the muscles of the thigh had been separated by extensive abscesses. . . . April 17th, . . . under the influence of ether, and the thigh amputated . . . at the middle third, by Surgeon D. W. Bliss, U.S.V.; the stump was dressed with water, and the patient placed in bed. April 18th, although twelve ligatures had been applied, haemorrhage continued to take place . . . and altogether about eight ounces of blood was lost. Applied liquor ferri persulphas by a camel's hair brush to the whole of the surface of the wound, which had been left open and exposed to the air. . . . [T]his, with the styptic, entirely checked all oozing. On April 20th, the granulations had become healthy; about two drachms of pus discharged daily. On the 30th the stump had nearly closed. June 23d, a piece of necrosed femur . . . four inches in length, was removed. August 8th, he was mustered out of service; his stump . . . was solid and in good condition.[19]

---

[17] Armory Square Hospital was constructed in the summer of 1862, on what was Seventh Street and opposite what is today the Smithsonian's National Air and Space Museum. Nearby was an open sewer reeking with the filth of the city. It was a one-thousand-bed hospital, one of the largest of the Civil War. Its location provided ready access to the major streets, the wharves, and the railroad depot. "Site of Armory Square Hospital," Historic Medical Sites in the Washington, D.C., Area, www.nlm.nih.gov/hmd/medtour/armory.html.

[18] Dr. Leale's care was said to have aided Lincoln's survival to the next day. Leale was born in New York in 1842 and was newly out of medical school when he was serving at Armory Square Hospital in April 1865. His notable efforts to record hospital cases and write about them may have stemmed from his inexperience in the actual performance of operations.

[19] Barnes et al., *Medical and Surgical History*, vol. II, chap. 10, 278. Walt Whitman spent many hours and days in the Civil War hospitals, and his opinion of the surgeons was, for the most part, very favorable. In a letter to a soldier's mother, he described Dr. Bliss as "one of the best surgeons in the army." Whitman, *Specimen Days* (London ed., 1887), 43.

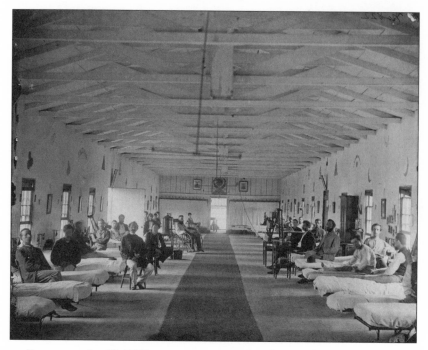

Representative Civil War–era patient ward at Armory Square Hospital,
Washington, D.C. *Library of Congress, Selected Civil War
photographs, 1861–1865, LC-DIG-cwpb-04246.*

Maxwell was left with only a ten-inch stump below the left hip, and
optimistic but vague promises of some sort of a prosthetic replacement.

Maxwell's survival was unusual; the complication of postoperative
hemorrhage after amputation, as experienced by Maxwell and many
others, so interested Leale that he authored a special publication that
was referenced in later scientific descriptions of problems encountered
in treating war wounds.[20] Because of the stress, blood loss, and risk of
infection, death was highly correlated with the level of the amputation.
A mortality rate of 30 percent has been cited for below-elbow or below-
knee amputations, but the rate was higher following amputations above
the knee. The death rate for those near the hip was 66 percent. For those

---

[20] Leale, "Intermediary Haemorrhage," 176.

Drawing of George R. Maxwell after leg amputation. *Barnes, Otis, and Huntington,* Medical and Surgical History, *vol. 2, part 3, fig. 192, p. 278, case 459.*

performed only a few inches distant from the hip, and those under-taken as a secondary procedure for gangrene or ascending infection, as in Maxwell's case, the mortality rate was more than 70 percent [21]

Military records list Maxwell as present at the surrender of the Confederate forces at Appomattox Court House, Virginia, on April 9, 1865, but this assertion is at odds with the degree of his injury and the hospital records.[22] It would also have been impossible for him to accompany the Michigan Cavalry Brigade and General Custer to the Grand Review of the victorious federal armies in Washington, D.C., on May 23, 1865.

---

[21] Bollett, *Civil War Medicine,* 256; Wegner, *Phantom Pain,* 1–18.

[22] In the Appomattox campaign records, Maxwell and Capt. Edward L. Negus are listed as co-commanders of the First Michigan Cavalry, indicating that Negus took command after Maxwell was hospitalized. They were under Maj. Gen. Philip Henry Sheridan, Army of the Shenandoah; Brig. Gen. Wesley Merritt, First Cavalry Division; and Brig. Gen. Thomas C. Devin, First Cavalry Brigade of Brig. Gen. Peter Stagg.

Taking the Measure of the Man

During the engagements of the First Michigan Cavalry over four years of service, Maxwell received gunshot wounds to both knees and his left forearm, had his left clavicle broken and left shoulder wounded from canister shot, was wounded by a bullet to the right shoulder, lost portions of the index, middle, and ring fingers of his left hand from a saber injury, and sustained saber wounds of the right groin. Because of these wounds, but especially because of his high thigh amputation, he was given an honorable discharge and a monthly disability pension of thirty dollars. Not yet twenty-three years old, and with his wounds in various stages of recovery, he was declared totally and permanently disabled and discharged August 4, 1865.[23]

Judged by the duration of his service, his dedication to victory interrupted only for recovery from wounds or for severe winter weather, his refusal to let even serious wounds or major disability deter his leadership, and his disregard for his own personal safety, this was not the record of any ordinary Civil War volunteer. Nor was his an ordinary unit. The First Michigan Cavalry was the oldest of the Michigan Cavalry forces and provided the stabilizing force of veterans, especially through the latter half of the war. They were also the heart of Gen. Ulysses Grant's cavalry under Gen. Philip Sheridan and Gen. George A. Custer. "Custer's Michigan Cavalry Brigade" was the term proudly applied to joining together of the First, Fifth, Sixth, and Seventh Michigan brigades during the period 1863–65.[24] Gettysburg was the defining battle that linked the names of Custer and the Michigan Cavalry Brigade, for this was the first battle under Custer's command after the formal organization of the brigade. The Michigan Brigade sustained the highest casualties of any mounted unit of the federal army, with 528 killed in battle or dead from battle wounds and 1,575 officers and men lost from all causes. Forty percent of these losses were at Gettysburg.[25] Gettysburg was the sentinel event for the Union cavalry; from that point to the end of the war, the Confederates were outgunned and outhorsed.[26]

---

[23] NA, Full Pension File for George R. Maxwells. Dr. Leale cited August 8 as the day of Maxwell's discharge.

[24] The Twenty-fifth New York Cavalry was added to the brigade for the Battle of Winchester. At times, other units were temporarily added.

[25] Boatner, *Civil War Dictionary*, 216; Kidd, "Michigan Cavalry Brigade," 24.

[26] Wert, *From Winchester to Cedar Creek*, 22.

Seven Union officers who survived major amputations after gunshot injuries in the spring and summer of 1865, photographed at Armory Square Hospital. (*left to right*) Capt. Charles H. Houghton, Capt. Edward A. Whaley, Lt. Moretz Lowenstein, Lt. J. G. Turke (*standing*), Lt. W. H. Humphreys, Gen. George R. Maxwell, with the left thigh amputation site exposed, and Lt. W. C. Weeks. Standing at the left is acting assistant surgeon C. P. Porter. (The men were misidentified in the original publication.) With magnification the Custer Medal can be seen on the lower edge of the white name tag on Maxwell's jacket. *Otis*, Histories of Two Hundred and Ninety Six Surgical Photographs, *GS63, fig. 24, no. 101.*

A surgeon of the 121st New York Infantry wrote of the Union cavalry in a letter to his wife in August 1864: "We really have something like cavalrymen now. General Sheridan . . . having his old reliable troops in the saddle, and he personally overseeing every movement. I like him first rate, and so do all."[27] In the words of the editor of the *New York Herald* in 1864: "Soldiering with the Michigan cavalry has been one

[27] Greiner, Coryell, and Smither, *Surgeon's Civil War*, 237.

continuous road of hard fighting. Both on foot with their carbines, and mounted, their sabres have carried terror in every charge."

Custer called his Michigan men his Wolverines. Each horseman could be readily identified, in battle or on parade, by the flapping of his blood-red neck scarf. Armed with Sharps carbines, Spencer rifles and carbines, or Burnside carbines, sabers, and Colt .36- or .44-caliber pistols, and well mounted on horses that Custer insisted be color-matched within each unit, the Michigan Cavalry Brigade fought in all but one of the significant battles of the Army of the Potomac.[28] Under Custer's command the Michigan Brigade earned a feared reputation among the Confederates and "achieved a reputation and secured for itself frequent and honorable mention in the history of war."[29] Custer historian Eric Wittenberg has high praise for the brigade in his evaluation:

> The Michigan Cavalry Brigade, known to the world as one of the best and most effective bodies of troops ever brought under the eye of the best commander in the service; selected as it was from the best material, and commanded by the best officers to be found; armed with the most approved arms; never really beaten in battle, but always pushing the enemy, it gained a renown equaled by few; excelled by none.[30]

The flamboyant, charismatic Custer appreciated the extraordinary acts of bravery of those under his command, and like several other military leaders of the war, he responded with a personal recognition:

> [He] commissioned the renowned New York jewelers, Tiffany and Company, to design and manufacture what became known popularly as the "Custer Badge." It was made with a solid gold Maltese Cross with the name "Custer" inscribed across it and surmounted by a single brigadier's star, with the motto of the state of Michigan in Latin inscribed below. It was only available on the Boy General's order, and those officers lucky

---

[28] The Union cavalry carried superior weapons. Short-barreled Sharps carbines were purchased in large numbers. Breech-loading, they were percussion cap ignited, and though single-shot, they could fire six or more rounds per minute. They were accurate to a range of 150 yards, and rifled weapons to 300 yards. They came in various calibers, .52 caliber being the most common. The Spencer was also .52 caliber, with a tubular magazine that passed through the butt of the weapon, and held seven copper, rimfire cartridges. Although rarely issued, ten extra magazines could be carried in a special box, giving the soldier seventy rounds of rapid fire. Boatner, *Civil War Dictionary*, 735, 782. The Burnside .54-caliber carbines required a special conical-shaped cartridge and, under the exigencies of the war, could become difficult to supply. Custer continued his practice of color-matching the mounts of different units in his Indian campaigns after the war.

[29] Congressman F. W. Kellogg, *Detroit Advertiser and Tribune*, October 11, 1864.

[30] Wittenberg and Husby, *Under Custer's Command*, 7.

enough to receive it called it a "beautiful present" or "a token of honor" and wore it with pride.[31]

This high honor was given very sparingly, only to the foremost Wolverine officers for distinguished and meritorious action in the field and under fire. Since this was a personal medal in the tradition of other personal Civil War medals such as the Kearny Cross and the Gillmore and Butler medals, there are no official records of its recipients. Tiffany does not maintain a record of the number of Custer Medals it produced or to whom they were awarded.[32] Neither do Custer's own writings contain a list of the recipients. Author John Peter Beckendorf cites what is thought to be the only surviving personal letter from Custer to Tiffany and Company requesting the making of one of the medals. This one was for Lt. Robert C. Wallace.[33] However, Maxwell left unequivocal evidence engraved on his tombstone that he was among those who received the Custer Medal in recognition of his meritorious service with the Michigan Cavalry Brigade.

Others besides Custer attested that Maxwell followed the example of his leader during his service with the Michigan Cavalry and early on earned a reputation for extraordinary bravery under fire. Col. James H.

---

[31] Urwin, *Custer Victorious*, 282.

[32] Louisa Bann, Research Department, Tiffany and Co., New York, pers. comm., May 2005. Present-day collectors of Civil War memorabilia claim that Custer Medals are very rare, and most vendors have never seen one or had one for public offering.

[33] Beckendorf is vice president of the Los Angeles Civil War Roundtable and a member of the West Coast Civil War Collectors. John Peter Beckendorf, "Maj. Wallace's Custer Medal," 29. Custer historians are divided on their view of the Custer Medal. Some agree with Beckendorf that the medal was given by personal order of Custer only to those officers he judged meriting it. Others say the award was initiated by Michigan Brigade officers, and then approved by Custer. Elizabeth Bacon Custer who was given a medal by her husband, records: "It was designed by the officers and had the Michigan motto and the name Custer." Arlene Reynolds, *Civil War Memories*, 83. General James Kidd and Major Wallace are the only two men, besides Maxwell, who have, directly or indirectly claimed to have been recipients. Kidd allegedly paid for his own medal. If the awards were strictly at Custer's choice, it would seem that Thomas Ward Custer, his brother, would have been a recipient, for he received two highly prestigious Medal of Honor awards. James Christiancy was also a Medal of Honor recipient and is not designated as a Custer Medal recipient. The design of the medal is also in dispute; at times the crossed sabers are pointed downward, possibly reflecting the recipient having retired. Frank Mercatante, pers. comm., Grand Rapids, Mich., August 2006. The engraving on Michigan Cavalry memorial on East Cavalry Field at Gettysburg shows the saber tips pointing upward. Of the hundreds of photos taken of Custer and his wife, only four show them wearing the medal. One is one taken with wife, Libbie, and former slave Eliza. Only the upper two-thirds of the medal, which is pinned on his red cravat, is visible. In this photo the medal has no crossed sabers. Swanson, *G. A. Custer*, 32.

REPLICA OF THE CUSTER MEDAL
Commissioned by Gen. George Armstrong
Custer and crafted by Tiffany & Co. of
New York, the medal was awarded by Custer
from 1863 to 1865 to the most deserving
officers of the Michigan Cavalry. In Latin,
Tuebor means "I will defend." The medal is
also depicted with saber tips pointed upward
or without the crossed sabers. *Photograph by
John Gary Maxwell.*

Kidd, another Custer Medal recipient and a Michigan Cavalry historian after the war, tells of Maxwell's role in the Battle of Buckland Mills near Brandy Station in October 1863:

> Captain George R. Maxwell of the First Michigan, whose regiment was
> . . . in the rear . . . asked permission to take a carbine and go on foot with
> the men of the Sixth, who were in front. . . . [G]iving his horse into the
> charge of an orderly, he was in a few moments justifying his already well-
> established reputation as a man of courage, by fighting like an enlisted
> man on the skirmish line of a regiment not his own . . . voluntarily
> exceeding any requirements of duty.[34]

The Custer Medal was a testimony of Maxwell's bravery in combat. Over the history of warfare, other emblems and rewards have been used for recognition. It is said that in ancient Greece a Spartan warrior was told to return with his shield or be carried home upon it. Returning without one's shield meant that his courage had failed and the shield was dropped. However, to be stretchered on his shield implied that, wounded or dead, he had fallen courageously and would be honorably returned. Not once did George R. Maxwell's courage fail through four years of unprecedented carnage. The shield he carried home was forever marked with the evidence.

---

[34] Kidd, *Riding with Custer*, 214.

PART TWO

1869 to *1892*

4

Turning West amid the Hostiles

The darkest places in hell are reserved for those
who remain neutral in times of moral crisis.
Paraphrased from Dante Alighieri's *Inferno*, Canto 3

AT THE END OF THE WAR, THE MEN OF THE MICHIGAN CAVALRY
units anticipated going home to be honored for their heroic record. Instead
they were ordered to Fort Leavenworth, Kansas, then to Fort Laramie, as
part of a force of two thousand soldiers sent against the Sioux, Arapahos,
and Cheyennes who were raiding in the western territories. They served,
neither willingly nor happily, in the Powder River Expedition under Brig.
Gen. Patrick Edward Connor, from July 1 to August 5, 1865.[1] Through the
winter of 1865–66, the First Michigan Veteran Cavalry was inactive, biv-
ouacked in snow and cold at Camp Douglas, near Salt Lake City; its men
were finally mustered out on March 10, 1866.[2] George R. Maxwell's close
friends Frank Hawley and James Kidd traveled west and were with General
Connor. However, three years would pass before Maxwell himself moved
west and had his first meeting with the general, in Utah Territory.[3]

---

[1] After his controversial and unsuccessful Powder River Indian campaign, Connor was removed
as commander of the District of the Plains and returned to his former command at Camp
Douglas. Varley, *Brigham and the Brigadier*, 229–59; Long, *Saints and the Union*, 268.

[2] *Union Army*, 3:416–18. The Michigan units sent west to join General Connor after the war were
known as the First Michigan Veteran Cavalry. They considered the western tour unjust after
the unit's long war service under great hardship. To add insult, no funds were given at time
of discharge for travel expenses to return to Michigan. Michigan governor Henry Howland
Crapo argued their cause until Congress provided $210 for each soldier. Longacre, *Custer and
His Wolverines*, 293–94.   [3] Longacre, *Custer and His Wolverines*, 283–92.

Back to Michigan

Recovered sufficiently from his amputation, Maxwell returned to Monroe County, Michigan. His height seemed accentuated because of the marked weight loss that accompanied his recovery. His father, Reuben Maxwell, was now forty-eight years old, and Reuben's third wife, Emeline, was now thirty-five. The elder Maxwell, though working by himself, was prospering on his farm.[4] George's half-brothers Edwin and Frank were ages six and four, respectively, and Willis was six months old. Another half-brother, Charles, had been born near Christmas 1864 but died at two months. Sister Emma, eighteen, was unmarried and living at home.

Though rail thin, handicapped by multiple injuries, and missing a leg, George Maxwell was seen by at least one young woman as attractive, with much to offer. On September 16, 1865, slightly more than a month after his discharge, he married twenty-five-year-old Emma Belle Turner, one of seven children of James Lawrence Turner, a wealthy grocer and merchant of Connecticut.[5] Maxwell had apparently courted Emma Belle during stays in Monroe County while on medical leave, recovering from his several wounds. She was considered a beautiful woman and was well known in the community for her pleasing singing voice.

Happily married and with his health improving, Maxwell continued his study of law, begun during intervals of quiet in the war. Now he made faster progress, for he worked under the tutelage of lawyer Otis Adams Critchett, a boyhood friend who had missed war service because of severe asthma.[6] Critchett had studied at Lodi Academy, a private preparatory school not far from the Michigan State Normal School in Ypsilanti, which Maxwell had attended. Following graduation from Lodi in 1862, Critchett completed his law degree at the University of Michigan in 1864 and then set up practice in Monroe. He was described as "a cautious and safe counselor [and] a clear advocate, depending on a logical and rational presentation of his case rather

---

[4] Reuben Maxwell did well in the postwar economy. Five years after war's end, the value of his real estate, as listed in the federal census, was $14,000.

[5] The Turner family descendants are unclear about why Emma Belle was living in Michigan rather than with the family in Connecticut.

[6] Otis Critchett suffered lifelong severe recurring asthma that had begun in childhood; however, his brothers, George Winslow Critchett and James C. Critchett, served in the Eighteenth Michigan Infantry.

George R. Maxwell's first wife,
Emma Belle Turner Maxwell.
*Courtesy of Maxwell Fisher Turner,
Elizabeth Jane Cunard Carey,
and Bruce Turner Cunard II.*

than oratorical efforts or sympathetic pleas."[7] Also the Monroe County prosecuting attorney, the Twenty-second Judicial Circuit judge, and a trustee of Albion College, Critchett was distinguished and respected and had an excellent practice.[8]

Maxwell soon became the register of deeds for Monroe, and because statutes at the time permitted him to "read the law" as an apprentice with Critchett, he became qualified without formal schooling in law. Before long, Critchett and Maxwell formed a law partnership in Monroe. Others within the legal community who may have helped in Maxwell's education included Isaac P. Christiancy and his son James, with whom Maxwell had served in the Michigan Cavalry; Frank Raleigh, who would later accompany Maxwell on his train ride west; and David A. Nobel, who later was elected mayor of the city of Monroe.[9]

---

[7] Wing, *Monroe County, Michigan*, 458–60.

[8] *Monroe Democrat*, June 15, 1893.

[9] Federal census records for Monroe County, Michigan, 1850, 1860, 1870. "Death of Frank Raleigh," *Monroe Commercial*, July 25, 1879.

Maxwell was on the path of achievement, likely to follow Otis Critchett to a comfortable life of taste and refinement, a home with a well-stocked library, the regard of the legal community, and the respect of the public for his war record, but tragedy intervened. Fifteen months after their marriage, Emma Belle died suddenly of unknown cause at the nearby city of Newport, on the shore of Lake Erie. Her body was taken by her grieving parents to the family's hometown of Montville, Connecticut, for burial.[10] Following his wife's death, Maxwell found strength to continue legal work in the city for a time. However, service to his country was the life he had known, and when struck with her loss, he soon returned to the familiar. In 1868 he exercised one of the options earned by his war service and requested a federal appointment from his former commanding officer, Ulysses S. Grant, now president of the United States. Maxwell was informed he would be superintendent of Indian Affairs in Arizona Territory, but this appointment was changed because Grant had previously promised the post to a citizen of his own home city in Illinois. Maxwell was assigned instead to Utah Territory as the Register of Land.[11]

Allegorical Hurricane

For George R. Maxwell and for Americans in general, both North and South, the Civil War had been a roiling cataclysm, the defining experience of their entire lifetime. It profoundly affected Maxwell's body and mind, touching every corner of his personal and public life. The war transformed the lives of millions on both sides for more than two

---

[10] New London County, Connecticut, records say that Emma Belle's death was due to "congestion of the brain." Viral encephalitis, bacterial meningitis, or rupture of a brain aneurism is the most likely medical diagnosis.

[11] According to his remarks at Maxwell's funeral, Ovander J. Hollister of the Internal Revenue Service in Utah repeatedly urged the general to make a written record his experiences in the war and in Utah. Although Maxwell never did, Hollister told the story that Maxwell was very angry at President Grant over the change of assignment from Arizona to Utah, thinking that his missing leg and physical limitations were the real reason for Grant's change. Maxwell may also have disliked the salary discrepancy between $1,500 per year for an Indian agent and $500 per year as Register of Land. Reportedly he challenged Grant in public; Grant replied only that the policy with the Indians was being altered and only clergyman would be sent to the territories as Indian agents, an explanation that Maxwell dismissed without comment. Hollister's account does not mention Grant's having previously promised the Arizona post to an Illinois resident. "Gen. Maxwell's Funeral," *slt*, July 4, 1889, 4, col. 4.

generations. Of a total population of thirty million, more than three million had served.[12] Death and mourning were everywhere. Half of all military-age males served. In the North, 6 percent of males age thirteen to forty-three died. In the South, the figure was 18 percent, and among the African Americans who fought, it was 20 percent.[13] It was, according to Faust, a virtual "harvest of death."[14]

> Men thrown by the hundred into burial trenches; soldiers stripped of every identifying object before being abandoned on the field; bloated corpses hurried into hastily dug graves; nameless victims of dysentery or typhoid interred beside military hospitals; men blown to pieces by artillery shells; bodies hidden by woods or ravines, left to the depredations of hogs or wolves or time; the disposition of the Civil War dead made an accurate accounting of the fallen impossible.[15]

On the Union side, the estimate was more than 700,000 battle casualties, with more than 360,000 battle-related deaths and more than 400,000 deaths from disease or other causes. The figure of an additional 258,000 Confederate military deaths can, at best, be an educated guess, for there was no postwar financing for recognition of service or reburial of the dead as there was on the Union side.[16]

Rare was the family, North or South, that was not touched by the death of a young man. The magnitude of casualties in individual battles is staggering: at Shiloh, in Tennessee, in April 1862 there were nearly 22,000 dead, wounded or missing. The Battle of Antietam in Maryland, in September 1862, was, and remains to this day, the most bloody single day in American history, with more than 23,000 men lost. In several days at Cold Harbor, Virginia, in May 1864, federal casualties were 44,000, and Confederate casualties about 25,000. Among the losses at Cold Harbor were more than 7,000 Union troops who died in less than sixty minutes when Gen. Ulysses Grant repeatedly ordered waves of infantrymen to storm into a direct frontal attack on

---

[12] James W. McPherson emphasizes that the number who fought in the Civil War can only be estimates. His best figures would be 2,100,000 for the Union, and 850,000 to 900,000 for the Confederates. McPherson, *Battle Cry of Freedom*, 306.

[13] David W. Blight, "Decoration Days: The Origins of Memorial Day in North and South," in Fahs and Waugh, *Memory of the Civil War in American Culture*, 94.

[14] Faust, *This Republic of Suffering*, xiii.

[15] Ibid., 102.

[16] Ibid., 255.

the entrenched Confederates, whose guns were pre-sighted for the field of fire.[17] Grant was denounced as a butcher, and there was great reluctance among Northern men to fill the calls for volunteers, as well as a strong disposition by many in the North for compromise. Even Lincoln lamented that "the heavens are hung in black."[18]

This war was a passage that forever altered America itself. In fact and in outcome it was the Second American Revolution. It mobilized the total resources of the two societies that fought it, and it utterly devastated the agrarian base, the infrastructure, and most of the resources of the loser. From the Deep South, one obscure, little-known example underscores this point: 20 percent of the entire budget for the State of Mississippi for the first year following the end of the war was spent exclusively on artificial limbs for its veteran sons.

The South was economically destroyed. At least $3 billion in wealth held by Southern white slaveholders vanished from their personal worth.[19] Union forces laid waste to crops, to bridges, to all infrastructure that supplied the Southern army. Gen. William Tecumseh Sherman resorted to "total war" against civilians and inflicted wanton destruction of private property. One can hear the only words that countless slave owners could find to say as they faced their former slaves: "I have *nothing* left to give you *but* your freedom."

Very touching are the words of William Colbert, a black slave born in Georgia, telling of the war's impact from his view and in his vernacular:

> De Yankees come in, and dey pulled de fruit off de trees and et it. Dey et de hams and cawn, but dey neber burned de houses. Seem to me lak dey jes' stay aroun' long enough to git plenty somp'n t'eat,' 'kaze dey lef' in two or three days, an' we neber seed 'em since. De massa had three boys to go to war, but dere wuzn't one to come home. All the chillun he had wuz killed. Massa, he los' all his money, and doe house soon begin droppin' away to nothin'. . . . De las' time I seed de home plantation, I wuz a-standin' on a hill. I looked back on it for de las' time through a patch of

---

[17] McPherson, *Battle Cry of Freedom*, 735. At Cold Harbor, Union soldiers pinned scraps of paper to themselves so their remains could be identified. The dread experienced by those preparing to attack entrenched earthworks, where their deaths were assured, was thereafter called the Cold Harbor syndrome.

[18] Ibid., 742.

[19] Aaron C. Sheehan-Dean, "A Fearful Lesson: The Legacy of the American Civil War," in Sheehan-Dean, *Struggle for a Vast Future*, 244.

scrub pines and it look' so lonely. Dere warn't but one person in sight—de massa. He was a-settin' in a wicker chair in de yard, lookin' out ober a small field of cotton and cawn. Dere wuz fo' crosses in de graveyard in de side lawn where he wuz a-settin'. De fo'th one wuz his wife.[20]

After two and a half centuries of slaveholding in North America, four million former slaves suddenly were cast adrift in freedom. This led to the reshaping of political, economic, and social relations within the nation and throughout the world.[21] From 1865 it was another one hundred years before the descendants of freedmen overcame, in even a strictly legal sense, the forces of white supremacy and racism in the South and elsewhere. Most of America continues to deal with the consequences of the Civil War and with the institutions of America that were shaped by them. Though the nation, once divided into North and South, was reunited and in many ways healed, our post-slavery racial division remains unhealed, and most of America continues to struggle with "diversity as the definition of America or as the source of its unraveling."[22]

What the General Did Not Know about the Mormons

Had Maxwell remained in any city of the Union, he would have been revered as a war hero, but among the Latter-day Saints in Utah Territory, he and other war veterans who brought federal rule were seen as a pox, a pariah. The causes of this reception were complex but in part originated from Mormon doctrine, prophecies of Mormon leaders, and the contradictory reality that the Saints had increasingly been required to face as the Civil War progressed. Maxwell's closest companion in the war, Frank Hawley, was among those sent west for the Powder River Expedition. Being in Salt Lake City among the Mormons and at Camp Douglas from the fall of 1865 to the spring of 1866, Hawley may have been able to warn Maxwell that the Latter-day Saints viewed the Civil War as an apocalyptic fire, justly consuming the wicked.

The stance of the Mormons on the matter of slavery and the place of

---

[20] Rawick, Hillegas, and Lawrence, *American Slave*, 1:104–105.
[21] Sheehan-Dean, "Fearful Lesson," 238.
[22] Blight, *Beyond the Battlefield*, 123.

blacks in Mormon theology is highly relevant to understanding affairs in Utah before and after the Civil War. Deliberate political and moral efforts were mounted by those outside Utah to equate polygamy in Utah with slavery in the South; polygamy enslaved Mormon women, it was asserted. Eradication of both slavery and polygamy had been a part of the Republican Party platform since 1856.

In the antebellum period, issues related to blacks and slavery were unique in Utah. Among the more than forty thousand people in Utah Territory in 1860, there were only thirty free blacks and twenty-nine black slaves. Although altering the national balance of slave and free states was of great concern in considering Kansas, Nebraska, California, and Texas for statehood, such concern was minimal outside or within Utah in its bids for statehood from 1853 to 1865. The Compromise of 1850 had given Utah the right, on admission to the Union as a state, to determine whether it would permit slavery or not. According to Lester Bush, one of several historians concerned with the LDS church doctrine regarding blacks and the author of several studies in the controversial field, one hundred black slaves were brought to the territory between 1847 and 1850.[23] Enslavement of blacks was legalized in Utah by an act of the territorial legislature in 1851: the buying and selling of slaves of African descent was permitted, but sexual relationships between blacks and whites—and thus intermarriages—were forbidden.[24] Some protections were stipulated for slaves, but they were required to "labor faithfully, and do such service as requested by master or mistress."[25]

The first Latter-day Saint prophet, Joseph Smith, dealt with the existence of the black race as a theological issue in his translation of an Egyptian papyrus, later published under the title *Book of Abraham*. In this work, which later became a part of the official Mormon scripture titled *The Pearl of Great Price*, Smith affirmed that the dark skin of blacks was a mark of the curse placed on them by God in a preexistent life for having chosen not to fight for the causes of good against the forces of evil. The curse was said to have been inherited through one of

---

[23] Bush, "Mormonism's Negro Doctrine," 23.

[24] Utah was not unique in this position regarding to racial intermarriage. Prior to the Civil War, all the Southern slave states had antimiscegenation laws banning the marriage of whites and blacks, as did several free states, including Indiana, Illinois, and Michigan.

[25] Sillitoe, *History of Salt Lake County*, 42.

Ham's sons, whose descendants were those who had not been valiant in the former spirit life. Smith and succeeding Mormon prophets allowed small numbers of blacks to join the LDS church; however, both Smith and many of his successors insisted that black men were "forever" to be denied the privilege of priesthood appointment given to white men.[26] Over his thirty-three-year rule as the second prophet of the Church of Jesus Christ of Latter-day Saints, Brigham Young repeated this doctrine of Joseph Smith's regarding the place of blacks within the church.[27] He stated that God's curse on blacks would extend to whites who intermarried with them: "If the white man who belongs to the chosen seed mixes his blood with the seed of Cain, the penalty, under the law of God, is death on the spot."[28] Mormon leader Orson Hyde explained the position of the Mormon church on slavery in 1851, with no hint that it was a deeply troubling moral issue of escalating importance in other states and territories of the continent, treating it instead as merely a matter of blandly adhering to existing laws: "The laws of the land recognize slavery—and we do not wish to oppose the laws of the country. If there is sin in selling a slave, let the individual who sells him bear that sin, and not the church."[29] The records of Mormon leaders from the time of the inception of their church to the period following the Civil War were silent on whether the LDS church, as an institution, held moral reservations regarding slavery, or whether its members struggled individually with slavery as a moral issue.[30]

---

[26] The prohibition of African Americans and other men of dark skin color being appointed to the second, higher-level Melchizedek priesthood positions within the LDS church lasted until 1978.

[27] Whether the Mormon church's position regarding blacks arose in the teachings of Joseph Smith or in those of Brigham Young has been a matter of serious historical debate. Bush and Mauss, *Neither White or Black*, 53–129; Taggart, *Mormonism's Negro Policy*, 34–35.

[28] Brigham Young, *Journal of Discourses*, 10: 110. Southern whites also held a biblical explanation of racial differences in which Ham and his son Canaan were black, Japheth was white, and Shem was American Indian. Because Ham had observed his own father, Noah, naked, Canaan was cursed to be "a servant of servants . . . unto his brethren." T. V. Peterson, *Ham and Japheth*, 45. "Ham sinned against his God and against his father, for which Noah, the inspired patriarch cursed Canaan. . . . This very African race are the descendants of Canaan, and have been the slaves of various nations, and are still expiating, in bondage, the curse upon themselves." Holland, *Refutation of the Calumnies*, 41.

[29] Orson Hyde, "Slavery among the Saints," *Millennial Star* 13 (February 15, 1851): 63.

[30] David Bailey deals with various Christian faiths and their struggle with slavery. Bailey, *Shadow on the Church*, 21–24.

A Unique Perception of the War

Mormons viewed the battles over slavery in Missouri and Kansas as only the beginning of God's punishment for the damage done to the Saints there.[31] Referring to the atrocity of the 1838 Missouri-Mormon war, in which eighteen Mormon men and boys were mercilessly slaughtered at Haun's Mill in Caldwell County by more than two hundred Livingston County Missouri militiamen, Elder George Q. Cannon, second only to Brigham Young in influence, wrote, "Missouri, whose soil is drenched with the blood of Saints!— . . . over whose surface Prophets and Saints were hunted and driven with cruel and fiendish violence—has become the theatre of stirring events. . . . A fearful retribution is being exacted from the wicked inhabitants of that poor State for their base conduct towards an innocent and unresisting people."[32]

Mormons believed that the mutual destruction of both Missouri and Kansas would open the way for Latter-day Saints to reclaim lands they had formerly owned there. It had been proclaimed by Joseph Smith that Christ's return to earth would occur in this area, which appropriately was the very site that had been the Garden of Eden. "Jackson County has been entirely cleared of its inhabitants . . . which is one of the greatest miracles manifested in our day[;] those who have driven the Saints out of Missouri are in their turn now driven out," wrote Apostle Wilford Woodruff.[33]

When it came to Mormons' view of the larger Civil War, Woodruff prayed: "Let the wicked slay the wicked untill [sic] the whole land is Clensed [sic] from the Corruption, sin, abomination, and wickedness which now reigns upon the face of the whole Earth. May thy Judgments Continue to be poured out upon this land of North America untill the Blood of Prophets and Saints is avenged before the Lord."[34] In Woodruff's personal journal entries for 1861 to 1865, the prevailing views of Mormon leaders relating to the unfolding events of the conflict were very consistent:

---

[31] As the Kansas-Missouri conflict over slavery intensified, U.S. senator David Atchison of Missouri boldly described to Jefferson Davis how his constituents desired to "Mormonize" the abolitionists of Kansas by shooting, burning, and hanging them as they had earlier done with the Mormons. McPherson, *Battle Cry of Freedom*, 145–46.

[32] George Q. Cannon manuscript, September 7, 1861, quoted in Bitton, *Ritualization of Mormon History*, 116.

[33] Wilford Woodruff, *Journal History of the Church* (hereafter "*JH*"), January 1, 1864.

[34] Kenney, *Wilford Woodruff's Journal*, 5:616–17.

December 11, 1861. I pray daily that the Lord will take away the reigns of Government of the wicked rulers and put it into the hands of the wise and good. I will see the day when those wicked rulers are wiped out. . . . I am not in league with such cursed scoundrels as Abe Lincoln and his minions.

December 31, 1863. . . . [T]he land is beginning to be bathed in blood and will continue until the words of the Prophet will be fulfilled.

March 6, 1865. . . . The North will never have power to crush the South. No never. The Lord will give the South power to fight the North until they will destroy each other.[35]

Neither were Mormons in sympathy with President Lincoln's 1863 Emancipation Proclamation; they contended that he did not have constitutional authority to fully abolish slavery. The Mormon *Deseret News* published their view, stating that they demanded "to be informed whence the President derives his power to issue any such proclamation," which was "in plain violation" of the provisions of the Constitution. Lincoln, they asserted, was "fully adrift on the current of radical fanaticism" and had been "coerced by the insanity of radicals, by the denunciation of their presses, by the threats of their governors and senators."[36]

Mormons were correct regarding Lincoln's authority. Legal sanctions for slavery in the several U.S. territories were abolished by Congress in 1862, and the Emancipation Proclamation applied to "all persons held as slave" within the rebellious states. Abolishing slavery across the Union awaited the Thirteenth Amendment in 1865, and even this was not ratified by Mississippi until 1995.

MAKING PROPHECY

The Civil War was a matter from which the Mormon people were insulated by distance, culture, and doctrine. Its occurrence and outcome had been predicted by their founder's prophecy. Mormons did not weigh in on the merits or evils of slavery. They did not debate the advantages or disadvantages of dividing the union of the states. Cuba entering as a slave state or the addition of Haiti and Santo Domingo as slave states was not the subject of discussion or of articles in Utah

---

[35] Susan Staker, *Waiting for World's End*, 264, 277, 280.
[36] "The Emancipation Proclamation," *DN*, October 22, 1862, 2, col. 2.

newspapers. Mormons considered the war an inevitable, deserved punishment by God for the persecution of the Mormon people. In September 1860, Brigham Young predicted a Mormon rescue: "While the waves of commotion are whelming nearly the whole country, Utah in her rocky fortresses is biding her time to step in and rescue the constitution and aid all lovers of freedom."[37] In January 1861 the *Deseret News* further proclaimed that Utah would receive those fleeing the bloodshed: "While the people and nations of the earth are warring[,] . . . peace according to the promise, may be expected to prevail in Utah; . . . those who will not take the sword to destroy their fellow man, shall flee hither for safety."[38]

Some Mormons predicted that war would create other problems for which the Saints and their practice of plural marriages had a ready solution. As Orson Pratt wrote,

> Many millions of fathers and brothers will fall upon the battle field, while mothers, and daughters, and widows, will be left to mourn the loss. What will become of these females? Answer—The gospel will be preached to many of them, and they will flee out from among the nations, and be gathered with the Saints in Zion. Under these circumstances, the number of females will far exceed the number of males. How are the overplus females to obtain husbands for eternity?[39]

An anonymous poet expressed it this way: "Fight on, till all your men are dead, And Mormon saints your widows wed."[40]

Immigrants from Europe traveling to Utah Territory during the period of 1861 to 1865 risked encounters with Confederate ships on the seas, and some experienced delays and inconveniences in rail transport and had to be wary of possible abduction and conscription as they crossed a war-troubled continent. Even so, more than eleven thousand foreign converts made their way to the relatively safe isolation of Zion during this period.[41]

The immense ideological gap that separated the Mormon people from the remainder of the non-slaveholding population is strikingly seen by

---

[37] Brigham Young's letters to Delegate Hooper, Coe Collection, Yale University Library, New Haven, Conn., quoted in G. O. Larson, "Utah and the Civil War," 56.

[38] "Passing Events," *DN*, January 2, 1861, 4, col. 1.

[39] Pratt, "Celestial Marriage" (1853), cited in Hardy, *Doing the Works of Abraham*, 83.

[40] Anon., *Mormoniad* (Boston: A. Williams and Co., 1858), cited in Deverell, "Thoughts from the Farther West," 8.

[41] Woods, "East to West."

comparing Michigan Supreme Court justice Isaac Peckham Christiancy's oration on May 21, 1861, with that of Mormon apostle John Taylor at the Fourth of July celebration that year. Christiancy described millions of people in a "moral earthquake" of indignation and patriotism, who had "resolved that treason shall be extinguished in blood." But Taylor denied that it was a matter that concerned his people: "We have been banished . . . and forced to make a home in the desert wastes. . . . Shall we join the north to fight against the south? No! Shall we join the south against the north? As emphatically No! Why? . . . [W]e have had no hand in the matter."[42]

As the war began in 1861, Brigham Young and Apostle Heber C. Kimball reminded the Mormon people of Joseph Smith's 1832 prophecy of a war that would begin in South Carolina, spread to involve Great Britain as a Southern ally, lead to a massive uprising of the Indians, and "terminate in the death and misery of many souls."[43] Many of the converted Saints had come from Great Britain and Scandinavia and may have been little acquainted with events in the South preceding secession. They may not have known that Smith had only to read the newspapers to make such a prediction with a high likelihood of being correct. The economic leaders in the South, particularly South Carolina's John C. Calhoun, had been troubled over issues of federal control for years. The South produced 80 percent of the world's cotton and balanced these exports with imports of manufactured goods from abroad. Factories in the North, rising in great numbers, wanted a tariff on imported goods that would force Southerners to use their products. South Carolina's tariffs began in 1816; by 1824 they averaged 33 percent, and by 1828 they were 50 percent. In opposition, South Carolina passed the Ordinance of Nullification in November 1832 to nullify congressional actions that placed duties on imported commodities. Contending that Congress was exerting power not granted under the Constitution, South Carolina declared that federal tariffs were void and that any collection of such taxes within its borders would bring immediate secession.[44] Teeth were added to this threat in January 1833 when South Carolina governor Robert Y. Hayne made preparations to form an army to challenge

---

[42] "Address by John Taylor," *DN*, July 10, 1861, 8, col. 1.
[43] Bushman, *Rough Stone Rolling*, 191–92; Long, *Saints and the Union*, 19, 30.
[44] Freehling, *Nullification Era*, 1–3.

the military enforcements sent by President Andrew Jackson to Fort Moultrie and the garrison called Castle Pinckney. Hayne aimed for a two-thousand-man horse brigade and a volunteer army of twenty-five thousand infantry. Agents from Charleston purchased more than $100,000 worth of arms.[45] In the South various states contended they "had a right to withdraw from a membership that they had voluntarily joined in the first place."[46] Smith's prophecy that a war would originate in South Carolina may have had its origins in divine revelation but could also have been predicted from the publicity given tariff fights, abolitionism, and threats of secession to which Smith and his fellow Mormons were exposed in the publications of the times.[47]

Although Brigham Young publicly professed loyalty to the United States, privately he had this to say of the impending conflict in the spring of 1861: "Mobs will not decrease, but will increase until the whole Government becomes a mob, and eventually it will be State against State, city against city, neighbourhood against neighbourhood, Methodist against Methodist, and so on . . . and those who will not take up the sword against their neighbours must flee to Zion."[48] Charles Carroll Goodwin, the fiery *Salt Lake Tribune* editor, credits Brigham Young as having made the following comment in an address in the tabernacle building at a time when the Civil War was raging: "The men of the South pray to God for the destruction of the men of the North; the men of the North beseech God to bring destruction upon the men of the South; I say amen to both prayers."[49]

Non-Mormon territorial governor Stephen S. Harding, who had begun his duties with a sympathetic view of the Saints, penned this summation of the Mormons' views about the Civil War in a private letter to Secretary of State William H. Seward:

> Brigham Young and other teachers are . . . constantly inculcating in the minds of the crowded audiences who sit beneath their teachings every Sabbath that the government of the United States is of no consequence; that it lies in ruins; and [that] the prophecy of Joseph Smith is being fulfilled to the letter. [According to his prophecy,] the United

---

[45] Ibid.; F. Bancroft, *Calhoun*, 91–126.
[46] R. Alexander, *Five Forks*, 67.
[47] Bushman, *Rough Stone Rolling*, 191–92.
[48] Brigham Young, *Journal of Discourses*, 9:5.
[49] Goodwin, "Mormon Situation," 758.

States as a nation, is to . . . be . . . destroyed . . . and then the Saints are to step in and quietly enjoy the possession of the land.. . . . and that "Zion is to be built up", not only in "The Valleys of the Mountains" but the Great Center of their power and glory, is to be in Missouri where . . . the Saints under the lead of their prophet, were expelled many years ago.

. . . I have sat . . . Sabbath after Sabbath, and heard many . . . declarations put forth, by those who claim to speak under the immediate inspiration of God[,] who "wink and chuckle" . . . when some intelligence of disaster reached them concerning the Great Army of the Union now fighting for the rights of humanity. . . . In all the meetings that I have attended, not one word, not one prayer, has been uttered or offered up for the saving . . . of our cause or for the restoration of peace, but on the contrary, the God of the Saints has been implored, to bring swift destruction on all nations, people and institutions that stand in the way of triumph of "this people."

Brigham Young . . . teaches [that] the Governments of the earth now in existence, are false, and ought to be over thrown[, that] no government ought to exist, without immediate authority from God—God has delegated the right to Set up a Government, only to the Priesthood and that one man appointed by God, should rule—that all persons . . . pretend[ing] to have the authority to govern, are usurpers . . . [, that] the Constitution of the United States is a . . . revelation from Heaven: but that it has fulfilled its purpose—It was merely . . . to form a Government, so that the Church of Latter-day Saints could be . . . organized. . . . Joseph Smith offered to become the President . . . of the United States but the people rejected him; . . . so the American people, . . . for the consenting of the death of the prophet at Carthage, Illinois is to be destroyed. . . . [S]*lavery has nothing whatever to do with the present disturbances; but they are in consequence of the persecutions that the Saints have suffered, at the hands of the American People.*[50]

Chiliasm was the additional dimension in the Mormon view of the war: it was the opening of events that would shortly lead to the cleansing of the earth in preparation for Christ's thousand-year return. Brigham Young was quite clear in his forewarning:

According to accounts, . . . not less than one million men, from twenty to forty years of age, have gone to the silent grave in this useless war. . . . Do you know that it is the eleventh hour of the reign of Satan on the earth? Jesus is coming to reign and all you who fear and tremble because of your enemies,

---

[50] Harding to Seward, ca. August 18, 1862, Utah Territorial Papers, 1860–73, 2:553–54. Emphasis added.

cease to fear them, and learn to fear to offend God, fear to transgress his laws, fear to do any evil to your brother, or to any being on the earth.[51]

Those Who Did Not Serve

In a war in which more than three million served, in which the number of dead equaled or surpassed the total number lost in all other of the nation's wars combined, Utah Territory provided the minuscule number of ninety-five men to serve, very briefly, for the Union.[52] By the official line, Brig. Gen. James Craig was the U.S. officer under whom the Mormons were organized; in reality, however, they were mustered under order of Brigham Young and Mormon Militia lieutenant general Daniel H. Wells.[53] They would serve three months under militia officers Lot Smith and Robert T. Burton to provide temporary protection of the telegraph along the North Platte and transport mail between Fort Laramie and Fort Bridger and to assure no interruption of travel on the Overland Trail.

Although it may be technically correct that Mormons served under federal directive *during* the war, neither Union nor Confederate efforts were supported in any capacity in the conduct of the war by the Mormon people of Utah Territory. It is amazingly incongruous that Wells, Smith, and Burton, the leaders of this expedition to protect six hundred miles of Overland Trail communication and passage, were the same men who had led Mormon guerrilla forces in destroying federal property and supplies worth millions along this path in the Utah War of 1857–58.[54] In fact, indictments for treason had been brought against these three, along with seventeen others, by the U.S. District Court in March 1858.[55]

Largesse, not tribulation, nor death or destruction, came to the Mormons from the Civil War. In May 1861, in preparation for the transfer of Utah's military forces to war purposes, Col. Philip St. George

[51] Brigham Young, an address under the Bowery, *Journal of Discourses*, 10 (October 6, 1863): 250.
[52] Dr. Gerald J. Prokopowicz, "Our Hearts Were Touched with Fire: The Men Who Fought the War," in Sheehan-Dean, *Struggle for a Vast Future*, 91; Hewett, "Utah Territory," in *Roster of Union Soldiers*.
[53] Long, *Saints and the Union*, 87.
[54] Hafen and Hafen, *Mormon Resistance*, 18, 218.
[55] A. G. Browne, Jr., Dispatch, "Indictment of Mormon Leaders for High Treason," *New York Daily Tribune*, cited in MacKinnon, *At Sword's Point*, 471–72.

Cooke was ordered to close up and dispose of the entire military post that had been built on the edge of Utah Lake in 1858 to house the 2,500 troops of Brig. Gen. Albert Sidney Johnston's forces. The inventory at Fort Crittenden (formerly Camp Floyd), including tools, wagons, food, and clothing, was sold to speculators and Mormon purchasers for an estimated $100,000, although it was worth $4 million.[56] "The bullets the troops brought to shoot us turned out to be gold Eagles and landed in our pockets," said one Mormon man, referring to the highly sought U.S. gold coins.[57]

As a result of the troop removal from Fort Crittenden, the population of Utah Territory experienced fourteen months without any U.S. military presence, from July 27, 1861, when Colonel Cooke handed LDS president Brigham Young the flag from Crittenden, to the arrival of Col. Patrick E. Connor and his California volunteers on October 19, 1862. The years of 1861 to 1865 in Utah Territory were a period of beneficent neglect of polygamy and the "Mormon problem" by the federal government. While 1862 saw the passage of the anti-bigamy Morrill Act, the hands of the nation's leaders were more than occupied with the conduct of the war, and so the drastic provisions of the Morrill bill were not enforced in the least.[58]

This was a war, not of professional soldiers, but of volunteers in which the obligation of the citizen to his nation was expressed in willingness to risk life itself. That this commitment fundamentally redefined the relationship of the individual to his nation was totally beyond the perception of the Mormons in Utah Territory.[59] It is an astonishing contrast that the central event of American history, the cataclysm engulfing twenty million other people, was for Utah's Mormons, no more than a teaspoonful sprinkling of tepid water in comparison with an unrelent-

---

[56] Long, *Saints and the Union*, 7. Hyrum B. Clawson, Brigham Young's son-in-law, was one of the principal buyers of the liquidated goods. T. G. Alexander, *Clash of Interests*, 8.

[57] William Laud, *Diary*, 6, Manuscript Section, Church Hostorian's Office, cited in Moorman and Sessions, *Camp Floyd*, 260.

[58] Justin Smith Morrill's bill was "to punish and prevent the practice of polygamy in the Territories of the United States, and for other purposes, and to disapprove and annul certain acts of the Legislative Assembly of the Territory of Utah." The act intended to stipulate that anyone engaged in polygamy would be guilty of bigamy, with up to $500 in fines and up to five years in prison. Additionally, it specified that no religious corporation could hold more than $50,000 in real estate. (Morrill also authored an 1862 act creating the Department of Agriculture.)

[59] Faust, *This Republic of Suffering*, 103.

ing, four-year deluge that enveloped the remainder of the nation. Both historians E. B. Long and Ray Charles Colton describe, at length and in detail, the events that transpired *inside* Utah during the Civil War, but neither has addressed the deep level of anesthesia that more accurately describes the disconnect, the state of minimal consciousness, of Utah's Mormons over the catastrophic events of the war.[60] Mormon apostle Ezra T. Benson, speaking on the temple grounds in Salt Lake City on April 6, 1863, exhibited a shocking degree of self-interest and detachment: "Though many have felt a little feint-hearted [*sic*] because of the war-cloud that has hung over us, but which has now burst without doing anybody any harm, yet I feel to say that if we go to war it will be in self defense, but at present there is no danger of any serious trouble."[61] By October 1863 the facts of Gettysburg hung as an undeniable reality on the shoulders of the Union and Confederate leaders, and on the families of the tens of thousands of men lost. Brigham Young, however, carried no weight of the war's losses nor of its consequences: "One portion of the country wishes to raise their negroes . . . and the other portion wishes to free them, and, apparently, to almost worship them. Well, raise them and worship them, who cares? I should never fight one moment about it, for the cause of human improvement is not the least advanced by the dreadful war."[62]

FACING REALITY

Throughout the course of the Civil War, Mormon leaders continued filtering its events through their concept of retribution, that North and South would persist to the mutual destruction of both. As late as the Sunday before Gen. Robert E. Lee's surrender at Appomattox, when the incapacity of the South to continue war was obvious, Brigham Young predicted the contrary, that there would be another four years of warfare.[63] Mormon writers and Young also raised the prospect of the war's spreading to Great Britain, and the church leaders discussed preparations if that were to happen.[64]

---

[60] Long, *Saints and the Union*, 310; Colton, *Civil War*, 1959.
[61] Ezra T. Benson, *Journal of Discourses*, 10:153.
[62] Brigham Young, *Journal of Discourses*, 10:250–51.
[63] H. H. Bancroft, *History of Utah*, 606.
[64] *Millennial Star* 27 (October 28, 1865): 681–82.

Most of the nation reacted to the assassination of President Lincoln on Good Friday 1865 as a personal and national tragedy. It evinced an "extravaganza of mourning."[65] Twenty-five thousand viewed his casket in the East Room of the White House; in Philadelphia his coffin lay in Independence Hall, where seventy-five thousand people marched with his cortege, and ten times that number watched from sidewalks and rooftops. Throughout Northern states "universal suspensions of ordinary avocations and a closing of places of business" took place.[66] Walt Whitman wrote for the millions who had served in the war: "Sing of the love we bore him—because you, dweller in camps, know it truly."[67] And Utah's non-Mormon journalist Frederick E. Lockley gave expression to what most of the nation felt at Lincoln's murder: "Men grieve for him as for the loss of a parent. He has carried us through the maelstrom of civil war with so undaunted and skillful a hand; he has shown such an impassibility to any human infirmity of temper, rising like the demigod above all the angry and senseless invective with which his name and character have been assailed."[68]

Among the Saints, however, Lincoln's death was not a tragedy but another opportunity to exclaim that the demands of justice had not been met in the murder of their prophet. The following appeared in the *Millennial Star*:

On the 14th day of April 1865, . . . the Chief Magistrate of the nation lay stricken dead by the hand of an assassin. Was there any dim recollection stirred in the minds of the people then, of a time when the chief and beloved head of a peaceful community lay dead on the soil that had given him birth, murdered by the connivance of that very people who now mourned the loss of their guide and ruler? Did the truth of the natural law then recur to their minds, whatsoever a nation soweth, that it shall also reap? . . . The blood of a servant of God has never been avenged in the same manner as the blood of a king or a statesman. Some of the supposed murderers of Joseph and Hyrum were placed upon trial before the judges of the land. A solemn farce, a mockery of justice was enacted. . . . The blood of the Prophets still calls for vengeance.[69]

[65] Faust, *This Republic of Suffering*, 161.

[66] Ibid., 156–57; *New York Herald*, April 20, 1865.

[67] Whitman, "Hush'd Be the Camps To-day," in *Civil War Poetry and Prose*, 34–35.

[68] Frederic E. Lockley to Elizabeth Metcalf Lockley, April 16, 1865, folder 10, box 2 (April 5–June 14, 1865), Lockley Papers.

[69] "Historical Contrast betwixt the 27th of June 1844 and the 14th of April 1865," *Millennial Star* 27 (July 1, 1865): 408–13.

Utah's Mormon leaders also entertained concern that the immense military forces of the Civil War might be turned to use against them. George A. Smith and John Taylor reported their understanding of a conversation with Representative James Monroe Ashley, chairman of the House Committee on Territories:

> Mr. Ashley said the religious feeling in the United States is more inten-sified against us than it had ever been before, and that the religious ele-ment now ruled the country, the clergy had it their own way and they were determined that the laws of the United States should be enforced in Utah, and that it would be terrible. . . . [T]he Army which would be ordered here, would be the refuse of Sherman's . . . army during his expedition south . . . [that] ravished every woman that was within 25 miles . . . and then burned their houses and that is what they intended to carry out here.[70]

When the collapse of the U.S. government as predicted by Mormon leaders did not occur, the beliefs of the leadership and of the Mormon rank and file in regard to millennial immediacy had to "yield to more conventional views of the future."[71]

STRANGER IN A STRANGE LAND

George R. Maxwell and other federal appointees sent to Utah during Grant's two-term administration were veterans of the conflict and also a reminder that was rarely discussed openly: the prophecies of Joseph Smith and Brigham Young had not come to pass. There remained a sovereign national government, not a federation wherein some could, in defense of beliefs or differences about such issues as slavery or polygamy, defy the majority. The North and South had not mutually devoured each other into nonexistence. Mormon leaders were not lifted into the ruling seats of the nation. Surviving women and children did not flock for protection to the Mormon elders in Utah. The federal army had not been withdrawn from Utah Territory. The millennium was not at hand. Instead, explorations for gold and minerals in Utah were begin-ning to create a new economy independent of Mormon agrarianism, and Mormons' self-sufficiency and isolation were diminishing.[72]

---

[70] Wilford Woodruff, *JH*, July 5, 1865.   [71] C. S. Peterson, *Utah*, 87.
[72] Arrington, *Great Basin Kingdom*, 195–96.

The federal appointees who came to Utah after the war were from states whose people had seen many thousands of their sons, brothers, and fathers die in the preservation of the Union and the dismemberment of slavery. Maxwell's state of Michigan saw ninety thousand of its men serve the Union, a number more than twice the total population of Utah Territory in 1860. Nearly fifteen thousand of Michigan's manhood perished, the equivalent of twice the population of Salt Lake City in 1860.[73]

Veterans knew that not only had Mormons remained neutral in the time of moral crisis, but many of them had also anticipated the destruction of the American people and their government as justified punishment. Veterans could not avoid having a biased view of Mormons; they observed that not a single Mormon life had been sacrificed in the titanic struggle. In Utah the preservation of the Union was neither expected nor desired, and the abolition of slavery was neither a moral issue nor an economic one but was viewed with indifference. As a consequence, polygamy in Utah became, in the minds of the federal appointees, analogous to slavery in the South. The Mormons' refusal to acquiesce to federal authority and law and disavow polygamy was directly compared to the Southerners' refusal to yield to the supremacy of the union of the states and to disavow slavery.

Many years after the war ended, some Mormon leaders in Utah still looked upon the Civil War as an event of divine retribution against the forces of an evil and corrupt government. In a prayer at the 1877 dedication of the Mormon temple at St. George, Wilford Woodruff, the fourth president of the LDS church, spoke of the United States as "the nation which shed the blood of the saints and prophets . . . which is making war with God and Christ."[74] After reading of the number of lives lost in the Civil War, Woodruff noted in his journal twenty years after the war's end: "This shows the inspired Man what it costs a Nation to Kill the Prophets and Apostles and shed the Blood of the Lords Anointed."[75]

Perhaps Maxwell's closest wartime friend, Frank Hawley, forewarned him of the Mormons' deeply rooted beliefs and their perceptions of the

---

[73] Verdoia and Firmage, *Utah*, 191.
[74] "Dedication Services at the Temple at St. George," *DN*, January 17, 1877, 8, col. 3.
[75] Kenney, *Wilford Woodruff's Journal*, March 5, 1885, 8:307.

war. However, Maxwell remained to some degree unaware or experienced some measure of denial that his war service would be met in Utah not with appreciation for his personal sacrifices and accomplishments but with responses ranging from apathy to open hostility.

Maxwell arrived in Utah as a competent lawyer, and shortly he became an assistant U.S. attorney.[76] As a patriotic hero and young lawyer from Michigan, he had ambitious goals. His federal appointment might become a stepping-stone to politics, a wealthy law practice, a lucrative business opportunity, or a mining bonanza. Western America was ripe with possibilities, even for a man severely maimed and disabled, a man recently widowed, a man accustomed to relying on himself.

---

[76] In 1869 lawyers were not regulated or licensed by examination in Utah Territory. "It shall be the duty of all judges of courts in the Territory to grant hearings as counsel to any person of good moral character, chosen by any person or persons to prosecute or defend a case." *Compiled Laws of Utah*, title XVII, chap. II, 354.

5

The Disputants in the Theologic War

So oft, in theologic wars,
The disputants, I ween,
Rail on in utter ignorance,
Of what each other mean,
And prate about an elephant
Not one of them has seen.

John Godfrey Saxe,
"The Blind Men and the Elephant"

Events in Utah Territory were inseparably interwoven, warp and woof, into the historical fabric of the Church of Jesus Christ of Latter-day Saints. To understand the world into which George R. Maxwell limped when he arrived in Salt Lake City, one must understand the organic polarity between the predominant American mores and institutions of the time, and the unique parochial assertions and unusual religious beliefs of the Mormons. From the moment of the founding of the LDS church in 1830, intense social, political, and religious conflict defined the interface between non-Mormons and Mormons until the end of the nineteenth century. Polygamy was sown like dragon's teeth in the soil of Illinois in 1842, and it emerged as a full-grown issue before the Mormons left on their trek westward.[1] This taking of multiple wives and the merging of the Mormons' religion and government were the primary, intensifying sources of this conflict.

---

[1] This early emergence of plural marriages is extensively covered in G. D. Smith, *Nauvoo Polygamy,* ix.

Difficult migrations characterized the early years of the Mormon church. Soon after the founding of the church near Palmyra, New York, its members relocated to Kirtland, Ohio, then to Daviess, Clay, and Jackson counties in Missouri. Conflicts in Missouri then led them to an Illinois city they named Nauvoo, on a sharp bend of the Mississippi River. Finally, under immense pressure from the State of Illinois and their non-Mormon neighbors, they abandoned their homes and property and, enduring great hardships, migrated into the vastness and isolation of the Great Basin, then part of Mexico. The viewpoint of a faithful Mormon believer was rooted in the revelations of founder Joseph Smith, the scripture he recorded, and the peregrinations of a people who saw themselves continually persecuted. However, the viewpoint of the unbelieving non-Mormon reflected the deep mistrust and hostility then held by the majority of Americans toward an alien, unyielding people and their peculiar belief system.

Describing and interpreting Utah history and that of the LDS church through the nineteenth century requires negotiating an interpretive minefield. Impartiality and objectivity may fall victim to either the proudly held Mormon perception or the diametrically opposite, harshly critical perceptions of the non-Mormon. Following are two attenuated histories of this period: one written from the Mormon viewpoint, as if taken from a deeply committed believer, and the other from the non-Mormon, or even anti-Mormon, perspective. The separate renditions have not been invented by the author, nor does the author extol one over the over. Both have been eclectically assembled from commonly held facts, stories, memories, and opinions, all having appeared in contemporary accounts or historical writings. Detailed documentation of specific issues is intentionally absent in both renditions because it is inappropriate to the purpose of their presentation. The two are contrasted, not to prove or disprove, nor to espouse one over the other, but to fulfill the single purpose of illustrating, point by counterpoint, their irreconcilable polarization. Perceptions were the reality for each group. Interpreting and understanding the happenings in territorial Utah up to statehood in 1896 must take into account the undeniable existence of these disparate views.

THE PERCEPTIONS OF THE MORMON BELIEVER

The Church of Jesus Christ of Latter-day Saints, composed of God's chosen people, holds the responsibility for a divinely driven restoration of the one and only true Gospel of Jesus Christ, which has been defiled of its true principles through time. God sent Christopher Columbus to open this promised land; the 1776 Revolution was part of his plan to achieve freedom in the New World. The U.S. Constitution was divinely inspired, expressly to protect those who would reestablish his church.

The founding prophet, the charismatic Joseph Smith, Jr., was chosen by God to receive new scripture, taken from the records of ancient inhabitants of the American continents. As related in Smith's *Book of Mormon*, six hundred years before the birth of Christ a group of Hebrew people living near Jerusalem were told to flee across the desert and the ocean. On doing so, they arrived on the continents now known as North and South America. Smith was given gold plates, long hidden in the ground by the angel Moroni, who had been a man descended from these emigrants. Mormon, Moroni's father, had recorded on the plates a new testament of Jesus Christ in the history of his people, the ancestors of present-day American Indians. With the information from this record, and from the instructional visits he received from God and angels, Smith was commanded to reestablish God's one and only true church.

The faithful had a unique opportunity for preparation for Christ's return, for a required physical gathering of true believers. From all corners of the earth they were to come to the location in Jackson County, Missouri, that had literally been the primordial Garden of Eden. Communal-like living in an agricultural society fostered their unity and mutual well-being.

Converts to this new religion suffered in every location in which they settled. In Missouri they were threatened with extermination by the sitting governor. Mormons saw the forces of evil in the foes that drove them from state to state, conspiring against the exercise of their religious liberties and the restoration of God's church. Because they received no protection from state or federal authorities, they formed an army, the Nauvoo Legion, for their own defense.

In 1843, Joseph Smith claimed a divine revelation, declaring that marriage to more than one wife was a restoration of one of God's most important requirements, a moral precept more difficult to live, one that would elevate men and women so joined to the highest level of Heaven. Smith and other early, high-ranking Mormon leaders engaged in multiple marriages.

Joseph Smith and his brother Hyrum were charged with destruction of the press of an opposition Nauvoo newspaper and were jailed in nearby Carthage, Illinois, in 1844. While they were awaiting trial and supposedly under state protection, Illinois militiamen and Masons, pretending to be a disorganized mob, murdered them in June 1844. Martyrdom of their prophet deepened the sense of persecution among the Saints. In the turmoil following Smith's assassination, Brigham Young assumed the mantle of leadership as their second prophet and guided their search for a safe haven, even an independent nation, in which to establish the social, economic, moral, and theocratic unity they named the Kingdom of God. Promising both eternal salvation and a better secular life, Mormons sought converts whose skills would also lead to a self-sufficient economy in their isolation.

With their faith tested by persecution and their unity fire-hardened in immense hardship, they migrated west. In August 1852, five years after his arrival in the Great Basin, Brigham Young publically affirmed the long-rumored practice of polygamy, claiming it as a major principle in the religion. Mormon men should take as many wives as their situation would allow and should father as many children as possible, for these souls would constitute their glory in the afterlife. This commandment and other revelations received through their prophets were "higher law" and superseded any laws made by men.

As they built their kingdom in the West, Mormons anticipated, in their lifetime, the destruction of the governments that had failed to protect the life of their prophet, and the imminent return of Christ for a millennial dispensation. Leaders of the Mormon church would rise to rule the United States, and then the world, through the principles of restored righteousness. Sustained by their prophet's revelations that a place of safety and reward awaited them in this life and that an exalted place in Heaven was reserved for the faithful, they not only survived but prospered and blossomed in the deserts of the basin.[2]

---

[2] Early Mormon history is extensively treated in Bushman, *Rough Stone Rolling*; and Quinn, *Early Mormonism*. A massive number of historical writings are found in Allen, Walker, and Whittaker, *Studies in Mormon History*; C. J. Flake, *Mormon Bibliography*; Campbell, *Establishing Zion*; T. G. Alexander, *Clash of Interests*; Arrington, *Great Basin Kingdom*; and Arrington and Bitton, *Mormon Experience*.

The Perceptions of the Nonbeliever,
the Anti-Mormon

Mormons were an alien, "peculiar people" who established a closed, authoritarian society inscrutable to outsiders. Joseph Smith was a charlatan treasure seeker, a necromancer, and an egomaniacal dabbler in the paranormal. A physically abusive man of explosive temper and the subject of many lawsuits, Smith was so egotistically driven that he petitioned Congress for an army of one hundred thousand men, with which he promised to subdue the territories from Texas to Oregon. He declared himself a king and an independent candidate for the presidency of the United States.

Mormons gained influence through unity and block voting and, without party allegiance based on principles, sold their vote to whoever most met their needs. Mormons sought to exclude non-Mormons from their agricultural and manufacturing endeavors; they advocated total boycott of non-Mormon businesses.

The symbolism and rituals of the Masons were expropriated into Mormon temple ordinances, and it was feared Mormons would control the Masonic lodges of Illinois. Secret Mormon temple oaths required sworn allegiance to God's law over man's law. Such oaths also carried a holy obligation to exact vengeance for their murdered prophet. They formed illegal banks, counterfeited stock certificates, printed bogus money, and fled their debts. Mormons threatened to take by force the land and property in Missouri that they said God intended for them as his favored people. They sent a gunman who attempted to assassinate the governor of Missouri, and they threatened a war of extermination against all who they believed abused them. Mormons could, within hours, assemble the largest army in Illinois, equipped with cannons.

As polygamists, Mormons took men's wives and daughters in a religion-based justification of aberrant, immoral sexual practices. Taking multiple wives was an outlet for male sexual energy, a ruse to give legitimacy to sexual excess. Little known when first practiced in Illinois, polygamy became increasingly abominable after 1852 when openly touted in Utah by Brigham Young as a basic tenet of the faithful. Yet, standing before Congress, Mormon men lied and denied their multiple wives and numerous children.

Mormons legally secured Illinois legislative approval for a charter that permitted a virtual independent theocratic oligarchy in the city of Nauvoo. A council of fifty Mormon men, whose identity was kept secret, solidified their rule. They formed a secret police force numbering eight hundred or more, who followed any orders, including murder. They obeyed only their religious leaders and ignored the laws of each state in which they lived, and the laws of their nation. In the first thirty years of their existence, Mormons were involved in three civil wars, embroiling their neighbors, a state militia, and ultimately the U.S. Army. Saints violated federal mail, especially in Utah, where it was intercepted, read, copied, or destroyed.

Through aggressive missionary work, large numbers of converts from the British Isles and Scandinavia swelled the Mormon population in Utah and replenished the numbers of young females available for Mormon plural marriages. Viewed as the flotsam and jetsam castoffs of foreign industrial society, they were a social element Mormons could mold to their own purposes. To strengthen unity, to solidify them in their peculiarity and isolation, Mormon leaders welcomed persecution, giving speeches that were deliberately provocative. Joseph Smith's successor, Brigham Young, was a ruthless tyrant, controlling the strings of his murdering puppets. Mormonism became politicized, and polygamy was entwined with slavery as an evil to be exterminated by force of law, at least, and by force of arms if necessary. Mormons were un-American, treasonous, dangerous misfits—a pseudo-Christian cult. They should at least be banished to the isolation, the spatial quarantine, they themselves sought in the West or in Russia, Vancouver, Texas, or Oregon— to the outer geographical and cultural limits of contemporary society.[3]

THE DICHOTOMY PERSISTS

Each of the conflicting viewpoints presented above can be considered offensive, extreme, and inflammatory, depending on the reader's own viewpoint. Either can stir the emotions; each can offend the reader's core beliefs and sense of identity. However, this unbridgeable chasm

---

[3] Extensive treatment of Mormon polygamy is found in Hardy, *Doing the Works of Abraham*; K. Flake, *Politics of American Religious Identity*; Gordon, *Mormon Question*; and Van Wagoner, *Mormon Polygamy*. The origins of polygamy in Nauvoo are treated in great detail in G. D. Smith, *Nauvoo Polygamy*. Mormon communal living is treated in Arrington, Fox, and May, *Building the City of God*. The Mormons' troubled path to statehood is described in Lyman, *Political Deliverance*; Bigler, *Forgotten Kingdom*; and Sessions, *Mormon Thunder*.

between believers and nonbelievers was the reality that existed from 1835 to at least 1896. Polar interpretations based on uncompromising and irreconcilable mind-sets influenced relationships at every level and, in lesser severity, continue to influence the writing and interpretation of the history of Utah and the LDS church. In 2004 highly regarded Columbia University emeritus historian of the early LDS period, Richard Lyman Bushman, said he was required "to fight on two fronts," against "unbelieving" historians who find his faith absurd and against "self satisfied" Latter-day Saints who expect their historians only to "confirm the traditional Mormon view."[4]

Addressing truth and faith, social scientist Paul M. Edwards observes, "It is not difficult to become confused between faith and truth. . . . Faith matters so much in time of crisis. One must have gone deep into history before reaching the conviction that truth matters more."[5] William P. MacKinnon, longtime student and historian of the 1857 Utah War, phrases this caution: "With a historiography already burdened by extensive scape-goating, vilification, ridicule and hagiography, neither side deserves anything but the truth."[6] Historian David W. Blight summarizes the risk of the problem: "Dichotomies have sometimes blurred more truth than they have revealed."[7]

According to author Mario S. DePillis, this divisive view is without equal in other historical venues: "This two-party group of scholars exists nowhere else."[8] Acclaimed western writer and historian Wallace Stegner places the responsibility for the divisiveness with both camps equally: "The literature on the Mormons is enormous, repetitious, contradictory and embattled. . . . [T]here is . . . Mormon opinion, Gentile opinion . . . and historians trying to allow for all the delusion, hatred, passion, paranoia, lying, bad faith, concealment, and distortion of evidence that were contributed by both the Mormons and their enemies."[9]

George R. Maxwell's time in Utah Territory coincides with the period of maximum conflict between Mormons and non-Mormons,

---

[4] Duffy, "Can Deconstruction Save the Day?" 23.
[5] Edwards, "Irony of Mormon History," 409.
[6] MacKinnon, *At Sword's Point*, 37–38.
[7] Blight, *Beyond the Battlefield*, 134.
[8] DePillis, "Bearding Leone," 79.
[9] W. Stegner, *Gathering of Zion*, 313.

and his biographic sources suffer from this dichotomy of perspective and perception. One capable historian responded abruptly to an inquiry about Maxwell with "May he rot in hell!" Another well-known author placed Maxwell as "a colorful and important figure who deserves honest recognition" in history's pages. One side may have described Maxwell a truculent, nefarious fanatic. Mormon apostle Moses Thatcher would have characterized him as "windfall only, with a worm in his core."[10] To that faction he was nothing more than a shot-to-pieces charity case, no more important than a stray street dog, another castoff sent by Washington officials to battle Mormon practices by any means, fair or foul. The opposing faction would say he was a devoted official who went to an alien land and remained, despite very trying circumstances, to follow his orders, to do his job, unwilling to quit. As he had given his professional best to end slavery and bring the people of the secession into compliance with the laws of the Union, he gave his best to end polygamy and bring the Mormon people in Utah Territory into the republican rule of the United States.

---

[10] Whitney, *History of Utah*, 3:408–409.

6

Register of Land

If there is anybody in this land who thoroughly believes
that the meek shall inherit the earth
they have not often let their presence be known.
William Edward Burghardt Du Bois,
The Gift of Black Folk

Frontiers are lines where one body of law stops
and another body of law begins.
Wallace Earle Stegner, *Wolf Willow*

ONLY NINE DAYS AFTER THEY HAD FIRST WALKED INTO THE
Great Salt Lake valley, Apostle Orson Pratt and fellow Mormon Henry
G. Sherwood, a skilled surveyor, began assessing and measuring the
land for distribution.[1] Religious leaders allotted the land, and planting
and building began. The ecclesiastical machinery of the Mormons was
integrated directly into their political government, including their land
distribution system. According to the principle that land could not be
bought or sold, each Mormon elder was entitled to as much land as he
could care for. The territorial legislature granted watercourses, graz-
ing tracts, timber stands, and other resources to church leaders, who
were expected, at least as the system functioned ideally, to make them

---

[1] The base meridian remains marked with a commemorative plate at the southeast corner of the
Temple Block wall in Salt Lake City.

equally available to all Mormon men.[2] Top-down distribution of land ownership through the authority of ward bishops worked very well for the most part, as there was little dissension among church members. Within a year of their arrival, 863 Mormons had either drawn lots by chance or had been allocated land tracts totaling more than eleven thousand acres.[3]

However, the 1848 Treaty of Guadalupe Hidalgo, which ended the U.S.-Mexican War, brought a blow to the Mormons. In the second-largest land acquisition in U.S. history, all of present-day Arizona, California, New Mexico, Nevada, Utah, and portions of present-day Colorado and Wyoming became, with a pen stroke and $15 million, the property of the United States. Immediately the Mormon people were deeply fearful, as this act again made them subject to an authority they believed had violated their lives and their civil and religious rights in Ohio, Missouri, and Illinois.

For the next two years land ownership for the Mormons sat in legal limbo. As they petitioned Congress for statehood in 1850, they were denied both statehood and their desired name of "Deseret." Instead, Congress created a territory named Utah and placed it under the same jurisdiction as other U.S. territories. The Compromise of 1850, which established Utah Territory, did not provide Utah's citizens with two important rights for the acquisition of land. First, the legislation did not incorporate the provisions of the Preemption Act of 1841, which specified that before land was offered for sale to the public, squatters who were heads of households, widows, or single men over twenty-one—citizens who had lived on the land there for at least fourteen months—could purchase up to one hundred acres at a price not less than $1.25 per acre. The Compromise of 1850 also failed to grant the territorial legislature the authority to distribute water, timber, and land. Although this legislation denied the legality of their earlier land allocations, Mormons were not deterred, and unwilling and unable to defer settlements while awaiting the required federal surveys, they continued to carry out their own surveying in Salt Lake City and the various counties of the territory. William W. Phelps was appointed surveyor

[2] T. G. Alexander, *Clash of Interests*, 8.
[3] G. O. Larson, "Land Contest in Early Utah," 311.

general of the Provisional State of Deseret in April 1849, and Henry G. Sherwood in 1850. Jesse W. Fox was appointed in 1853 and worked in Salt Lake, Davis, Box Elder, and Millard counties.[4] Other Mormon surveyors included Chandler Holbrook in Millard County, William M. Lemon in Summit County, William M. Dame in the city of Ogden, and James Henry Martineau in Cache County.[5]

Despite their well-intentioned efforts, Mormons were still faced with meeting the same three basic requirements that applied to all American citizens seeking to own land in their states and territories. The land had to be first declared clear of Indian claim, then surveyed by federal surveyors, and finally purchased from its owner, the federal government.[6]

FIRST FEDERAL SURVEYS

On September 2, 1849, First Lieutenant John W. Gunnison, heading the advance party of Capt. Howard Stansbury of the U.S. Army Corps of Topographical Engineers, arrived in Salt Lake City, having been commissioned to survey the area of the Great Salt Lake.[7] They were to explore the region, seek a better path between Fort Bridger and Salt Lake City, and evaluate the area for a route for the planned transcontinental railroad.[8] Although surveying land for purchase by settlers was not within Stansbury's objectives, the Mormons were suspicious, especially since the War Department (under whose jurisdiction Stansbury fell) had not notified Brigham Young that Stansbury's group was being dispatched. Certainly the Mormons had no wish for lands they already occupied to be resurveyed by outsiders, by untrusted non-Mormons. They considered ownership already established. William P. MacKinnon notes that "Stansbury and Gunnison had to use all of the diplomacy they could muster before a suspicious, offended Brigham Young would

---

[4] Sillitoe, *Utah Centennial County History*, gives a detailed account of each county.

[5] Carmack, "Running the Line."

[6] It is beyond the scope of this work to examine the complex and charged issues of land ownership by American Indians.

[7] Camped on Utah's Sevier River, Gunnison and seven members of his topographical party were killed on October 26, 1853. Pahvant Indians were blamed, but Mormons were accused of involvement. Bigler, *Forgotten Kingdom*, 82–84.

[8] The rush of gold seekers wishing to travel the best route to California was also behind Stansbury's being sent. Stansbury, *Exploration and Survey*, x–xi.

accept and agree to assist their mission."[9] It may have been helpful that
Stansbury included Albert Carrington—not a surveyor by education
but a Dartmouth College graduate who was among the first Mormons
to enter Salt Lake valley in 1847—as an assistant on the survey team.[10]
However threatened they felt, Mormons were increasingly faced with
the reality that secure and lasting title to land required a federal survey,
not simply a territorial one. No legally binding federal distribution and
ownership of land, by public sale or preemption, could take place until
the federal work was completed.[11]

In February 1855, Congress established the federal office of surveyor
general of Utah Territory. By July, David Hugh Burr had arrived in
Salt Lake City as the first individual with federal credentials to survey farmland and homelands already occupied by Governor Brigham
Young and thousands of Mormons. Burr was a respected engineer and
surveyor and already a renowned cartographer for his mapping of the
United States, the British Isles, and India. Two sons, Frederick H. Burr
and David Auguste Burr, assisted him as deputy surveyors. Historian
David Bigler has pointed out that even one Burr was "one burr too
many under the Mormon saddle," for "the duty to divide the Mormon
homeland into townships and sections before it was put on the market
. . . , as provided by federal law, placed David H. Burr in a continuous confrontation with religious leaders."[12] "Abrasive" is an appropriate
but understated adjective describing the Burr-Mormon interaction that
ensued. Brigham Young accused Burr of not performing the surveys
he purported to have done. According to Young, the work of Burr's
team was sloppy and inaccurate: "They stick down little stakes that
the wind could almost blow over. . . . Not a vestige of all they do will
be left to mark where they have been in five years."[13] Burr countered
that Mormons were secretly removing his well-placed markers.[14] In a
January 1857 letter to Mormon leaders, Young wrote: "[Burr] was never

[9] MacKinnon, *At Sword's Point*, 42.

[10] Carter, *Heart Throbs of the West*, 2:273–78.

[11] The Homestead Act of 1862, which came under Lincoln's signature, also required that land be
federally surveyed before homesteading could take place.

[12] Bigler, *Fort Limhi*, 142.

[13] Brigham Young to John H. Bernhisel, cited in G. O. Larson, "Land Contest in Early Utah,"
315–16.

[14] G. O. Larson, "Land Contest in Early Utah," 316.

anything else than a snarling puppy, snapping and biting at everything that comes in his way. He is . . . swindling the Government extensively, all the surveying that has been done by his party is not worth a groat."[15] Burr riled Mormons with his criticisms relating to their land distribution. Three of Burr's complaints were especially troublesome and would remain for George R. Maxwell and others to resolve. First, Burr said (correctly) the Utah territorial legislature had exceeded its authority by improperly giving federal land, water, and timber to the Mormon leadership. Second, the City of Salt Lake claimed an area far exceeding that allowed by Congress for a township. Third, Mormons had transferred their land titles to their president and prophet, Brigham Young, who was simultaneously trustee-in-trust for the LDS church, governor of the territory, and commissioner of Indian affairs. This was seen by Burr as an unprecedented move that furthered the impenetrable fusion of church and state.[16]

Brigham Young suspected Burr as being President Buchanan's spy, providing information to the administration about Mormon doings. Burr's letters to Buchanan describing the Mormons to be in open rebellion were influential in Buchanan's ill-fated 1857 decision to send troops to install a new governor in Utah. Another Burr letter to Washington describing Mormons in Utah as preparing for war was intercepted and read by Mormon leaders. As a result, the Burr survey team became a target of violence from angry Mormons, with one of their team, Joseph Troskowlawski, suffering a life-threatening beating in Salt Lake City.[17] Nonetheless, more than two million acres were surveyed before Burr and his team, believing their lives in danger in the tumult preceding the Utah War, left the territory in April 1857.

Two additional surveyors followed Burr; Samuel C. Stambaugh arrived in 1859, and Samuel R. Fox in 1861. Fox was reminded by General Land Office officials in Washington that despite two million acres having been surveyed, not one had been sold to the Mormon inhabitants. Since there appeared to be no demand for land purchase, no

---

[15] MacKinnon, *At Sword's Point*, 66.

[16] G. O. Larson, "Land Contest in Early Utah," 316.

[17] MacKinnon, *At Sword's Point*, 58–60, 66. The spelling of Troskowlawski's name has been as abused as was the man, but Hosea Stout describes the two responsible for the beating on August 4, 1856, as Emery Meecham and John Flack. Brooks, *On the Mormon Frontier*, 599.

further surveying was planned, pending sale of lands already surveyed, and all surveying records were consolidated in 1862 with those of Colorado Territory. For seven years, until 1869, no further surveying progress was made in Utah Territory.

The population of Utah Territory could not indefinitely remain uniformly Mormon, nor would Mormons always remain fully compliant to their leaders' wishes regarding land. Bluntly stated, Mormons occupied the land, controlled its ownership, and had developed no plans for change, even as the demographic makeup of the population changed. From the federal perspective, both Mormons and non-Mormons were illegal squatters on land that had neither been properly surveyed nor purchased from its legal owner, the U.S. government.

Mineral explorations in the nearby Wasatch and Oquirrh mountains by Gen. Patrick Connor and his troops resulted in land claims for gold, silver, and precious minerals. Most claims were by non-Mormons, though a small number were submitted by Mormons, and all wanted secure title. With the transcontinental railroad nearing completion and non-Mormon emigration increasing, land jumping of property by non-Mormons began challenging the Mormons' existing, exclusionary land system.

Violence over Land Disputes

To no surprise, several instances of violence resulted from land disputes: Capt. Albert Brown and surgeon Jonathan M. Williamson, both former Second California Cavalry officers, were beaten and threatened with drowning after they made claim on land near what was considered by the Mormons their military parade grounds. John Deaver and J. C. Emerson, thinking they could preempt land on the west bank of the Jordan River, were also threatened with drowning until they promised to leave the territory.[18]

In 1866 the brutal murder of a non-Mormon doctor, John King Robinson, was attributed to his attempt to claim title on eighty acres that included Warm Springs. This land had, for some time, been a municipal bathing resort, and Dr. Robinson was said to be planning a hospital

---

[18] Federal survey of land was required before preempting, and the land described had not been surveyed.

on the site.[19] Mormons were firm that Robinson could make no valid claim because the land had previously been taken by Mormon leaders for the City of Salt Lake.[20] Dr. Robinson was lured into a dark street by a false report that an injured man needed his urgent attention, and there he was struck with a sword and shot. Non-Mormon Salt Lake attorney Robert Newton Baskin, to whom Robinson had come for legal counsel, described the man in warm terms:

> Dr. Robinson was an educated gentleman of courteous manners and affable disposition. His deportment was in every respect exemplary. He was superintendent of the first Gentile Sunday School in Salt Lake City; was a skillful physician and surgeon; had an extensive practice, and it was generally known that his attendance could always be obtained by anyone, even when compensation was out of the question. He was charitable and humane motives alone induced him to begin erecting a hospital.[21]

A December 1866 letter written by Capt. Stephen E. Jocelyn of the California Infantry in Salt Lake City cited the thoughts prevailing among the non-Mormon element:

> Brigham Young is the author of Dr. Robinson's assassination, and in this I do not go one iota beyond the public opinion of all gentiles in Salt Lake City. . . . [S]ome of his satellites—probably Daniel H. Wells—made the detail for the execution; and not the least hideous feature of the whole affair is that . . . the perpetrators of that most atrocious crime feel no guilt for this deed, have no visitations of remorse or compunctions of conscience, but . . . proved their faith in thus obeying the behests of their Prophet.[22]

The vitriol of Brigham Young when interviewed by a *New York Evening Post* correspondent brought no comfort to the non-Mormons:

> Dr. Robinson was one of the worst men he [Brigham] ever knew. "He was saucy and impudent, and pushed himself right against us." He said he was sorry the doctor had been killed, for he wanted him to live and die in

---

[19] In a letter to his parents, David Eugene Cross wrote: "I suppose you have heard about the assassination of one Dr. Robinson in this city by some of Brighams destroying angles. . . . He was shot by some of the mormons one night and was burried at Camp Douglas cemetery with Odd Fellows honors." Ellis, "Common Soldier," 55. Robinson had married Ellen "Nelly" Kay, daughter of John Kay, a well-known Mormon iron- and silversmith and formerly a popular musician in Nauvoo and a territorial marshal in Salt Lake City.

[20] The death of Dr. Robinson against the background of land ownership is addressed by Bigler, *Forgotten Kingdom*, 247–58.   [21] Baskin, *Reminiscences of Early Utah*, 14.

[22] *Chicago Republican*, January 4, 1867, reprinted in Waite, *Mormon Prophet*, 306–309.

the ditch like a dog, as he would have done if he had gone on[;] . . . that instead of going by night to destroy [Robinson's] building, they should have gone through it in broad day. "I'd have gutted it at noon, torn it down and destroyed it in the light of day, so that every man might see me."[23]

Young said the accusations of Mormon instigation of Robinson's murder were "for the purpose of raising an excitement here, through which they hope to accomplish their ends, and have an army brought here."[24] Young warned from the pulpit that land was not free for the taking by those who had not worked to earn it: "We have spent hundreds of thousands of dollars in taking out the water of our mountain streams, fencing in farms and improving the country, and we cannot tamely suffer strangers, who have not spent one day's labor to make these improvements to wrest our homesteads out of our hands."[25]

Other unsolved murders possibly relating to land claims took place during this period, including those of Thomas Coleman, in Salt Lake City, and John Howath, in Beaver. Coleman (also known as Thomas Colbourn and "Nigger Tom") was found behind the arsenal of the Nauvoo Legion on Capitol Hill on December 11, 1866; he had been stabbed and castrated, and his neck sliced ear to ear.[26] A note attached to his body warned black men of the dangers of "meddling with" white women, implying a racial, sexual motive for the crime. Contemporaries insisted that the note was a ruse; Coleman may have been silenced because he had witnessed Dr. Robinson's murder.[27] Coleman worked as a live-in attendant for Brigham Young and Feramorz Little at the Salt Lake House hotel, located at 143 South Main, and Dr. Robinson was murdered nearby, at about 200 South Main. Historian Connell O'Donovan has noted multiple similarities in the modus operandi of the murders of Robinson and Coleman, leading him to conclude that the lead assailant in both murders was the same person.[28]

Another land-related murder was that of John Howath, who had been a soldier at Camp Cameron, near Beaver, and remained there after

[23] *New York Evening Post*, November 7, 1867, quoted in Baskin, *Reminiscences of Early Utah*, 15–16.
[24] Brigham Young to Orson Pratt, Sr., October 29, 1866, in "Correspondence," *Millennial Star* 28 (December 15, 1866): 795.   [25] G. O. Larson, "Land Contest in Early Utah," 320.
[26] Thomas Coleman was a black slave owned by Col. J. H. Johnson. Lythgoe, "Negro Slavery in Utah," 48; Mason, "Prohibition of Interracial Marriage," 116.
[27] Schindler, *Orrin Porter Rockwell*, 345. Coleman had been convicted of manslaughter for killing a fellow slave during a fight over a slave woman and served prison time in 1859–60, which complicates the questions of motive in his murder. "Court Proceedings," *Valley Tan*, September 21, 1859, 2.
[28] O'Donovan, "Life and Murder of Thomas Coleman."

discharge. In October 1873 he was crossing an area locally called the Field to visit a friend, Morgan Paden, who had built a shanty there. Howath made known his intention to erect his own squatter's shanty on the field. This was a serious error. Mormon colonies were patterned after the settlement of New Jerusalem, in Jackson County, Missouri, with a "big field" at their geographical heart. The central field was considered community property, and Mormons understood that it was off-limits for individual ownership.[29] As Howath walked the field, several men in hiding along his course fired at him and killed him. Philo T. Farnsworth, Jr., Isaac Riddle, Charles Oakden, and Samuel Porter, all Mormons of the city of Beaver, were charged with the murder. None were ever convicted.[30]

RESUMPTION OF LAND SURVEYS

Threats to land ownership from the enlarging non-Mormon population brought urgency to a renewal of federal land surveying and the establishment of a land office in Utah. Through the efforts of Mormon elder William H. Hooper, Utah's congressional delegate, an act was passed in July 1868 that reopened the Utah Territory survey and made the Pre-emption Act of 1841 and the Homestead Act of 1862 applicable in Utah. Twenty-one years after the first settlers had come, people in Utah Territory now had land acquisition laws that other states and territories enjoyed. Consequently, John A. Clarke arrived in Utah in the fall of 1868, as the territory's fourth surveyor general. The first U.S. land office in the territory opened in Salt Lake City on March 9, 1869, with non-Mormon Courtland C. Clements as the first Register of Land, and L. S. Hills the first receiver of land. Clements was soon succeeded by George R. Maxwell, who officially began duty June 15, 1869.[31]

---

[29] Bigler, *Forgotten Kingdom*, 38–39.

[30] Arrington, "Crusade against Theocracy," 20–22. Philo Taylor Farnsworth, Jr., was the grandfather of the person of the same name who is credited with the invention of television.

[31] Clements was appointed surveyor general. He was accused by congressional delegate Hooper, a Mormon, of using his office to facilitate claim jumping. L. B. Lee, "Homesteading in Zion." An unsigned item in *New York World*, November 25, 1871, entitled "Brigham Young's Janissary," described Maxwell: "Samuel's land office register . . . [was] a worthless vagabond, whose neglected appearance would . . . [lead a lawman to] at once arrest him for vagrancy. . . . He . . . informed me that the papers had been ridiculing his wooden leg. . . . He cautioned me not to say anything against his private character, . . . seemed to take special delight in vomiting forth obscene ribaldry mingled with crudest of blasphemy, and boasted of a villain's intimacy with Mormon girls."

In anticipation of the land office's opening, Mormons reconvened the dormant School of the Prophets in March, April, and May. In these meetings ward bishops and local leaders were instructed on the land office procedures and were exhorted to complete the processes as soon as possible.[32] From March to the end of June, more than 148,000 acres of land were processed for ownership. Nearly 52,000 acres had been sold for $1.25 an acre, and nearly 97,000 acres had been disposed of under the terms of the Homestead acts of May 20, 1862, and June 21, 1866.[33]

Maxwell's Arrival among Many

George R. Maxwell arrived in Salt Lake City on June 8, 1869, in the company of his friend Frank Raleigh, a well-to-do fellow lawyer from Monroe, Michigan. Maxwell had first come to know Raleigh during recovery visits to Monroe in 1863 where Raleigh acted as a notary and assisted in efforts to have Maxwell's medical leave visits extended. Raleigh had kindly traveled as Maxwell's companion, to assist his disabled friend in his trip on the recently completed transcontinental railway. Raleigh was known in Monroe as an unconventional sort, for he had publicly announced himself an atheist. He had been admitted to the bar in Michigan about 1859 and had twice been elected prosecuting attorney for Monroe County. He left his busy office and planned to remain in Salt Lake City "for a few weeks" after he had deposited Maxwell in his new situation.[34] Maxwell was quick to make friends within the non-Mormon element and, less than a month after his arrival, was asked to give the dedicatory oration at the recently completed Corinne Opera House as part of that city's Fourth of July celebration.[35]

The completion of the railroad in May was followed by a clamor to travel on this new convenience, and June, July, and August saw visits of several groups of high-ranking federal officials, the majority of whom were very unsympathetic to Mormon views and practices. Whether the

---

[32] L. B. Lee, "Homesteading in Zion," 30.

[33] House Documents, 41st Cong., 2d sess., 1869–70, no. 1, part 3, Serial Set 1414, 40–41; Linford, "Land Ownership in Utah."

[34] *JH*, June 17, 1869. Raleigh died ten years later in Quincy, Illinois, while en route to relocate his practice to Pueblo, Colorado. The coroner listed acute alcohol intoxication as the cause of death. "Death of Frank Raleigh," *Monroe Commercial*, July 25, 1879.

[35] B. D. Madsen, *Corinne*, 225.

Gen. George R. Maxwell, photographed in Utah, probably in 1869 or 1870. *From the Library of Congress, Brady-Handy Collection,* LC-DIG-cwpbh-04270.

timing of Maxwell's arrival with those of a number of anti-Mormon politicians was coincidence or planned is not known.

On June 14, ten distinguished men arrived, led by Benjamin Franklin Wade, a U.S. senator from Ohio and recently president pro tem. As the chairman of the Joint Committee on the Conduct of the War, Wade had been highly critical of Lincoln and the military, and he was fiercely against the South after the war.[36] Neither was he a friend to the Mormons, for Wade had introduced a bill in 1866 to circumvent Utah territorial courts. Other visitors with Wade included Gen. Philip Sheridan; Gen. Henry Van Ness Boynton, formerly of the Thirty-fifth Ohio Infantry and also General Sheridan's son-in-law, and Gen. David

---

[36] This committee was formed in December 1861, at the instigation of Senator Zachariah Chandler of Michigan. It had broad investigative powers and pushed aggressive war policies.

Henry Rucker of the Quartermaster Corps.[37] Also with them was Senator Roscoe Conkling of New York, who shared Benjamin Wade's radical Republican and Mormon views, and John A. Campbell, recently appointed as the territorial governor of Wyoming.[38] The evening of their arrival, the ten were visited by George A. Smith, of the First Presidency of the LDS church, along with Utah's former congressional delegate, Dr. John M. Bernhisel.

On June 16, one week after his arrival and one day into his new federal position in the land office, Maxwell also merited a visit by George A. Smith, who was accompanied by Elder John Taylor, one of the twelve Mormon apostles. As with the Wade, Sheridan, and Conkling group, the substance of their discussion in the visit is unknown. Notably, it was later that evening when Smith and Taylor called, for the second time in as many days, on Gen. Philip Sheridan in his rooms at the Townsend House.[39] Whether Sheridan was in the city solely for the purpose of accompanying the Wade delegation or whether his objective was also to renew his acquaintance with Maxwell, or to relay certain instructions from Washington, or both, is not known.[40] Visits of high-ranking Mormon dignitaries to both Maxwell and Sheridan on the same evening suggest the latter.

June 16 also marked the arrival of a newly appointed associate justice in the Second District, Cyrus Myron Hawley. The report in the *Deseret News* was disparaging: "He has found it necessary to change his occupation for a while in order to obtain rest. . . . [I]f there is a place in the world where a judge has little to do, and plenty of time to do it in, Utah certainly is that place." Despite the pejorative editorial, Hawley was later asked to be the orator of the day for the Mormon celebration of July 4. He gave a lengthy discourse on the Civil War, a topic not dear to the hearts or interests of his Mormon listeners.[41] June 14 also brought

---

[37] Floyd A. O' Neil, a historian of Utah's Indian groups, finds no evidence that Sheridan's presence had to do with a starving group of Utes under Tabby-to-kwana who were being placed on the eastern Utah reservation. O'Neil, pers. comm., May 2008.

[38] *JH*, June 23, 1869. Campbell had been appointed territorial governor of Wyoming on April 15, 1869.   [39] *JH*, June 17, 1869.

[40] In March 1869, Gen. Philip Sheridan had been made lieutenant general of the army. In the preceding November, George Armstrong Custer, serving under Sheridan, led men of the Seventh Cavalry in the killing of Black Kettle and a hundred Cheyenne men, women, and children in a raid on Washita River, in what is now Oklahoma. Morris, *Sheridan*, 323–26.

[41] "The New Associate Justice," *DN*, June 16, 1869, 11, col. 2; July 7, 1869.

a pleasant morning visit by Maj. Gen. W. S. Hancock and his staff with Brigham Young, as they stopped in the city for a few days on their way to Montana.[42]

About June 20, nine members of the House Ways and Means Committee, on their way to business in California, also stopped in Salt Lake City. Chairman Samuel Hooper, of Massachusetts, and his group lodged in the Townsend House. At the same time, California congressional delegate Samuel B. Axtell arrived, along with Anna E. Dickinson, a celebrated lecturer and women's rights advocate. Rather than leave with Axtell, Miss Dickinson, and her brother, Rev. J. Dickinson, decided to stay so they could learn more of the Mormons.[43] In the later part of June another political visitor, Representative George Washington Julian of Indiana, a Republican and a social reformer, was also in Salt Lake City. His relationship with the group from the House Ways and Means Committee is not clear.[44]

In mid-July, Senator Lyman Trumbull of Illinois, as part of a commercial excursion party of Chicago merchants, arrived in Salt Lake City and met with Brigham Young at his residence. At this encounter Young told Trumbull that he might hear word of federal officers being sent out of Utah Territory. Trumbull warned Young that President Grant would not allow the molesting of federal officers in the discharge of their duties. The lively exchange between the two reportedly caused "considerable sensation" in the group.[45] When Trumbull reported Young's words, they "gave Vice President Colfax the advantage to push General Grant almost to the verge of actual war against Mormon Utah."[46]

August saw the stopover of the ten-person Congressional Committee on Retrenchment, a committee concerned solely with governmental expenditures, on their way to California. This group included Senators Allen Granberry Thurman of Ohio and Justin S. Morrill of Vermont, both well known to their host, Brigham Young, as opponents of the Mormons.[47]

---

[42] "From Wednesday's Daily," *DN*, June 16, 1869, 1, col. 2.

[43] "Miss Anna E. Dickinson," *DN*, June 23, 1869 8, col. 4. Axtell would later serve briefly as the Utah territorial governor.

[44] "Distinguished Arrival," *DN*, June 23, 1869, 7, col. 3.

[45] "An Unfair Report," *DN*, July 14, 1869, 6, col. 2.

[46] Tullidge, *History of Salt Lake City*, 397.

[47] "Our Distinguished Visitors," *DN*, August 25, 1869, 8, col. 4.

With the remarkable string of influential, anti-Mormon visitors the first summer of transcontinental railroad travel brought to Salt Lake City, Brigham Young and Mormon leaders were glad to see the season end.

His Daily Routine

It took extra time and help for George R. Maxwell to fasten on his wooden leg and to get his trousers over the artificial leg and foot. He had learned he must plan ahead and begin early. His wife, Mary Ann—or Mamie, as he endearingly called her—washed him, and John Burns, his barber and hairdresser, combed his hair and adjusted his necktie. His left arm was nearly useless, even if it could have been brought up. As the day wore on, he always looked less tidy. Alone, he could not repair the rearrangements caused by the wind and the day's doings.

By midmorning his amputated stump was moist from perspiration and the prosthesis was irritating. Dressings that absorbed the drainage of his forearm would be soaked. Thick yellow pus drained from chronic infections in the flesh and bones near the elbow. Medical wisdom of the time said that pus forming was indispensable to healing. Termed "laudable pus" when it appeared four to ten days after surgery, it was not recognized as a bacterial infection or seen as a medical complication, as is now known. When the dressings would fill on long days out of the house, Maxwell himself would begin to notice the odor that others around him had probably detected hours earlier. Most of the time friends and colleagues were too polite to complain, but there was the occasional sotto voce comment.

Perhaps Mary Ann learned to save the muslin cottons that, after repeated bleaching and washing, served as soft and absorbent dressings. At times the pink "proud flesh" around the edges of the wounds bled briskly, despite her gentleness, but she learned to apply a styptic stick, which stopped the bleeding even as it turned the tissue black. Ulcers on the stump of the amputation would heal for a week or two but, irritated by the prosthesis, always returned. Maxwell may never have heard the medical term "phantom pain," but he experienced it. Pain emanating from a limb that seemed still present had been his companion for some time, although over the years its intensity had diminished.

Once into the street he appeared much like other professional men of the city. He wore the customary dark gray or black wool broadcloth jacket and pants, with a starched white shirt collar. The chain of a gold pocket watch, a gift from his fellow lawyers of the Salt Lake bar, was strung from one vest pocket to another, completing the professional attire. A Colt revolver, a remnant of his cavalry days, might be worn, mostly hidden beneath the jacket, but the right hand, which would have commanded it, was now preoccupied with aiding ambulation.

Walking was more of a problem than dressing, with the prosthesis on the left leg strapped in place with leather belts around his waist and only the painful right knee and leg capable of sustaining weight for long periods. The crude knee joint of the prosthesis allowed only limited flexion. Some days it was better to simply leave the prosthesis at home and try to make do with a cane or crutches, but all options were difficult because his left arm could not support more than a few pounds.

THE LAND OFFICE

At the General Land Office, Maxwell did not avail himself the privileges of the position to get first access to prime real estate, as land officers in other states or territories are reported to have done. If such opportunities arose, he did not act on them. His critics later commented on his poor business skills, and indeed Maxwell never achieved financial security or prosperity. He immediately found himself fully occupied with land disputes and enmeshed in their cross fire. Mormons wanted clear title to lands they had occupied, in many cases for decades, and the growing minority of non-Mormons feared being excluded from land ownership by entrenched Mormons and by various Mormon actions.[48]

Good relations with the community seemed to mark Maxwell's start in the land office, evidenced by a complimentary entry in the *Deseret News*:

> We are indebted to General Maxwell, Register of the Land Office for this Territory, for information pertaining to the land question that will be of importance to many of our citizens. The General informs us that

---

[48] L. B. Lee, "Homesteading in Zion," 37. By 1878, Mormons were by far the predominant owners of agricultural land, and non-Mormons predominated in the ownership of mining claims.

on Monday last a number of plats were turned over to the Land Office in this city in which the settlements of Parley's Park, Rhode's Valley, also called Kamas Prairie, Provo Valley, Heber and Kamas Cities, and the towns of Wasatch, Rockport, Snyder's Wallsburg, Ithaca, Peoa, Midway and Kimballs were included.[49]

As is evident in this report, Maxwell was addressed as "General" in Salt Lake City, as he also had been in Michigan after the war, but the historical record contains a number of conflicting details regarding Maxwell's rank. Historian Leonard J. Arrington mentions that Maxwell was a "distinguished Union soldier who became a Brigadier General by the time he was twenty-one."[50] Pension office papers, notations by history writers, and his photo in the Library of Congress indicate that he was a brevet brigadier general. However, National Archive records say that he was "allegedly" promoted to that rank. In affidavits attesting to Maxwell's medical condition, Dr. John D. Thompson of Salt Lake City listed his patient as a brevet brigadier. Given that the single star of a brigadier general resides atop the Maltese Cross on the Custer Badge, Custer may have used the presentation of the medal to Maxwell to announce the bestowal of the brevet general rank upon him. Historian Mark Grandstaff notes that brevet ranks were awarded for gallantry and that often the full explanation for the award was provided only in the officers' meetings or in private social gatherings of the officers.[51] In a speech before the Grand Army of the Republic in Salt Lake City in 1884, Maxwell said his brevet general promotion had followed a gallant charge against an entrenchment made from stacked railroad ties, but confirmation that this promotion took place at Five Forks was not included in his remarks.[52] Had Maxwell not fully merited the title "General," his intrinsic honesty, which was amply attested to by his peers, would have prevented its use. And if the title had not been properly awarded, this would have been readily disclosed during his many trips to Michigan and to Washington, D.C., where he was personally acquainted with Ulysses Grant, many former Civil War

---

[49] "Important to the Settlers on Railroad Land,' *DN*, January 19, 1870 5, col. 1.

[50] Arrington, "Crusade against Theocracy," 12.

[51] Grandstaff, "General Regis de Trobriand," 210. Since pay remained at the level of his non-brevet rank, paperwork for the brevet position may have been of little concern in the turbulence of Maxwell's emergency evacuations to City Point and Washington, D.C.

[52] "GAR Entertainment," *SLT*, April 27, 1884, 4, col. 6.

officers, and later the entire congressional delegations from Michigan. The most compelling confirmation is that in his history of the medical aspects of the war, Confederate army surgeon Thomas Fanning Wood records Maxwell's injuries and his medical history and independently cites Maxwell as being a brigadier general at age twenty-one.[53]

While thousands of acres were acquired by citizens in the first six months of the opening of the land office, five areas of dispute were soon apparent to General Maxwell: First, Mormons did not reside on their lands. Second, plural wives filed for land and shortly transferred ownership to their husbands. Third, non-Mormons claimed that Mormons never sold their land, except to other Mormons. Fourth, townships were dramatically enlarged beyond their residential areas, a matter previously raised by Burr in 1857. Fifth, by preferentially awarding water and timber rights to Mormons, the Mormon-controlled legislature had exercised an authority it had not been granted. It was Maxwell's leviathan task as Register of Land to apply federal laws in answer to these issues.

CITY OF ZION VERSUS THE HOMESTEAD

When most farmers in the American West were fiercely independent, following a pattern of establishing isolated, scattered individual farmsteads, Brigham Young's "village," or "New Jerusalem," model called for Mormons to reside in centrally located communities and perform farmwork in outlying agricultural fields, often several miles distant. Young inherited this concept both from his New England background and from the teachings of Joseph Smith and early Mormon leaders regarding the concept of the city of Zion.[54] Often the "big field" was communal but subdivided and brought under cultivation.

This concept was very well suited to the agriculturally based colonization that Brigham Young implemented. Centralization permitted efficient use of irrigation waters. It enhanced social interaction of church members, reinforced their "unity against persecution" theme, insulated them against encroachment by non-Mormon settlers, and increased their safety. The village structure assured, even demanded, that individual behavior would conform to the teachings and standards

---

[53] Wood, "Wood's Recollections," 39–40.
[54] L. Nelson, *Mormon Village*, 34–40.

of the Mormon theocracy. As late as 1882, Mormon church president John Taylor continued to press these advantages:

> The Saints should be advised to gather together in villages. . . . By this means the people can retain their ecclesiastical organizations, have regular meetings of the quorums of the priesthood, and establish and maintain day and Sunday Schools, Improvement Associations, and Relief Societies. They can also co-operate for the good of all in financial and secular matters. . . . [Villages] are a mutual protection and a source of strength against horse and cattle thieves, land jumpers, etc., and against hostile Indians.[55]

However well suited and advantageous, this Zion model did not conform to the federal homestead statute, which required, as a condition of title, a continuous five-year residence on the land as proof of settlement and cultivation. The editors of the *Salt Lake Tribune* offered sound advice to their Mormon neighbors:

> The people . . . should rely upon themselves and the proper officers for information, and not be governed by the advice of the Bishops who are not apt to be very well posted on the Land Laws and regulations of the United States. . . . The Legislature of Utah has, therefore, no control or influence over it. It must be understood now, that nothing but a personal and exclusive residence upon the land gives any one possession. . . . All persons who have entered land in Utah who are residents of this city . . . have done so fraudulently according to the opinion of the Government officials. Among these persons are a large number of dignitaries of the [Mormon] Church.[56]

Mormons often compromised by moving onto the land temporarily and living out of wagons, hoping that their partial compliance would suffice. However, in so doing, the Saints ran the risk of perjury. Concerned with loss of ownership arising from this residency requirement, Mormon leaders, through the Utah territorial legislature, asked Congress to allow the substitution of irrigation works for the residence requirement of the Homestead Act.[57]

---

[55] President John Taylor to Stake President William B. Preston of Logan, Utah, cited in W. Stegner, *Mormon Country*, 31.

[56] "Important to Homestead and Other Land Claimants," *slt*, April 26, 1871, 2, col. 1.

[57] The Desert Land Act of 1877 fulfilled this demand and was later used in Utah. L. B. Lee, "Homesteading in Zion," 32–33.

LAND AND PLURAL WIVES

Certain provisions of the federal land statutes of the Preemption Act of 1841 and the Homestead Act of 1862 further aggravated the conflict between Mormons and non-Mormons regarding land acquisition. The acts allowed a male of twenty-one years, who was a citizen (or had filed a declaration to become one), or any head of family of either sex, to make entry on 160 acres at $1.25 an acre. "Head of family" was interpreted by Mormons to include plural wives, and several instances of apparent abuse were publicized in the Salt Lake newspapers. The *Salt Lake Tribune* addressed the matter:

> [There is] a pretty lively business being done in the Land Office by the "heads of families" in obtaining homesteads of 160 acres each. These "heads of families" are in every instance the wives of one man, who has already acquired a homestead, but who is anxious to increase his acres by fresh acquisitions obtained through a loop-hole left in the Homestead bill. . . . In one day 1250 acres of public land were gobbled up by the wives of two men in clear violation of the spirit of the homestead law. . . . [T]he lands taken up are in the vicinity of a located station on the proposed Utah Southern Railway, to be built by the Church of Jesus Christ of Latter-day Saints. Any one familiar with the tendency of the faithful to deed over their property to the Church, will have no difficulty in suspecting where this land so curiously obtained from the Government, will eventually go. . . . Shall the United States Laws be so construed as to give the Saint an advantage over the Gentile? . . . [T]he man having a plurality of wives is the recipient of as many homesteads as he has wives, while the genuine head of one family can take only one quarter section of land.[58]

When asked to rule on this interpretation, federal land commissioner Willis Drummond clarified the official position, which was based on the lack of legal status for undocumented plural marriages: "Under the laws of the United States, this woman is not the wife of the man to whom the usage referred to relates her; therefore her affidavit whereby she is shown to be a citizen of the United States and the head of a family, must entitle . . . acceptance."[59]

Although the practice does not seem to have involved large numbers of people, Maxwell and other non-Mormons objected to women

---

[58] "How They Gobble Up the Land," *SLT*, May 14, 1871, 2, col. 1.
[59] Drummond's letter was published under the inflammatory title "Rights of Prostitutes" in the *Corinne Daily Reporter*, July 29, 1872.

obtaining and transferring a land title under a marriage not recognized by U.S. law. Maxwell believed that two elements of federal law were violated: first, polygamous marriages were not legal, and second, land was provided and intended for the use of the applicant, not for immediate transfer to another person or to the trustee-in-trust of the LDS church.[60] In 1876 Maxwell recounted that Mormons instigated his removal from the land office over this issue, recalling an episode in which Elder Allsop and his plural wives applied for and obtained 1,260 acres at Sandy Station, land that was later claimed by Brigham Young and Feramorz Little. The issue of plural wives vying for land was brought before Congress by the U.S. land commissioner in testimony during the *Maxwell v. Cannon* contest for Congress.[61]

This was not a conundrum that Maxwell could readily solve, but his efforts led to the *Lyon v. Stevens* decision in 1879 that plural wives were not eligible to enter separate tracts.[62] As the *Salt Lake Tribune* reported, "Credit is to be awarded to a faithful officer of the Land Department for untiring efforts in resisting and responding to these fraudulent entries. When Register of Land, General Maxwell, ten years ago made up a case where a polygamist wife had filed a declaratory statement and submitted it to the Land Commissioner [Joseph S.] Wilson."[63] Maxwell had been unsuccessful in his earlier appeals to U.S. land commissioners Wilson and Drummond, but "General Maxwell is not the man to give up beaten," the *Tribune* noted. When James A. Williamson succeeded Drummond as commissioner of the General Land Office, Maxwell prepared the papers of the Lyon case and found a more receptive ear. "It was high time this burlesque upon statesmanship, this outrage upon justice and common sense—was put a stop to," said Williamson. The *Lyon v. Stevens* case was carried to Interior Secretary Alonzo Bell, who ruled that such practice "will not be permitted under homestead and preemption laws."[64]

LAND AND WATER DISPUTES

Eager to establish ownership of the towns and farms they had founded, Mormons were aided by the provision of the Mormon-dominated

---

[60] L. B. Lee, "Homesteading in Zion," 33.   [61] "Sandy Station," *SLT*, May 19, 1876, 4, col. 4.
[62] L. B. Lee, "Homesteading in Zion," 33.
[63] "The Lyons–Stevens Decision," *SLT*, October 11, 1879, 2, col. 2.   [64] Ibid.

territorial legislature that "allowed liberal boundaries . . . to include the surrounding fields as well as the residential areas."[65] This was justified, according to Mormon historian Gustave O. Larson, as "a defensive movement on the part of the Mormons to preserve as much land as possible for the original settlers in Utah."[66] As in most matters, the non-Mormons interpreted the actions differently, knowing that land could not be preempted or homesteaded inside of incorporated cities, thus excluding all settlement within cities by non-Mormons. Maxwell put it in these words: "The corporate limits of some city or town extends over all the available arable lands of Utah[,] . . . the reason of which is obvious, *viz.* in plain terms, it is to prevent the Gentiles from acquiring title to the public lands."[67]

The availability of water also determined land value, and control of creeks and canyons was given to trusted Mormon leaders in high standing. The territorial legislature gave Ezra T. Benson control of the water of Tooele Valley. Brigham Young was given the timber, rocks, minerals, and water of City Creek Canyon, and Heber C. Kimball the waters of North Mill Creek Canyon. Apostle George A. Smith was given ownership and exclusive control of "all the timber in the mountains west of the Jordan [river]."[68] The County Court of Great Salt Lake granted the petition of Daniel H. Wells for the "wood, timber, lumber, poles, grass, stone, road and water of the kanyon [*sic*] commonly known as emigration kanyon, including the entire control and privilege of said kanyon, and its tributaries."[69]

When Wells and other city officials applied for 5,700 acres for the city of Salt Lake, Maxwell's efforts to oppose this amount of land caused the city officials to make special application to the General Land Office in Washington for granting of the oversized allotment. Mayor Wells said:

> It is no fault of the United States Government that we are not now peacefully possessing titles to the ground we have redeemed, and which Congress wishes us to retain. It is the fault of the unrelenting Land Register

---

[65] The city of Fillmore was an example of the allocation of excessive city size; in 1852 it encompassed thirty-six square miles, nearly one square mile for each of the original colonizers. Bigler, *Forgotten Kingdom*, 55.

[66] G. O. Larson, "Land Contest in Early Utah," 323.

[67] Ibid.

[68] Morgan, *State of Deseret*, app. B, 158, 160, 163; Bigler, *Forgotten Kingdom*, 54.

[69] Alter, *Utah*, 144.

here, Maxwell, who has entertained and abetted every petty and malicious claim contesting our right to the site and who hinders the entry of our city, apparently with the object of being bought off or of discouraging us, or even of robbing us of it. . . . The General Land Office ought to instruct this devilish Maxwell not to entertain these paltry claims.[70]

Indeed, it was only by a special congressional act in November 1871 that the Salt Lake City townsite was awarded as the Mormon leaders wanted.[71]

Maxwell and other federal officers further angered Wells when they subsequently charged him with illegal timber cutting in Little Cottonwood Canyon, seized the disputed lumber, and engaged him in a prolonged legal battle over ownership of the materials.[72] Maxwell was acting on instructions he had received from the General Land Office of the Department of the Interior:

> There is no authority of law to permit anyone to cut timber from the public lands for the purpose of speculation or sale. Parties who have made settlements under the pre-emption and homestead laws are entitled to cut and use the timber on the lands embraced in their settlements to the extent necessary for domestic purposes . . . but not for sale. . . .
>
> You will discharge with energy the duty devolved upon you. . . . [Y]ou are authorized to compromise with the parties committing the trespass on their paying all expenses incurred and a reasonable stumpage to be fixed by you according to the condition of the market, but not to fall below the minimum rate of $2.50 per M feet. . . . In cases where no compromise, you will seize the timber cut on the public lands . . . and sell the same, after due notice, at public auction, to the highest bidder.[73]

With the authority provided by these instructions, Maxwell found, seized, and publicly advertised for sale, in the *Salt Lake Tribune*, a large amount of lumber harvested in Big Cottonwood Canyon by those in the employ of Daniel H. Wells, much to the consternation and anger of Wells and the Mormon leadership.

While in office, Maxwell pointed out other exclusive franchises given to Mormon leaders and cited the instance of Congressman William H.

---

[70] Whitney, *History of Utah*, 2:626–28.

[71] "City News," *SLT*, July 8, 1872, 3, col. 2.

[72] Keller, *Lady in the Ore Bucket*, 82–89.

[73] Letter from Jos. S. Wilson, Commissioner, General Land Office, published with comment by the editors in the *Salt Lake Herald*, November 16, 1870.

Hooper, who was given, under territorial grants, thirty thousand acres of land.[74] By December 1871, Maxwell's actions over land matters had become sufficiently troublesome that efforts were being mounted from some source to remove him; indeed, reports came from Washington seemingly confirming that it had been done. Northeastern political analysts and some Mormons saw it differently: "The appointment of W. B. Irving as Register of Land Office in Utah is regarded by the 'Mormon' delegation here as indicating that the Administration intends to modify its policy toward polygamy. Maxwell, the former incumbent, and who is now a contestant for Hooper's seat as delegate, was active in his persecution of the Mormons and was chiefly instrumental in bringing the late suits against their leaders."[75] Oscar G. Sawyer, the pugnaciously anti-Mormon editor in chief of the *Salt Lake Tribune*, sent a telegraph to the Associated Press on December 7, 1871, and it was printed in the *Washington Capital* and repeated in the *Corinne Daily Reporter*: "Much surprise is caused by the removal of General Maxwell from the Land Office. The Gentiles universally regret it, and the Mormons rejoice."[76] The *Deseret News* did not explain its access to the telegraphed message but expressed delight at Maxwell's removal, while denying that it was newsworthy:

If anything is required to bury the Western Union telegraph monopoly to an end and insure postal telegraphy[, it] is the fact that . . . statements like the above are sent over the wires . . . and palmed upon the public as news. Hon. Willis Drummond, Commissioner of the Land Office, Secretary Delano, and President Grant are entitled to praise for removing the being Maxwell, named above, for the causes of interference, loafing, foul language, neglect of business and petty tyranny.[77]

However, unknown forces were operating; the nomination of Irving was withdrawn, and Maxwell retained his post.[78] The *Salt Lake Tribune* announced the news, albeit incorrectly, as Maxwell had not been

[74] George R. Maxwell, in *Corinne Daily Reporter*, May 17, 1872.

[75] "General Maxwell Suspended in Land Office," *Corinne Daily Reporter*, December 7, 1871, 2, col. 2; "By Telegraph—New York," DN, December 13, 1871, 5, cols. 2–3.

[76] *Corinne Daily Reporter*, December 8, 1871, 2, col. 2.

[77] JH, December 17, 1871.

[78] In May 1879, General Sheridan traveled to Corrine, Utah, via the Union Pacific Railroad. This would have given Maxwell an opportunity to discuss his difficulties concerning the Mormons with someone who would transmit them upward to Grant.

removed from office: "We are pleased to learn that General Maxwell has been re-installed in the Land Office in this city. Ulysses needs talking to, as Maxwell will do his duty every time."[79]

The *Corinne Reporter* correctly phrased its congratulations:

> The innumerable friends of General Maxwell, Register of the Land Office, will be delighted to learn that he is to continue in his present position for four years to come. Had it been otherwise our faith in the judgement of the President might suffer a skate; but as it is we reiterate Maxwell is an honor to the administration, and General Grant knows this just as well as we do. That's why the battered hero is to remain with us despite the power of the lecherous kingdom.[80]

Accusations of fraud and corruption for personal gain began against Maxwell while he was in the land office. Lawyer George Caesar Bates alleged fraud over "certain coal land." Maxwell responded with the challenge that in fifteen minutes he could obtain a written statement from Bates that all accounts were in good order. Compelling evidence of his lack of personal gain came from the description of Maxwell's appearance by the *Tribune*'s editors: "Maxwell looks so poor that even a Young Men's Christian Association could not help but rejoice to hear that he had stolen enough to make himself comfortable."[81]

Despite the efforts to remove him from the land office, Maxwell continued his attempts for change, and as late as December 1873, after he had become a U.S. marshal, he went with attorney William Carey to Washington, where they worked for legislation and testified before the Committee on Territories for solutions to the conflicts between Mormons and non-Mormons over land ownership in Utah.[82]

During the first ten years of the Salt Lake City land office, 4,100 homestead entries were made, and only twenty-six legal contests were filed. William Clayton, the Mormon representative to the federal land office, had the assignment of assisting Mormons with filing their claims in order to prevent lawsuits from developing among the brethren, for such disputes would encourage non-Mormon "land sharks" to intervene.[83]

---

[79] "Re-installed," *SLT*, December 14, 1871, 3, col. 2.

[80] *Corinne Daily Reporter*, December 13, 1871, 2, col. 2.

[81] "Exposures in Utah," *SLT*, August 30, 1873, 2, col. 3.

[82] George Q. Cannon to Brigham Young, Washington, D.C., December 17, 1873, Brigham Young Collection (hereafter "BYC").

[83] L. B. Lee, "Homesteading in Zion," 33–34.

UTAH PENITENTIARY OR UNITED STATES PENITENTIARY?

The Utah Territorial Penitentiary, completed in 1855, had been commissioned and money furnished by the U.S. government. Up to 1871, funding was supposed to come from territorial monies provided by the Mormon-controlled legislature. In January 1871, Congress passed the Act in Relation to Certain Territorial Penitentiaries, which placed the care and control of each penitentiary under the U.S. marshal for the territory in which each penitentiary was situated. From this point, the prison in Salt Lake City was the United States Penitentiary. Territorial prisoners were not to be taken there and instead were to be housed in facilities rented or supplied at territorial expense. All expenses of this United States Penitentiary and its prisoners were to be borne by payments from the U.S. marshal. To the marshal's minuscule salary of two hundred dollars a year was added an additional one hundred dollars a month for the additional expenses. Despite the provision that territorial prisoners would remain separate from the other prisoners, they were frequently, if not routinely, housed together, resulting in chronic contention over who would pay. Argument over payments for court costs and for prisoner's housing and maintenance would become the bane of all three U.S. marshals of the Utah Territory during this period: Marshal Mathewson T. Patrick, followed by Maxwell and then Marshal William Nelson.

During Maxwell's time as Register of Land, Mormon elder Albert Perry Rockwood filed a claim for a quarter section of land. Rockwood was at the time warden of the Utah Territorial Penitentiary, and unknown to Maxwell the piece for which Rockwood filed was the land on which the prison stood. Mormon historian Orson Whitney contends that Rockwood was attempting to gain title to the penitentiary because of disputes with Marshal Patrick over the custody and expenses of territorial prisoners.[84] Rockwood, for years one of Brigham

---

[84] Albert Perry Rockwood joined the Mormon church in Kirtland, Ohio, in 1837, gathered with the Saints in Missouri, and then settled in Nauvoo. In December 1845 he was ordained one of the First Presidents of Seventies. In 1847 Rockwood was among the first body of pioneers to enter the Great Salt Lake valley. He served in the territorial legislature and headed several committees of that body. He later wrote a history of the Utah Penitentiary, but his account omitted many matters of great interest to historians. The imprisonment of John D. Lee and William Dame, any mention of George R. Maxwell, the murder of Warden Matthew Burgher, and any investigation of the events that led to a total of twelve men being killed while attempting escape are all absent from his account. Rockwood, "Report."

Young's most trusted assistants, planned to turn the land over to Mormon ownership so that the church would control the prison.[85] In a letter to Brigham Young, George Reynolds—Young's secretary and later known for his conviction for polygamy—reported that Judge Zerubabbel Snow, acting as attorney for the Mormons, deemed that they had a strong chance at winning the case.[86] At Maxwell's urging, the matter was solved by Secretary of the Interior Columbus Delano and Attorney General George H. Williams; they instructed U.S. attorney William Carey to vacate Rockwood's claim.[87]

Despite the overall satisfaction Mormons experienced in expeditiously acquiring land, the land ownership disputes involving Maxwell spurred Brigham Young to single him out in 1872. Young said that Maxwell, "without the least provocation[,] had striven for three years to hinder this people from entering their land."[88]

OTHER CONFLICTS

Simultaneously with his land office duties, Maxwell operated in other capacities that resulted in conflict with Mormon leaders. According to Mayor Wells, Maxwell worked pro bono for claims against the Mormon leaders: "Maxwell spends his time acting as a volunteer counsel against us in criminal cases before the United States Court."[89] Maxwell did assist several men in their attempts to file on land claimed to be city property. One was Salt Lake lawyer James Milton Orr, who filed on eighty acres near Ensign Peak and Arsenal Hill, and a man named

---

[85] Brooks, *On the Mormon Frontier*, 524.

[86] George Reynolds to Brigham Young, June 3, 1876, BYC.

[87] Attorney General George H. Williams to U.S. attorney William Carey, May 23, 1874, General Records of the Department of Justice, Record Group 60, National Archives, Washington, D.C. (hereafter "RG 60"), Chronological Files, 1871–84, box 1015. The $1,200 paid to the U.S. marshal to run the penitentiary was the same amount that had been paid to Rockwood as salary as the territorial warden. Paid from territorial funds, this was for Rockwood's personal use and not for prison expenses. "Territorial Auditor and Treasurer's Reports," *SLT*, January 13, 1876, 2, col. 2.

[88] Minutes of a meeting of Brigham Young and Mary Ann Sprague, May 16, 1872, BYC.

[89] Whitney, *History of Utah*, 2:627. Juanita Brooks cites the diary of Samuel Whitney Richards, wherein he and Hosea Stout, at the request of Mormon president Daniel Wells, "called upon Mrs. Tate at the Delmonica Hotel and inquired into the circumstances by which she was there and making application to G. B. Maxwell [*sic*] of the Register's office, for property from her divorced Husband to support her children." Brooks, *On the Mormon Frontier*, 738.

Slosson, who had been forcibly ejected as he attempted to claim a quarter section on the road to Camp Douglas. Neither man was successful, and the lands claimed were retained by the city.[90]

Methodist minister John Philip Newman, chaplain of the Senate and pastor of the Metropolitan Methodist Church in Washington, D.C., arrived in Salt Lake City in April 1870, for the purpose of engaging Mormon church president Brigham Young in a personal debate on the topic "Does the Bible Sanction Polygamy?"[91] Maxwell, along with four other non-Mormons, had written to Newman asking for confirmation of his willingness to proceed.[92] Newman answered by sending a letter of challenge directly to Brigham Young, indicating that Dr. James P. Taggart had become his Utah representative in the endeavor. Young did not himself engage in the debate but sent the capable, knowledgeable apostle Orson Pratt in his stead to take on Newman. Debate occupied three days in the Tabernacle; both Mormons and non-Mormons claimed to have had the better argument.

In February 1872, Maxwell was one of a group of non-Mormon businessmen and federal officials who provided the visiting Japanese delegation of the Iwakura Mission with an elaborate dinner and celebration in the Townsend House. The welcome did not include any Mormon attendees.[93]

On March 27, 1872, a large number of professionals and businessmen met in the Liberal Institute to draft a memorial to Congress, protesting Mormon plans to seek statehood at that time. The epistle they drafted listed several reasons for this opposition, among them that the population of Utah did not meet the required number and that a large majority of the citizens entertained doctrines antagonistic to the fundamental ideas of free government and followed a religious head whose law was claimed to be superior to all other law and civil authority. Polygamy was, of course, also listed as a serious impediment, but

---

[90] Hinckley, *Daniel H. Wells*, 157.

[91] Notables among Newman's church congregation were President Grant, Vice President Colfax, Chief Justice Salmon Chase, and James G. Blaine, Speaker of the House. Hardy, *Doing the Works of Abraham*, 254.

[92] Others signing the letter to Newman were John P. Taggart, of the Internal Revenue office; J. H. Wickizer; G. B. Overton, land office receiver; and J. F. Woodman. Whitney, *History of Utah*, 2:450–51.

[93] Iwakura Mission visitors had been stranded in Salt Lake City when heavy snow blocked railroad travel to the east. Butler, "Iwakura Mission," 31.

the greatest emphasis was on the problem of theocratic rule, which overrode the plural marriage issue. A series of speakers were heard, and the wording of the lengthy memorial was fashioned. The *Salt Lake Tribune* reported: "General Maxwell was then called for and he gave a withering rebuke . . . and spoke on the situation in terms that 'certain parties' would not liked to have listened to. After which he moved for the reading of the Memorial to Congress, which was accordingly done by Mr. Edward Tullidge as Secretary."[94]

In his history of Salt Lake City, Tullidge reported that a later ratification meeting, held July 22 in the Liberal Institute, was "well toned, but General Maxwell quickly broke the harmony of the occasion" by declaring, "The supremacy of the law, the safety of life and property in Utah to-day, is owing to the Liberal party." Maxwell then was "cheered to the echo." He went on to speak of the "corrupt party in power[,] . . . mismanagement of the city affairs, . . . using up the people's taxes[, and] Danites as policemen [who do the] murderous and dirty work of the Mormon Church." Again he was cheered as he took his seat.[95]

Maxwell served as the assistant attorney, along with U.S. attorney Robert N. Baskin, in Judge James Bedell McKean's Third District Court, in the prosecution of Mormon police officers Andrew H. Burt and Brigham Y. Hampton for the 1866 murder of Dr. John King Robinson. Also accused were storekeeper John L. Blythe, gunsmith James Toms, and a man named John Brazier (or Brasher) of Salt Lake City's Fourth Ward.[96] Witnesses reported that the night of the crime was brightly moonlit and that Robinson was first struck in the head with a short sword and then, as he was falling, shot in the eye. The prosecution contended that his murder was instigated from within the LDS hierarchy. In the *Deseret News* were listed the names of thirty-eight witnesses who were called for their testimony.[97] The editor of the paper

---

[94] "Local Matters," *SLT*, March 28, 1872, 3, col. 1.

[95] Tullidge, *History of Salt Lake City*, 506–507.

[96] The *Corinne Daily Reporter* for December 15, 1871, 2, col. 2, says that John Brazier or Brasher (image illegible) had been arrested December 14 in Salt Lake City for Robinson's murder. Robert Baskin and Maxwell appeared for the people, and Charles H. Hempstead and Thomas Fitch for the accused. In 1883 Burt, by then police chief, was himself murdered by a black laborer, Sam Joe Harvey; a mob promptly lynched Harvey. Andrew Burt's son, of the same name, also served in the city police and in 1885 was involved in an altercation with Deputy Marshal Henry F. Collin. Robert Kirby, *Salt Lake Tribune* journalist, pers. comm., May 2006.

[97] "Court in Chambers," *DN*, December 27, 1871.

did not identify Maxwell as the prosecuting attorney but described the argument for the prosecution:

> On this occasion, as on all others, whenever he has had the opportunity to harangue against "Mormons[,]" did it with a seeming most hearty good will; what he lacked in grace and style and elegance of diction being counter-balanced by vehemence and effort to prove his case and convict. He insinuated that the whole police force were now on trial and got through his "piece" in about an hour.[98]

Witness Charles W. Baker gave testimony regarding the guilt of the police officers, but twelve days later he recanted his statements, indicating that he had been bribed by Deputy Marshal Samuel Gilson. Defendants Burt, Hampton, Blythe, and Toms were confined for a period, but their level of concern appears not to have been high, as their wives feted them to a jailhouse surprise party for the occasion.[99] Later these four and Baker were among a large number of individuals absolved of all charges as a result of the Supreme Court ruling in *Englebrecht v. Clinton*. Despite a special investigating committee, a $9,500 reward, and the lifelong efforts of Maxwell and Baskin, no conviction was ever obtained for Dr. Robinson's murder.[100]

HAWKINS AND POLYGAMY

In 1871 Maxwell also assisted U.S. attorney Robert Baskin in the trial for adultery of a young Mormon convert from England, Thomas Hawkins. Since plural marriages were not a matter of available public record, conviction for the specific crime of polygamy was nearly impossible. Baskin and Maxwell were able to secure a guilty verdict on adultery, based on its definition in Section 32 of the 1852 Utah Territorial Code and the testimony of the first wife, Harriet. She told of having been married in England, with a happy relationship for a number of years, until her

---

[98] *DN*, December 27, 1871, 8, col. 1. A boisterous, loud, confrontational manner, as described in this report, would have been at odds with the court conduct taught Maxwell by his mentor Otis Adams Critchett, but it would have been consistent with the forceful oratory for which Maxwell was known.

[99] George A. Smith to the Honorable William H. Hooper, *JH*, March 22, 1872.

[100] Members of the committee to investigate Robinson's murder were a mix of Mormons and non-Mormons. They were Seth M. Blair, Hosea Stout, *Union Vedette* editor and attorney Charles H. Hempstead, and John B. Weller, the ex-governor of California.

husband brought into their home another women whom he claimed to have married as a second wife. She described how, through a thin curtain, she could hear the sounds coming from the amorous union of her husband and his new wife in the bedchamber they occupied.[101] Writing in October 1871, the Mormon-friendly correspondent for the *Cincinnati Commercial*, George Alfred Townsend, wrote in Hawkins's behalf:

> The command 'Thou salt not commit adultery' was delivered to a polygamous people, and engraved upon stone by the husband of three wives. The same public opinion . . . which enacted the statute against adultery married the prisoner to his wives. . . . The man is tried for adultery and lewd and lascivious conduct in living with a woman to whom he was married according to the customs of the society which enacted the law.[102]

Hawkins's second marriage was indeed in accord with the customs of his society but was not within the territorial laws to which that society was subject. The implications arising from the first conviction for polygamy based on a law against adultery that had its origin in the Mormon-controlled territorial legislature were not lost on the Mormons, for at this time their church president Brigham Young was under arrest for lewd and lascivious cohabitation.[103]

---

[101] Baskin, *Reminiscences of Early Utah*, 39–41; Bigler, *Forgotten Kingdom*, 291. Baskin omits any description of Maxwell's role in the prosecution.

[102] Reprinted in "Correspondence—Utah Affairs," *DN*, May 20, 1874, 10, col. 1.

[103] The verdict in Hawkins's trial was rendered on October 28, 1871. Hawkins was among those later set free as a result of the *Englebrecht v. Clinton* decision. Bigler, *Forgotten Kingdom*, 291, 295.

7

Indispensable Opposition

He ought also to pray never to be left without opponents;
for they keep him on the path of reason and good sense.
Walter Lippmann, "The Indispensable Opposition"

MOST OF THE FEDERAL JUDGES AND FEDERAL MARSHALS SENT to territorial Utah were judged by Mormon leaders as merely patrons of the spoils system, men of limited capacity, political hacks, and carpetbaggers.[1] They had "in common only an intense feeling begotten of conviction and interest against every feature of the Mormon Church," said historian Orson F. Whitney.[2] Brigham Young's words were sharp: "No sensible person would accept such offices, contrary to the known and expressed wish of the people, only to serve their own selfish purposes, regardless of the rights of others."[3]

Maxwell's disputes with Mormon leaders in the land office, his role as assistant prosecutor in the Thomas Hawkins trial, and his representation of non-Mormons in court cases quickly earned him the same classification.[4] Antagonism deepened as the list of Maxwell's further actions to bring republican rule grew to be a long one: (1) his role in

---

[1] G. O. Larson, *Americanization of Utah for Statehood*, 33–34.
[2] Whitney, *History of Utah*, 2:624–26.
[3] Brigham Young to President Buchanan, January 6, 1857, cited in MacKinnon, *At Sword's Point*, 70.
[4] George A. Smith counseled Mormon Mary Gillett of Tooele not to continue a lawsuit against the "factory Company" with General Maxwell as her lawyer. Smith advised her to settle her differences and not go to the law, and he told her that if she did not heed his words, she would be standing on the "brink of an abyss the bottom of which she could not fathom." George Q. Cannon to Brigham Young, June 19, 1870, BYC.

helping organize the first non-Mormon political party; (2) his candidacy as the second non-Mormon to run for territorial office against the
Mormon majority; (3) his twice contesting the seating of Utah congressional delegates, first against William H. Hooper and later with George
Q. Cannon, thus bringing unwanted scrutiny of Mormon polygamists,
theocratic oligarchy, and voting processes, each uniquely unfavorable to
the image of the Mormons; (4) his role in prosecuting Brigham Young
for murder and for lewd and lascivious cohabitation; (5) his involvement in the Gentile League of Utah; (6) his assistance to Ann Eliza
Webb Dee Young in her divorce proceedings against Brigham Young;
(7) his role in the polygamy convictions of Thomas Hawkins, already
described, and later of George Reynolds, in a case that went to the U.S.
Supreme Court and stands, to the present day, as a precedent-setting
case; (8) his efforts to correct the inequities produced by the legislature's granting voting rights to Utah's polygamous wives; (9) his work
in Congress supporting passage of the Cullom, Frelinghuysen, Christiancy, Poland, and other anti-polygamy and anti-theocracy bills; (10)
his role in attempting to unravel who was responsible for the Mountain
Meadows mass murders; and (11) his role in the arrest of John D. Lee,
the man charged with the Mountain Meadows murders, and in con-
ducting the first properly managed oversight of Utah jurors, in Lee's
trial.

THE LIBERAL PARTY

A mix of non-Mormon and Mormon men were the prime movers in
forming the new Liberal Party in Utah. Several dissident Mormons,
prominent in business and professional activity in Salt Lake City, had
been labeled "the Godbeites," or the "Godbeite protestors," the name
derived from that of the most prominent among them, businessman
William Samuel Godbe. Other Mormons joining Godbe in protesting the actions of Brigham Young in Utah's economic, theological,
and practical affairs were Elias Lacy Thomas Harrison, Edward William Tullidge, Eli Brazee Kelsey, Henry W. Lawrence, and William
H. Shearman. Also described as the New Movement, these men were
sophisticated intellectuals, and their challenge to Brigham Young's
leadership was formidable; according to Bancroft, it had the potential

to be the most damaging Young ever experienced.[5] With considerable influence in Washington, these Mormon reformers aspired to leadership of the Mormon church and threatened Young's tight-fisted control.[6] Their disaffections were deep and complex; they were estranged from the Mormon concept of the Kingdom of God with its stress on the personal leadership by an individual prophet—from required unwavering conformity in thought and actions, to the inability to question and discuss its precepts—and at odds with the religious hierarchy's economic decisions that excluded mining development.[7] Because of their opposition to Young's economic priorities, their demands for freedom of thought and expression within the church, and their criticisms of Mormon policy, Godbe, Harrison, and Kelsey were brought before a tribunal of church leaders in October 1869. Upon their refusal of obedience in "all subjects—secular and spiritual" to the priesthood authority and to Brigham Young, they were excommunicated from the LDS church on October 25.[8] The Godbeites formed a new church—the Church of Zion—and started an opposition press, *Utah Magazine*, which would eventually become the *Salt Lake Tribune*.[9] They advanced spiritualism in their intellectual forums at the Liberal Institute and were influential in setting the tone for life in Corinne. Known as the "Gentile City of Utah," Corinne was established in Box Elder County in 1869 by a bevy of business leaders in anticipation of a railroad-induced boom that would follow the completion of the transcontinental link at nearby Promontory Summit. Corinne was the site of the first non-Mormon church house to be built in Utah Territory and was the only city in the territory where polygamy was against the law.[10]

---

[5] H. H. Bancroft, *History of Utah*, 655.

[6] In an 1870 visit to Utah, Gen. Philip Sheridan said, "The President has charged me to do nothing without consulting Mr. Godbe and his friends." Tullidge, *History of Salt Lake City*, 481.

[7] The complex details of the schism between these men and Brigham Young are described in R. W. Walker, "Commencement of the Godbeite Protest"; and R. W. Walker, *Wayward Saints*, 344.

[8] Bigler, *Forgotten Kingdom*, 267.

[9] Initially named the *Mormon Tribune*, it began with the high aim that "no intemperate article will be allowed to appear in its columns," but when ownership changed, its pages carried stinging words that were far from temperate. *Utah Magazine*, November 27, 1869.

[10] Several works describe the boomtown of Corinne and its short-lived but unique place in Utah: Anderson, "Gentile City of Corinne," 141; B. D. Madsen and Madsen, "Corinne, the Fair," 105; Frederick M. Huchel, "Corinne, the City of the Ungodly," in *History of Box Elder County*, chap. 7, 123–45; and B. D. Madsen, *Corinne*.

The non-Mormon celebrations of the Fourth of July of 1869 were in Corinne, and George R. Maxwell was the invited, featured speaker. He complimented the group, saying that the assembly of non-Mormon men and women represented more gathered loyalty to the nation than had ever before been manifest in the territory. He censured Brigham Young for not sending men and arms in the war with the South and remarked that he would prefer to write Brigham Young's name in letters as "a stigma and scorn that could not be erased as long as our language should last." Maxwell added that he would "place the Mormons in a stone ship with lead sails, iron spars and a paper rudder, and put them in some dark sea and place the prophets, seers and revelators to steer them to hell by the shortest route!"[11]

A public meeting of independent voters, made up of non-Mormon businessmen and professionals, and Godbeite former Mormons, was also attended by George R. Maxwell. It had been advertised as a "Come one, come all" meeting to select a ticket for the upcoming Salt Lake City municipal election. Mormon leaders urged mass attendance by their members to overwhelm the dissidents and "defeat the purpose of the meeting." As the doors of the Walker Brothers building were opened on the evening of February 10, 1870, a rowdy crowd rushed in, screaming and breaking seats. Led by territorial marshal John D. T. McAllister and Bishop J. C. Little, the Mormon mob "forcibly entered and took control" of the meeting.[12] Godbeite Eli B. Kelsey remained calm, waiting for the Mormons to leave. When they did so, the independents voted to select their candidates, who would run under the label of the yet to be officially organized Liberal Party. The first person nominated was Godbeite Henry W. Lawrence, as the candidate for Salt Lake City mayor.[13] The first political party in the Utah Territory to oppose the Mormons, the Liberal Party was officially formed in Corinne, on July 16, 1870.[14] The party was generally aligned with the national Republican Party but

---

[11] In a telegram letter to Brigham Young, Apostle Lorenzo Snow attributes Maxwell's words to the sworn statement of Wilford W. Lewis before Justice of the Peace J. T. Packer of Brigham City, Utah. Letter dated July 28, 1870, 4:45 P.M., BYC; *Salt Lake Herald* (hereafter "*SLH*"), July 29, 1879.

[12] Maxwell, who was present at the meeting, later confirmed that McAllister was the leader of the group. "Liberal Meeting," *SLT*, February 13, 1876, 4, col. 2.

[13] Tullidge, *History of Salt Lake City*, 428–30; McCormick, "Hornets in the Hive," 237.

[14] The economic, political, and women suffrage issues that were inter-twined into the motivation to form a party opposing the Mormons are dissected in detail by B. D. Madsen, *Corinne*, 93–121.

held special opposition to the environment of polygamy and theocracy in which its members lived. Prior to the formation of the Liberal Party, a separate political machine was superfluous to the Mormons; elections were simply directed through the existing church lines. In response to the creation of the Liberal Party, the Mormons gave their existing party a name, the People's Party.

John Hanson Beadle, who would later lobby vigorously for the anti-Mormon Cullom Bill, was nominated on a radically anti-Mormon platform of no compromise. General Maxwell presented a platform with some elements of compromise, and Beadle withdrew to avoid dividing the fledgling party. The party's first chairman, Gen. Patrick Connor of Camp Douglas, rose to speak and nominate Maxwell for the delegate seat for the Utah Territory.[15] The Liberal platform opposed Brigham Young's isolationist economic policies and promotion of polygamy (even though Godbe and several men of the New Movement held plural wives) and encouraged the development of mining, which Brigham Young had repeatedly warned Mormons to avoid. Historian Whitney was acerbic in his appraisal of the opposition party. Deeming the Liberal Party as anti-Mormon and filled with "bitterness and rancor to the heart's core," he declared that any "elements of respectability" it might have had were "breaking away" and were "poisoned by the exudations of its own encysted venom."[16]

Despite the efforts of Maxwell and the Liberal Party members, the 1870 election was lost to Mormon incumbent William A. Hooper by an impressive margin, as both parties had predicted. In a move that he would later repeat after a loss to George Q. Cannon, General Maxwell contested Hooper's seating with the limited goal of exposing the oath of allegiance that Mormons took in the endowment house that superseded the vow of allegiance to their nation. He also wished to publicize what he considered an illegal voting practice, in which every Mormon ballot was numbered and thereby identified the person cast-

---

[15] In addition to their contact in Corinne, Connor probably knew of Maxwell from Michigan cavalryman James Kidd, who commanded the Michigan Veteran Cavalry soldiers in Connor's Powder River campaign. Maxwell's relationship with Connor was likely influenced by information from Kidd, who had considered Connor's dealings with the Michigan volunteers at the end of the war too heavy-handed, given that the men felt very unfairly treated by having been sent west instead of being allowed to return home. Longacre, *Custer and His Wolverines*, 283–92.

[16] Whitney, *History of Utah*, 2:540.

ing it.[17] James Jencks, a stalwart Mormon, wrote in the *Millennial Star*
that Maxwell was one of the Mormons' more rabid enemies:

MAXWELL ON THE RAMPAGE

Perhaps one of the most rabid present enemies of Utah and her people
is General Maxwell who holds an appointment in the land office of that
Territory, but who imagines it to be his special mission to "regulate" and
control the politics of the whole Territory. If President Grant has as much
common sense as he is credited with, he would say to the officious Maxwell, "Mr. Maxwell, you were appointed to attend to certain duties at Salt
Lake City. If you choose to go there and quietly, peaceably, effectually,
and faithfully discharge those duties, good." . . . This Maxwell wants to
represent Utah in Congress, although what he has ever done to induce
the people of that Territory to put any confidence in him, any more than
in hundreds of other political hacks, does not appear. . . . Maxwell is in
Washington contesting the election, and the wonder is, to the uniniti-
ated, why Congress stoops for a moment to entertain his claim. Maxwell
foists a great amount of claptrap upon the public to the effect that Captain Hooper is a Mormon, that Mormons are law defying enemies of the
country, that people in Utah dare not vote as they please, that the women
of Utah voted, which is not according to common custom, that polygamists voted, that the Utah system of voting is peculiar. . . . All of which
shows that Maxwell is more fit for a lunatic asylum than [to] be left to run
free in a peaceably disposed, law-abiding community.[18]

On May 20, 1871, the Central Committee of the Liberal Party met in
the quarters occupied by the District Court in Salt Lake City to organize statewide efforts to nominate local non-Mormons as candidates for
the territorial legislature. Representatives of ten counties in Utah were
present when General Maxwell was "called for and made a brief but
eloquent and patriotic speech," which undoubtedly included comments
relating to the efforts to unseat Hooper. More patriotic speeches were
made, plans were drawn up, and duties were assigned to members of

---

[17] In testimony given in Salt Lake City, Hooper denied "in toto" the charges relating to Endowment House oaths. "The Contested Territorial Delegate Election," *SLT*, April 21, 1871, 3, col.
1. Hooper's seating as the Utah representative had been previously contested by non-Mormon
William H. McGrorty after a similar one-sided loss to Hooper in the 1867 election. Bigler,
Forgotten Kingdom, 277–79. At this time, mileage and per diem were paid by the federal treasury to those individuals who traveled to Washington to contest congressional seats. Remuneration for contestants was later rescinded.

[18] *Millennial Star* 33 (March 28, 1871): 201–202.

the committee in anticipation of the upcoming contests.[19] Maxwell's appeal was not heard in Congress until December; it did not prevent the seating of Hooper and, according to the account of Thomas B. H. Stenhouse, Hooper's being seated further convinced Maxwell that Mormon elders were un-American and "disloyal to government."[20]

THE WOODEN GUN MARCHING EPISODE

According to Utah territorial law, the sitting governor was also the commander of the militia of Utah Territory. This sat well with the militia and pleased the Mormon population when Brigham Young was their governor; however, when a series of non-Mormon men replaced Young in the gubernatorial seat beginning in the 1857–58 Utah War, a number of divisive issues shortly arose. One of these was Governor John Wilson Shaffer's 1870 prohibition of marching, musters, drills, or gatherings of the Utah militia. In actual practice, the command of Utah's troops, uniformly Mormon men, remained with Gen. Daniel H. Wells, the powerful Mormon leader who was also a counselor in the First Presidency of the LDS church. This disjunction of jurisdiction became a friction point in two confrontations between Mormon and non-Mormon elements in Salt Lake City in the fall of 1870 and summer of 1871: the so-called Wooden Gun Marching Episode and a Fourth of July holiday dispute. (Following Judge John W. Shaffer's sudden death, another non-Mormon, Vernon H. Vaughn, then territorial secretary, was named to replace him.)

In November 1870 the Third Regiment Band gathered on the grounds of the Twentieth Ward house in Salt Lake City. Recently acquired musical instruments were their plausible reason for the drill, but they were deemed in violation of Governor Shaffer's earlier order. George M. Ottinger, a former city fire department chief, and Andrew Burt, the chief of police, were prominent among the ward officers involved.[21]

---

[19] Counties represented included Salt Lake, Tooele, Box Elder, Piute, Utah, Summit, Juab, Beaver, Morgan, and Cache. "Meeting of the Central Committee of the Liberal Party," *SLT*, May 22, 1871, 2, col. 1.

[20] Stenhouse, *Rocky Mountain States*, 686.

[21] The others arrested in the marching were C. R. Savage, A. Livingstone, C. Livingstone, John C. Graham, W. G. Phillips, and James Fennamore. "That Rebellion—The Evidence in the Case," *DN*, November 30, 1870, 1, col. 1.

In the preliminary investigation following their arrest, Burt was interrogated by George Maxwell. The two were well known to each other,
as Burt had been accused and interrogated by Maxwell for the 1866
murder of Dr. John King Robinson. Under bail, the accused men were
housed at Camp Douglas under the supervision of Gen. Henry Andrew
Morrow. Maxwell and Robert N. Baskin, as the prosecuting attorneys,
established that the men were in uniform, played military music, carried the American flag, and carried arms, including sabers, and that
between one hundred to two hundred spectators were present.[22] Mormon historians B. H. Roberts and Edward William Tulledge treated
the episode as farcical.[23] However, the *Deseret News* was incensed: "A
clearer instance of malicious, and vexatious prosecution never existed,
and []the men who have been active in it were not already so low that
they cannot very well be made more contemptible. . . . [T]his is the first
time in the history of the United States that training under the waving
folds of the stars and stripes . . . has been punished as treason."[24]

On the contrary, Baskin, Maxwell, and Justice Cyrus Myron Hawley treated it as a potentially serious violation of a legally issued federal
injunction, given by the highest civil authority of the state. Testimony
established that some of the officers who were drilling were in the
possession of carbines, cartridge boxes, and swords. Shaffer, Hawley,
Baskin, and Maxwell were attempting to implement federal control as
President Grant had instructed, but the Mormon leadership's response
was to trivialize the event. Of itself, the matter was of small consequence, but it was characteristic of the frictional jurisdictional disputes
between the Mormons and non-Mormons at the time that would continue for years.

SEGREGATED HOLIDAY CELEBRATIONS

As noted, Mormons regularly treated the Twenty-fourth of July with
greater respect and fanfare than they afforded the Fourth of July. In
early June 1871 a number of prominent citizens of Salt Lake City and

---

[22] One witness remarked that boys with wooden guns were present, and that has given title to
this episode.
[23] B. H. Roberts, *Comprehensive History*, 5:353–57; Tullidge, *History of Salt Lake City*, 492–98.
[24] "That Rebellion—The Evidence in the Case."

Corinne announced their intention to hold a patriotic celebration of the nation's founding holiday in Salt Lake City. Twenty-one men, mostly non-Mormons, were named to a Committee of Arrangements. Miners outside Salt Lake City were encouraged to come and participate. Shortly, the Mormon-run city council followed suit and began making its own holiday plans. The two factions could not agree on a common program and concluded that celebrations would be held in separate locations, with separate themes and events. Mormons would hold forth in their Tabernacle on the temple grounds, and the non-Mormons would meet at the Liberal Institute, "the new building of the reform movement, . . . which is not so familiar with disloyal sentiments uttered against 'that government' whose flag we shall march under."[25] The Liberal Institute had celebrated its official opening ceremony only two days earlier. Located on Second East between First and Second South, it was three blocks from Brigham Young's home and boasted a seating capacity of a thousand, with amenities such as a heating system. Next door was the octagonal home of William Samuel Godbe, who had provided most of the $50,000 for the institute's construction. On other occasions, visiting speakers addressed spiritualistic issues from its lectern.[26] Historian Ronald W. Walker describes the role of the Liberal Institute:

> There stood in the very heart of Brigham Young's Zion, the Liberal Institute, a free thought forum dedicated to radical reform and the overturning of the Mormon commonwealth. The Institute would survive less than 15 years, but . . . it would serve Mormon opponents as a court room, political hall, school, entertainment center, and radical lyceum. The Institute also became a religious counterweight. Utah's earliest congregations of Protestants, Jews, Spiritualists, and "Reorganized" Mormons used its facilities, sometimes to challenge dramatically Utah's prevailing faith. . . . [T]he Liberal Institute represented Utah's growing cultural pluralism as the territory matured from its pioneer isolation and Mormon exclusiveness. This is precisely what the founders of the Liberal Institute intended.[27]

---

25 "The Coming Fourth of July," *SLT*, June 16, 1871, 4, col. 1; "The Work Goes Bravely On," *SLT*, June 16, 1871, 4, col. 1; "Miners Attention," *SLT*, June 16, 1871, 4, col. 2.

26 R. W. Walker, "When the Spirits Did Abound."

27 R. W. Walker, "Godbeite Protest" (PhD diss., University of Utah, 1977), 149. According to Walker, the completion of the Walker Opera House spelled the end for the faltering Liberal Institute, and it was sold by Godbe to the First Presbyterian Church in 1884.

For the July Fourth event, the Institute was handsomely decorated with flags, mottoes, and a large representation of the Goddess of Liberty, draped in a star-spangled banner, as well as portraits of George and Martha Washington. George R. Maxwell was the president and officer of the day; included as speakers were Susan B. Anthony and Elizabeth Cady Stanton. The crowd was "rejoicing over the emancipation from the thrall of the Theocracy of Brigham."[28] Maxwell's featured oration was followed by remarks from prominent businessmen and professionals of the city. Nat Stein read an original poem, and Amasa Mason Lyman spoke. Additional speeches were given by Maj. Charles H. Hempstead, William Samuel Godbe, Judge Dennis J. Toohy of Corinne, Col. Stephen E. Jocelyn, and Elias Lacy Thomas Harrison.[29] The *Salt Lake Tribune* reported: "The entire population of Salt Lake and neighboring towns were in our street, and the rejoicing was general. . . . Never in the history of Utah was the anniversary of the Nation's Birthday more enthusiastically and universally celebrated than on Tuesday last."[30]

Meanwhile, the Mormon speaker, George Q. Cannon, was addressing the Mormon crowd at their Tabernacle. His message and tone started out in praise and gratefulness but shortly became strikingly antipodal to that expressed by Maxwell and was openly rancorous toward the federal officials. Cannon referenced, not the Fourth of July and its tie to independence and freedom, but the Twenty-fourth of July, which marked the entry of the Mormon emigrants into the valley. He castigated the federal government. The priority of patriotic remembrances and honoring of the national Independence Day was forgotten:

> My mind reverts to the time . . . twenty two years ago, . . . the anniversary of the arrival of our pioneers in this valley. . . . [W]e can see how visibly God over-ruled circumstances to raise up a free people[;] . . . a people had been prepared by persecution to inhabit the land. . . . When we take into consideration the many falsehoods that have been circulated against us,

---

[28] Ibid., 152. R. W. Walker, "Liberal Institute."

[29] Amasa Mason Lyman was an early convert to the LDS church, served fifteen missions, was a colonizer, mission president, counselor to Joseph Smith and an Apostle. He aligned himself with the spiritualists of the New Movement for he believed truth must be pursued above all else and that Mormonism was only a part of universal truth. He was excommunicated from the church on May 12, 1870. Heffner, "Amasa Mason Lyman."

[30] "The Celebration," *SLT*, July 6, 1871, 2, col. 3.

and how widely and extensively they have been spread, our preservation is something remarkable[;] . . . we endured the insults of mean, low-lived men, beggars of office many of whom, incapable of making a decent living elsewhere, were willing to give Utah the benefit of their presence. History will do us justice; therefore my closing remark is "Let us bide our time."[31]

As the day's parade was to begin, a confrontation developed between President Brigham Young, Gen. Daniel H. Wells of the Mormon Militia, or Nauvoo Legion, and Col. P. Regis de Trobriand. Only three days earlier, de Trobriand had replaced Gen. Andrew Morrow as the commander at Camp Douglas. Now de Trobriand had the challenge of enforcing the order of Acting Governor George A. Black that the Nauvoo Legion was not to march in the parade.[32] Mark R. Grandstaff relates the event, when de Trobriand said simply:

> "Gentlemen, I am not here to argue or discuss the questions with you. I have orders to obey, and I will obey them; you have seen my preparations, if your militia, under arms, parades tomorrow, I will pitch in." Young, not at a loss for words, assured De Trobriand that the Nauvoo Legion would easily destroy the 13th Infantry. If that was to happen, came De Trobriand's cheerful reply, "[it] would not inconvenience the United States in the least, but would ensure the prompt and thorough destruction of Mormonism."[33]

Both Young and de Trobriand were correct. Wells had under his command approximately 6,000 men, most of them drilled, equipped, and armed. The troops under de Trobriand numbered fewer than 250.[34] Colonel de Trobriand followed his orders but wisely transferred the

---

[31] For the full text of Cannon's address, see "Independence Day," *DN*, July 5, 1871, 6, col. 4.

[32] Morrow had been commander at Fort Rawlins in Provo, Utah, and was warmly received by non-Mormons. The July 8, 1871, issue of the *Salt Lake Tribune* described him as "a thorough soldier, a strict disciplinarian, honored in his profession, a brilliant conversationalist, a true and reliable gentleman." Another tribute, signed by seventy-two prominent officials, professionals, and businessmen was published on July 27. P. Regis de Trobriand was a West Point graduate and professional officer. He served the Union in the Civil War and, like Morrow and Maxwell, was present at Gettysburg. His Camp Douglas assignment was strongly protested by federal officials in Utah, as he was viewed as overly aligned with Mormons. Dwyer, *Gentile Comes to Utah*, 72–73.

[33] De Trobriand said his men would be "ineffective against thousands of armed religious fanatics ready to lay down their lives." Grandstaff, "General Regis de Trobriand," 221.

[34] Mahon, *History of the Militia*, cited in Grandstaff, "General Regis de Trobriand," 212.

responsibility to the politicians when he indicated that his troops would be present as ordered, but that orders to fire on any Mormon marchers would rest with Governor Black and nonmilitary federal authorities.[35] Eyeball to eyeball with the authority of this U.S. officer, and with treason and rebellion to be the charges if U.S. troops were killed, Wells backed down, emotions were defused, and bloodshed was averted. The *New York Times* allowed this episode unusual significance, saying: "The supremacy of the United States laws over the decrees of the Mormon Church was for the first time fully vindicated."[36] The *Salt Lake Tribune* added: "The most gratifying feature . . . of the day to every right thinking patriotic man, was the vindication of the supremacy of the United States laws in this community."[37]

The Cullom Bill

Among the Mormons' complaints about Maxwell was his support of anti-polygamy legislation. The 1862 Morrill Anti-bigamy Act had resulted in no change in polygamy in Utah, but several postwar bills were proposed to do so. In 1866 the Wade Bill was introduced by Ohio senator Benjamin F. Wade, in 1869 the Ashley Bill by James Ashey of the same state, and in 1867–69 the Cragin Bill by Abram H. Cragin of New Hampshire.[38] The Cragin Bill was withdrawn in favor of the Cullom Bill, introduced by Shelby Cullom of Illinois. However, the latter bill had been "concocted in Salt Lake City by a pettifogger named Baskin," said Brigham Young, who added, "If government will only give Baskin some lick-spittle office here, I think our sisters would be very apt to show him his walking-papers in the shape of a forest of broomsticks."[39] Young's charge was correct: Baskin and another Salt Lake lawyer, Reuben Howard Robertson, had coauthored the bill and sent it to Cullom, who introduced it in the House.[40] By its provisions, probate courts would be denied criminal jurisdiction; believers in plural

---

[35] C. S. Peterson, *Utah*, 94–95.

[36] "The Fourth in Utah," *New York Times*, July 6, 1871, front page.

[37] "Our Fourth of July Celebration," *SLT*, July 6, 1871, 2, col. 1.

[38] Mormons viewed the Morrill Act as an ex post facto action, for Mormon men had publicly admitted engaging in plural marriages ten years before passage of this law against it.

[39] Brigham Young to Honorable W. H. Hooper, January 11, 1870, BYC.

[40] Baskin, *Reminiscences of Early Utah*, 28–31.

marriage would be excluded from jury duty in polygamy cases. Additionally, wives would be permitted to testify against their husbands when the men were charged with polygamy; polygamists were proscribed from holding public office; and various fines and punishments were stipulated.[41] The bill passed the House in March 1870 but languished and died without action in the Senate. While some observers thought railroad lobbyists and southerners had been responsible for its demise, Baskin's opinion was that Senator James Nye of Nevada had not allowed it to leave his Committee on Territories. Baskin thought Nye had held the bill to benefit his fellow congressman Thomas Fitch in making his mark as a pro-Mormon politician.[42] Historian Will Bagley contends that Nye was simply corrupt and for sale.[43]

While waiting for Senate action on the Cullom bill, Godbeites and prominent non-Mormons gathered "by invitation only" in a meeting in the Masonic Hall in Salt Lake City. They discussed asking Congress to modify the act to make polygamous marriages exempt if the marriage had taken place prior to its passage. Several Godbeite men, though only quasi-Mormon, had multiple wives and did not warm to the requirement of severing ties with their families. Whitney claims that Baskin was among the most vehement of non-Mormons, along with U.S. Internal Revenue collector Col. Ovander J. Hollister. Maxwell, however, reportedly urged some moderation: "General Maxwell stated his unwillingness to make any such request of Congress, but . . . would join in any effort to have the land and disenfranchising clauses so modified as not to injure any who were disposed to be loyal to the government."[44]

Failure of the Cullom Bill stimulated President Ulysses Grant to deal more aggressively with the Mormons. To this purpose he appointed Gen. J. Wilson Shaffer as governor of Utah Territory (previously discussed) and James Bedell McKean as its chief justice.[45]

---

[41] Van Wagoner, *Mormon Polygamy*, 107–10.

[42] Baskin, *Reminiscences of Early Utah*, 48–51.

[43] Bagley, *Blood of the Prophets*, 283.

[44] Whitney, *History of Utah*, 2:433–38.

[45] Born in Bennington, Vermont, McKean, the son of a Methodist minister and a leading Republican in New York State prior to the Civil War, adamantly opposed slavery and polygamy. Elected to Congress in 1858, he resigned in 1862 to lead the Seventy-seventh New York Volunteers. He was practicing law in New York City when he was appointed by Grant to his Utah Territory position.

Arrests of Brigham Young and
Other Mormon Notables

Judge McKean, assisted by Maxwell, charged President Brigham Young with two separate counts: one for "lewd and lascivious cohabitation," and shortly afterward one for the 1857 murder of Richard Yates, who was killed for having sold supplies to U.S. troops who were en route to Utah Territory.[46] U.S. marshal Mathewson T. Patrick served the first arrest warrant on October 2, 1871, and the warrant for the murder charge on October 28. Daniel H. Wells, who was mayor of Salt Lake City at the time, and Mormon leaders Hosea Stout and William H. Kimball were also charged and arrested for Yates's murder. Notorious Mormon hit man William Adams "Bill" Hickman, admitted to the murder but, in confession to prosecution lawyer Robert N. Baskin, claimed he had acted at the instigation of the named Mormon officials. Hickman had served for some time on the dark side for the Mormons, but fortunes had changed and his motives as an accuser were to be carefully evaluated.[47]

Before he could be taken into custody, Brigham Young opted to "take his usual winter journey to the south for protection of his health."[48] A legal contest ensued over the granting and the amount of bail for Wells and Stout. Maxwell and Baskin argued that a first-degree murder charge was not an offense for which bail was allowed. Judge McKean was willing to consider a departure from this practice, ostensibly because Wells would have difficulty discharging his mayoral duties if not free on bail. Maxwell offered that bail should be set at the surprisingly high figure of $500,000, but to the delight of the Mormons, Judge McKean countered with $50,000.[49] According to Edward Tullidge, Maxwell's reaction "was . . . savage and preposterous."[50] A similar confrontation

---

[46] The case was officially titled *The People v. Brigham Young*. It was illustrative of the two divergent views among Utah residents that Judge McKean unofficially editorialized the title to *Federal Authority v. Polygamic Theocracy*, and the Mormons countered with their view, *Utah Ring of Imported Officials v. Religious Liberty*.

[47] Hickman had been part of the elite, white-uniformed, twelve-man bodyguard of Joseph Smith in Nauvoo. Other notables among the guards were Orrin Porter Rockwell, Hosea Stout, and John D. Lee. Brodie, *No Man Knows My History*, 272.

[48] Tullidge, *History of Salt Lake City*, 546. Young considered other options, including soliciting Colonel de Trobriand for protective custody should he be housed at Camp Douglas. Grandstaff, "General Regis de Trobriand," 204–22.

[49] Bail of $50,000 in 1871 would equate to between $909,000 and $95 million in 2008 dollars, depending on whether the comparison was based on the consumer price index or the gross domestic product. MeasuringWorth, www.measuringworth.com/uscompare/.

[50] Tullidge, *History of Salt Lake City*, 545.

took place in November, when the case of Brigham Young was called, for he remained in southern Utah. Maxwell and Baskin, as they had previously done, requested the forfeiture of the bond because of his failure to appear.

The charges against Brigham Young were still in dispute in early 1872, when the U.S. Supreme Court's deliberations relating to the Englebrecht case were in progress. Young remained in his home under U.S. marshal–supervised house arrest, when a Japanese delegation stopping in Salt Lake City paid him a visit.[51] On April 15 the proceedings against Young were stopped by the Supreme Court *Englebrecht v. Clinton* decision, ruling that criminal issues were within the jurisdiction of the territorial officers and not the federal officials.

This Supreme Court case began when Paul Englebrecht and two other men brought suit in October 1870, in Utah's Third District Court under Judge McKean, against Salt Lake City police officers Jeter Clinton, John D. T. McAllister, and Andrew Burt. Citing malicious destruction of more than $20,000 worth of liquor, they sought a judgment of three times the value of the destroyed goods. Attorneys Maxwell, Hempstead, and Baskin represented the liquor dealers.[52] Judge McKean had ruled against the policemen, but the result was overturned by the 1872 U.S. Supreme Court decision cited, which also invalidated 130 separate pending actions of the district court. Mormons celebrated; non-Mormons were devastated and dismayed. Utah governor George Lemuel Woods wrote to President Grant: "To say that the Decision is diastrous [*sic*] to us only, in part, expresses our condition. It leaves us powerless, ties us, and all the authority of the Government hand and foot, and pitches us into the Mormon Camp. . . . [L]aw will be a farce, and the Officers of the Govt mere ninnies."[53]

Preparations by Mormon leaders for another bid for statehood become focused and intense in January 1872. Governor Woods vetoed their request for $50,000 to finance a constitutional convention to prepare their appeal to Congress and reminded the Mormons that statehood was a privilege granted on merit, not an automatic right given to those who continued to rail against federal law. Two petitions were sent by non-Mormons of Utah Territory, pleading for denial of statehood.

---

[51] Butler, "Iwakura Mission," 42.
[52] "Legal Decision," *DN*, September 28, 1870, 7, col. 1.
[53] Hesseltine, *Ulysses S. Grant*, 213–14.

One carried the signature of 2,700 citizens complaining that Mormon rulers were "antagonistic to the fundamental ideas of free government" and would remain so after statehood.[54] A second petition from more than four hundred women in Utah, warned that "the rule of the Mormon priesthood is a bloody despotism" and that "the history of Brigham Young's reign is written in characters of blood." The *San Francisco Chronicle* asserted that most of the women signing were Mormons, but this seems disingenuous. However, George Q. Cannon, writing as editor of the *Deseret News*, countered that the Mormon women simply did not understand what they were signing.[55] Statehood was again denied, and this outcome contributed to Maxwell's decision for another run for Congress, this time against Cannon.

The Gentile League and the Mormon Richelieu

Edward Tullidge contends that one response to *Englebrecht* decision rendering the district courts toothless was the formation of a quasi-secret society known as the Gentile League of Utah (GLU), organized in Salt Lake City and in mining camps to carry out President Grant's mission to break up Mormon theocracy. Tullidge asserts that General Maxwell was very prominent within this group, if not its leader.[56]

On July 30, 1872, the Salt Lake City Council expelled Joseph Salisbury, a *Salt Lake Tribune* reporter, allegedly because he had misrepresented Brigham Young's remarks at a previous meeting. Salisbury planned to seek readmission to the council and was assured by the manager of the paper, Frederick Thomas Perris, that Maxwell had promised to be at the council meeting with one hundred men from the GLU.[57] That the presidentially appointed Register of Land to Utah Territory would threaten an official city meeting with a force of one hundred armed men is an incredulous assertion.

By midsummer 1872, Maxwell and the Liberal Party began another run against the popular and powerful Mormon leader George Q.

---

[54] Bigler, *Forgotten Kingdom*, 293.

[55] "Startling Disclosures of Four Hundred Mormon Women," *Corinne Reporter*, May 28, 1872, 2, col. 2, reprinted from the *San Francisco Chronicle*.

[56] Tullidge, *History of Salt Lake City*, 591.

[57] Ibid. Perris was appointed general manager of the *Tribune* on July 24, 1873, under the new ownership of the paper by Frederick Lockley, George F. Prescott, and A. M. Hamilton. Malmquist, *First 100 Years*, 31.

Cannon, described as "one of the most widely known men in America" and "the Mormon Richelieu."[58] Realists as they were, Maxwell and the Liberals were confident they could not outvote the majority under the control of Mormon leaders. The *Salt Lake Tribune*'s description of the election process was colorful: "Brigham Young wagged his 'big toe' by which he himself boasted he could move the Territory, and Daniel H. Wells in the City Council has wagged his, and the Bishops throughout Utah, taking their cues to the political farce, have wagged theirs, and our city and Territorial elections have gone like clockwork."[59] Short of winning, Liberals had in mind to continue bringing the issues of polygamy and theocracy before the American public. In August 1872 at an outdoor meeting to support Maxwell's candidacy on the Liberal ticket, speakers decried the Mormon theocracy and spoke of the Mormon people as "dupes," "serfs," and "down-trodden." Allegedly, armed members of the Gentile League circulated among the crowd, hoping to incite the Mormons to violence and thereby begin "the work of revolution," drawing in troops from Camp Douglas for "the execution of a common vengeance."[60] Tullidge's objectivity is lost in this speculation about actions of a federal officer inciting riot through a cabal in the tinderbox atmosphere of Utah Territory. The *Salt Lake Tribune* gives an entirely different story, describing Mormon efforts to disrupt the meeting as having originated in the Mormons' School of the Prophets. The hecklers attempted to drown out the speeches of Robert N. Baskin, of his co-author of the Cullom Bill, Reuben H. Robertson, and of Gen. Maxwell. One celebrant, a Mr. A. S. Gould, was heard to call out: "Maxwell, Truth, and Liberty is our war cry!"[61] Shortly thereafter, the *Tribune* reported, "the un-natural excitement caused by the near collision of our citizens at the ratification meeting of General Maxwell is gradually subsiding and our city is being restored to its usual quiet and good feeling."[62]

---

[58] Landon, Cannon, and Turley, *Journals of George Q. Cannon*, 1:xi. The designation "Mormon Richelieu" refers to French clergyman and statesman Armand Jean du Plessis de Richelieu, or Cardinal-Duc de Richelieu (1585–1642), who became the secretary of state and was widely known as the influence behind the scenes to King Louis XIII. The *Salt Lake Tribune* editors frequently used the term "Cardinal" disparagingly in reference to Cannon, and "Profit," rather than "Prophet," in reference to Brigham Young.

[59] "Elections in Utah," *SLT*, August 3, 1872, 2, col. 3.

[60] Tullidge, *History of Salt Lake City*, 593.

[61] "The Most Peaceable, Orderly, and Law Abiding Community," *SLT*, August 5, 1872, 2, col. 1.

[62] "Our Quiet City," *SLT*, August 9, 1872, 2, col. 3.

Maxwell's major support came from the city of Corinne, from places where mining activities were beginning to take hold in Summit and Beaver County, and from the cities of Stockton and Tooele, in Tooele County. Speaking in Corinne, he "opened his batteries on the Hell-born system of the theocracy" and "with strong arguments and irresistible logic" demonstrated the differences between his candidacy and that of the "ecclesiastical libertine set up for Congress by the bandit priesthood."[63]

On a fall evening in October 1872, a third incident involving the Gentile League allegedly took place in front of the Walker House hotel. Tullidge reports that members of the league moved through the crowd in pairs, hands on their pistols, threatening those who dared to object to the stinging denunciations of Mormon leaders: "Had there been any counter demonstration, the G.L.U.s . . . would have fallen back . . . in front of the Walker house and a volley from them and others stationed in the windows above would have fulfilled the caution [of] . . . Attorney Baskin . . . [for] a hundred coffins.[64] Associate Justice Obed F. Strickland is credited with calling out a warning and defusing what could have resulted in casualties. Credibility is strained by Tullidge's biased account.

FRELINGHUYSEN BILL

February 1873 found Maxwell in Washington, D.C., lobbying for the passage of the Frelinghuysen Bill, which carried the name and sponsorship of the New Jersey senator and contained a number of anti-polygamy and anti-theocracy measures.[65] Maxwell accompanied the Reverend Norman McLeod and Thomas B. H. Stenhouse and wife, Fannie, on this mission. Former members of the LDS church, the Stenhouse pair were now opponents of the Mormons; Fannie lobbied by lecturing on their views of the adverse conditions of Utah's women under polygamy.[66]

---

[63] "Corinneville's Reception of General Maxwell Last Night," *Corinne Reporter*, August 1, 1872, 3, col. 2.   [64] Tullidge, *History of Salt Lake City*, 395–96.

[65] From a distinguished Germany family in New Jersey, Frederick Theodore Frelinghuysen was elected to the Senate in 1871 and served on the Judiciary and other committees. A devoted religious man and longtime member of the Dutch Reform Church, he served, as had several of his ancestors, as a lifelong member of the American Bible Society and, for thirty-four years, as a trustee of Rutgers College. He was later secretary of state under President Chester A. Arthur.

[66] George Q. Cannon to Brigham Young, February 27, 1873, BYC.

In the Frelinghuysen Bill were provisions returning jurisdiction in the courts to the federal level, impartial impaneling of juries, removal of the "spy ballot" by requiring unmarked election ballots, requirement for proof of a marital relationship, and the nullification of many of the acts of the territorial legislature, including the incorporation of the Mormon church, the 1870 women's suffrage, the granting of public domain and land, timber and water rights, all of which had been flash points of contention for which General Maxwell and many non-Mormons had long been seeking solution. After receiving a synopsis of the bill by telegraph, the *Salt Lake Herald* expressed its deep concerns, noting that if the Senate Judiciary Committee—George F. Edmunds, Roscoe Conkling, Matthew Carpenter, F. T. Frelinghuysen, John Pool, George C. Wright and Allen G. Thurman—had "consented to such a measure, it must have been with the understanding that every principle of liberty was to be deliberately violated." The *Herald* stated that the bill "virtually abolishes all local legislation, would produce chaos out of order, and make Siberia a more desirable residence . . . than the Territory of Utah.[67]

Pressure for passage was being exerted by President Grant, with the full support of Senators Samuel Augustus Merritt and William Horace Clagett, and by representatives of the Methodist Church, in addition to McLeod. The bill passed in the Senate, but in the House it faced four days of ebb and flow between Mormon and non-Mormon factions. Maxwell, Merritt, Clagett, and Judiciary Committee chairman John A. Bingham pushed to bring the bill to a vote, with the Mormons privately giving credit to God for each distraction that displaced its presentation. On the calendar for action early Saturday morning, March 4, 1873, a representative from California objected to the bill's being considered without a quorum present. The bill was informally laid aside and never retrieved. Mormons were ecstatic. According to Hooper's report, Maxwell and his associates were devastated:

> Maxwell said he would take out British papers and be an American citizen no longer. Clagett asserted that we [the Mormons] had spent $200,000 on the Judiciary Committee, and Merritt swore that there had been treachery, and we had bribed Congress. But I praised and thanked God, who was our friend and mightier than they all. By seemingly small

---

[67] "The Frelinghuysen Bill," *SLH*, February 18, 1873, 2, col. 3.

and insignificant means he had brought to pass marvelous results and to him all the glory was due.[68]

Edward Leo Lyman claims that the Frelinghuysen Bill did not pass because of the efforts of James Gillespie Blaine, chairman of the Committee on Territories and Speaker of the House, who Lyman says was very likely "lavishly bribed by the Mormons."[69] A special Washington correspondent to the *St. Louis Republican* asserted: "Brigham Young boasted that Benjamin F. Butler was paid $10,000 to defend the Mormon cause, that other Congressmen were paid smaller amounts, and that by this means Frelinghuysen's bill . . . was defeated."[70] Tullidge suggests that money was involved but that there was a more efficient, subtler method in use:

> Z. C. M. I. [Zion's Cooperative Mercantile Institution] has not only a commercial significance . . . but also a political one. It has long been the temporal bulwark around the Mormon community. Results which have been seen in Utah affairs, preservative of the Mormon power and people, unaccountable to "the outsider" except on the now stale supposition that "the Mormon Church has purchased Congress," may be better traced to the silent but potent influence of Z. C. M. I. among the ruling business men of America.[71]

Judge Jacob Smith Boreman also described these economic pathways used by the Mormons:

> They worked through the Pacific Rail Road companies and through the wholesale houses of New York. It was amusing to learn that the rail-road and the wholesale merchants of the east, should do their bidding. In the days when the Gentiles were struggling for recognition in Congress, Leland Stanford and A. A. Sargent in the U.S. Senate were always ready and willing to do the bidding of Brigham Young and his leading men in the Mormon Church.[72]

---

[68] Quoting from "the diary of a Mormon leader who was sent to Washington to assist Delegate Hooper in his unexpired term and to prepare the way for Delegate Cannon's work in the next Congress." Tullidge, *History of Salt Lake City*, 605–607.

[69] Lyman, "Mormon Quest for Utah Statehood," 28.

[70] Reprinted as "Maxwell and Cannon" in *slt*, December 4, 1873, 2, col. 2. Benjamin F. Butler was a representative from Massachusetts and served as chairman of the Judiciary Committee in the Forty-third Congress. A Union major general in the Civil War, he was known as "the Beast of New Orleans" for his stern actions as military governor of the city in 1862.

[71] Tullidge, *History of Salt Lake City*, 734.

[72] Arrington, "Crusade against Theocracy," 27.

Utah's non-Mormons waited two years before the provisions lost in the Frelinghuysen Bill were enfolded into the Poland Act in 1874. According to President Grant, that act was also intended to correct what non-Mormons uniformly considered the serious and obvious judicial error made by the Supreme Court in the Englebrecht case.

Adding to Maxwell's woes over the failure of the Frelinghuysen Bill were injuries he sustained in a carriage crash involving his wife. Both were thrown from their carriage when it was struck by a runaway streetcar at Walker Brothers' corner. The streetcar, drawn by "Spanish mules," came at them at a "furious rate of speed," upsetting and badly breaking their carriage. Mary Ann Maxwell was the most seriously hurt, sustaining a severe arm injury, as well as head and shoulder injuries. The general sustained cuts about the head and face and bruises over his body, no doubt adding discomfort to his already damaged extremities.[73]

When President Grant removed George Caesar Bates as U.S. district attorney because of his pro-Mormon alignment, Maxwell anticipated being appointed to the post, in large part because of his support of and friendship with Judge McKean.[74] However, William Carey of Illinois received the position.[75] In December 1873, Grant nominated Willett Pottenger, of Provo, Utah, formerly a lawyer and mayor of Plattsmouth, Cass County, Nebraska, to be Register of Land, simultaneously asking that George R. Maxwell be made U.S. marshal. Pottenger's appointment was likely requested by the politically powerful Algernon S. Paddock, soon to be a Nebraska senator. Maxwell was selected as marshal over several other nominees.[76] Maxwell prepared for the change by promptly and publicly delegating to his friend and fellow Civil War veteran Amos K. Smith major responsibilities in the office: "Notice: All papers for the United States Marshal must be delivered to Deputy A. K. Smith at the

[73] *DN*, October 7, 1873; "Accident to General Maxwell and Lady," *SLT*, October 7, 1873, 4, col. 4.

[74] Bates's pro-Mormon stance is supported by Brigham Young's later selection of Bates as part of the defense in the trial of John D. Lee.

[75] Although Maxwell knew that Carey was from Illinois, it was unlikely he knew that Carey hailed from the city of Galena, where he and Ulysses S. Grant were childhood playmates and the two would "swap jack-knives" and "slide down cellar doors" together. This relationship may explain Grant's choice of Carey for U.S. attorney over Maxwell. "Washington," *SLT*, January 26, 1876, 4, col. 2.

[76] Brown, "United States Marshals." Other candidates included Emory P. Beauchamp of Terre Haute, Indiana, and Alford S. Gould, a newspaperman from San Francisco, nominated by former *Salt Lake Tribune* editor Oscar Sawyer and Utah governor George Lemuel Woods.

marshal's office, and all general business must be done through him."[77] Given the power vested in the Mormon-run probate courts, Marshal Maxwell's appointment made him, until the passage of the Poland Act, a toothless tiger in a hostile territory.

Contesting Cannon's Congressional Seating

The 1872 election of George Q. Cannon had again been massively one-sided, with Cannon tallying 20,969 votes to only 1,942 for Maxwell. Undeterred by these numbers, Maxwell and the Liberal Party had gone on to their next objective. Federal law required that notice be given to any person whose seating in the House of Representatives was to be contested, and therefore a lengthy list of allegations made by Maxwell toward Cannon was printed in the *Salt Lake Herald*:

> You are hereby notified that I, George R. Maxwell, will appear before the House of Representatives . . . and there contest your right to hold a seat as Delegate from Utah Territory in said Congress . . . because:
>
> 1. You did not receive a majority of legal votes cast in a legal manner at said election.
> 2. That said election was not a free and fair expression of the voters of Utah Territory, they, the voters, having been influenced by fear of one Brigham Young. . . .
> 3. That at said election each and every ballot was numbered and a corresponding number was kept by your confederates for the purpose of intimidation.
> 4. All numbered ballots should have been thrown out of the returns of said election, thus giving me a majority of the legal votes cast in a legal manner in precincts where no numbers were used.
> 5. . . . I received one thousand legal votes in the county of Beaver and other parts of the Territory of Utah, which were illegally thrown out because you and your confederates willfully neglected and refused to establish election precincts in places where the miners could vote. . . .
> 6. That fifteen thousand women, whose votes are illegal, voted for you; that . . . five thousand of them were of foreign birth and not naturalized, and about five thousand of the women were under the age of twenty-one years.
> 7. That the male and female voters in all the precincts voted together, using the same poll-lists and ballot-boxes, thus rendering it impossible

---

[77] Notice signed by George R. Maxwell, Register of Land, published in *slt*, November 20, 1873.

to separate the male and female vote. . . . That you are personally disqualified, having heretofore taken the oath to obey Brigham Young, and his successors, in all things, temporal and spiritual, upon pain of death, and an oath of disloyalty to the United States, and that you would do all in your power to thwart and overthrow the government. . . .

8. That you . . . declared upon oath heretofore . . . that you considered the revelations of polygamy paramount to all human law, and that you would obey said revelations rather than the law of any country.

9. That you are further personally disqualified because you are a bigamist, and living in open and continued violation of the law of God, man, your country, decency, and civilization, and the act of Congress of 1862, entitled "An act to prohibit polygamy in the Territories."

10. That you are now living and cohabiting with four pretended wives, in defiant and willful violation of the law of Congress of 1862. . . .

11. That you have declared upon your oath. . . that you considered polygamy, or the revelation authorizing it, paramount to all human law; that no oath of allegiance to the Government of the United States would be binding in your case because of these promises, and the voters of Utah Territory had full and ample notice of these disqualifications; therefore the votes cast for you were void and to no effect.[78]

Cannon's reply to Maxwell's long list was published in the newspaper on November 23. Cannon denied each allegation, also pointing out that numbering of ballots was done by authority of laws passed by the Utah territorial legislature. Most notably, he specifically denied "that I am living with four wives, or that I am living or cohabiting with any wives in defiant or willful violation of the law of Congress in 1862 entitled 'An Act to Prohibit Polygamy in the Territories.'"[79]

When Cannon appeared at the opening of the First Session of the Forty-third Congress in Washington, D.C., in December 1874, Maxwell was there to personally contest the seating.[80] Congressman Clinton Levi Merriam of New York introduced a resolution containing the multiple charges against the legality of Cannon's seating. For this audience, Cannon admitted that the ballots were numbered, but he emphasized the legality of this practice under Utah territorial law. Before Congress, he again denied his status as a man with more than one wife.[81]

[78] "The General Protests," *SLH*, October 31, 1872, 2, col. 2.

[79] "Geo. Q. Cannon's Rejoinder," *SLT*, November 26, 1872, 2, col. 3; *SLH*, November 23, 1872.

[80] By this date, federal regulations no longer allowed reimbursement for travel and per diem, and travel expenses to Washington were Maxwell's responsibility.

[81] Tullidge, *History of Salt Lake City*, 600.

The text of Maxwell's challenges to Cannon in the House of Representatives was published by the *Salt Lake Tribune*, whose editor said of Maxwell: "The fearless champion of liberalization in Utah shows himself as powerful in the use of his tongue as of his sword."[82] Indeed, Maxwell's words in reference to a report from the Ashley Committee on Territories were strong:

> This testimony shows that Brigham Young, in the presence of thousands of people to whom his voice is more potent than the voice of Deity, boasts of the power of his instructions to juries. . . . Here you flaunt your foul polygamy in the face of a nation—a Christian nation—yea against the moral decency of the world, but which now, in another room, and before another committee of this House you have the pliable audacity to deny it.

When Cannon rose to interrupt, Maxwell responded heatedly:

> I will not be interrupted again. . . . During three entire days I sat a patient though not a willing listener to his false statements and only once arose to protest against his insolent personalities. Now he has branded his wives with the stoma of shame and his children as—I cannot, will not, pronounce this terrible word—I cannot help it. The gentleman has placed his families, his offspring, under the bane of social and domestic disgrace and the responsibility is all his, not mine.

Maxwell then provided examples of Cannon's avowed allegiance to his religion above federal law and questioned Cannon's honesty and fitness for performing in the office to which he had been elected.

> Mr. Cannon admits the existence of Blood Atonement as part of his Mormon faith. He confesses that "a few men have been killed for adultery." Therein I am sure he spoke the truth, though the term "few" should be construed to mean legion. . . . On page 7 of *Maxwell vs Cannon* you will see his declaration under oath that if on a jury he would not convict for adultery where the defendant acted this part of adulterer under the usage of the Mormon Church. Of course not. What are the laws of the Republic to him? What cares he for legal interpretations of capital crimes and other felonies when the higher law of the Church overrides the statutes of the land? . . . [A]t Salt Lake City Mr Cannon swears he would not convict an adulterer, and behold, here before a committee of Congress he says he would convict! . . . Look at his words, gentlemen, and stand aghast at the man's reckless mendacity.

---

[82] "Maxwell and Cannon," *SLT*, February 10, 1874, 4, col. 2.

Next, Maxwell took up the matter of Cannon's criticism of Judge McKean. Cannon had contended that no conflict with the judiciary had existed in Utah until McKean arrived on an apparent mission focused against the Mormons:

> Every Judge that goes upon the bench ought to be on a mission to enforce his country's laws. . . . Judge McKean . . . may well be proud of his "mission" among the malefactors of the Rocky Mountains, for while the hot furnace of priestly calumny emits its blast of hate upon his name, there are forty million of his loyal countrymen exclaiming: "Well done, thou good and faithful servant." . . . The annals and traditions of the Territory show that . . . judges found Utah an uncomfortable place to administer justice, most of them having been forcibly driven from their jurisdictions. As Mr. Cannon can tell you, and probably in many cases by his own advice, in accord with the decree of his chief, Brigham Young.

Having brought up the name of the Mormon leader, Maxwell went on to tie Young's name with the troublesome issues of polygamy and the massacre of the Arkansas emigrants at Mountain Meadows. The general then moved to his final argument as to why he should be seated as congressman rather than Cannon:

> Brigham Young not long ago declared he would need his pet and filthy tenet in the National Councils, that Polygamy should occupy the seats once honored—immortalized—by the Clays, the Websters, the Lincolns. . . . Shall we not also prepare to offer homage to the dogmas ratified at Mountain Meadows? . . . [Cannon] charges that the men of Utah who pray for legislation to Congress are not land owners. . . . [On the petitions before you] you will find the names of Walker Brothers, Henry W. Lawrence, Godbe and Company, R. N. Baskin and 8,000 others representing millions of dollars in real estate, mineral properties, merchandise, etc. . . . And at last this legate of our Utah Pontiff ventures the further prevarication that only the United States marshal desires legislation. In that assertion he is not the victim of delusion, but only guilty of deliberate mendacity.[83]

Maxwell drew favorable comments while at this task in Washington, according to a special correspondent to the *Tribune*: "Mr. Maxwell, the contesting delegate, is genial and popular, and is believed to be worthy of the high respect which he has universally gained."[84] Meanwhile,

---

[83] Ibid.
[84] "Affairs at the Capital," *slt*, February 11, 1874, 1, col. 2.

rumors circulated that Mormons were resorting to bribery to influence the outcome of the contest: "The rumor is rife over the town that
the Mormon Delegate is attempting to secure his seat through corrupt
means. That he has command of any necessary quantity of funds and
does not hesitate to use them wherever they can be made effective,
there can be little doubt."[85] Despite intense, in-person lobbying efforts
by Maxwell, Myron Hawley, William Carey, and others, Cannon was
seated. The legal argument rested on the principle that he had met
the three minimal requirements of the Constitution: he had attained
thirty-five years of age, had been a citizen for seven years, and had
been duly elected. "The Lord be praised for His goodness," and "I
never enjoyed greater calmness and serenity of mind," wrote Cannon to
Brigham Young.[86]

---

[85] "Cannon's Money and Purchasable Congressmen," *Washington Republic*, April 7, 1874, reprinted
in *SLT*, April 16, 1874.

[86] George Q. Cannon to Brigham Young, December 2 and 15, 1873, BYC. Cannon would later
receive the same challenge from Robert N. Baskin, Maxwell's friend, fellow Salt Lake City
lawyer, and fellow member of the Liberal Party.

8

Ann Eliza's Next Best Friend

In the courts women have no rights, no voice; nobody speaks for them.
I wish woman to have her voice there among the pettifoggers.

Sojourner Truth, remarks at
American Equal Rights Association meeting,
New York, 1867

ANN ELIZA WEBB DEE YOUNG IS WIDELY KNOWN AS THE PLURAL wife of LDS church president Brigham Young who engaged him in a highly publicized, salacious divorce, thereby becoming a spectacular Mormon apostate. Less known is her relationship with Marshal George R. Maxwell and her extended, nationwide speaking tour on what was called the Chautauqua Circuit. While it is impossible to measure the effect of her lectures quantitatively, they contributed significantly to the passage of the Poland Act, the elimination of polygamy, and federal legislation regarding Mormon theocracy. Over ten years, she delivered more than two thousand lectures about her experience in Utah. The reactions of her audiences both directly and indirectly influenced their representatives in Congress.[1]

LEGAL ACTION AGAINST THE LION OF THE LORD
Ann Eliza Webb's father, Chauncey G. Webb, was an early Mormon convert and polygamist while in Nauvoo. He was also Joseph Smith's gram-

---

[1] Ivins, review of *Twenty-seventh Wife*.

mar and English instructor while they were together in Kirtland, Ohio. In Webb's own account of his long history within the church, he wrote:

> I have been thoroughly acquainted with the Mormon Church *for over fifty years.* . . . [I]n the winter of 1834 and 1835, [I] assisted in teaching Joseph Smith, the prophet, English grammar. I witnessed the history of the Church in Kirtland, Ohio, in Caldwell and Davies counties, Mo., in Nauvoo, Ill., and in Salt Lake City. I was intimately acquainted with Joseph Smith and his family for *eleven years*; also with the leading men of the Church down to the present time.[2] (Italics in original.)

Webb migrated to Utah as a prosperous and well-equipped early settler. A skilled wagonwright, he was a tireless director of the building of the handcarts used by all five of the companies of Mormons migrating from Iowa to Utah in 1856. He was also among the few who voiced opposition for the launch, very late in the season, of the last company of Saints that year. As he feared, the members of the Edward Martin company suffered mercilessly, and more than 250 died from exposure to the cold and snow and from starvation.[3] Following his move to Utah, Webb continued to manufacture wagons and buggies.[4]

In April 1863, at age nineteen, Ann Eliza Webb married James Leech Dee in Salt Lake City. Two children were born, but because of her husband's physical abuse, she took her case to the Mormon elders. On the advice of none less than Brigham Young and George Q. Cannon, she received a divorce in the Utah territorial probate court in 1865. She insisted her divorce had nothing to do with amorous feelings for Brigham Young and that, to the contrary, she was not attracted to him.[5] Accounts differ as to who was interested in whom. However, a period of negotiation between Young and her parents followed, and Ann Eliza was married to Brigham Young on April 7, 1868, in the Endowment House.[6] Initially she lived with Young's other wives but then was housed by herself in what was called the Forest Farm House.

With time, Ann Eliza claimed that her marriage was in name only,

---

[2] Wyl, *Mormon Portraits*, 7; Brodie, *No Man Knows My History*, 169, 459, 498.
[3] Bagley, "'One Long Funeral March,'" 108.
[4] After his daughter's divorce suit, Webb was excommunicated, but he was eventually restored to membership. He was featured in interviews about Utah history by Dr. Wilhelm Ritter von Wymetal, who wrote under the pseudonym "Dr. Wilhelm Wyl." Brooks, *On the Mormon Frontier*, 313. [5] Young, *Wife No. 19*, 437.
[6] The Endowment House was a special building reserved for the performance of this sacred, nonpublic (Mormons-only) marriage ceremony.

that she lacked material support to the point of having to take boarders, and that she had been virtually abandoned by Brigham Young. Lack of commitment and support from her husband, added to the reluctance she had in entering the marriage, compelled her to "change her circumstances." She sought advice from the Methodist minister C. C. Stratton, whose church she had visited. His advice was "[that she should] sever the connection, . . . that the laws of the United States did not recognize the validity of her marriage and could afford her no relief, [and] that as she had a good house and a partial support it would be best for her to remain where she was."[7] She did not follow Stratton's advice but met with a lawyer, Albert Hagan, who was recently from California and boarding at her home at the time. Hagan conferred with two local Salt Lake City lawyers, F. M. Smith and Judge Frank Tilford, and the three men agreed to take her case and look to Brigham Young for remuneration.[8] Stratton had recommended Tilford, saying he "knew Judge Tilford, . . . and understood him to be a lawyer of ability and integrity, and thought she could trust him."[9] The reverend's opinion was that Mrs. Young did not need to seek safe refuge in the Walker House hotel, but in the event she went there to be careful to "see nobody on business without the consent of her attorneys and especially to see no gentleman alone."[10]

Ann Eliza may have been somewhat hasty in considering Stratton's recommendation of Tilford to be fully trustworthy, for the three attorneys demanded a $20,000 retainer and a 50 percent contingency fee of all proceeds won from the defendant.[11] They indicated if she did not

---

[7] "Mr. Stratton's Statement," *SLH*, August 22, 1873, in *JH*, January 1–November 17, 1873.

[8] Albert Hagan had served in the Confederacy. In Santa Cruz, California, he practiced mining law before moving to Salt Lake City, where he married Brigham Young's daughter Eudora. He later served as a judge in Coeur d'Alene, Idaho, where he died in 1895. Steven L. Staker, "Mark Twain v. John Caine, et al.," 361.

[9] "Mr. Stratton's Statement."

[10] Ibid.

[11] Tilford's allegiance is difficult to unravel and may have vacillated with time. He was employed by George Q. Cannon in the contest of his seating in Congress brought by Maxwell. The *Salt Lake Herald* editor addressed him as "Brother Tilford" and asked why his name was on the list of speakers in Corinne to *oppose* Cannon's seating. "Will Judge Tilford Explain," *SLH*, November 14, 1873, 3, col. 3. Tilford was a pallbearer at Judge McKean's funeral in 1879 and the grandmaster of Utah's Freemasons in 1880. In California near the time of the gold rush, he was elected to the ayuntamiento of San Francisco, along with Samuel Brannan. Tilford, Hagan, and Sumner Howard represented John D. Lee in the Utah Supreme Court appeal of his 1876 conviction for the Mountain Meadows murders. Steven L. Staker, "Mark Twain v. John Caine, et al.," 361. A retainer of $20,000 in 1873 would range from $371,000 to $33 million in 2008 dollars, depending on the index used for comparison. MeasuringWorth, www.measuringworth.com/calculators/uscompare/.

agree to such a contract, they would not represent her.[12] She discussed
the fee arrangements with George R. Maxwell, who found them totally
unacceptable, saying he wished no part of such "rascality":

> I then asked her if she had signed such an agreement; she said "No," and
> gave me what she said was her understanding of the case. I then told her
> if she had signed that paper, I would have withdrawn from the case; also
> what I had thought in the matter as to the purpose for which the suit was
> commenced, and was not yet satisfied that it was not so; that I should
> watch that case, and no rascality of any kind, name or nature, should be
> . . . perpetrated over my shoulders by anyone.[13]

Maxwell advised her to seek a compromise from her lawyers if she
intended to continue the legal course of action. Stratton indicated that
the actions of the three lawyers remained more aggressive than Mrs.
Young had intended, and the pastor reported that the lawyers further
attacked his own character for having impeded their proposed remuneration: "As they thought I had stood in the way of their schemes, I must
be blackmailed. Newspaper correspondents, telegraphic dispatches, and
private ears were filled with their rights and my wrongs. Through different channels threats have come to me that I must keep quiet or my
past history would be overhauled."[14] Stratton described events in Oregon eleven years earlier and claimed that he had been fully vindicated,
both civilly and ecclesiastically, of the scandal of which he been at the
time wrongly accused. Although Mrs. Young had intended to have the
reverend stand as her representative in the formal filing of papers, the
possibility that his past might be resurrected, to his and her mutual
detriment, led her to ask Maxwell to take Stratton's place. On July 19,
1873, divorce documents were served by the U.S. marshal to the much-
married prophet of the Mormon church, President Brigham Young.[15]

Next Best Friend

Whether Marshal Patrick or Marshal Maxwell served the papers to
Brigham Young is not clear. Ann Eliza Young's words of praise for

---

[12] The claim was made that Brigham Young was worth several million dollars and had a monthly
income of more than $40,000. Young countered that his worth was only $600,000 and his
monthly income about $6,000. Ivins, review of *Twenty-seventh Wife*.
[13] "General Maxwell Explains," *slh*, August 26, 1873, 2, col. 3.
[14] "Mr. Stratton's Statement."   [15] Young, *Wife No. 19*, 553.

Maxwell, however, would by themselves have earned him enmity from Mormon leaders: "Through General Maxwell, who was so kind as to come forward with offers of assistance, I brought suit for divorce against Brigham Young."[16]

Maxwell would certainly have had no doubt that his actions would further antagonize Young. Historian B. H. Roberts records that the suit was brought "at the instigation of the Utah 'Ring'—George R. Maxwell being named in the initial and subsequent pleadings of the case as 'her next best friend.'"[17] This phrase is defined in *Black's Law Dictionary* as "a person who appears in a lawsuit to act for the benefit of the incompetent or a minor plaintiff, but who is not a party to the lawsuit and is not appointed as a guardian." Now antiquated, the term was frequently used in legal proceedings of the era and is at the heading of all legal papers of Ann Eliza Young's case. Its usage did not imply a personal or intimate relationship, as a nonlegal context would suggest, but indicated that the person named was a trusted representative, often appearing for a child or for someone not capable of acting on his or her own behalf. It was applied for both male and female plaintiffs, but particularly in relation to women when they were not allowed to stand in legal proceedings without male representation.

Maxwell's taking a role in this personal action against the man who remained the de facto governor and unquestionably the most powerful man of Utah Territory, was an attention-getting end to his career in the land office and a provocative beginning of his marshalship. It could only generate further ill will among Mormons. Young moved to quash the service of the subpoena on the grounds that the territorial marshal, not the U.S. marshal, was the proper officer. Judge Philip H. Emerson of the First District Court reversed a prior ruling by Judge James Bedell McKean, and held Young's motion good.[18] The papers were quickly reserved, this time by the territorial marshal.

Ann Eliza Young was urged by Hyrum B. Clawson, Brigham Young's

---

[16] Ibid., 551.

[17] B. H. Roberts, *Comprehensive History*, 5:143.

[18] Frederic Lockley, editor and part owner of the *Salt Lake Tribune*, believed that Emerson was of "coarser moral fiber" than his fellow Judges Jacob Boreman and James McKean, who were "fearless, upright." When Lockley was about to publish an editorial highly critical of Emerson, Patrick H. Lannan, part owner of the paper, intervened and, with great effort, convinced Lockley not to do so. Lockley manuscript, 34–35.

son-in-law, to accept a $15,000 settlement that also carried assurance of safe passage out of Utah Territory in return for dropping the suit.[19] At the urging of Maxwell, Stratton, and her lawyers, Mrs. Young rejected Clawson's offer, but her experiences in Utah, combined with the implied threat that her safety would be assured only if she accepted the offer, left her fearful of death at the direction of the Mormon faction.[20] From the time of the initiation of her suit to her clandestine departure by horse and buggy from Salt Lake City in the dark hours of November 28, 1873, an attractive wife of polygamist Brigham Young suing for divorce attracted much media attention.[21] Articles concerning Mrs. Young appeared in newspapers and publications across the United States and stirred public appetite for more: "Her name was on the lips of millions—to some a virtuous heroine, to others, a scarlet woman. But no matter how she was regarded by her fellow citizens, there was unanimity on one point—everyone, without exception, it seemed, wanted to see her and hear her. In four weeks she had become a commodity of value. Show business courted her."[22]

Chautauqua Circuit and More

Leaving Utah, Ann Eliza Young traveled toward Denver. It was from there, under the business management of James Burton Pond, she would shortly set out on an extensive Chautauqua-type tour, speaking against polygamy and Mormon theocracy.[23] The name "Chautauqua" arose from meetings on the shores of the lake of that name in New York. The concept of Chautauqua evolved as a social and cultural phenomenon

---

[19] Clawson was also a participant in other monetary transactions to achieve desired Mormon ends. He paid $25,000 in 1887 to three New York City newspapers—the *New York Times*, the *New York Sun*, and the *New York Evening Post*—to produce articles favorable to Utah. Another $30,000 was promised to the same papers if Utah gained statehood. Other "investments" of more than $150,000 were made in the 1880s to influence publishers to soften their anti-LDS rhetoric. Verdoia and Firmage, *Utah*, 162. The public relations favors purchased by the Mormons are described in Lyman, *Political Deliverance*, 33–95.

[20] Wallace, *Twenty-seventh Wife*, 27.

[21] On her night journey from Salt Lake City, Mrs. Young had as her traveling companion and chaperone Sarah Ann Cooke, who, like herself, was in an active legal dispute with Brigham Young.   [22] Wallace, *Twenty-seventh Wife*, 268.

[23] Mrs. Young had first became acquainted with James Burton Pond when he and his daughter were boarders at her establishment. Pond had been a Civil War veteran, fighting for the Union against Quantrill's Raiders.

that had its beginning in the lyceum movement in the mid-1800s. For
millions of rural Americans a Chautauqua program coming to town
meant entertainment for the whole family and the entire community.
It was part circus, part music, with laughter, relaxation, religion, and
education in various mix, often with women playing featured roles. It
experienced a resurgence after the Civil War, when commercial lyceum
bureaus were founded, and traveling teams were centrally controlled
and organized; among them was the 1868 Redpath Lyceum Bureau of
James C. Redpath, who later succeeded Pond in sponsoring Ann Eliza
Young. Redpath was only one of many organizers and producers of the
traveling tents of the Chautauqua tours.[24] By 1871 no fewer than 150
lady lecturers were speaking on contemporary topics such as suffrage,
Negro integration, and temperance. By 1875, more than five hundred
groups were circulating. Students of the Chautauqua movement assert
that no other American institution, with the possible exception of the
Model T auto, had a greater impact on the social and cultural life of
rural communities. Victoria and Robert Ormond Case write, "Beyond
computation are the indirect effects of Chautauqua's greatest single
contribution: The awakening of rural areas to consciousness of the part
they were both entitled and expected to play in the affairs of the nation
and the world."[25] And John E. Tapia notes, "The information and
issues presented in such public forums were subsequently discussed and
argued in countless farmhouse kitchens, dry goods stores, and barber
shops."[26] Chautauqua tours long outlasted Ann Eliza Young's involvement; they continued into the 1920s and died only with the onset of the
Great Depression of 1929.[27]

    The first stop for Ann Eliza Young on the road to Denver was Lara-
mie, Wyoming, where she was joined by Pond. They used this stop for
a warm-up before her upcoming stint in Denver. Gaining confidence
and self-assurance at stops in Cheyenne and Fort Russell, Young was

---

[24] Tapia, *Circuit Chautauqua*, 14–15. Among the Redpath Lyceum speakers was George Armstrong Custer, who needed money to cover his stock market losses. Leckie, *Elizabeth Bacon
Custer*, 176.

[25] Case and Case, *We Called It Culture*, v, 239.

[26] Tapia, *Circuit Chautauqua*, 11.

[27] The role of the Chautauqua Circuit in developing American culture is the subject of serious scholarship. Charlotte Canning (University of Texas, Austin) has compiled an extensive
online bibliography at http://sdrc.lib.uiowa.edu/traveling-culture/guides/tcbibl.htm.

a financial success and was well reviewed in Denver and in a host of cities on her way toward the destination she considered most important, Washington, D.C. In Kansas she spoke in Topeka, Lawrence, and Leavenworth; in Missouri, at St. Louis. Audiences in Iowa, Wisconsin, then Illinois, warmed to her speaking skill and the sincerity she communicated.

Thought to have been instigated by Mormons, rumors of a sexual relationship between James Burton Pond and Ann Eliza Young were published first in the Bloomington, Illinois, newspaper, later to be picked up and enhanced by the *Chicago Times*.[28] According to *Salt Lake Tribune* editor Frederic Lockley, thousands of extra copies of the *Times* article were distributed by Mormon agents at doorsteps in advance of Mrs. Young's arrival in the cities on the tour. Only by hiring an investigator and having a tour agent contact leading clergymen in each city to explain the integrity of the falsely accused parties were Pond and Young able to attract a sizable audience.[29] Upon proving the allegations false, Pond and Young continued to Boston, then to Springfield, Massachusetts; Titusville and Philadelphia, Pennsylvania; Williamsburg, Virginia; then to New York City, Rochester, Buffalo; and finally, Toronto and Baltimore. At last, with their chaperone, they arrived in Washington in mid-April 1874.

She was met there on April 13 by her friend and adviser General Maxwell. He had come to Washington for the opening of the first session of the Forty-third Congress—to formally accept his appointment as U.S. marshal and to contest the election of George Q. Cannon to Congress—and he also wanted to be present for Mrs. Young's arrival.[30]

Maxwell escorted Ann Eliza Young to the House of Representatives, where she was invited into the House chambers by Speaker James Gillespie Blaine.[31] Thronged by representatives, she conversed with them for two hours, passing out photographs of polygamous wives and

---

[28] Ann Eliza Young laid the responsibility on $20,000 furnished by Mormons and on their Salt lake attorney George Cesar Gates. Young, *Wife No. 19*, 573.

[29] Lockley manuscript, 63.

[30] Maxwell was in Washington as early as January 1874, according to a letter from George Q. Cannon in which he tells of two of "Maxwell's strikers" approaching him to "sell out." Cannon did not identify them, but, according to him, both were critical of Maxwell, and each was unaware of the other's plan to sell out. Cannon to Brigham Young, January 21, 1874, BYC.

[31] Although a Republican, Blaine was opposed to many of President Grant's policies.

discussing polygamy's effects in Utah.[32] The next evening, in a lecture hall filled largely with congressmen, government officials, and their wives, she made her point:

> I know that you come to hear me from curiosity. I do not know why there should be anything curious in my being the nineteenth wife of Brigham Young. Polygamy is sanctioned by you in the national councils. While George Q. Cannon, of Utah, a polygamist with four wives, sits there, the peer of delegates from the other territories, Congress is responsible for the system which makes a plurality of wives possible in the Mormon country.[33]

At her second Washington lecture, prominently seated near the front were President Ulysses S. Grant and his wife, Julia, for whom Young fired the second Cannon barrel:

> The Congressional delegate from Utah has four wives. . . . It is now commonly reported in Utah that he has put away all but one to gain his seat in Congress, but the report is without foundation whatever. He denied through the newspapers that he was living in violation of the law, and explained it to his wives by saying the law was unconstitutional and the lawmakers were the transgressors, not him.[34]

After the lecture, President Grant shook Young's hand and allegedly said, "It will be an everlasting disgrace to the country if Cannon is allowed to take his seat in Congress."[35]

The efforts of Young and her advocates—Maxwell and lawyers Cyrus M. Hawley and William Carey—were not fruitful.[36] On behalf of Maxwell, Representative Clinton Levi Merriam of New York filed a resolution for a committee to investigate allegations against Cannon. The resolution was supported by George C. Hazelton of Wisconsin but was not formally considered by the House. The question was settled, however, when newly appointed Utah governor Samuel Axtell made his first act of office the issuance of a certificate of election to Cannon, an act that the previous governor, George Lemuel Woods, had refused

---

[32] Other outspoken women had appeared before Congress. On January 16, 1864, Anna Elizabeth Dickinson, a vocal critic of Lincoln and Republican causes, had also spoken to the combined houses. She would visit Utah in 1869, speaking on polygamy and Mormonism. J. Matthew Gallman, "Is the War Ended? Anna Dickinson and the Election of 1872," in Fahs and Waugh, *Memory of the Civil War*, 158.   [33] Wallace, *Twenty-seventh Wife*, 329.
[34] Ibid., 330.   [35] Ibid.
[36] George Q. Cannon to Brigham Young, Washington, December 15, 1873, BYC.

to do. With this, Cannon was seated.[37] The *Salt Lake Tribune* expressed the disappointment of the non-Mormons: "We are still bound with the chains of a dominant priesthood. Our children are denied the privilege of education. . . . And our legislative assembly are mere registers of His Mightiness' edicts. We have no voice at the polls, no returns of the use made of our money, and justice is denied us in all the Courts." But the editor found baroque words of praise for Maxwell, describing him as "one of the daring souls who refused to wear the mark of the beast, who, finding public opinion prostrate and asphyxiated under the terrorism and cursed delusion that prevailed, appealed to the manhood of his fellows to assert their rights and invoke the protecting folds of the starry banner under which he fought, bled and triumphed."[38]

In July 1874 Ann Eliza Young returned to Salt Lake City from her lecture engagements in the East and was again met by General Maxwell. Her arrival occasioned a reception in her honor at the Walker House hotel, where she thanked those who had helped her: Judge McKean, Maxwell, Col. Joseph H. Wickizer, and the Reverend and Mrs. C. C. Stratton.[39] Young asked Maxwell to speak on her behalf, and he recounted her lecture tour, her visit to the House of Representatives, and the other happenings in Washington as all being very successful despite "the assaults and libels levelled at her by the mercenary hirelings of the Mormon Priesthood." Maxwell went on to make accusations that the *Denver Tribune* and Washington's *National Republican* had been offered substantial sums of money ($1,500 to the *Tribune*, with the *National Republican* being able to name its price) for the use of their columns to publish the stories of an illicit relationship between Young and James Pond that had previously run in Illinois newspapers.[40] Both the Denver and Washington editors reportedly refused such publication.[41] The *Salt Lake Tribune* accorded Young great credit for favorably influencing passage of the Poland Act:

---

[37] During his brief tenure as governor, Axtell was subjected to many comments critical of his alliance with Brigham Young and George Q. Cannon. Non-Mormons referred to him with a fictitious but pejorative Mormon title, "Bishop Axtell."

[38] "The Utah Question in Washington," *SLT*, January 15, 1874, 2, col. 1.

[39] "Welcome to Ann Eliza," *SLT*, July 15, 1874, 1, col. 2. Walker House was to become Salt Lake City's finest hotel of the time. Built in 1871 at a cost of $80,000, it was located on the west side of Main Street between Second and Third South. Four stories high, it had an elevator, 105 sleeping rooms, and a large dining room. "The Walker House," *SLT*, September 12, 1871, page 2, col. 2.

[40] "Ann Eliza," *SLT*, July 16, 1874, 2, col. 2.   [41] Wallace, *Twenty-seventh Wife*, 337.

Mrs. Ann Eliza Young, the eloquent advocate of liberty for her sex[, returns] from . . . a glorious mission among the people of the States, where she told the story of her wrongs to listening thousands. . . . In the great struggle at Washington, . . . Mrs. Young's influence, more than any other, aided in securing the enactment of a salutary law. The discarded wife of a tyrant became the honored guest of the best and noblest in the land.[42]

Lockley reported that Mrs. Young had returned from this first tour an unqualified success in appeal and reception, but she was rendered "penniless" from the efforts of the Mormons to subvert this appeal with claims of sexual impropriety. She lived with the family of *Salt Lake Tribune* editor George F. Prescott while she and Pond refitted for another campaign.[43]

Following her Walker House reception, Ann Eliza Young continued with speaking tours across Utah and Nevada, bringing her message to the mostly non-Mormon audiences of the developing mining cities of Alta, Park City, Bingham, Tooele, Ophir, and Stockton. She also spoke in Provo, Utah, and was then off to Virginia City, Nevada; Oakland, San Jose, Sacramento, and San Francisco, California; and Nebraska. She enunciated the evils she saw existing in Utah to eight cities in Iowa and to St. Paul and Mankato, Minnesota. November of 1875 found her in Cincinnati, Ohio:

> Mrs. Ann Eliza Young, familiarly spoken of as Ann Eliza, ex-consort of Brigham Young, will lecture . . . to tell the "Story of a Ruined Life," to devote herself to the emancipation of the enslaved women of Utah, and combat the most monsterous delusions of this or any other age. Mrs. Young is good looking, a pleasant speaker, and her missionary efforts will no doubt commend her to the good wishes of our community.[44]

To the wife of President Rutherford Hayes, Young wrote a long and virulent letter in March 1879 to counter the message conveyed to Mrs. Hayes by the visits of Mormon wives Emmeline B. Wells and Zina Williams. Wells and Williams had favorably portrayed women's lives under the polygamy practiced in Utah, and said that women in Utah could vote independently of their husband's opinions. Young sent a copy of her letter to the press for publication, but no public response

---

[42] "Welcome to Ann Eliza," *SLT*, July 15, 1874, 1, col. 2.
[43] Lockley manuscript, 63.
[44] *Cincinnati Enquirer*, reprinted as "Ann Eliza vs. Brigham," *SLT*, November 14, 1875, 1, col. 4.

was made by Lucy Hayes. However, in his message to Congress, President Hayes said: "It is the duty and purpose of the people of the United States to suppress polygamy where it now exits in one territory and prevent its extension." Hayes's personal diary reveals a much harsher view regarding Utah and its government:

> Now the territory is virtually under the theocratic government of the Mormon Church. The union of Church and State is complete. The result is the usual one—the usurpation or absorption of all temporal authority and power by the Church. Polygamy and every other evil sanctioned by the Church is safe. To destroy the temporal power of the Mormon Church is the end in view. This requires agitation. The people of the United States must be made to appreciate, to understand the situation. Laws must be enacted which will take from the Mormon Church its temporal power. Mormonism as a sectarian idea is nothing; but as a system of government it is our duty to deal with it as an enemy to our institutions and its supporters and leaders as criminals.[45]

After nine years of a highly successful but exhausting lecture career, Ann Eliza Young delivered her last lecture, titled "Utah's Curse and the Nation's Shame," on April 24, 1883, in Napoleon, Ohio. Records of the cumulative size of the audiences that heard Ann Eliza do not exist, and it is not possible to calculate her impact on the public attitude toward polygamy and government in Utah. If the overall impact of the role of Chautauqua programs on the moral and social milieu of the time is correct, her influence was important and substantial.

Shortly after her final lecture, she was married, in Manistee, Michigan, to businessman Moses R. Deming. This marriage was never more than a troubled union, and they were divorced in 1893. She lived for four more years in Manistee, then followed her son to New York City, where her history became obscure. The story of the remainder of her life, and her death and burial, is unknown.

RUMORS

An intimate relationship between George R. Maxwell and Ann Eliza Young was very unlikely, but nevertheless there was speculation and

---

[45] Rutherford B. Hayes, personal diary, January 13, 1880, cited in Williams, *Life of Rutherford Birchard Hayes*, 2:225.

George R. Maxwell's second wife,
Mary Ann Sprague Maxwell.
Courtesy of Maxwell Fisher Turner,
Elizabeth Jane Cunard Carey, and
Bruce Turner Cunard II.

rumor, as evidenced from the journal of Mormon pioneer wife Alma
Elizabeth Mineer Felt:

> I think Ann Eliza was bitterly disappointed when he [Brigham Young]
> did not pay more attention to her. She filed her divorce suit and went to
> live at the Walker House. I used to sew for Mrs. Patten [*sic*] in the room
> just across from Ann Eliza's and I have often seen her go into her rooms
> with a man named Maxwell. . . . He later traveled with her on her lecture
> tours throughout the East and he helped to get up her book with all the
> mean things about Brigham Young.[46]

Maxwell had married for a second time and was a father, however,
prior to his friendship with Ann Eliza Young and prior to meeting
her in Washington. His marriage took place on July 21, 1872, in Salt
Lake City to Utah-born Mary Ann Sprague, the daughter of Samuel
Lindsey Sprague. A well-known Mormon, Maxwell's father-in-law

---

[46] Daughters of the Utah Pioneers, *Journal of Alma Elizabeth Mineer Felt*, 217, 225.

was the first doctor in the valley and later practiced medicine in Salt Lake City.[47]

Born in Boston in 1807, Samuel Sprague was one of the earliest Mormon converts who attached himself to the banner of Brigham Young. The diaries of early Mormon midwife Patty Bartlett Sessions cite her several contacts with Dr. Sprague in the period 1846 to 1852.[48] He came into the valley in 1848, with the second wave of Saints. In his journal, Thomas Bullock relates a number of instances when Sprague ministered to patients with broken bones, fevers, contagious disease, lung complaints, and a host of problems consistent with the traveling body of Saints. Sprague was Brigham Young's close companion and was with him in his travels, except when sent away on detached assignments. His movements "formed a constant pilgrimage serving the Saints."[49] Like several other Mormon men of the period, Sprague was an "adopted" spiritual son of Brigham Young. Sprague officiated for years in the Endowment House and acted as family physician to the residents of President Young's homes.[50] John D. Lee said that Sprague was also, for some time, Brigham Young's personal physician.[51] In December 1856 he was privileged to be one of two doctors attending Jedediah Morgan Grant, the "Mormon Thunder" and first counselor in the LDS church presidency, in his final illness in Salt Lake City.[52] It was Sprague who attended the severe head wound inflicted on Mormon farmer Howard Orson Spencer by Sgt. Ralph Pike in Rush Valley in 1859.[53] Sprague was well regarded in Mormon circles for his ministrations both to the Mormons and to the Indians of the territory.[54]

---

[47] An affidavit letter submitted to the U.S. attorney general by her brother in support of Mary Ann Sprague Maxwell's pension benefits placed the marriage in the Sprague home in Salt Lake City. However, an announcement in the Corinne newspaper said the marriage was performed there. Utah Genealogical Society, *Historical and Genealogical Register*, record 224825, 41. General Maxwell undoubtedly met Mary Ann and Samuel L. Sprague, Jr., while boarding in their home. The younger Sprague served as bailiff of the Third District Court and as a deputy marshal, eventually following his father's course and becoming a physician.

[48] In 1846 Dr. Sprague treated Omaha chief Big Head, who had been shot. At a March 1852 church meeting he spoke in tongues; in August 1852 he performed some type of "painful surgery." Smart, *Mormon Midwife*, 68, 140, 173, 183, 189–90, 196, 218.

[49] Rose, "Early Utah Medical Practice."

[50] Endnote editorial comment added by J. Cecil Alter, quoting Mrs. Catherine V. Waite, in her book *Adventures in the Far West* (1857, 1866, 1882), cited in Rose, "Early Utah Medical Practice," 33. [51] Cleland and Brooks, *Mormon Chronicle*, 345.

[52] *Journal of Wilford Woodruff*, December 2, 1856, cited in Sessions, *Mormon Thunder*, 250.

[53] Sadler, "Spence-Pike Affair," 84. [54] Rose, "Early Utah Medical Practice."

In 1863 Sprague served in the state legislature. In April 1864 he was a member of a grand jury, which presented a complaint to the U.S. District Court, of grievances growing out of conditions at Camp Douglas, Utah. Corrals and stables had been erected, and waters had been diverted from Red Butte Creek. The jury regarded these corrals and stables as a public health menace, an interference with irrigation, and an economic loss to the community.[55] Sprague also took an active interest in civic affairs—he was the vice president of the Horticultural Society of Utah, a member of the Flower Committee, and a member of the Deseret Agricultural and Manufacturing Society. He planted the first flower garden in Salt Lake City, using seeds and bulbs brought from Boston. The mix of a gentle, flower-raising doctor and long-suffering, dedicated Mormon with the assertive war veteran and Brigham Young critic who was his son-in-law seem an unfertile environment for love and matrimony, especially in light of the warning given by the prophet.

THE LION INTIMIDATES

On October 27, 1869, Samuel Sprague, Sr., left Salt Lake City, having been called to the Eastern States Mission. George R. Maxwell, who had arrived in Utah in June took lodgings with the Sprague family near this time. This was an understandable move by Sprague in view of the loss of income during his absence. It is estimated that he returned to the city in the fall of 1871.[56]

In January 1872, six months prior to her marriage to George R. Maxwell, Mary Ann Sprague and her father presented themselves, as they had been instructed, to the offices of Mormon president Brigham Young in the east room of the Beehive House for a personal interview. Mary Ann came prepared to contradict information that had come to Young—that she had told General Maxwell that she had seen a sword at the Young house that had been used to kill Dr. John King Robinson. She assured Young that the Sprague family kept boarders and that nothing of the kind had been said to Maxwell while he boarded with them. Now that the tiny young woman was face-to-face with the president of the

---

[55] Ibid.
[56] *DN*, October 27, 1869, 5, col. 4.

Mormon church, the supreme authority in Utah and, in this position, he answered to no man, she asked Young not to believe other reports he may have heard. President Young asked Dr. Sprague his opinion of Maxwell, and the reply was that he was hated and was a "mean person." Mindful of the unchecked power wielded by Brigham Young, both father Samuel and daughter Mary Ann disclaimed having any respect or regard for Maxwell. Young issued a stern warning against the Sprague family for associating with General Maxwell, saying that if they had "regard for the priesthood and love of the Gospel," they "would not board or harbor a person of his sentiment in the family."[57]

Despite the immense intimidation that surely accompanied the warning of Brigham Young as he looked at her, despite the ostracism that marrying outside the church promised for Dr. Sprague and his daughter, Young's counsel was not followed.[58] A serious relationship had developed during Maxwell's stay with the Spragues, and to their jeopardy, the marriage of George R. Maxwell and Mary Ann Sprague took place six months later; the birth of their first child followed eleven months after that, on June 6, 1873.

The juxtaposition of the dates of the Maxwell-Sprague marriage, the birth of their first child, and the subsequent birth of two additional children against the dates of Ann Eliza Webb Young's legal actions and her demanding lecture-touring life suggest neither a troubled marriage nor opportunities for Maxwell to have had clandestine meetings with Young. The only associations between Maxwell and Young for which there is factual support are those in her divorce action in Salt Lake City, by which the absence of any protection or standing under the law for polygamist wives was illuminated to a national audience; the brief period of their being together in Washington, D.C. in their mutual effort for anti-polygamy and anti-theocratic laws; and his encouragement and support of her embarking on a sustained lecture circuit. The evidence is that the two were respectful friends who shared the common purpose of influencing affairs in Utah.

---

[57] Memo of interview of Mary Ann and Dr. Samuel Sprague by Brigham Young on January 3, 1872, BYC.

[58] Annie Clark Tanner relates, "It was an extremely serious thing for girls to marry outside of the Church, both socially and religiously. It jeopardized their personal salvation, that of their children, and resulted generally in social ostracism." Cooley et al., *Mormon Mother*, 23.

9
Devils and Angels

Dancing at the rascal fair,
devils and angels all were there,
heel and toe, pair by pair,
dancing at the rascal fair.

Ivan Doig,
Dancing at the Rascal Fair

ON FEBRUARY 16, 1874, MARSHAL MAXWELL PETITIONED U.S. attorney general George Henry Williams for an extended leave of absence. The contest over George Q. Cannon's congressional seat was languishing in committee, and Maxwell insisted that his presence in Washington was needed on this matter. He also asserted he was needed in the nation's capital because he was "the only representative of mining interest in Utah except Mr. Carey" and was "immensely interested in procuring [mining] legislation for Utah."[1]

Maxwell brought to Washington affidavits from his wife, contending that, in his absence, their home had been broken into and its contents destroyed. Maxwell asserted that this act was vengefully done by Mormons.[2] Despite the attack on his home and property, Maxwell remained

---

[1] Many of Maxwell's friends and contemporaries (Robert N. Baskin, William Samuel Godbe, Amos K. Smith, James Bedell McKean, Courtland C. Clements, J. M. Moore, Patrick Connor, and Alonzo G. Paddock, at least) were involved in mining. With borrowed money, Maxwell invested in a mine in the Lincoln District known as the Rollins Mine, or the Lincoln Mining and Smelting Company, but financial success in any mining venture apparently eluded him. Fielding and Fielding, *Trials of John D. Lee*, 63.
[2] George Q. Cannon to Brigham Young, March 21, 1874, BYC.

in Washington until April, working in part on legislation relating to mining but, more importantly, continuing to assist congressmen William Horace Clagett of Montana, Samuel Augustus Merritt of Idaho Territory, and John Scott Negley of Pennsylvania, as well as attorney Robert N. Baskin of Salt Lake City and others, for passage of legislation to resolve "the Mormon problem." Introduced in January by Luke Potter Poland of Vermont, his was the bill Ann Eliza Young had also worked to support. For eight months, at his own expense, Maxwell lived in Washington and lobbied for the bill, meeting with congressmen to urge its passage.

From their efforts, and those of many others, the Poland Act passed in June 1874. The act eliminated the territorial positions of attorney and marshal, giving those duties to the U.S. attorney and U.S. marshal. Its provisions also returned exclusive civil and criminal jurisdiction to U.S. courts, and an especially important provision was that probate courts were limited to estate and divorce settlement. The *Salt Lake Tribune* reported on the passage of the act in glowing terms:

> Gen. Maxwell and [Idaho congressman] Col. Merritt arrived home from Washington last evening. . . . [T]hese two valiant champions of popular rights and justice for Utah are deserving of such an ovation as never yet did Saint or sinner receive in the ex-capital of the Kingdom. . . . They stood at the guns until the Poland Bill knocked the foundations from under the last relic of barbarism, and today we are satisfied with offering to Maxwell and Merritt a modest welcome to their home.[3]

The following day, the *Tribune* added: "The energy with which General Maxwell . . . has labored to obtain the legislation is worthy of all commendation. . . . [N]ever, till the last moment, did he relax his efforts . . . and it did not get through until the very last day of the session."[4]

Passage of the Poland Act was a major victory for non-Mormons. For Marshal Maxwell it was additionally a life-changing event and a two-edged sword. It gave him the authority to do his duty—to hire deputies and perform the functions intended of a U.S. marshal. This authority also opened him to the dangers of financial disaster because of the disjunction, unique from other territories, between the Mormon-run legislature and the federal authorities. The territorial legislature depended on federal dollars to run its lawmaking sessions, and when monies were

---

[3] "They Are Here," *SLT*, July 9, 1874, 4, col. 3. Merritt later became chief justice of the Utah Supreme Court.   [4] "The Poland Bill," *SLT*, July 10, 1874, 4, col. 4.

not sent by Washington (as they were not sent to territorial secretary George A. Black in 1876), Utah legislators were ill disposed to appropriate money for the expenses of inmates, prisons, and courts.[5] It was also true that Mormon lawmakers had no interest in providing funds to federal officers to lock up fellow Mormons, especially when the charge was polygamy. Maxwell would have been wise to have had the necessary funds in hand before he acted on his responsibilities, but he did not. Like Marshals Peter Kessler Dotson and Mathewson Patrick before him, and Marshal William Nelson after him, Maxwell was continually left holding the bag, a bag filled with enormous debts but no money.

On the totally mistaken presumption that in Utah an immense groundswell was forming among the women to rise from the bondage of polygamy and vote against the practice and against their abusive Mormon husbands, Congress naively suggested in 1869 that women's suffrage would be beneficial in Utah Territory. Mormon men jumped on this as the political opportunity it was. The Utah territorial legislature was quick to act, and in February 1870 Utah became the second territory, after Wyoming, to grant women voting rights.[6] The addition of seventeen thousand Utah women strengthened the Mormon vote. Within days the unofficial government of Deseret met, and with the approval of the elected "president" Orson Hyde and Brigham Young, woman suffrage was given the stamp of higher ecclesiastical approval by this shadow governing body.[7] Any woman of age twenty-one or older who had been a resident of the territory for six months, was born or naturalized in the United States, or was the wife, widow, or daughter of a citizen was now entitled to vote in any election.[8]

Historian Thomas G. Alexander asserts that women were given the vote only out of a sincere wish to provide them with deserved equality, an assertion that appears at odds with the generally unequal status that Mormon society and its theocratic oligarchy assigned to women in this era.[9] Whatever the motivations of territorial legislators for enacting this law, many non-Mormons, and certainly Maxwell, saw it as

---

[5] Black's problems with the forwarding of monies from Washington are described in T. G. Alexander, *Clash of Interests,* xv.

[6] T. G. Alexander, "Experiment in Progressive Legislation," 20.

[7] "In reality . . . the State of Deseret was the *de facto* government; and the Council of Fifty . . . was the policymaking body for the civil government of Utah from 1848 to 1870." J. R. Clark, "Kingdom of God," 143. See also Morgan, *State of Deseret,* 111.

[8] T. G. Alexander, "Experiment in Progressive Legislation," 26.　　　　[9] Ibid., 29.

a plot to swamp the polls with the ballots of monogamous and plural wives of Mormon men. Ann Eliza Young held a strong opinion of Mormon women's voting privileges: "Women in Utah are but child-bearing slaves. Every time they vote, they . . . vote into office, such men as George Q. Cannon, who are using all their powers to perpetuate Polygamy. The ballot is no protection to these women, for they vote in utter ignorance of what they are doing, and for whom they are voting."[10] Particularly cutting was the comment made later by the editor of the *Salt Lake Tribune* when describing the women who were voting in Utah: "Women with the odor of the emigrant ship still upon their clothes, without ever having taken an oath of allegiance to the United States, without the slightest idea of the meaning of the act . . . cast their votes as they are instructed to, in some tongue unknown to ordinary Americans and go away dazed."[11]

Not for ten years—after the Poland Act, after his second contest with George Q. Cannon in Congress, when the Liberal Party had strengthened substantially—did Maxwell and the other attorneys of Salt Lake feel sufficiently prepared to confront the matter of women's suffrage. In this he was supported by legal advice from several men of the bar (Jabez Gridley Sutherland, John R. McBride, Joseph B. Rosborough, and Samuel A. Merritt, at the least) that a Utah territorial law of 1878 superseded the 1870 law. The language of the 1878 bill limited entitlement to voting to male citizens of the United States who were taxpayers, but it did not mention women. On this basis Maxwell filed a complaint, resulting in a writ of mandamus to Judges John A. Hunter, Jacob Smith Boreman, and Philip H. Emerson.[12] The writ instructed Robert T. Burton, assessor and register of voters for Salt Lake County, to remove Emmeline B. Wells and Maria M. Blythe (prominent Mormon women), Mrs. A. G. (Cornelia) Paddock (a prominent and vocal non-Mormon), and any and "all women" from the voting registration lists of the Salt Lake County.[13] The three territorial Supreme Court judges heard the case immediately, with Judges Emerson and Hunter holding the majority opinion that the court had no jurisdiction in the matter, nor was it within Burton's scope

---

[10] Wallace, *Twenty-seventh Wife*, 349.   [11] Goodwin, "Mormon Situation," 758.

[12] *Maxwell v. Burton*, 1880-018, 2 Utah, 595–605.

[13] Ibid. Burton, together with Lot Smith, was responsible for the multimillion-dollar sabotage of the U.S. Army supply trains in 1857, was in the contingent sent by Daniel H. Wells to guard the telegraph lines in 1862, and in the same year led a group of Mormon men in putting down a rebellion by a group of Mormon dissenters led by Joseph Morris in which a number were killed.

of authority to remove women from the voter list. Judge Boreman wrote a dissenting opinion, noting that the 1870 legislation, in not requiring women to be taxpayers or citizens, treated the requirements for voting by women differently from those for men, and in his judicial opinion the requirements should be the same.[14]

Attempting other tactics by which Utah voting practices could be brought into compliance with those in other states and territories, Maxwell worked with his friend Republican senator Isaac Peckham Christiancy from Michigan. Mormons readily identified that Christiancy was potentially dangerous. In their view he was "a careful, accurate man, and a thoroughly trained lawyer," not an emotional attention seeker as earlier critics had been seen, but a man of a "practical turn of mind," one who knew the law and was "bitterly opposed to Mormon institutions."[15] Christiancy introduced two bills bearing his name that were aimed at regulating Utah voting.[16] In 1876 Maxwell and Robert N. Baskin returned to the problems of plural marriage and worked with Christiancy for a bill directed at that practice: "to declare ineligible for juror in any trial for bigamy or polygamy the pious Saint who has polluted his household with this filthy crime . . . or who has scruples of conscience against finding a verdict of guilty where this offence has been proved."[17]

---

[14] Jacob Smith Boreman, whose brother was Arthur Inghram Boreman, U.S. senator and governor of West Virginia, came to Utah in April 1873 as an appointee of President Grant. Boreman was a native of antebellum western Virginia. He had served in the Kansas state legislature and was an editor of the Kansas City *Evening Bulletin*. In Kansas City, Missouri, he had been a city attorney, a private attorney, and a judge of the Court of Common Pleas. His experience in Jackson County, Missouri, likely influenced his attitude about Mormons, for he was described as "a man of integrity and rectitude, a legal scholar of considerable brilliance, and a devout churchman and loving father" as well as "an implacable enemy of Mormonism." Arrington, "Crusade against Theocracy," 2–3.

[15] "A New Departure," *slh*, February 14, 1876, 4.

[16] The absence of a democratic election process in Utah Territory is seen in the 1857 letter of Brigham Young to Isaac C. Haight in Iron County, July 15, 1857: "Dr. John M. Bernhisel is nominated for re-election to the office of Delegate to Congress which we presume will met [*sic*] with the united and hearty support of all the People—It is also our wish that George A. Smith should be returned a member of the Council of the Legislative Assembly of the Territory at the August election from Iron and Washington Counties. You will please to shape things accordingly." In Moorman Papers, box 7.

[17] "Senator Christiancy's Bill," *slt*, January 22, 1876, 2, col. 1. Christiancy proved a poor model of decorum. At age sixty-four he was divorced and then married a woman of nineteen, bringing embarrassment to his party. Sent to the hinterlands as ambassador to Peru, he later divorced again and returned alone to Michigan.

A VICTORY FOR LIBERALS: THE TOOELE REPUBLIC

By 1874 the mining ventures initiated by Gen. Patrick Connor in Tooele County, in the mountains west of Salt Lake City, had burgeoned into the creation of the wealth-producing towns of Ophir, Lewiston, Jacob City, Rush Lake, and Stockton:

> Mines were opened all along the western slope of the Oquirrh Range. Tramways and stamp mills and smelters were built and operated. Every man and team in the county were kept busy with remunerative employment, and a shining stream of precious bullion was poured forth over the newly built Pacific railroads to the markets of the world that caused a return flood of wealth that increased three-fold the value of every man's labor, every bushel of grain and vegetable, every acre of arable land and every head of stock in the county.[18]

The changed demographics that resulted from these new, largely non-Mormon communities led the Liberal Party to judge that it might be successful in an election against the long-dominant People's Party of the Mormons. In Tooele County, non-Mormon Lawrence A. Brown was nominated to be probate judge against John Rowberry, the Mormon bishop; E. S. Foote, to be representative to the territorial legislature against George Atkins, the bishop's counselor; E. C. Chase to be select-man over George Bryan, also a bishop's counselor; and James Lynch to be sheriff, against William H. Lee. All of the Liberal Party candidates won election; the average margin of victory was more than two hundred votes, in a county with an estimated population of four thousand.[19]

The People's Party countered this outcome by declaring over a thousand Liberal Party voters ineligible. These were men not included as taxpayers on a list drawn up by William H. Lee, who defined a taxpayer as one who had already paid taxes rather than one who was liable for taxation. Reportedly on the orders of President Brigham Young, the People's Party leaders refused to turn over the offices, books, and records of the county to the non-Mormons. On September 10, 1874, Third District Court judge McKean issued a mandamus for surrender of these materials and the occupancy of the court to the newly elected men. No action was forthcoming, and on September 17 the court sent Marshal Maxwell with instructions to enforce the Third District

---

[18] Col. M. M. Kaighn's Reply to Apostle F. M. Lyman, Campaign Document 6, "The Republic of Tooele: How the People's Party Wrecked the County," 1, in Reed Papers.

[19] Kaighn's Reply to Lyman, 1–2.

Court's ruling, along with laying a $450 fine against each of the two noncompliant leaders, John Rowberry and Richard Warburton. Traveling by afternoon stagecoach, Maxwell, in the company of his wife, editor Frederic Lockley, and Deputy Marshal J. H. Kingsley, arrived late in the day, and the group took quarters in the Oquirrh House. An account from the time described the events of the following morning:

> [Maxwell] found the court house, a large blacksmith shop adjoining, and the Co-op store filled and surrounded with armed men, numbering 200 to 300. Tooele was an exclusively People's Party town, but Maxwell gathered a posse from the Liberal [Party] town of Stockton, personally cowed [and arrested] ex-judge Rowberry who was in command of the armed mob and served his writ. Bloodshed seemed imminent, but the coolness and intrepidity of Maxwell prevented it.[20]

Another report also referred to the diffusion of tensions during the incident: "During this crisis, Maxwell's revolver accidentally dropped to the floor but did not discharge. Lysander Gee [a lawyer of Tooele] picked it up and quietly handed it to him. The crisis passed without bloodshed."[21] Rowberry remarked to General Maxwell: "If you and I had not shown good sense in this affair, we could have had a first class fight; my boys were hankering for it."[22] Rowberry kindly delivered a basket of fruit from his own orchard to Mary Ann Maxwell, and the parting was smooth. In December, Alexander Frazer, Matthias Nelson, Charles Waters, and Lysander Gee, all of the People's Party, were indicted, tried, and convicted of illegal voting practices. Gee was sentenced to one month in the penitentiary and served his term.[23] Out of this first win of any consequence in Utah, the Liberal Party took temporary control of the county offices in what became known for a time as the Tooele Republic. Short-lived was the victory, as the People's Party regained control when its candidates swept the 1878 election.

DIFFICULTIES FOR THE MARSHAL

In March 1874, Maxwell was supplied with a warrant for the arrest of Martin M. Allred of Sanpete County for federal violations of the Internal Revenue Law. After a first deputy marshal was unable to complete

---

[20] Ibid.   [21] Daughters of the Utah Pioneers, *Journal of Alma Elizabeth Mineer Felt*.
[22] Reed Papers.   [23] Kaighn's Reply to Lyman, 1–2.

the arrest, Maxwell sent another deputy marshal, Myron J. Brockway, disguised as a miner to make the arrest. Brockway did so but was then surrounded by a "howling mob of Mormon men and women who by force took the prisoner from him." Brockway gave up his prisoner to save his own life. Maxwell wrote to Attorney General George H. Williams, explaining that a posse comitatus to assist in carrying out federal laws cannot be summoned in an area of fifty miles of the Utah Territory.[24]

The inability to assemble a posse was one of Maxwell's lesser worries. Even before returning from Washington, D.C., to Utah in the spring of 1874, he had begun searching for sites for housing prisoners from Utah courts. In February he petitioned Gen. Henry Andrew Morrow, then commander at Camp Douglas, asking to bring prisoners there as he had "no place suitable" for them. Maxwell was well acquainted with Morrow, who was from Michigan and had served in the Civil War, and they were social friends.[25] Additional letters from Maxwell followed to inform Morrow that Attorney General Williams was in the process of asking the secretary of war to make a special provision at Camp Douglas for nonmilitary prisoners. Morrow had previously allowed Maxwell's predecessor, Mathewson Patrick, to house his prisoners at Camp Douglas, so the reason for special permission from the War Department for Maxwell to do so is unclear.[26] It was clear, however, that Maxwell was under significant stress, as a message two days later to the attorney general said it was "absolutely necessary that some arrangement be made" for prisoners. By August 1874, not only space for prisoners but also payment for their upkeep were major issues for Maxwell. His letter to Attorney General Williams of that date said:

> In all Districts there [are] an unprecedented number of cases arising under the laws of the Territory. In the last session of the [Utah] Legislature no appropriation was made for expense in such cases. . . . If there is any money in the [territorial] treasury it can only be reached by an order of mandamus which would be fought by the local authority to the bitter end thus involving ruinous delay that would defeat the ends of justice and would ruin any Marshal that would advance costs even if he were pecu-

---

[24] Maxwell to Williams, May 18, 1874, RG 60, Chronological Files, 1871–84, box 1015.

[25] Morrow had been severely wounded as he carried the colors on the first day of battle at Gettysburg, fighting with the Black Hats of the Twenty-fourth Michigan Iron Brigade on McPherson Ridge, and he was awarded a brevet general promotion.

[26] Cresswell, "U.S. Department of Justice," 207.

niarily able to do so. (Which I certainly am not.) . . . I have not one jail in this territory and all sheriffs refuse to accept my prisoners unless I become personally responsible . . . at $1.00 to $1.76 per diem which I . . . cannot do. I am incessantly opportuned to take into my custody every prisoner in this Territory, the object of which is plain and needs but little explanation. The local and antagonistic authorities know I cannot keep prisoners for two reasons: 1st, no place to keep them, 2nd, no money with which to do it.[27]

His pleas for financial aid and jail space fell on unreceptive ears, however, as Williams curtly replied, "Congress has made it your duty to execute all writs and process issued out of the courts of your territory." After noting that the costs "of the laws of the Territory shall be paid by the Treasury of the Territory," Williams stated that he knew of "no remedy unless you can obtain a mandamus upon the Treasury of the Territory." He added that regarding "the support and safe keeping of prisoners" at Camp Douglas, he had "heard nothing from the Secretary of War."[28]

Attorney General Williams was intensely preoccupied with his own troubles, which may explain in part his deafness to Maxwell's urgent pleas for financial relief. Williams was being subjected to serious criticism after being found using Department of Justice funds for his own lavish personal expenditures. Gold pens, expensive carriages, and extravagant household items were on the list. Although these allegations of illegal practices were not pursued with formal charges, William's expenditures were all the more in poor taste because of the financial panic of 1873, which had beset the nation. He came under stinging public rebuke from Washington newspapers, as did his defender, President Grant. This criticism culminated in Williams's resignation not long after the time of his exchange of letters with Marshal Maxwell regarding funds in Utah.[29]

Despite the unsuitable conditions of the prison in Salt Lake City (which became the subject of a grand jury investigation later the same year), Maxwell housed prisoners there and unwisely accepted the costs.[30] From doing so, Maxwell received, rather than support or praise for cre-

[27] Maxwell to Williams, August 25, 1874, RG 60, Chronological Files, 1871–84, box 1015.
[28] Ibid.   [29] Cresswell, *Mormons and Cowboys*, 8.
[30] As early as 1858, wardens emphasized that the prison was dilapidated and in great need: "The Penitentiary in this Territory is wholly inadequate. . . . I would respectfully recommend that an appropriation be made by the Territory for the repair of the Penitentiary and . . . that Congress be memorialized to contribute to this object." Letter by S. A. Mann, Acting Governor, Utah Territory, in *SLT*, January 11, 1870. The pleas of several wardens—Alexander McRae, James A. Little, and Albert Perry Rockwood—for money for the facility were all in vain.

ative solutions to vexing problems, further criticism from Williams, who told him that notification and permission to house territorial prisoners at the penitentiary must come from the attorney general's office. By October 5, Maxwell again wrote in frustration that he had fourteen prisoners at Beaver and thirty more in Salt Lake City and that he was being charged $1.00 per day for each. He pointed out his obvious dilemma: "If I fail to comply with the order of the court [to pay for support,] I am liable for contempt. If I cannot comply for want of funds, I dare not turn prisoners loose . . . for in that event [I would] be guilty of malfeasance in office."[31]

The attorney general remained unrelenting and in letters dated October 14 and 16 indicated he could not provide financial aid, that the secretary of war would not allow prisoners at Camp Douglas, and that nothing could be done to aid Maxwell financially until Congress convened the following December. He again criticized Maxwell for not making prior arrangements for the use of the prison, for charging too much for the number of prisoners, and for the "complaining and censorial tone" of his letters.[32]

In his next letter Maxwell wisely returned to the overly courteous, officious construction of formal letters that was then the fashion. He continued, however, to insist that his financial situation was untenable: "I respectfully report that the Grand Jury of the Third Judicial District . . . has brought in 64 indictments, the most of which were for violations of the laws of the Territory." He went on to say that he currently had fifteen prisoners in the penitentiary and warrants for the arrest of thirty other "accused persons," besides having in "constant employ ten Deputies, one clerk, three guards, and bailiffs and criers for courts." Maxwell concluded: "I respectfully refer you the enclosed documents and by leave to state that unless something is done at an early day by Congress, I cannot see what I can do."[33]

A POLYGAMY CONVICTION

Amid this battling with Attorney General Williams and with territorial officials for the funds to carry out his duty, the passage of the Poland Act allowed Maxwell another role that brought him further

---

[31] Maxwell to Williams, October 5, 1874, RG 60, Chronological Files, 1871–84, box 1015.
[32] Ibid.   [33] Ibid.

abrasive interaction with the Mormons. This involved the first successful prosecution in Utah for polygamy. In the summer of 1874, George Reynolds, then secretary to Brigham Young, was arrested, tried, found guilty, fined $500, and sentenced to two years of hard labor. According to attorney Robert N. Baskin, it was Marshal Maxwell and Deputy Arthur Pratt who, in a surprise move, brought Reynolds's second wife to the trial, where her testimony resulted in conviction.

It has been repeatedly written that Mormons leaders, particularly George Q. Cannon, instigated the arrest and trial of Reynolds, with the express purpose of having the case reach the level of the U.S. Supreme Court. There, they believed, Mormons would be vindicated and precedent would be established in their favor that polygamy fell under the aegis of freedom of religion.[34] Robert N. Baskin, who had been an observer, not a prosecutor in the trial, left this report:

> Daniel H. Wells and other witnesses by whom Carey [the prosecuting attorney] expected to prove the second marriage, testified that they knew nothing respecting the alleged plural marriage of Reynolds. While Mr. Wells was being examined, and had positively denied all knowledge of such a marriage, General Maxwell, who was United States marshal, stated to me that Carey had failed to prove the second marriage; that there were no other witnesses in attendance, and that the court would have to instruct the jury to acquit the accused. I asked the marshal if the plural wife had been subpoenaed, and he said she had not. I then secured a subpoena for the plural wife . . . and it was placed in the hands of Arthur Pratt, a deputy marshal, with instructions to procure a buggy and bring the witness to the court house as soon as possible. . . . Marshall Maxwell left the court room and in ten minutes brought in the second wife by a side-door, from which she could be seen by the entire audience. As the marshal stepped aside from the door and revealed the person of Mrs. Reynolds No. 2 framed in the doorway, the consternation in the Mormon crowd was startling. . . . The polygamous wife took the oath . . . and the following facts were elicited: . . . "I was married to George Reynolds in the endowment house in this city in August last by General Wells. Mr. Orson Pratt was present. . . . I have lived with George Reynolds ever since our marriage."[35]

---

[34] Orson Ferguson Whitney also contends there was a pretrial agreement expressly to establish a Supreme Court precedent and that the prosecution reneged on its promise that no significant punishment would be affixed. Whitney, *History of Utah*, 3:47–50.

[35] Baskin, *Reminiscences of Early Utah*, 61–72. Arthur Pratt, Orson Pratt's son, was in agreement with his mother's opposition to polygamy, which explains his willingness, though he was the son of an apostle, to assist as a deputy marshal with this case.

Wells refused to answer certain of the questions put to him, stating that he considered "the keys and powers and mysteries of the church" were being invaded. As a result he was sentenced to forty-eight hours in the penitentiary, and the city experienced these hours as a potentially explosive period, with intemperate talk on both sides of the street. On Wells's release, a long procession of Mormons escorted his return; as they reached the courthouse, the U.S. flag was lowered into the dust of the road and was trampled upon. Newspaper editor Frederic Lockley observed, "This gross indignity heated the blood of the war veterans mixed in the crowd of onlookers, but self restraint was strictly enjoined them by the U.S. marshal [Maxwell.]"[36]

The outcome of *Reynolds* was appealed to the U.S. Supreme Court, and in January of 1879 the Court ruled that religious beliefs were protected under the First Amendment, but that religious practices arising from those beliefs were subject to law. The case is cited to the present as a precedent.[37] Mormons were as shocked by this decision as the non-Mormons had been at the outcome in the Englebrecht case, and predictions circulated that *United States v. Reynolds* would eventually deal polygamy a lethal blow.

What remains untold are the details of the Reynolds case, provided by Maxwell in 1879, that contradicted that Mormon leaders had any intention to instigate the suit.[38] Maxwell related his recollection of what occurred after names had been called to serve on various upcoming grand juries:

> One of the number, Mr. James Horrocks of Ogden, happened to attend Sunday afternoon services in the Salt Lake Tabernacle. There he listened to an address from Elder George Reynolds in the course of which the speaker boasted of his polygamist relations and avowed his constitutional right to take all the wives he had a mind to. This naturally incensed Mr. Horrocks as a local citizen, and he came to my office the same afternoon to ask if the Government could be defiled in this manner

---

[36] Lockley manuscript, 70–71. Restraint against Mormon mistreatment of the flag would again be required of Maxwell and the Civil War veterans in a later episode in 1885, in which the flags were lowered to half-mast on July Fourth. In the Reynolds encounter, Lockley described Maxwell as "an untamed fire eater" and said that despite his having been "shot all to pieces," his "undaunted soul yet animated what remained of his shattered body." Ibid., 67.

[37] Baskin, *Reminiscences of Early Utah*, 62; Bigler, *Forgotten Kingdom*, 305; *Reynolds v. United States*, 98 U.S. 145 (1879).

[38] "That Test Case," *SLT*, June 28, 1879, 4, col. 3.

with impunity. Seeing he was in earnest, I told him that as a Grand Juror it lay with him to procure an indictment against Reynolds on his own admissions. Mr. Arthur Pratt, one of my deputies, being present at the time, and I knowing his intelligence and having full confidence in his official integrity, gave him full charge of the case. Handing him a blank subpoena I instructed him to hunt up his own witnesses, and such others as Mr. Horrocks might desire to have summoned.

. . . Mr. Horrocks in the Grand Jury room repeated some of Mr. Reynolds' sayings in the Tabernacle and presented his name [Reynolds's] for indictment. . . . Whatever action Mr. Cannon and his friends may have taken, in no way affected the Grand Jury nor did their desire to furnish a test case in any way instigate the judicial inquiry. Witnesses were summoned, Cannon, Wells, Orson Pratt, the relatives of wife No. 1, and others, but these refused to furnish a single fact to prove the second marriage, and I will state to that contradiction of Mr. Cannon, that the defense did not furnish a single witness to prove the defendant's first marriage or any other fact.[39]

Maxwell went on to record for the public several new facts regarding the calling of witness Amelia Jane Schofield:

Deputy Pratt spent fully a week in a fruitless endeavor to find her. At Reynolds' house he would be told she was not in, or . . . he would be told insolently to go. . . . I changed my tactics, begged my Deputy terminate his search for awhile, and gave out in conversation that the prosecution would not use the second wife for a witness.

While the trial was on . . . Mr. Pratt came to me in the courtroom to inform me that he could now lay his hand upon the hitherto invisible witness. This I mentioned to Mr. Baskin, who was a listener in the trial, and he passed a written message to Mr. Carey suggesting summoning the second wife as a witness. . . . Whereupon my Deputy secured a carriage, drove rapidly to Reynolds house, and found the woman employed at the wash tub. He told her she was wanted in the Courtroom as a witness. Wife No. 1 said that No. 2 was busy and couldn't go. Deputy Pratt replied that her reputation as a married woman was at stake as the Gentile lawyers were trying to prove that she was not married. Finding there was still some hesitancy he further urged that General Wells and Elder Pratt desired her presence.

"Who are you" was the inquiry of the perplexed woman. "My name is Arthur Pratt and the Deputy, son of Orson Pratt, and father and General Wells in the courtroom want your testimony."

---

[39] Ibid.

This determined the pair. No. 2 attired herself in a few minutes, entered the carriage. . . . Being placed on the stand, she swore to her marriage with Reynolds, and pointed out Mr. Wells as the man who had performed the sealing ceremony. Upon this testimony George Reynolds was convicted. . . .

The above is a plain statement of the case, and I ask its publication to refute the lies which the Church organ is disseminating in the community in regard to this being a test case, and also the flagrant misstatements which Cannon has been guilty of in his letter to the President [Hayes].[40]

Shortly after the publication of Maxwell's account, the *Ogden Junction* published Horrocks's complete denial of the story. This was countered by the *Tribune*'s publication of a corroboration of Horrocks's original statements by clergyman Robert G. McNiece and by two other of Horrocks's fellow grand jury members.[41] There followed accusations that Horrocks was an outspoken apostate Mormon, having suffered financially because of his departure from the church, and that his denial was made to somewhat repair himself with Mormon leaders. Maxwell reiterated the validity of his recounting of Horrocks's role, with further corroborating statements from McNiece and juror William F. James.[42]

BAYONET RULE

Besides the conviction of George Reynolds for polygamy, another event that involved Maxwell had the potential of disrupting the fragile peace of the territory. In August 1874, George Q. Cannon and Robert N. Baskin were rival candidates for the Utah's congressional delegate. "To see that no citizen was hindered in freely casting his vote," Maxwell employed a large number of deputy marshals and sent them to monitor the polls.[43] The authority for this action on Maxwell's part derived from the congressional act known as the Bayonet Rule, or the

---

[40] Ibid. The published statement was signed by "George R. Maxwell, former U.S. Marshal for Utah," attested by Arthur Pratt, and dated June 27, 1879.

[41] "General Maxwell's Statement," *SLT*, July 10, 1879, 2, col. 2. William F. James and I. Watters were named as the two jury members.

[42] "The Closing Argument," *SLT*, July 13, 1879, 2, col. 2.

[43] B. H. Roberts, *Comprehensive History*, vol. 5, chap. 139, 377.

Force Act, passed during Reconstruction. It was intended to assure the voting rights of the black freedmen in the South after the Civil War. From 1870 to 1892 this act granted special powers to U.S. marshals and deputies in cities with more than twenty thousand inhabitants, when candidates to the national Congress were to be elected. In Utah, as elsewhere, local civic authority was temporarily suspended and "United States' law" took precedence.[44] Maxwell and his deputies compromised with local factions and agreed to work together with local police to maintain order during the 1874 election. Lockley reports that "Maxwell swore in a dozen or more deputies—sober, discreet men, and instructed them to protect every voter . . . to resist aggression, but not to resort to violence if peaceable means would serve."[45] However, Mayor Daniel Wells hired on an even greater number of special police. When city policemen attempted to remove a man ejected by the election judge, the U.S. deputies opposed the removal of the man. (Of note, there was no registration policy in force, and both sexes were legally invested with suffrage.)

Sources differ as to the precipitating event leading to what followed. Editor Lockley reported that the city hall doors were inexplicably closed. The *Salt Lake Tribune* reported that policeman Jeter Clinton had removed the ballot box and was tampering with the contents.[46] Mormons claimed they were simply closing for lunch. Contention between the enforcement groups escalated, with Wells's city police and Maxwell's deputy marshals vying over who properly had responsibility for maintaining the peace. Mayor Wells challenged U.S. deputy James Milton Orr, denying him entry to the balloting place, and allegedly raised his cane to strike Orr. Andrew Burt and others responded, and fighting broke out between the police and the marshals. Wells had his clothing torn but was not harmed. On the order of Mayor Wells, the city police suddenly burst out upon the crowd, armed with metal clubs and raining blows on the heads of the deputy marshals. Two of Maxwell's deputies were severely injured. With difficulty, Marshal Maxwell and his deputies took control and

---

[44] Edward W. Tullidge, "The First Government: Story of Municipal Election of 1874," in Carter, *Heart Throbs of the West*, vol. 10.

[45] Lockley manuscript, 72.

[46] "The Election," *SLT*, August 4, 1874, 4, col. 2.

arrested police magistrate Clinton, police chief Andrew Burt, and officers Brigham Y. Hampton, Charles Ringwood, W. G. Phillips, Charles Crow, and J. Livingston.[47] Governor George Woods was present and spoke to the gathered crowd and was successful in dispersing the men.

During the investigation that followed, the Mormons accused Maxwell of being drunk, but several witnesses, including Dr. Samuel L. Sprague, Fred Lockley, and Governor Woods, all denied any such evidence.[48] U.S. attorney William Carey ruled that federal law officers were the correct authority responsible for election day, that Mayor Wells was injudicious in his instructions to the police, and that his police officers resorted to uncalled-for violence.[49] The editors of the *Tribune* later claimed that Burt had two or three score of armed policemen hidden from view, and had the marshals initiated violence, escalation would have "drenched the streets in blood."[50]

As in previous encounters with Maxwell and Salt Lake policemen, thinly veiled antagonisms were operating: Burt and Hampton were among the police officers who had been unsuccessfully prosecuted by Maxwell in Judge McKean's court in 1871 for the murder of Dr. John King Robinson.[51] Burt and Maxwell had been opponents in the Wooden Gun Marching Episode, and Clinton and Maxwell had previously faced one another in the dispute over the matter of destruction of property in the Englebrecht liquor case and in another episode involving water rights issues in which Clinton twice shot a fifteen-year-old Negro boy in Salt Lake City and on the grounds of Camp Douglas.[52]

---

[47] Lockley quotes an unidentified attorney as having said: "It is a common thing to praise the heroic forbearance of the U.S. marshal's aides in allowing themselves to be beaten over the head by armed ruffians in the employ of the city, without offering resistance; and thereby averting a massacre." Lockley manuscript, 73.

[48] Whitney, *History of Utah*, 2:747–48; "Election Troubles," *slt*, August 13, 1874, 4, col. 2.

[49] "Election Troubles."

[50] "Giving Up Their Religion," *slt*, September 21, 1874, 1, col. 2.

[51] In 1885 officer Hampton authored a scheme to bring about the arrest of non-Mormon officials. He hired a madam to establish a house of prostitution, complete with peepholes for Mormon police to observe in flagrante delicto. T. G. Alexander, "Charles S. Zane," 300–302.

[52] Apparently a fifteen-year-old boy named Carrigan and his mother diverted water that flowed through the grounds of Camp Douglas. The *Tribune* contended that Clinton shot the young man twice, arrested him, and then charged him with a fine of $5. The *Tribune* editors raised the question of the jurisdiction of Clinton on the federal property of Camp Douglas. However, Gen. George R. Maxwell posted bail of $100 when the boy could not pay the fine. "Jeter Clinton and the Water Question," *slt*, July 11, 1871, 2, col. 2.

New Quarters, New Expenditures

Near the time of the 1874 congressional election, Maxwell was able to secure space for his office and for others of the judiciary at the Clift House. Maxwell and deputy Dr. Amos K. Smith were on the ground level together with the courtroom and jury rooms. Second-story accommodations housed the chief and associate justices, the U.S. commissioner, and U.S. attorney Carey. These offices were "a positive improvement on all the places hitherto occupied for judicial purposes in Salt Lake City," the *Salt Lake Tribune* noted. Credit for obtaining them was given to "the exertions of Gen. Maxwell and his very able Deputy," the *Tribune* added.[53] Shortly after making these arrangements in Salt Lake City, Maxwell leased Thompson Hall in Beaver for the courtroom and appointed William McAusland as the deputy marshal in that city.[54] Maxwell also secured quarters for judicial functions in Provo.[55]

Having incurred substantive expenditures for these several district court facilities before having the monies in hand, Maxwell should have foreseen the beginnings of the destructive fiscal vortex of inadequate or nil reimbursement that would shortly be his undoing. He was told by Attorney General Williams to present his expenses to the territorial treasurer as provided for in the Poland Act and, "should that official neglect or refuse payment of same, then to proceed without delay to enforce disbursements by mandamus or such other proceeding that in the marshal's judgement will furnish a prompt and speedy remedy." To this the *Tribune* added: "We hope the General will put [it] to the test by sending a statement of the expenses already incurred to the Treasurer of the Territory. Mr. Jack should be holding that balance of $35,000 reported on hand last winter for the drafts which are to be made on them. There is no authority by law, by appropriation, or otherwise for paying out any part of the public funds into the strong box of Utah. This is one of the stings of the Poland Bill."[56] That James Jack was simultaneously territorial treasurer and financial secretary of the LDS church was a fact of which Attorney General Williams was possibly unaware. There would have been no question which master Jack would serve when required to choose.

---

[53] "New Court House," *SLT*, August 12 and 20, 1874, 4, col. 6.

[54] "Beaver Notes," *SLT*, August 23, 1874, 4, col. 5.

[55] "Court House at Provo," *SLT*, August 29, 1874, 4, col. 3.

[56] "Territorial Court Expenses," *SLT*, September 26, 1874, 4, col. 3.

The defense lawyers and the judge at the first trial of John Doyle Lee for his role in the Mountain Meadows massacre. Previously not identified is Gen. George R. Maxwell, then the U.S. marshal, on the far right. Note the left leg prosthesis covered by his trousers and the missing fingers of his left hand. John D. Lee, seated at center, is flanked by (*left to right*) attorney William W. Bishop; Jacob Smith Boreman, the presiding judge; and attorneys Enos Dougherty Hoge and Spicer Wells. The prosecution team of U.S. attorney William C. Carey and Salt Lake City attorney Robert Newton Baskin is not in the photograph. *Used by permission, Utah State Historical Society, all rights reserved.*

10

Mountain Meadows, John Doyle Lee, and Marshal Maxwell

It breaks his heart that kings must murder still,
That all his hours of travail here for men
Seem yet in vain.
Vachel Lindsay,
"Abraham Lincoln Walks at Midnight"

IN ADDITION TO ENABLING FEDERAL OFFICERS IN UTAH TO DEAL
with the matter of polygamy, the passage of the 1874 Poland Act cleared
the way for justice that had been delayed seventeen years for a crime of
mass murder of monstrous proportion. In September 1857 the Mormon
population of Utah Territory felt threatened by a military expedition
ordered by President James Buchanan, whose purpose was allegedly
to escort a new territorial governor to replace Brigham Young. These
troops were also to act as a posse comitatus in asserting federal authority
and protecting federal officers in a territory believed to be in rebellion
against and insubordinate to the laws of the United States. However,
Brigham Young and the Mormons saw in this military action a specter
of renewed persecution, a commencement of another religious pogrom,
as they anticipated the arrival of 2,500 soldiers then under the command
of Col. Edmund B. Alexander.[1] Having started from Fort Leavenworth

---

[1] Col. Albert Sidney Johnston did not take command at Fort Bridger and Fort Supply until
November 1857. Johnston replaced Brig. Gen. William S. Harney, initially assigned to lead
the expedition.

and gone through Fort Laramie, their course along the Mormon Trail of the North Platte would bring the troops near Fort Bridger, northeast of Salt Lake City, in present-day southwestern Wyoming. They would then be able to traverse the well-traveled Echo Canyon and enter the valley of the Great Salt Lake. The complex events preceding and following this march of troops constitute the Utah War and have received much attention and concentrated study, especially around the time of its 150th anniversary.[2]

On September 7, in another portion of Utah Territory, a company of 120 to 140 individuals, mostly women and children, led by trail captains Alexander Fancher and John T. "Jack" Baker, were four hundred miles southwest of Fort Bridger.[3] Coming from prosperous farms in Arkansas, they were traveling on the Old Spanish Trail to a destination in southern California. They were attacked at daybreak in the beautiful, grassy valley called Mountain Meadows in the far southwestern corner of Utah, three hundred miles from Salt Lake City.[4] On September 11, the fifth day of the siege, without a water source, with many of their men already killed and their ammunition nearly spent, the surviving company of exhausted, terrified travelers was lured from the scant protection of the rifle pits beneath their wagons by a white-flag promise held in the hand of a white man. This man talked of safe transport to nearby Cedar City, Utah. Thinking they were safe at last from an attack by Utah Indians, they relinquished their arms. Shortly after their surrender, the adult men were marching single file when a Mormon militiaman signaled "Halt!" Each emigrant man was killed, shot at arm's length, by the Mormon guard walking immediately beside him. Hearing the gunfire from the backside of the low ridge they had just

---

[2] MacKinnon, *At Sword's Point*, 2008.

[3] The *Arkansas Sunday Post-Dispatch* stated in 1895 that the wagon train "numbered about 140 souls, connected by various kindred ties." Cited in Bigler, "Terror on the Trail." A precise number of those killed at Mountain Meadows is not possible, because the numbers making up the Baker and Fancher groups, like most of the westward emigrant groups, were fluid as some left and others joined. Novak, *House of Mourning*, 51–56.

[4] Many authors have dealt with this extremely troubling event. The study by Juanita Brooks remains a classic. Brooks, *Mountain Meadows Massacre*. More recently published is the painstakingly documented book by Bagley, *Blood of the Prophets*. Three historians of the Church of Jesus Christ of Latter-day Saints, along with numerous Mormon researchers also contributing, have produced a work from the limited-access sources within the church archives. The authors claim they have not withheld any relevant material contained in the records; see R. W. Walker, Turley, and Leonard, *Massacre at Mountain Meadows*.

crossed, the women and teenage boys rushed back toward their men, only to be systematically slaughtered as they attempted to flee or hide. Only seventeen children, all under eight years of age, were not killed.

This crime is little known and little remembered by the public at large, even in Utah, or perhaps especially in Utah.[5] It represented, in magnitude of lives lost, the worst terrorist act against U.S. citizens by U.S. citizens until the bombing of the Murrah Federal Building in Oklahoma City by Timothy McVeigh and Terry Nichols in 1995.[6] In the view of historian David L. Bigler, the Mountain Meadows massacre remains the most heinous, repugnant atrocity in America's history, not simply from the body count of those murdered but as measured by its deceit and premeditation, its brutal, up close and personal one-on-one executions.[7] The complex interconnection of the U.S. Army's advance to Utah, and the reasons and responsibility for the mass murder of the Arkansas travelers, have both become the subject of intense research and interest as the history of the Utah War and the LDS theocracy is untangled.[8]

For seventeen years, suspected Mormon perpetrators and leaders of this massacre were in hiding; no responsibility was legally placed, no arrests were made, and no court was impaneled.[9] Maj. James Henry Carleton of the First United States Dragoons had visited the site of the massacre in May 1859 and submitted a lengthy report of his findings and interpretation of the event, with a number of names of suspects. Judge John Cradlebaugh of the Second Judicial District also traveled to southern Utah in 1859, initiated a grand jury investigation, and issued warrants for the arrest of almost one hundred suspects.[10] In June 1859,

---

[5] News of the massacre traveled quickly, and from California, a month afterward, came a call for military action: "If the government was incapable of handling the Mormon question, from this state alone, thousands of volunteers could be drawn, who would ask no better employment than the extermination of the Mormons." *San Francisco Daily Evening Bulletin*, October 12, 1857.

[6] In Oklahoma City, 168 people died, and about 500 were wounded. Both descriptions fail, as we usually fail, to consider the massacres of American Indian peoples.

[7] Bigler, "Terror on the Trail." For a detailed narrative, see Bagley, *Blood of the Prophets*.

[8] The aforementioned publications by Bagley, Bigler, MacKinnon, Turley, Leonard, and Walker all deal, from different perspectives, with the question of the causes and responsibility for the massacre within the larger framework of the Utah War.

[9] Paiute Indian spokespeople insist that there was no involvement of Indians after the first day. Of note is that no contingent of U.S. soldiers had been sent to annihilate the men, women, and children of the American Indian tribe thought to be responsible, as routinely occurred elsewhere in the western territories during this era.

[10] These investigations and the information from Indian agent Jacob Forney is covered in detail in Bagley, *Blood of the Prophets*.

U.S. marshal Peter Kessler Dotson wrote to Cradlebaugh, explaining that, given the hostile Mormon population he faced, it was not within his power "to execute any of these processes."[11]

Under the Poland Act, U.S. attorneys and marshals were finally empowered with jurisdiction to deal with this crime. The grand jury convened in Salt Lake City on September 7, 1874, and authorized the arrest of nine Mormon men in southern Utah: John Doyle Lee, William Horne Dame, Isaac Chauncey Haight, John Mount Higbee, Philip Klingensmith, William Cameron Stewart, George Washington Adair, Jr., Samuel Jewkes, and Ellott Willden.[12]

ARRESTING THE SUSPECTS

George R. Maxwell was the U.S. marshal responsible for making the arrests of those indicted for the Mountain Meadows murders, and the decision was made that John D. Lee would be the first taken. Because of his physical limitations, Maxwell needed the help of a deputy marshal who was physically able and trustworthy. He wisely selected William Stokes. Thirty-one years old, from Oshkosh, Wisconsin, Stokes was also a Civil War survivor, having served with the Eighth Wisconsin Infantry under Gen. George H. Thomas in Tennessee.

Five additional assistant deputies served with Stokes under Maxwell's command. Two were older, former Mormons: Thomas LeFevre, age forty, who "once belonged to the church," and Thomas Winn, thirty-eight, who "was also once a Mormon." Two were younger men whose parents were active Mormons: Franklin R. Fish, age twenty-five, and David Evans, twenty-four, whose father was a Mormon bishop in the city of Lehi. Samuel S. Rogers, who was "about forty" and "not a Mormon," was also listed among the deputies.[13]

---

[11] Marshal Dotson's experience in attempting to arrest men in 1859 was the same as that of other marshals. Dotson spent his own money, as did other marshals, for "neither the Territory nor the Federal Government provide for the payment." Dotson to Cradlebaugh, June 3, 1859, Moorman Papers, box 10. Thomas G. Alexander lays out the Mormon view that Brigham Young tried repeatedly over the seventeen years to implement justice, where Young cited the inability to secure an impartial judge and trial as the obstacle. Alexander, *Brigham Young.*

[12] Fielding and Fielding, *Trials of John D. Lee,* 48–49 (Ellott Willden was incorrectly identified in this work as Edward Weldon, and Samuel Jewkes was incorrectly identified as Samuel Duke); R. W. Walker, Turley, and Leonard, *Massacre at Mountain Meadow,* 256–64.

[13] Fielding and Fielding, *Trials of John D. Lee,* 9.

Because Lee had repeatedly proclaimed throughout his years in self-imposed exile that he would not be taken alive, the arrest on November 7, by Stokes and his five assistant deputies while Lee was hiding in a straw-covered animal pen at his home in Panguitch, Utah, was almost miraculously uneventful. That a bloodbath between the Lee family and the arresting deputies did not take place was due to the skill and judgment of Deputy Marshal Stokes and to John D. Lee's restraint when he found his capture imminent. Maxwell received word from Stokes on November 9 that Lee had been taken into custody.

Philip Klingensmith, at the time of the massacre, had been a Mormon bishop in Cedar City, Utah, and a Mormon militiaman who admitted participating with John D. Lee in the killing and in the disposition of the surviving children.[14] Klingensmith was the only man known to have left the Mormon Church over the massacre; he had confessed in April 1871, before a court in Lincoln County, Nevada, to his actions at Mountain Meadows. Maxwell had instructed the Lincoln County sheriff, who knew where to find Klingensmith, to bring him to Pioche, Nevada. Maxwell was to send for him there, but the plans fell apart, as the *Salt Lake Tribune* recounted:

> That official [the Lincoln County marshal], not understanding that secrecy was necessary, telegraphed the General for money to pay his expenses and mentioned the name of the man he was to go for. This rendered his services useless, as his dispatch would pass through the hand of one or more Mormon telegraph operators. Maxwell telegraphed the Sheriff that he didn't want the ex-Bishop [Klingensmith], and instantly dispatched Deputy [Jerome B.] Cross to bring him in.[15]

When Cross telegraphed Maxwell that he had his man at Riverside, "Maxwell hitched up his roan ponies and headed north with military celerity." the *Tribune* continued. "The party arrived at Beaver yesterday [July 16]."[16] Klingensmith came willingly, to serve as the star witness for the prosecution. Of the role of deputy marshals serving warrants on those accused in the massacre, Maxwell said: "You must remember that nowhere in the United States are such obstacles to be surmounted. We

---

[14] There are multiple variations of Klingensmith's name: P. K. Smith, Philip K. Smith, and Philip Klingon Smith. Backus, *Mountain Meadows Witness*, 302.

[15] "Our Beaver Letter," *slt*, July 20, 1875, 4, col. 2. The entry is signed "F.L." (Frederic Lockley).

[16] Ibid.

are surrounded by a people who have nothing in common with the spirit of free republican institutions, and no regard or respect whatever for federal officials, but who are controlled by a priesthood whose power is more absolute than that of the most despotic Monarchy of the Old World."[17]

Maxwell perceived his situation in Utah Territory to be unique, but his was an experience shared by other U.S. marshals and their deputies who were challenged in their local enforcement of unpopular federal law. Before the Civil War this was the case with the enforcement of the Fugitive Slave Law in the North. In the South after the Civil War, the marshals dealt with civil rights, voting rights for blacks, and revenue laws taxing whiskey.[18]

Once John D. Lee was in custody there was substantial concern about his safety as a prisoner, for it was suspected that Mormons might silence the man who knew so much about the massacre. The *Tribune* reported:

> There is at present quite a disturbed feeling among the . . . Saints over the arrest of Lee, and for a few days, well grounded fears were entertained of an assault upon the jail and the assassination of the prisoner. . . . Lee holds terrible secrets locked in his breast, and the error committed by Brigham in suffering him to live could even now be repaired by a sudden dash and a bold stroke. I hear strange thoughts in out of the way places, half whispered and the rest merely indicated. . . . Lee is well guarded. Marshal Stokes and his men are true blue and not easily scared. But a sudden dash of half crazy fanatics upon the jail might overpower them, and the murderer Lee would be put beyond the power of telling tales.[19]

On November 18, Deputy Marshals Benjamin A. Spears and David Evans arrested William H. Dame and brought him to Beaver. With two prisoners now in hand, Maxwell wrote to Governor George A. Black, asking his aid in arranging with Col. George A. Woodward of Fort Cameron to move Lee and Dame from the Beaver jail to this federal facility at the mouth of nearby Beaver Canyon. Dame did not remain in Beaver, however, for he was removed to the U.S. Penitentiary in Salt Lake City. Far from his family and home, Dame was not silent about the conditions of his incarceration. His attorneys, Jabez Gridley Sutherland and George Caesar Bates, wrote to Attorney General Williams that the

---

[17] Maxwell to Attorney General, June 27, 1875, RG 60, Attorney General Papers, Utah Territory (hereafter "AG Papers, Utah Terr."), roll 4, part 3, file 5/87.

[18] Calhoun, *Lawmen*, 123–24.

[19] Fielding and Fielding, *Trials of John D. Lee*, 11.

Utah prison was a "disgrace" and that it was the "most brutal, loathsome and infamous prison in the country."[20] Dame protested his innocence and asked to be returned to Beaver or to be released on $50 bail.[21]

Maxwell and Stokes were responsible, along with Deputy B. L. "Pony" Duncan, for supervising the prisoners from the time of arrest to the beginning of the Lee's first trial in Beaver in July 1875.[22] Maxwell and his deputies were quite lenient with the men in their charge and allowed Lee's wife, Rachel, to see him frequently and even to have a family portrait photograph taken. For this leniency allowed to Lee, Maxwell later came under stinging criticism from one of his deputies, Benjamin Spears, for allowing "women or concubines to co-habit with them in this place of confinement."[23]

SERVING SUBPOENAS

About five o'clock on October 12, 1874, in Salt Lake City, Maxwell sent Deputy Marshal Arthur Pratt to serve Brigham Young with a subpoena to appear as a witness in court in Beaver in the Mountain Meadows proceedings. Being told that Young was not accessible, Pratt fetched Marshal Maxwell to the Lion House, Young's home, where they found Mayor Daniel Wells and a large contingent of Mormon guards. On the porch, conversation took place with gatekeeper Joseph Shaw; Maxwell instructed Pratt to arrest Shaw, and an altercation ensued, with Shaw and Pratt engaged in a scuffle. Maxwell was struck from behind by either Elias Morris or a man named Cushing and, having only one good leg and one good arm, was knocked to the ground. Morris, an Iron County militiaman, was also among those suspected of participation in the murders.[24] According to the *Salt Lake Tribune* account, Maxwell was set upon by several Mormon men intent on killing him.

---

[20] Sutherland and Bates, William H. Dame to Attorney General Williams, April 19, 1875, RG 60, Chronological Files, 1871–84, box 1015.   [21] Ibid.

[22] Maxwell paid a fee of $600 per year (three times his annual salary) to rent the space above Edward W. Thompson's store in Beaver for holding the Second District Court proceedings.

[23] Spears accused Maxwell of drunkenness, complained of dereliction of duty by attorney William Carey and Deputy Duncan, expressed dissatisfaction with poor compensation, and complained his reports to superiors had been ignored. Benjamin A. Spears to Attorney General Edwards Pierrepont, January 20, 1876, RG 60, Chronological Files, 1871–84, box 1015. Spears was, for a time, the Beaver correspondent for the *Salt Lake Tribune*, writing under the code name "Royal."

[24] R. W. Walker, Turley, and Leonard, *Massacre at Mountain Meadows*, 261.

Maxwell was not armed but, had he been, would likely have shot his attackers.[25] Morris was arrested for resisting a U.S. marshal but was soon released. Cushing and Shaw were conveyed to the penitentiary, where each was held on a $5,000 bond.[26] Marshal Maxwell returned to the premises accompanied by a half dozen deputies, whereupon Mayor Wells accepted the subpoena and indicated that Young would appear to give testimony.[27] Brigham Young is said to have relayed an apology to Maxwell for the incident.[28]

Despite having been served with subpoenas, neither Young nor Apostle George A. Smith traveled to the Second District Court in Beaver, as required of witnesses in the Lee trial. Judge Jacob S. Boreman ruled against the request for the court's indulgence in not requiring Young or Smith to attend the trial in that city. According to defense motions made on July 28 by Lee's lawyers, both witnesses were too ill to travel; the trip would be perilous. "It would be a great risk, both to my health and life, for me to travel to Beaver at the present time. I am and have been for some time an invalid," replied Brigham Young. Smith's sworn assertion said that he was presently, and for several months had been, "suffering from a severe and dangerous illness of the head and lungs" and that "to attend the court in Beaver . . . would in all probability end his life."[29] Despite Boreman's ruling to the contrary, depositions were taken in Salt Lake City from both leaders and then sent to Beaver, where they were filed with the trial records but not allowed to be officially entered into the proceedings of the first trial.

---

[25] "Commissioner's Court," *SLT*, October 14, 1874, 1, col. 2; "The Jibbering Serfs," *SLT*, October 14, 1874, 1, col. 3. Other accounts cite Maxwell as having a handgun; "Local Matters—A Misunderstanding," *DN*, October 21, 1874, 10, col. 2. However, as the strident, highly visible, and well-known critic of the Mormons, Maxwell, even acting with the authority of a U.S. marshal, would not have been so foolhardy as to invite his own death by arriving at Brigham Young's home with a concealed gun. Pratt's demeanor may have been influenced by the fact that only a week earlier he and his mother, Sarah M. Bates Pratt, first wife of Orson Pratt, had been excommunicated for their opposition to polygamy. Van Wagoner and Van Wagoner, "Arthur Pratt," 24.

[26] Shaw had died before the trial began eighteen months later, and Cushing was sentenced to twenty-four hours imprisonment and fined $125. "Sentenced," *SLT*, February 27, 1877, 1, col. 3.

[27] "Resistance!" *SLT*, October 13, 1874, 4, col. 2; "Where the Responsibility Lies," *SLT*, October 14, 1874, 2, col. 1. Young may have been ill at this time, suffering from prostatic enlargement, for which catheterization was begun by his nephew Dr. Seymour B. Young. Bush, "Brigham Young in Life and Death."   [28] "Where the Responsibility Lies."

[29] Fielding and Fielding, *Trials of John D. Lee*, 152, 154.

Young's contention of being an invalid was at the least an overstated claim and, according to his activities for the period, an outright lie.[30] George A. Smith's assertion about his own health, however, was not far from the truth. Notations in the church record for July confirm that he was ill, and on September 1, 1875, at age fifty-eight and notably obese, he sat in his parlor, fighting for breath, and died. He had been generally acknowledged to be a close friend and one of the most trusted of confidants of President Brigham Young.

General Maxwell was the featured speaker at the Camp Douglas celebration of Decoration Day in May, but otherwise April to September of 1875 saw Maxwell involved with important but financially draining marshal's duties before, during, and after John D. Lee's murder trial. In early April, Maxwell returned William H. Dame to Beaver, for at this time it was still uncertain whether Dame or Lee would be the first brought to trial.[31] Maxwell and his deputies found a "scarcity of Saints" as they attempted to serve warrants to Mormon men to appear as witnesses. One observer of the marshal's efforts recorded: "The appearance of the marshal or his officers in any settlement to serve process, causes a general stampede and thus it becomes difficult to get hold of men. Maxwell and his deputies are having an exceedingly lively time getting in their witnesses. They are scattered over an immense range of country and hide like deer when an officer approaches."[32]

Approximately 260 subpoenas for 160 individuals were issued and served by George R. Maxwell and deputy marshals working with him. Benjamin Backman, A. J. Kirby, William Stokes, J. A. Barton, and B. F. Brown are named in the records of the Second District Court as assisting with delivering the papers.[33] Many of those to be served were

---

[30] Young's actions were those not of an invalid but of a vigorous man. He went to the Tabernacle on July 24 to celebrate the holiday. On August 1 he was in Provo for meetings. On August 12 he dealt with the immense financial disaster of the federal government's reneging on its mail contract and issued orders closing all the stations that had been built; on the same day, he left with Bishop Sharp to travel by carriage to Cache Valley. *Journal of History*, reel 33, July 20–May 10, 1875.

[31] Mormon leaders may have wished John D. Lee to be tried first and not William Dame, for Lee may have had only secondhand knowledge of orders, whereas Dame, who had met with George A. Smith, publicly threatened that if he was tried, he would "put the saddle on the right horse!" Bagley, *Blood of the Prophets*, 299.

[32] Fielding and Fielding, *Trials of John D. Lee*, 71, 73.

[33] The court records also indicate that D. P. Whedon served as an assistant district attorney under Baskin and Carey.

impossible to find, for many of them were likely participants in the massacre. Others with information relevant to the investigation of the charges against Lee and Dame or others did not wish to testify against their Mormon neighbors.

Court clerk James R. Wilkins often cited Maxwell's expenditures as part of the court record. Frequently the "actual expenses" were twenty-five to fifty dollars or more for each attempted subpoena, substantial amounts for the times. In Wilkins's records are repeated notations in the book margins that Maxwell had insufficient money to pay these expenses, and moreover Wilkins wrote that territorial funds for these expenses had been repeatedly denied.

Not only did Maxwell and his deputies have trouble finding the witnesses and serving their papers, but once the witnesses were in Beaver, many of them petitioned Judge Boreman to take their testimony in chambers and allow them to return to their farms to participate in the harvest and care for their families. Additionally, they petitioned Boreman to require Marshal Maxwell to pay them subsistence allowances for their time away from their farmwork. Boreman declined to authorize the payments, but even had he done so, Maxwell did not have the funds to pay them, and such a requirement would have further complicated his financial conundrum.

Johnny Reb, Billy Yank, and the Carrot Eater

During his preparations for the John D. Lee trial, Maxwell took a tour to the Lincoln Mining area near Cedar City, to the site of the former Rollins Mine, which he and three friends had purchased. Their mining venture had been incorporated on May 10, 1875, with C.C. Clements as president, George R. Maxwell as vice president, John M. Moore as secretary, and John Dupraix as treasurer.[34] General Maxwell opted to visit the property to see how the dig was going. By a strange twist, the hands employed at the mine were mostly ex-Confederate soldiers, and

---

[34] The mine's future production was estimated at five tons of bullion per diem, on average. The mine was said to be "one of the most valuable in southern Utah," "constantly increasing in gold and silver," and to have "proved itself a valuable property." However, there is little evidence that Maxwell received any significant profits from it. "Our Beaver Letter," *slt*, May 18 and July 22, 1875, 4, col. 3.

the foreman, Alfred Healington, was a devout Latter-day Saint. Wanting to see the operation below ground, Maxwell "placed himself in the bucket and bade the man at the windlass [Healington] unwind." As Maxwell descended, one of the workers heard the foreman say, "I wish he would break his d——d neck." The *Salt Lake Tribune* reported on what transpired next:

> At night, the employees were all gathered in their boarding house, General Maxwell . . . being present as a guest. The [comment] of the foreman was brought up for discussion. When reported around it gave great offense and three or four of the hardy drivers were prompt with their offers to put a head on the churlish overseer. Bad feeling was generated in an instant. . . . "Here boys, none of this" commanded [Maxwell,] the United States officer, humping to the front. "No fighting here; I command the peace." But the boys seemed to regard the General as off-duty, so they gave but slight heed to his summons. "I don't care a d——m . . . for his being [a] United States marshal, but I ain't going to stand by and hear a soldier abused." "And by an [adjective] carrot-eater," chimed in a second. "These [adjective] Mormons took no part in the war on neither side, but stood off [like timid, carrot-munching rabbits] and enjoyed the sight of Federal and Johnny Reb cutting one another's throats. Such men can't wish no harm to a soldier—no matter which side he fought—while I'm by. And these men chewed over the insult to the mutilated Federal officer, until they lost temper over it, and then a self appointed champion took to pounding the offender pretty roughly. The General quelled the trouble finally, but he had to do some loud talking to get them apart. . . . Federals and Confederates hated each other . . . during the "late unpleasantness" . . . but the two parties, when they meet, entertain respect for each other, and in social intercourse readily sink all past differences. Not so the Mormon. . . . [H]e must be treacherous and revengeful, vowing eternal vengeance for the assassination of Joseph Smith.[35]

LEE'S FIRST TRIAL

The trial of John D. Lee for murder began in the city of Beaver on July 23, 1875. Attorney William Carey led the prosecution team, assisted

---

[35] "General Maxwell and the Mines," *SLT*, May 15, 1875, 1, col. 2 (expletives were partially elided, deleted, or replaced by "[adjective]" in the original). Healington sent letters to the *Salt Lake Tribune* and *Salt Lake Herald*, denying the event, but Maxwell reiterated the story as fact and added that Healington trailed him, insulting him over his mutilations and his physical disability. "Another Tribute Lie Exposed," *SLT*, June 6, 1875, 1, col. 3.

by attorney Robert N. Baskin of Salt Lake City.[36] It was Carey who delivered the opening salvo. In his first sentence is found what others would later judge as the prosecution's downfall—its focus on "leaders" and "they" and not on the individual sitting at the bar:

> For 18 years the leaders of this terrible tragedy have borne this fearful secret. They have shunned the light of civilization. They have feared the investigation of the courts. They have skulked and hid from the gaze of their fellow men. Gradually as civilized immigration came into the territory and pressed south they have fallen back! Back! Back! Until Utah is no longer a safe hiding place. And many of them are today seeking concealment and skulking from the officers of justice in the wilds of Arizona; but not long will even that protect them. . . . If they make their beds in hell their own guilty conscience will still follow them. There is no peace for them.[37]

As the trial began, the streets of Beaver were awash with people, and federal officials were aware of threats made by some in the crowds. Presiding judge Boreman "suggested" to Marshal Maxwell, who was responsible not only for security of the prisoners and the jury but for the safe conduct of the entire trial, that he might "hint" to the crowds that federal officials were prepared to deal with them. Maxwell's remarks were well above the level of a hint: "We are ready to meet you—come on and do your best—and we will hang any G——d——Bishop to a telegraph pole and turn their houses over their heads—We'll show them who is going to run things down here."[38] This warning was allegedly followed by a string of profane and blunt oaths, and the bailiff calmly confirmed to Judge Boreman's satisfaction that "whole crowd knew that Maxwell was utterly fearless and brave as a lion."[39] The crowd became and remained suitably quieted.

By July the prosecution's star witness had wandered away, disappearing into the deserts of Nevada, and again Deputy Cross was sent to

---

[36] Editor Frederic Lockley wrote to his wife that Carey was a "weak and inefficient lawyer" who could not handle the opposition's legal team. Lockley was relieved that Baskin had joined the prosecution. Baskin was eager and said he had waited years for the opportunity. Maxwell brought offers from Star District miners that they would pay for additional attorneys to assist Carey. Frederic Lockley to Elizabeth Metcalf Lockley, Beaver, Utah Territory, July 26, 1875, Lockley manuscript, 87.

[37] Court records, Beaver County Courthouse, cited in Backus, *Mountain Meadows Witness*, 30. Spicer Wells and Enos Dougherty Hoge initially defended Lee, and Jabez G. Sutherland, George Caesar Bates, William W. Bishop, and John McFarlane were added to the team. Bagley, *Blood of the Prophets*, 291.   [38] Arrington, "Crusade against Theocracy," 38.
[39] Ibid.

apprehend Klingensmith. For sixteen days Maxwell heard nothing. In the extreme midsummer desert heat, his horses dying of thirst, Cross finally found and brought his man back to Beaver under extraordinarily difficult conditions. Cross reported that he had suffered "twenty days and nights without sleep, traversing barren wastes where his life was in danger from Mormon desperados, Indians, and scarcity of water."[40]

On the opening day of the trial, the role of witnesses was called; forty-one answered, and twenty-four were absent. Klingensmith and Joel White were the principal witnesses, and Lee's lawyers, in a countermove, persuaded a local justice of the peace to issue warrants for the arrest of Klingensmith and other witnesses for complicity in the murders, a move that would have made them unavailable to the prosecution.[41] Judge Boreman contended that not only would they have been unavailable but they would have killed. Boreman immediately released word that he would order, and Maxwell swore he would carry out, the arrest of any local constable who interfered with federal witnesses.[42] Considering Klingensmith's life at risk, Maxwell brought him into his own marshal's quarters while awaiting the call for him to testify. Great anticipation accompanied Klingensmith's journey to the stand and his swearing in: "[When he] was called to the witness stand and sworn in '. . . there was a general movement in the audience. Every eye and ear was strained, and the man was thoroughly photographed by every attendant.' Philip stood six feet tall, he was broad, but 'well-muscled,' not fat, weighing about 175 pounds."[43]

Not withstanding John D. Lee's confession, Klingensmith's damning testimony, and that of Joel White and other witnesses, the prevailing opinion at the proceedings was that Lee would not be convicted by the

---

[40] Maxwell to Attorney General, June 27, 1875.

[41] In September 1857, Capt. Joel White was a lieutenant in Company D of the Iron County Militia, the former Nauvoo Legion.

[42] Arrington, "Crusade against Theocracy," 37.

[43] Backus, *Mountain Meadows Witness*, 32. The *Pioche (Nev.) Journal* reported what was thought to be an assassination attempt before the Lee trial. The item was reprinted in the *Tribune*: "Philip Klingensmith now stopping at Mineral Park about a week ago received quite a scalp wound from a rock thrown at him from some parties unknown. We are told he was unconscious for several days afterwards from the effects of the blow, and was given up as dead, but he is now in a fair way to recovery." "Attempted Assassination," *SLT*, November 27, 1875, 4, col. 5. The *Tribune* shortly afterward printed a retraction of its statement that it was not an attempted assassination, saying that "Johnny Weaver, a renegade Mormon," was responsible. "City Jottings," *SLT*, December 21, 1875, 4, col. 1. Frederic Lockley describes Klingensmith's ultimate fate: "California papers told of a man answering the ex-bishop's description being found brained by the roadside. He had been hauling ore from abandoned lead workings in the southern part of the state, and the avenger had overtaken him when no help was nigh." Lockley manuscript, 102.

jury, which was composed mostly of Mormons. Lee's family and supporters did not fully share that optimism, for in late July, hatchets, knives, a
rope, percussion caps, a gimlet (a screw-tipped hand tool), and compasses
were found hidden in Lee's cell. Out of fear of an escape plot, Lee's family and wives were denied access to him for the remainder of the trial.

That the Mormons of Beaver were not pleased with the U.S. marshal understates the matter. Lockley described the situation for the *Salt
Lake Tribune*:

> The young Mormon hoodlums of Beaver, when filled with rye, flourish
> their six shooters and Bowie knives and talk sportively about blowing off
> the top of his head, letting his bowels out, etc. Meantime, the Marshal
> keeps a wakeful eye on the assassin, Lee, battles his schemes to break
> jail, and sees that he is well supplied with bracelets. No wonder that
> young Mormondom has bestowed upon him [Maxwell] the pleasing
> title of "The Carpetbagger from H———l!"[44]

In his closing arguments, Baskin named Lee as "in connection and
concert of action with other persons" and focused on "Brigham Young,
first as an accessory," and then as "having violated his oath of office . . .
and the common dictates of humanity."[45] On August 5, after eleven days of
trial and three days of deliberation, the jury was deadlocked and unable to
reach a verdict. Nine jurors—eight Mormons and one ex-Mormon—stood
for acquittal, and three non-Mormons voted for conviction. In a mistrial,
declared by Judge Boreman, the first opportunity in seventeen years to fix
responsibility for the murder of 120 or more human beings was lost.[46]

The prospect of a second trial was faced with ambivalence. *Tribune*
editor Lockley considered the advantage of a non-guilty verdict, as
he envisioned that the resulting attention of the public would high-
light the insufficiency of the Poland Act and lead to additional, more
severe legislation.[47] On the other hand, few anticipated that a second
jury impaneled with Mormon members would be any more receptive
to facts and evidence than had this one. Newspapers across the United
States cried foul at the failure of the jury to arrive at what would have

---

[44] "City Jottings," *slt*, August 3, 1875. The entry is signed "F.L." (Frederic Lockley).

[45] Transcript of the First Trial of John D. Lee, ms 8191, lds Church Archives.

[46] Orson Ferguson Whitney charges that the prosecution deliberately courted a hung jury in the
expectation that it would pave the way for action against Mormon leadership. Whitney, *History of Utah*, 2:801–802.

[47] Frederic Lockley to Elizabeth Metcalf Lockley, July 31, 1875, Lockley Papers.

been a just verdict.[48] Even Ann Eliza Young, the outspoken former wife of President Brigham Young, took up her pen and wrote to the *Boston Globe* from her lecture circuit:

> I ask the Christian people of the United States to read the news that comes today from Utah—John D. Lee is acquitted! . . . His crimes have been proven. . . . [H]e reddened his hand with the warm blood of women. . . . [T]he blood of murdered Americans and their wives and daughters and little ones that cries out for vengeance has been spit upon by the remorseless despotism that rules Utah.[49]

She did not stop here but reserved a special invective for President Ulysses S. Grant, who she thought should have intervened in the Lee trial rather than taking his summer respite at the New Jersey beach retreat of Long Branch: "If he [Grant] is indifferent to the shrieks of the women slaughtered by Lee and Young, let your voice be heard in tones so stern and loud that it will startle him from his slumbers at Long Branch. When assassins are crowned with laurels, it is no time for our rulers to loaf by the seaside."[50]

At around two or three o'clock of the night on August 7, Maxwell and Stokes were treated to a pistol serenade on the porch of their quarters at Fort Cameron, perhaps in celebration of the Mormon victory, perhaps to draw them out of the building for a "blood atonement."[51] The *Tribune* had unusual praise for Maxwell and his marshals:

> Now that the Lee trial is over . . . we are at liberty to speak of the excellent conduct of the United States Marshal and his deputies. . . . [T]hey have done themselves great honor in the performance of such duties as fell to them. . . . [N]ever danger nor fatigue has daunted those who had to travel hundreds of miles through an inhospitable region, often among a hostile people, in arresting criminals and in bringing in witnesses. . . . Special commendation is bestowed on General Maxwell for his careful management of affairs immediately about the court. For the first time, perhaps, in the history of Utah courts, the jury has been guarded as the law directs. Their every move was under the General's eye. . . . [W]hatever personal faults he may have been accused of, his sharpest critics forgive them all for his excellent conduct in this case. . . . The lovers of justice in Utah, and all the loyal people of the United States, owe a thousand thanks to the Marshals in attendance in Beaver.[52]

---

[48] Lockley, *Lee Trial!* 53–64.   [49] Ibid., 61.

[50] Wallace, *Twenty-seventh Wife*, 343.   [51] Fielding and Fielding, *Trials of John D. Lee*, 179.

[52] Ibid.

Frederic Lockley, the *Salt Lake Tribune* editor of the time, is almost certainly the author of the above, given that he shared similar praise with his wife in a letter to her: "Maxwell and his deputies have acquitted themselves like heroes, but for their untiring exertions, the array of testimony which has set the Mountain Meadows butchery before the world in all its heart-sickening details, could never have been presented to the world."[53] This was high praise for Maxwell from Lockley, a man who tended to take an uncompromising and critical view of men and events and who dispensed kind words only sparingly. Lockley's comment about John D. Lee near the end of the trial is far less harsh than many statements made by others of the time about Lee: "Sitting at his elbow day after day, and seeing his deep affliction, I cannot help but be a little moved at it."[54]

From Beaver to Salt Lake City

At an altitude of about 6,200 feet, on the north side of the crystal waters of the small stream optimistically called the Beaver River, about a mile from its exodus from steep-walled corridors in the Wasatch Mountains, sat Fort Cameron. Located in a recess between the foothills, about two miles east of the city of Beaver, its buildings had been fashioned from locally quarried volcanic stone.[55] It was from here, at about 9:30 P.M. on the cool night of August 9, that John D. Lee began his journey to the U.S. Penitentiary in Salt Lake City, to await further trial. Transported in an open wagon, Lee was sitting next to Marshal Maxwell, with three deputy marshals—William Adams Hickman, Jack Kirby, and Tom Wiem—riding alongside.[56] The editor of the *Tribune* guessed at the motive for their leaving at night, accompanied by six heavily armed, mounted guards: Maxwell was anticipating an attempt to rescue Lee. "A great dissatisfaction exists among the Mormons," the editor wrote, noting that Mormons viewed the Mountain Meadows investigation "in the light of persecution" and that they asserted that "more money

---

[53] Frederic Lockley to Elizabeth Metcalf Lockley, July 31, 1875.

[54] Ibid.

[55] The buildings of Fort Cameron were subsequently used by the Murdock Academy, now defunct. As of April 2009 only one of the original buildings survived.

[56] "Bear, the Brewer" was the carriage driver. Cleland and Brooks, *Mormon Chronicle*, 2:343. The other guards were apparently members of the military encampment at Fort Cameron.

should have been spent on the jury" to obtain an outright acquittal. He added, "They openly threaten to rescue Dame and Lee."[57]

Historians Cleland and Brooks take from the diaries of Lee the following account, which tells of some mutual acceptance, even fondness, between Lee and Maxwell:

> Strongly guarded, we drove to Pine creek ranch for the Night. The Gen and I Bunked down together. At the Daun of day I went in search of wood and when I had a fire burning I called up the General to warm. The guard was enraped and soundly sleeping in the arms of Morphiues. The Gen. looked arround seeing the guard all asleep turned to Me with a smile said I believe you are the best guard I have. The truth is the whole party was past the Maredian in Liquor.[58]

The next day, some comment of Maxwell's annoyed the driver, who was called Bear, and Lee intervened and protected Maxwell from the "Dutchman's" physical advance.[59] On their second day out, Maxwell entrusted Lee with a gun, and they shot ducks and waterfowl.[60] Lee remained armed until they boarded the railroad in Nephi. On the journey from Beaver to Nephi they were met by a carriage carrying Maxwell's wife, Mary Ann; her father, Dr. Samuel Lindsay Sprague; her brother, Samuel Lindsay Sprague, Jr., acting as deputy; and "Mrs. Robinson," very likely the widow Mrs. John King Robinson. The junior Samuel Sprague would later make a number of visits to John D. Lee at the Utah prison. If Maxwell armed Lee in anticipation of an attempt by Hickman or others to assassinate him, it seems contradictory, even foolhardy, for Maxwell to have arranged for his wife and in-laws to meet his party on the road.

An incongruous collection of people were now assembled on the road northward from Beaver. Three of them had been among the faithful of the Mormon Church from its early days in Nauvoo, but their lives had gone in widely diverse paths. First was William Adams "Wild Bill" Hickman, who had been converted to Mormonism and baptized by John D. Lee.[61] Hickman had practiced law in Nauvoo and later in Utah and, along with Lee, was a former member of Joseph Smith's elite bodyguard and an alleged leader of the Danites, or, in Mormon terms the Destroying Angels. In January 1857, in the midst of the Utah

---

[57] Fielding and Fielding, *Trials of John D. Lee*, 196.
[58] Cleland and Brooks, *Mormon Chronicle*, 343–44.
[59] Ibid., 344.
[60] Lee's diary says, "We had W. S. Lake improved needle guns." Ibid., 345.
[61] Bagley, *Blood of the Prophets*, 20.

War, Brigham Young wrote to President Buchanan, complaining that federal officials sent to Utah had been unsuitable in the extreme and requesting that federal appointments be made from locals, from among the Mormons of the territory. Young named Hickman as a candidate for Utah's U.S. attorney.[62] At the time, Hickman was widely acknowledged as acting outside the law, willing to carry out any directive that Young gave him.[63] Hickman had transported the first cash payment of Brigham Young's Y. X. Express mail contract from the federal government, served in the guerrilla forces who destroyed federal property in the Utah War, and admitted to killing Richard Yates for selling supplies to federal troops. He was a spiritual "adopted" son of Brigham Young, but to one newspaper correspondent he was "a Missouri border ruffian, a polygamist, and a human hyena."[64] Now sixty years old, Hickman had recently been released from jail and was regarded as a Mormon outcast. In addition to the murder of Yates, Hickman was widely suspected of involvement in the murders of Sgt. Ralph Pike in 1859 and Dr. John King Robinson in 1866 and in the death of John Varah Long, Brigham Young's former scribe, in 1869.[65] Hickman had been appointed to the task of guarding Lee by Governor George W. Emery, who had been in office only a little more than a month. Apparently Emery did not recognize the incongruity of having a man widely considered as having murdered under the instigation of Mormon leaders now guarding Lee, widely considered to have killed a number of the Arkansas emigrants at the instigation or complicity of Mormon leaders.[66]

---

[62] MacKinnon, *At Sword's Point*, 67–73.

[63] MacKinnon, review of *Camp Floyd and the Mormons*, 231. Hickman's status changed dramatically. He had been a territorial legislator representing Green River County at the first legislative session in Fillmore, Utah, and in January 1855 a bill was passed giving the entire Rush Valley to him and to Luke S. Johnson, Brigham Young, Orrin Porter Rockwell, and other prominent Mormons. At the 1857 legislative session, however, the gift to Hickman and the others was rescinded. Blanthorn, *History of Tooele County*, 288.

[64] Schindler, *Orrin Porter Rockwell*, 359. Brigham Young's "adopted" spirit-sons had been "sealed" in the Mormon temple to be his sons in the afterlife.

[65] Hickman, with George A. Stringham, was linked to the murder of army sergeant Ralph Pike. In 1859 Pike was patrolling in Tooele County when, during an altercation with a young Mormon farmer named Howard Orson Spencer, he inflicted several serious head wounds on the farmer. Dr. Samuel Sprague treated Spencer, who eventually recovered, but some months later Pike was killed while walking on the streets of Salt Lake City. Quinn, *Mormon Hierarchy*, 245, 530. The most recent treatment of this episode is found in Sadler, "Spence-Pike Affair."

[66] The First Presidency of the LDS church authorized the posthumous rebaptism of Hickman on March 21, 1934, and all of "his former blessings restored" by proxy on May 5, 1934. Quinn, *Mormon Hierarchy*, 768.

The second in this trio of Mormon faithful was, of course, John D. Lee, who had been an early, zealous convert to the church, a member of Joseph Smith's special bodyguard, also an adopted spirit-son of Brigham Young, and a member of the ultrasecret Council of Fifty in Nauvoo. During the 1846 trek of the Mormon Battalion, Young had entrusted Lee to carry the cash of the first service pay for the battalion from Santa Fe to Omaha. Lee's diary recording the battalion's march made him, according to Bigler and Bagley, "one of the best Mormon journalists of his day."[67] Young later picked Lee to be one of the principal colonizers of southern Utah. But now Lee was in limbo, somewhere between revered, abandoned, and possibly marked for death.

The third adopted spirit-son of Brigham Young in the group was General Maxwell's father-in-law, Dr. Sprague. Born in Massachusetts, he was an early Mormon convert and pioneer. As the first doctor to come to the Great Salt Lake valley, he had been the personal physician for Brigham Young and his family and had ministered to the health needs of many of the Indians in the area.

Among the others traveling with the Lee assemblage, Samuel Lindsay Sprague, Jr., had been a court bailiff, a U.S. commissioner, and a sometime deputy marshal. His wife, Anna Marian Kimball, was the daughter of pioneer Indian fighter and Pony Express rider William Henry Kimball and the granddaughter of Mormon apostle Heber C. Kimball. Added to this already strange list was Mrs. Robinson, probably Ellen "Nellie" Kay Robinson, Dr. John King Robinson's widow. The doctor had been murdered in 1866 at the alleged instigation, if not by the very hand, of Hickman, who now accompanied the group as a guard.[68] Also present was Mary Ann Sprague Maxwell, who, along with her father,

---

[67] Bigler and Bagley, *Army of Israel*, 107–108.

[68] Ellen Kay was the daughter of John Kay, a faithful Mormon polygamist who had been for a time a Utah territorial marshal, but in 1859 Chief Justice Delana R. Eckels and U.S. marshal Dotson refused to appoint him as a deputy U.S. marshal, for he was a "notorious Mormon." Alexander, *Brigham Young*, 22. It is very unlikely that the Mrs. Robinson on the trip from Beaver was the wife of a little-known lawyer of that surname with whom Maxwell may have been briefly affiliated. A man named W. F. Robinson advertised in the *Tribune* in 1871 as a dentist in Salt Lake City, but no relationship with the Maxwells can be found. *SLT*, December 11, 1871, 3, col. 3. According to the 1880 census, widowed Nellie Kay Robinson, age thirty-one, was living with her mother only two blocks from twenty-nine-year-old Mary Ann Sprague Maxwell, who was also in her parents' household. Her husband, George R. Maxwell, was not in town. Indirect evidence supports the two women having developed many areas of common interest.

had been accused by Brigham Young of spreading rumors that Young possessed a sword that had been used in Robinson's murder.

Lacking a large contingent of soldiers, Maxwell may have planned this strange assembly of people to make it utterly incredulous for an armed attack or rescue mission on the person of John D. Lee to take place. Maxwell may have armed Lee out of fear that Hickman was under secret order to kill Lee before he could be brought to another trial. Maxwell and the widow Robinson may have reasoned that John D. Lee or Hickman had knowledge of Dr. Robinson's killer or of Brigham Young's complicity in Robinson's fate, and hoped the protection and secluded circumstances of the trail would facilitate unburdening one or both of them of such information. At the evening campfire, if the bottle was passed, it was possible that the talk might turn to Mountain Meadows. The existence of the sword alleged to have been used in Dr. Robinson's murder might arise, and perhaps Hickman would admit to the details. But the reality was that Hickman was traveling in the company of a U.S. marshal and, even if he could have provided enlightenment, would have been unlikely to put himself at risk of arrest.

Both General Maxwell and John D. Lee had at times been active Masons, Lee during the early history of the LDS church in Illinois.[69] Maxwell had joined while in Michigan during a lull in Civil War service, but his name is absent from the Masonic attendance records of the Salt Lake City lodges, and Lee's Masonic activities probably ended when he came to Utah. If their shared membership in Freemasonry enhanced their relationship or led to any increase in Lee's trust in Maxwell, there is no evidence to substantiate it.[70]

At a saloon and trading establishment near the Sevier River, Maxwell treated the group to food and drink; at evening the junior Mr. Sprague insisted on placing Lee in irons. The next morning, Maxwell removed the irons and insisted on leaving them off for the remainder of their passage. By midday on August 12 they arrived in Nephi, where Lee had his first sight of a railroad train. Maxwell "called for a Gill of the best brandy" for Lee, who "enjoyed the ride into the city all the

---

[69] Novak, *House of Mourning*, 142–44.

[70] Maxwell spoke before the Improved Order of Red Men while in Utah and may have been a member of this group. Other fraternal groups active in Salt Lake City at the time were the Odd Fellows, the Knights of Pythias, and the Knights Templar, but there is no evidence of Maxwell's having joined any of them.

more because General Maxwell, still sitting beside him, pointed out improvements, new buildings and businesses, and told him something of who owned them and what they typified."[71] The group transferred to the train to continue their journey, and Lee later wrote about their arrival by railroad car in Salt Lake City: "Gen Max sat down by me, and talked verry [*sic*] kindly, pointed out the Principle Buildings and their owners. . . . [He] was careful to avoid any demonstrations and . . . took [me] to a fine carriage with matched sorrell [*sic*] horses."[72] A crowd met the train at the Salt Lake depot, but the fine carriage of President Brigham Young was not among them.[73] Marshal Maxwell put Lee into the care of his friend, fellow Michigan cavalryman, and now penitentiary warden, Matthew B. Burgher, and returned to see Lee on August 31. Juanita Brooks describes that visit:

> [Maxwell] took Lee down into the city in a carriage drawn by a span of fine mares and allowed him to shop in different stores for items that he wanted—pills, hair tonic and a silk handkerchief among them—and bought him a box of cigars and a flask of whiskey with which to treat his friends. Best of all, he advised Lee as to his future, warning him that Sutherland and Houge had "an object to accomplish, aside from mine, which is more important to them than mine, hense they would use me as a tool and keep me lingering in prison for year to year."[74]

Maxwell's chief argument was that Lee should make himself a witness against Dame and others, and Maxwell promised him that if he would do that, he could return to Beaver, have his wife live with him, and get a trial within a month. Lee considered this and tentatively promised to comply. On September 23, Maxwell again visited Lee, bringing with him Deputy Marshal Stokes. According to Fawn Brodie's account, it was Stokes "who promised to take Lee out immediately if he would tell his story in full." Brodie added that "both of these men had been kind to him and had shown such a real interest in his welfare that Lee knew them to be sincere."[75] Again Lee resolved that he would not testify against anyone. In October, Lee said of Maxwell: "He had never tried to befriend a Man more than he had Me with as little success." Juanita

---

[71] Brooks, *John Doyle Lee*, 344.   [72] Cleland and Brooks, *Mormon Chronicle*, 2:348.
[73] "City Jottings," *slt*, August 13, 1875, 4, col. 1.
[74] Brooks, *John Doyle Lee*, 345. Typographical errors in the original have been preserved in this quotation.   [75] Quoted in ibid., 346.

Brooks notes that Maxwell had decided to set Lee free, as Klingensmith had been, "if he would only tell his story."[76]

Marshal Maxwell and Warden Burgher made an arrangement that Lee was not required to live in the regular prison cells but could reside with his wife, Rachel, in an area near the warden's quarters. This was done in exchange for chores performed by Lee, for cooking done by Rachel, and five dollars a month in cash paid to Warden Burgher. When Lee first arrived at the prison, he said that Burgher "appears to be a gentleman" and told further of the kindness he was afforded: "I feel under a thousand obligations to Capt Burgher and Maxwell and to Mr. Ward and lady, for heaven knows that I dreaded to go back in that prison."[77]

Oliver Andrew Patton accompanied Maxwell on some of his visits to Lee in the penitentiary. Willett Pottenger, Maxwell's successor in the land office, had in turn been succeeded by Patton, whose wife Rachel Ellen Tompkins was first cousin to President Ulysses Grant.[78] The Patton family became close friends of George R. and Mary Ann Maxwell, and Patton had written strong letters of support to the U.S. attorney general, attesting to Maxwell's integrity and capability as marshal.[79] During a visit to Lee in early September 1875, Patton had spoken to him and promised to keep him informed of the happenings in the city and the territory by sending him the *Salt Lake Herald*. Shortly thereafter, Lee commented that the newspaper came in the mail with his name printed on the wrapper. In thanks, Lee composed the following acrostic poem dedicated to Patton:

[76] Brooks, *John Doyle Lee*, 347.
[77] Letter from John D. Lee to his children, January 18, 1876, quoted in Kelly, *Journals of John D. Lee*, 239.
[78] President Grant would not have been entirely comfortable with his cousin's marriage, as Patton had fought with the Confederacy in the Civil War. He founded Patton's Rangers in Morgan County, Kentucky, in the spring of 1863. The six companies operated for the most part behind federal lines in Kentucky. In October 1863, Colonel Patton was in command when the units were captured near the Cumberland River. Maxwell and Patton's relationship had the same obstacle to overcome, that of being former Civil War adversaries.
[79] The Pattons were also close friends of Jacob S. Boreman, who had attended law school at the University of Virginia in Charlottesville and, while there, was the roommate of William Tompkins, Rachel's brother. Rachel's sister Virginia was also the object of Boreman's attention at the time she attended the French Seminary school in Washington, Pennsylvania. Arrington, "Crusade against Theocracy," 35.

Col., I gratefully accept your generous gift
Only found in a true manly heart.
Long may you live in memory of the Just,
On Syophants to cast a frowning Dart.
Lo, you met me in a Prison cell,
In sadness, deep sorrow and grief.
Verry Kindly you came with a spirit that Tells
Every moment that I sighed for Relief.
Regardless of fear, frowns or Position,
As an act of Benevolence you sent me the Paper,
Presed with the sense of my lonely condition,
And lighted my mind in a clear burning Taper.
This little kiness produced a sensation
That Tonge would fail to express.
Once more I acknowledge with true aceptation.
Nothing more can I give while in Distress.[80]

While Lee remained in the penitentiary in Salt Lake City, Maxwell continued his pursuit of others charged with the Mountain Meadows crimes. About September 19, 1875, Marshal Stokes and a posse comitatus attempted to arrest Haight, Higbee, Stewart, and Willden at St. George in southern Utah but failed because of telegraphed warnings to the men. George W. Adair was captured in Richfield in early November by deputies Barton, Fish, and Winn.[81]

Lee's detailed account of prison life in November 1875 confirms the validity of messages Maxwell had been sending to Washington, conveying that he had insufficient funds to supply food, coal, and other provisions for prisoners at the penitentiary. Lee shared his food ration with a man named Tracy, who was awaiting trial for murder. Men were burning benches and bunk boards, breaking up anything that would burn, in order to generate heat. Inadequate food and other deprivations from underfunding were in part the motive for a jailbreak on March 14, 1876, that resulted in the fatal beating of Warden Burgher.[82] Burgher's head and face were smashed by the escapees with a stone encased in a sock and swung. Burgher, who had been Maxwell's Civil War companion, the

---

[80] The spelling errors in the poem are unchanged from its publication in *slh*, October 20, 1875.
[81] Cleland and Brooks, *Mormon Chronicle*, 365–83.
[82] Escapees were James Gaines, Charles Williamson, Charles Patterson, Joseph Smith, W. T. Bell, W. D. Phelps, and J. H. Davis. Burgher's murder is treated by Robert Kirby in his book of Utah officers killed in the line of duty. Kirby, *End of Watch*, 17–21.

man with whom he had survived as a prisoner of the Confederates and whom he had awarded the post of prison warden, died in the early hours of March 16, 1876, from severe brain injury.[83] At the request of the officers of the penitentiary, John D. Lee, even though he was a prisoner awaiting his own trial for mass murder, kindly attended Warden Burgher through the coma that marked his final hours.[84] Burgher was buried in the Camp Douglas military cemetery overlooking the Salt Lake Valley.[85]

May 30 of the year marking the one hundredth anniversary of the nation's birth was accompanied by more than an ordinary honoring of fallen veterans in Salt Lake City. Despite heavy rain, a large crowd formed in front of the Federal Courthouse and proceeded north to the South Temple Street, then east to Camp Douglas. Notables on the parade stand were Judge James B. McKean, General Maxwell, Colonels Albert Hagan and Ovander J. Hollister, and Sumner Howard.[86] The ceremonies were inaugurated by General Maxwell, who introduced Michael Schaeffer, the recently arrived chief justice of the Third District Court, as president of the day. After a brief address by Schaeffer, Judge McKean was the orator of the day. As McKean's speech ended, the storm abated, allowing members of the Grand Army of the Republic to decorate the graves with floral tributes. All veterans' graves were honored, but the graves with the greatest profusion of flowers were those of the murdered Dr. John King Robinson, the recently buried Capt. Matthew Burgher, and Lt. Robert P. Warren, the younger brother of noted Civil War general Gouverneur Kemble Warren. The junior Warren served in Company F of the Fourteenth U.S. Infantry until he died suddenly of a stroke at Camp Douglas.[87]

---

[83] Burgher served in the Michigan Cavalry, reaching the rank of lieutenant. In June 1864 near Lexington, Kentucky, he received a commendation. *OR*, I, 39, part 1: 45. After the war, Burgher was a mail carrier in Pittsburgh before coming west to Colorado and Utah. Kirby, *End of Watch*, 17–21.

[84] Brooks, *John Doyle Lee*, 351; Cleland and Brooks, *Mormon Chronicle*, 437–42.

[85] "Burial of Capt. Bergher," *SLT*, March 21, 1876, 4, col. 7, noted that "the body of Captain Berger was carried . . . to Camp Douglas cemetery for interment." Reference kindly supplied by Su Richards, research archivist, Fort Douglas Military Museum, Salt Lake City.

[86] Albert Hagan, who married Brigham Young's daughter Eudora, was the law partner of Frank Tilford and had acted in behalf of Ann Eliza Webb Young in her divorce from Brigham Young. It was also Hagan who, with Sumner Howard, represented the state prosecutors in the Utah Supreme Court appeal of John D. Lee's conviction for murder at Mountain Meadows.

[87] "Decoration Day," *SLT*, June 1, 1876, 4; "Death of Lient [*sic*] Warren," *SLT*, January 25, 1876, 4, col. 6.

LEE'S SECOND TRIAL

Oliver Andrew Patton and General Maxwell were not the only visitors John D. Lee received at the penitentiary. Lee recorded that Marshal Stokes, an attorney named Robinson, attorney John R. McBride, a deputy named McArty, and Samuel Lindsay Sprague, Jr., came to see him.[88] However much Lee appreciated the kindness offered him, he was adamant that he would maintain silence about other individuals involved in the massacre. Even when fellow Mormons William Adams Hickman and George Stringham visited, Lee responded to them as he had to others: "The Same old Storry was harped upon, that for Me to Make a clean sweep of all & be free. Our interview was Short, as I replied I would Stand by Record. I would never PurJure Myself to get out, & thus we parted."[89]

The first trial for the mass murders of Mountain Meadows ended with a mistrial. The single man who had been tried, John D. Lee, was awaiting retrial. The prosecution team of U.S. attorneys and the U.S. marshal responsible for the trial were released from their appointments and replaced. William Nelson, George R. Maxwell's successor in both the marshalship and the prosecution team, claimed, as did others, that the first legal team of Carey, Baskin, and Maxwell had failed to convict Lee because it focused unduly on the involvement of Brigham Young and other high Mormon authorities. Either the aim of the first team was too high and they got nothing, or the leading men of Zion were not yet convinced that Lee should become their sacrificial offering to appease justice. Whether either or both were true, the American public was outraged at the failure to secure a measure of justice for crimes that could not have been committed by one man acting alone.

Lee's second trial lasted only six days. Mormon witnesses regained clear memory; Daniel H. Wells testified and cast his eye over the all-Mormon jurors who unanimously found Lee guilty of first-degree murder. Lee was sentenced to death, unsuccessfully appealed, and was executed by a firing squad on the site of the Mountain Meadows murders on March 21, 1877. No one else was ever tried for the crimes.[90]

---

[88] Cleland and Brooks, *Mormon Chronicle*, 376–77.   [89] Ibid., 382.

[90] John D. Lee and Isaac C. Haight were also "punished" by formal excommunication from the Mormon Church on October 8, 1870. However, Haight's membership and full standing were restored in 1874, twelve years before he died. John D. Lee's status was restored posthumously on April 20, 1961, by action of the First Presidency of the Church of Jesus Christ of Latter-day Saints and the Quorum of the Twelve Apostles. William H. Dame, the highest-ranking officer of the local Utah militia officers, was released from federal custody and remained officially in good standing with the LDS church until his death in 1884.

II

Marshal Maxwell's Muddle

It is good to kill an admiral from time to time
to encourage the others.
Voltaire

MARSHAL GEORGE R. MAXWELL HAD FOUR LEVIATHANS TO FACE
simultaneously. The first was the trial of John Doyle Lee, and the second
was his transfer to the penitentiary in Salt Lake City, both treated in
the previous chapter. The third was Maxwell's desperate need for large
sums of money for the various expenses of federal activities incurred at
Beaver and in the other two districts of the territory. His battle against
efforts, from powerful sources he did not clearly identify, to have him
removed from the marshalship during Lee's trial and transfer was the
fourth.

FINANCIAL PROBLEMS

In December 1874, Maxwell received criticism from U.S. attorney general George H. Williams, who claimed—incorrectly—that the First
National Bank of Utah was not the designated place for the deposit
of U.S. Treasury funds. Maxwell had carefully documented deposits
going to the First National of Utah, as well as the transfer of the funds
to a New York City bank. Maxwell reminded Williams that his predecessor, Marshal Mathewson Patrick, had received special instructions

to make deposits at the First National and that all of the marshals' reports were clear about where the money had been routed.[1]

Neither Williams nor Maxwell appears to have known of the convoluted financial actions involving Treasury Department officials, Utah territorial secretary George A. Black, and U.S. attorney William Carey that had placed Maxwell in fiscal jeopardy and alienated those he dealt with in Washington. Historian Thomas G. Alexander gives this account: "In September, 1873, Black received a federal bank draft of $10,000 as an advance on the legislative expenses for 1874. As he was required to do, Black deposited it in the First National Bank of Utah, a designated United States depository."[2] Carey had heard local rumors suggesting that the bank was in a precarious financial status and so advised Black, who then went to the bank president and demanded payment on the draft. After reporting to Washington officials that the bank president refused payment, Black was ordered to return the draft to Washington for deposit in the New York subtreasury. Black later wrote a check for $10,000 on the New York subtreasury and deposited it in the Salt Lake City National Bank, which was solvent but not a designated federal depository. Reprimands came from Washington, and Black was again instructed to deposit the money to the First National Bank of Utah. Apparently unknown to Washington officials was that this bank was now beset with involuntary liquidation. For a second time, Black transferred the funds to the New York subtreasury. By 1876 Black's successor, Moses M. Bane, was still required to keep funds at the New York bank.[3] Williams's criticisms of Maxwell's financial transactions were clearly invalid, but their letters of disagreement may have set a tone of ill will against Maxwell within the already troubled Justice Department by the time allegations of money mismanagement were brought by Maxwell's opponents in Utah Territory.

---

[1] This exemplifies problems in communication that plagued the Justice Department. Attorney General Williams clearly did not know of the March 15, 1872, letter from George S. Boutwell, secretary of the treasury, naming the First National Bank of Utah as the agent for safekeeping and disbursing of public funds. The failure of the First National Bank of Utah initiated Maxwell's financial woes, while wiping out the fortune of its owner, Warren G. Hussey. Arrington, "Taxable Income in Utah," 29.   [2] T. G. Alexander, *Clash of Interests*, 19.

[3] Utah's congressional delegate George Q. Cannon very likely knew a great deal about the financial dislocations described, as he had intervened in 1874 when territorial secretary Black was short of money for legislative expenses. Cannon approached President Garfield and helped obtain a deficiency appropriation for Utah. Ibid., 16–20.

An additional instance when federal parsimony and inefficiency affected financial affairs in Utah that coincided with those of Marshal Maxwell is recorded by Alexander. Federal appropriations paid expenses of territorial legislative sessions, including per diem and travel compensation for legislators. The 1874 legislative session in Utah expended $24,786; however, only $20,000 had been appropriated, leaving territorial secretary Black short $4,786. Utah's congressional delegate George Q. Cannon appealed to James Garfield's Appropriations Committee for additional money, but this was not approved until four months after the legislature had adjourned.[4]

In December, Attorney General Williams had letters in hand from Ohio senator Allen Granberry Thurman and Mormon-aligned Utah attorney George Caesar Bates, alleging discrimination by Utah marshals against seating on juries of those "holding the Mormon doctrine."[5] Williams demanded an explanation from U.S. attorney William Carey that he or Marshal Maxwell may have had regarding the matter. Without mentioning Maxwell, Carey explained that polygamists had not been denied seating by marshals and that any perceived discrimination was the result of their conduct in answering questions during jury selection.

Immediately after Christmas 1874, Maxwell and Utah governor George L. Woods traveled to Washington, D.C., with the goal of obtaining money for the marshal's office. Derision and innuendo characterized the reports published in the two Mormon newspapers, the *Salt Lake Herald* and *Deseret News*:

AFTER DOLLARS

U.S. Marshal Maxwell has gone to Washington to urge upon Congress the necessity of appropriating $25,000—more or less—to grease the wheels of the federal courts in this territory. The bills have been coming into the marshal's office just a trifle fast of late, and there was danger of the establishment being swamped. The "gineral" has got an elephant on his hands, and it requires some lively skirmishing to gather provender for the beast.[6]

---

[4] Ibid., 16–18. Before 1873 such funds came from Treasury appropriations; after 1873 they came from the Department of Interior.

[5] RG 60, Chronological Files, 1871–84, box 1015. Bates was, by now, on the Mormon payroll.

[6] "After Dollars," *SLH*, December 30, 1874, 3, col. 3; "Marshal Maxwell," *SLH*, December 30, 1874, 3, col. 4.

Gone to Washington

Governor George L. Woods and the high-toned U.S. Marshal Maxwell
are now en route for Washington, having departed for that point yesterday morning as emissaries of the crusading ring.[7]

Over a three-month period, Woods encountered great difficulty in
obtaining $23,400 from the general appropriations bill, as the amend-
ment passed through five conference committees. Congressman Cannon
succeeded in having it struck in all instances but the last. Woods also was
able to procure an allowance for General Maxwell to defray some of the
expenses associated with his contest of the seating of Cannon.[8]

Judge James B. McKean, seeing more clearly than Maxwell where
the financial stringency to which he was being exposed would end,
advised him to "come into Court and make his statement, setting
forth his inability to pay the expenses of administering justice, and
. . . adjourn the Court."[9] Marshal Maxwell, it will be seen, rejected
this advice, choosing to carry out his duties while either ignoring his
personal liability or believing that Washington funds would be forthcoming.

As the months of early 1875 passed, Maxwell's financial difficulties
reached a crescendo. In January he asked Attorney General Williams
for $30,000 in court expenses and an additional $4,000 for repair of the
penitentiary. By February 18 there was an urgent, almost frantic tone in
Maxwell's sparingly worded telegram to Williams: "Penitentiary full
of territorial cases. No supplies. Telegraph instructions. I cannot hold
out much longer."[10] Maxwell was now reeling from the financial impact
caused by the territorial legislature's failure to fund the activities of law
officers. The reception of his appeals in Washington was not sympathetic. Local observers of the Utah scene declared their understanding of what was taking place: "If money is sought from the Territorial
Treasury to pay Court expenses, the answer comes 'we will do this, if

---

[7] "Gone to Washington," *DN*, December 19, 1874, 3, col. 3. The criticism continued: "It is reported
that two [federal] officers [Maxwell and Woods] have just left on this annual log-rolling
business. Have they obtained leave of absence? . . . If they have not, they [ought] to be made
examples of for their audacious neglect of duty." "Absent Without Leave," *DN*, December 30,
1874, 2, col. 3.

[8] "A Friend in Need," *SLT*, March 21, 1875, 2, col. 2; "Appropriations for the Courts in Utah," *SLT*,
March 5, 1875, 1, col. 5.

[9] "Marshal Maxwell Chepes In," *SLT*, December 15, 1875, 2, col. 1.

[10] RG 60, Chronological Files, 1871–84, box 1016.

Utah Territorial Penitentiary/U.S. Penitentiary,
in Sugarhouse, near Salt Lake City, about 1870. *Used by permission,*
Utah State Historical Society, #6138, all rights reserved.

you do this.' If pay for prisoner's keeping is demanded the condition is
'we will pay the money if you will do so-and-so.' This is the common
practice with the Priesthood and their tools."[11]

In March 1875, Maxwell was involved with the trial of Thomas E.
Ricks of Logan, accused of the 1860 murder of Elisha David Skeen.
Ricks, a Mormon of high standing, was not convicted, and church
influence was suspected in the outcome. Important to the matter of
Maxwell's finances was the trial expense of approximately $2,000,
adding to his already mounting financial woes.[12]

Ann Eliza Webb Young Revisited

In the latter part of February and the first weeks in March 1875, Maxwell returned to the divorce of Ann Eliza Webb Young and delivered
a court order to Brigham Young to pay her support of $500 per month,

---

[11] Fielding and Fielding, *Trials of John D. Lee*, 52.
[12] "Marshal Maxwell and His Accounts," *SLT*, February 2, 1876, 2, col. 1.

Matthew B. Burgher, a former
Michigan Cavalry lieutenant, was
with Maxwell when both were taken
prisoners during the war. He was
later the Utah prison warden and
was murdered by prison escapees.
Courtesy Archives of Michigan.

as well as $3,000 in attorney fees within ten days and another $9,500
within twenty days. Young failed to do this, and on March 10, Judge
McKean ordered the U.S. marshal to arrest him and bring him to court
to answer charges of contempt. Deputy Marshal Amos K. Smith was
the person who responded to this order, for Marshal Maxwell had been
urgently called to Michigan by his father, and he did not return to Salt
Lake City until March 12.[13] James Jack, the church financial secretary,
paid the $3,000 in attorney's fees and Young's fine of $25, and Young
was imprisoned in the penitentiary for one day. Edward W. Tullidge
reports that the Utah populace was agitated by his imprisonment, but
no violence ensued.[14] A very different description of the people's mood
was reported by Frederic Lockley:

> [Young's] fanatical followers regarded this as persecution, and hundreds
> of armed men turned out with their families to encamp all night round
> the penitentiary, bivouacking in the snow. Some of the squads placed

---

[13] "Personal," *slt*, March 13, 1875, 4, col. 1. The nature of the emergency that called Maxwell to
Michigan is unknown.

[14] "Prometheus Bound," *slt*, March 13, 1875, 2, col. 1; Tullidge, *History of Salt Lake City*, 616.

themselves so near to the entrance that passage was obstructed, and the warden [Matthew B. Burgher] supposed this was part of a design of meditated assault. He had given up a dwelling room to his prisoner and attendants, and entering the apartment, he made this announcement: "Mr. Young, your people are camped outside the prison wall by the thousand, and I find myself hindered in exit and entrance. I don't know what their intention is, but one thing is certain: If violence is resorted to, you'll be the first man to fall."[15]

Within two days of Brigham's imprisonment by Marshal Maxwell, James C. Burke of New York submitted an application to the U.S. attorney general, stating his understanding there was "a decided probability of removal of the Marshal of Utah."[16] Also within days of Young's imprisonment, James B. McKean, the initial judge in the *Young v. Young* case, was notified by telegram from President Ulysses Grant that he had been removed from the bench.[17] In the opinion of the non-Mormon historian Robert Joseph Dwyer, the handling of the Brigham Young divorce action by McKean and Maxwell generated criticism against them rather than against the accused: "The Ann Eliza case, with its ludicrous implications and its attempt to embarrass in his age a man for whom the nation, with all its disapproval of his moral code, felt a certain respect as a pioneer, and a colonizer, was . . . a blunder."[18]

That the reaction time against Maxwell and McKean was measured in days seemingly confirmed that their actions had triggered major ill

---

[15] Lockley Papers, 58.

[16] In 1863 Col. James C. Burke attempted to reorganize the Eleventh New York Infantry, made up of firemen (Fire Zouaves.) This was not successful, in part because of riots in New York City over the draft. New York State Military Museum and Veterans Research Center, Unit History Project, "11th Infantry Regiment, Civil War," www.dmna.state.ny.us/historic/reghist/civil/infantry/11thInf/11thInfMain.htm.

[17] Frederic Lockley said McKean "was remiss in not visiting Washington occasionally, to renew acquaintance with his former chief [Grant]" and "lacked the arts of the courtier, resting content with the belief that a faithful performance of duty was sufficient." Lockley manuscript, 60. McKean wrote a pleading letter to B. R. Brown of the Department of the Interior, and another to Attorney General Edwards Pierrepont, asking why he was removed and seeking a personal meeting with the president. This was never granted. Judge Jacob Boreman reported that Stephen J. Field, associate justice of the Supreme Court and Timothy O. Howe, Wisconsin's senator, both asked President Grant for McKean's removal while Grant was preoccupied over matters of the Reconstruction. Thomas Alexander asserts that McKean's censure of Salt Lake City lawyer George E. Whitney, the brother-in-law of both Field and Howe, was the inciting event in McKean's discharge. Boreman claimed that Grant later regretted his removal of McKean. McKean was urged to apply for other positions but refused. T. G. Alexander, "Federal Authority versus Polygamic Theocracy," 96–97; Arrington, "Crusade against Theocracy," 33–35.   [18] Dwyer, *Gentile Comes to Utah*, 92.

will from those in the East who had power to influence their removal.[19] McKean had been a critic of, and an impediment to, Mormon leaders, polygamy, and theocracy from his arrival in Utah Territory. Contemporary accounts of his tenure by his opponents describe an almost evangelical fervor against Mormons and their beliefs.[20]

Justice Alexander White had taken office in late September 1875 but was allegedly taken ill and functioned only intermittently. Judge Jacob Boreman was standing in for White on October 19 and ordered Brigham Young to appear on October 23 before the Third District Court to show just cause why he should not be held in contempt for failure to pay alimony to Ann Eliza Webb Young as ordered by Judge McKean. Brigham Young sent his counsel Jabez G. Sutherland to answer the charge, asking that the matter be delayed. On November 1, General Maxwell reported to John D. Lee that Young was confined to his home, guarded by Deputy Marshals Pratt and Porter.[21] On November 3, Maxwell remarked to John D. Lee that Young was a very sick man whose recovery was doubtful.[22]

In the midst of criticism directed at Maxwell and the marshal's office, the writ that he received on November 12 for delivery to Brigham Young was an ill-timed challenge:

> You are hereby commanded to have the body of Brigham Young . . . before the undersigned Alexander White, Chief Justice of the Supreme Court of said Territory at the Judge's chambers, . . . in the Federal Court house in Salt Lake City . . . on Wednesday, the 17th inst., at ten o'clock A.M. of said day, . . . to be dealt with according to the law, and to abide such order as the said Judge shall make in the premises.[23]

---

[19] The *Salt Lake Herald* accused McKean of judicial misconduct relating to litigation about mining ventures in which he had a personal interest. Allegations were also raised that *Salt Lake Tribune* editor Oscar G. Sawyer had allowed McKean to write anonymous editorials that prematurely revealed information from cases pending before the court. T. G. Alexander, "Federal Authority versus Polygamic Theocracy," 96–99.

[20] Careful reading of a letter written by McKean in November 1873 to Attorney General Williams provides an example that McKean was capable of a cautious, reasoned approach against the theocratic oligarchy. George Q. Cannon was the single most influential force in Washington who likely worked for the removal of Maxwell and McKean.

[21] Brigham Young's son complained that the demands of guards checking on his father every hour through the night was excessive and harsh and asked that they stop. Maxwell granted the request. "Brigham's Body Guard," *SLT*, October 31, 1875, 4, col. 2.

[22] Cleland and Brooks, *Mormon Chronicle*, 2:385.

[23] "Habeas Corpus," *DN*, November 15, 1875, 3, col. 3.

This matter was temporarily resolved when White freed the ailing Brigham Young on the grounds that Boreman's previous order was void.

The Ann Eliza Young divorce action was finally settled only a few months prior to Brigham Young's death in 1877. Alexander White's successor, Judge Michael Schaeffer, ruled that the marriage to Ann Eliza Webb Dee was not a valid contract, and she was awarded only the wages of a menial servant.[24] The case had taken four years and involved five judges; Brigham Young had been held in contempt twice and had spent one day in jail. This made it clear that under the Mormon system of polygamy all but the first wife had less than a full marriage and lacked protection under the law.

THE MOVEMENT TO REMOVE MAXWELL

In addition to criticism over his involvement in Brigham Young's divorce, other events indicated that a movement was afoot to remove Maxwell from the office of U.S. marshal. On March 24, Maxwell dismissed Alonzo G. Paddock as warden of the penitentiary for general incompetency and for bringing criticism on Maxwell by allowing prisoners to escape. Through March, April, and May, several letters were sent to the U.S. attorney general nominating individuals for the post of Utah Territory's U.S. marshal. Paddock himself was nominated by his influential cousin, Nebraska senator Algernon S. Paddock.[25] George Q. Cannon nominated James A. Williamson, the land agent for the Union Pacific Railroad and later the commissioner of the General Land Office.

On March 30, 1875, Attorney General Williams notified Maxwell that the $23,400 appropriated by Congress in early March for court expenses in the territory would not be available until after July 1875. Maxwell replied on April 20, "I will try to hold out until the 1st of July on my personal credit."[26] On the same day, the following appeared in the *Salt Lake Tribune*: "Marshal Maxwell is incurring considerable expense in supporting and guarding this felon [John D. Lee], and as it is the invariable policy

[24] Ivins, review of *The Twenty-seventh Wife*, 377–78.
[25] Senator Algernon Paddock to Grant, telegram, July 13, 1875, RG 60, Chronological Files, 1871–84, box 1017.
[26] "Appropriations for the Courts in Utah," *SLT*, March 5, 1875, 1, col. 5; Maxwell to Williams, April 20, 1875, RG 60, Chronological Files, 1871–84, box 1017.

of the Church to hamper Federal officers and impede the execution of the law, this official [Maxwell] is kept without the means of running his office, paying penitentiary and jail expenses."[27]

Attorney General Williams retired under duress in August, and in September, S. F. Phillips, then the solicitor general, was made acting U.S. attorney general. Like Williams, Phillips was unreceptive to Maxwell's financial plight and again incorrectly accused Maxwell of "grave error" for drawing money on the New York bank after the closure of the National Bank in Salt Lake City, for incurring extraordinary expenses, and for evading letters of inquiry regarding spending. Maxwell may have known of the rumor that Phillips, along with George Q. Cannon, was energetically pushing for Maj. Edmund Wilkes to attain the marshalship, for on September 18, Maxwell bypassed Phillips and wrote directly to the newly appointed U.S. attorney general, Edwards Pierrepont:

> Pardon me for writing . . . without a personal acquaintance. Let the contents be my excuse. . . . I entered the service of the Public . . . at age 18 years, . . . and with but six months rest, have continued in it in a variety of ways. . . . I never had a position that is as difficult as my present one. I assumed the duties of this office under the most trying of circumstances: no court house, no prison, no money, and almost an entire community adverse to enforcement of the Law. I got the Attorney General to see the necessity and the "Poland Bill" passed. I spent eight months in Washington to get it through, at my own expense, and paying the personal expense of other citizens of Utah at the same time to remain in Washington to aid in the matter. . . . I carried the Courts, repaired the penitentiary, furnished court rooms . . . at my own cost and expense, in a *very* good measure.[28]

Noting that there seemed to be a change in personnel each time he managed to get officials to understand his predicament, Maxwell asked that an inspector be sent to Utah to assess matters so that the attorney general could recommend to Congress that Maxwell receive relief. In concluding his letter, Maxwell wrote: "Officers are not usually anxious for inspections. *I am.*"[29]

---

[27] "John D. Lee," *slt*, May 30, 1875, 4, col. 3.

[28] Maxwell to Pierrepont, September 18, 1875, RG 60, Chronological Files, 1871–84, box 1017. Emphasis in original.

[29] Ibid. Emphasis in original.

If Pierrepont had himself received this letter requesting an investigation of Maxwell's circumstances, the marshal may have found a receptive and sympathetic ear, for Pierrepont had described the Mormons and their polygamy as "a social system corrupting and degrading, abhorrent to the principles of the Christian religion, and never yet permitted by any Christian nation."[30] However, Pierrepont was not yet functioning in the attorney general's position, and Maxwell received his answer in another letter from Acting Attorney General Phillips, condemning him for not having paid a deputy at the penitentiary, for allegedly being drunk, and for allegedly being abusive to a deputy. Phillips had made no inquiry to investigate these allegations yet puzzlingly insisted to Maxwell that it would require "more than his word" that such allegations were not true.[31]

GRAND JURY INVESTIGATIONS

In October 1875 a grand jury made up of fifteen men was called in Salt Lake City by Judge Jacob Boreman. They were to evaluate the First Judicial District for such matters as crimes and misdemeanors, polygamy, and illegal voting and to inspect the financial records and accounts of the officials of the district.[32] With this charge to the grand jury, and to a second grand jury that he shortly thereafter called in the Second District in Beaver, Boreman was directing their efforts both toward examining Mormon practices and toward scrutinizing the non-Mormon federal judiciary and officers of two court districts in the territory.

On October 27 four members of the jury, accompanied by General Maxwell and a *Salt Lake Tribune* reporter, toured the federal penitentiary, the Lunatic Asylum, the Salt Lake County prison, and the city jail. The visit found the penitentiary warden Matthew Burgher efficient and industrious, having made many improvements and replacements of the things "stolen from the premises by A. P. Rockwood," the Mormon elder who had attempted to lay claim to the land on which the prison

---

[30] Cummings and McFarland, *Federal Justice*, 253.

[31] Phillips to Maxwell, RG 60, Chronological Files, 1871–84, box 1017.

[32] The grand jury members in Salt Lake City were Lorenzo Petit, Augustus Podlech, Stephen Hunter, W. R. Jones, W. Rench, Jacob Engler, Joseph Kierman, H. Bliss, Jacob Moritz, Edward Morgan, George E. Reid, Alfred Lemmon, James Godfrey, Joseph Smith, and Andrew Kloppenstein.

stood. The jurors reported the prison to be an "old shell, which might be blown away by a stiff breeze," but it was clean and well kept, and, they added, "with the exception of paying the guards, but little fault can be found with the management of the institution."[33] The *Tribune* wished to have other records examined as well:

> Some persons have expressed doubt about the correctness of United States Marshal Maxwell's accounts, with a sensetiveness [*sic*] over the allegation which speaks well for his honesty, that officer has submitted his books to the inspection of the Grand Jury and invited rigorous search. Let there be no whitewashing, the search should be made by experts in accounts, and the result given to the public. . . . General Maxwell's friends (and they are legion) have implicit confidence in his integrity, but since suspicion has arisen in the midst of some others of irregularities in the Marshal's office, it is due to all that his accounts should be fully searched and the result unreservedly made known. Let the City Books next be examined, the examining committee will find richness in store for them in that den of thieves. The accumulated corruption of a quarter of a century requires to be exposed, and the exploitation will be the death blow to Mormonism.[34]

The grand jury reported that it had free access to the books of the marshal's office and found them "correctly kept" and showing "in detail the amount of fee received in each case." Vouchers for expenditures and disbursements were on file, and the charges were "legal, reasonable and just." They examined the correspondence and found that the marshal had "used every occasion in his power to forward the ends of justice."[35]

In late October the *Tribune* carried an article critical of Marshal Maxwell following the escape of a prisoner from the penitentiary. Maxwell's rejoinder, including a free-verse ditty, was published in the paper the next day:

> The Almighty will never have a Judgement Day without a throne;
> Satan will never have a h——l without combustibles;
> The Tribune can never censure successfully without foundation;
> The Marshal cannot hold prisoners without a jail.
>
> The Deputy marshals will recapture at any expense all escaping prisoners; the Marshal has paid from his own means over $2,000 for recapturing

---

[33] "Investigation," *SLT*, October 27, 1875, 4, col. 2.

[34] "A Good Work Begun," *SLT*, October 28, 1875, 2, col. 1.

[35] "The Marshal's Books," *SLT*, November 2, 1875, 4, col. 2.

prisoners. The Marshal has never been paid one dollar for guards for the penitentiary, and has never been authorized to employ any, not one cent for subsistence of prisoners has yet been allowed. The Marshal has advanced every dollar in the extraordinary expense of the Lee trial; the Attorney General informs him that he must confine himself to his official duties, but he would be sustained as far as practical.[36]

To evidence their support in the midst of the criticism directed at him, members of the legal community feted Maxwell in November and gave him a generous tribute:

A number of friends assembled at General Maxwell's house, to spend the close of the festive day in social intercourse. A memorable incident . . . was the presentation of an elegant gold watch and chain to the General, Judge Robertson[] very happily expressing the kind feelings of the company to the recipient. This was responded to by the General in his usual unstudied off-hand manner. The watch and chain were purchased of Joslin & Park, the former bearing the following inscription very beautifully engraved:

Presentation to General George R. Maxwell
by his many friends
on Thanksgiving Day, 1875.[37]

"This very flattering compliment has been honestly earned by the General in a long course of services rendered to the public during his official life in Utah," said the *Tribune* in its report.[38]

A Second Grand Jury

On December 9, 1875, Judge Boreman called another grand jury, this time in Beaver, in the Second Judicial District, which shortly before had seen the extraordinarily expensive trial of John D. Lee.[39] Fourteen non-Mormons and one Mormon made up the jury, whose foreman was H. H. Lull.[40] Three days later the jury charged Marshal Maxwell with financial mismanagement and fraud and stated that he had stolen federal funds for his own pocket. The extensive notations of clerk James R. Wilkins, who

---

[36] "The General to the Front," *slt*, October 23, 1875, 1, col. 2.
[37] "Presentation," *slt*, November 28, 1875, 4, col. 3.   [38] Ibid.
[39] "Misc.," *slt*, December 10, 1875, 1, col. 3.
[40] The members of the Beaver grand jury were Michael Monahan, Jared Taylor, Thos. J. Smith, Jas. H. McCarty, James Black, Hugh Hewson, G. W. Hill, Henry H. Smith, Sidney Manning, Lorenzo Barton, David Pollock, Wm. R. Crawford, Robert Keyes, and Samuel Augell, with H. H. Lull as foreman. *DN*, November 14, 1875.

entered numerous comments in his court records that Maxwell had no money and that his reimbursement requests had been repeatedly denied, apparently were not seen by the jury members. Not only did the written record of the trial verify Maxwell's financial predicament, but deciphering of transcripts of the original trial shorthand records indicates that Maxwell frequently made statements in the courtroom about his monetary crisis. He warned the court many times that he had incurred a large indebtedness from the expenses of gathering witnesses and housing prisoners and that territorial authorities had refused to pay.[41] Citizens of Beaver were kept well informed of such details of the trial by those who attended the sessions, so Maxwell's finances were common knowledge. The report from this grand jury was inexplicably harsh on the man who was anything but secretive or obtuse about his financial status as would be expected if his goal was to steal for personal gain.

Maxwell's own deputies claimed they had observed fraud in the marshal's office. Jerome B. Cross, who had retrieved the witness Philip Klingensmith during the Lee trial, wrote that money paid for that trial did not go for those expenses. Cross claimed that expenses to witnesses, jurors, deputies, and others had not been paid, although affidavits had been made out to the contrary. He accused Maxwell of naming witnesses who were not present in the court and said that the marshal's office was a "robbing arrangement."[42] Maxwell countered that Cross brought these accusations because he knew he was about to be discharged from his position for being drunk on the job and consequently had planted materials falsely incriminating Maxwell. Arthur Pratt was more subdued, stating—as had Maxwell—that the marshal's office was bankrupt, owing "nearly every man in the county." He said, "Personally I like General Maxwell but that is no excuse for the steals that have been and are being perpetrated every day, for which I hold Gen. Maxwell less guilty than is Dr. A. K. Smith who runs the office and the General." Smith had induced other deputies to sign blank vouchers so the amounts could be collected at will.[43]

---

[41] Translation of the Rogerson version of the transcript was kindly furnished by LaJean Purcell Carruth, PhD, June 2007.

[42] Jerome B. Cross to Attorney General, December 8, 1875, RG 60, AG Papers, Utah Terr., roll 4, part 3, file 4/119.

[43] Ibid.; "Marshal Maxwell on the War-Path," *SLT*, January 14, 1876, 4, col. 4. To the contrary was the evaluation of Amos K. Smith by *Salt Lake Tribune* editor Frederic Lockley: "I knew Deputy Smith to be a vigilant, fearless officer, and he was classed among the stanchest gentiles." Lockley manuscript, 100.

Another deputy, H. L. Porter, claimed that Maxwell had not paid his expenses when he was sent to Provo as a deputy. Yet Porter had subsequently taken a position as bookkeeper with the Lincoln Mining and Smelting Company, of which Maxwell was a co-owner. Initially Porter alleged that Maxwell had instructed him to withhold financial records from the jury, but his own father "did not believe a word of his son's affidavits," and in a report published by the *Tribune*, Porter denied having made the accusations, saying the statements sent by the *Tribune* editor from Beaver concerning his allegations were "false, scandalous and libelous."[44] The *Beaver Enterprise*, however, repeated Pratt's assertion that the marshal's office was indebted to all or nearly all of his Beaver deputies for amounts from $200 to $1,000 and that officers of the court and guards at the prison had not received pay.[45] Although the accusations made by his employees were extremely disturbing, they confirmed that the messages Maxwell had been conveying to Justice Department officials regarding the massive financial crisis in the U.S. marshal's office were not exaggerated. Missing from all of the incriminations was any evidence or indication of how Maxwell had benefitted personally.

From December 13, 1875, to February 8, 1876, at least twenty-one articles were published in the territorial newspapers in response to the grand jury's report.[46] The *Deseret News*, for instance, was quick to reach its verdict and to launch an opening salvo on December 13: "OFFICIAL EMBEZZLEMENT IN THE SECOND JUDICIAL DISTRICT." Charges of financial mismanagement and possible fraud on Maxwell's part were repeated, the tone varying according to the sympathies of the newspaper. A large volume of newspaper space and many harsh words were directed against Maxwell. The more severe of the criticisms were published in the *Deseret News* on December 13, 14, and 21 and in the *Salt Lake Herald* on December 15 and 21. While also critical of Maxwell, the *Tribune* editors, having personally experienced the events of the

---

[44] "Marshal Maxwell on the War-Path"; "Mr. Porter Explains," *SLT*, January 15, 1876, 4, col. 4.

[45] *Beaver Enterprise*, December 14, 1875, RG 60, AG Papers, Utah Terr., roll 4, part 3, file 5/97; articles from *SLT* and *Beaver Enterprise*, December 13, 1875, RG 60, AG Papers, Utah Terr., roll 4, part 3, file 4/119; "The Alleged Defalcation in the United States Marshal's Accounts," *DN*, December 14, 1875.

[46] Seven pieces were published in the *Salt Lake Tribune*, six in the *Deseret News*, and eight in the *Salt Lake Herald*. Editions of the *Beaver Enterprise* have not been preserved, except as they are quoted in other publications.

trial in Beaver, was more moderate in their features that were published December through February.

Brigham Young hastened to inform George Q. Cannon in Washington as to the progress of the affair: "Nothing more than what I have already told you and what has appeared in the newspapers has come to light with regard to Marshal Maxwell's muddle. It is said he is about to submit his books and accounts to the scrutiny of the Territorial Auditor. If this be true, we may learn something that will be reliable on the subject."[47] Writing to his sons Ernest and Arta in England, Brigham Young conveyed his high spirits regarding the matter: "The Grand Jury at Beaver . . . has presented a stinging arrangement against the conditions of things in the U.S. Marshal's Office, which plainly charges wholesale speculation and organized stealing on the part of Maxwell, or whoever acts for him. . . . This doubtless will give rise to a very pretty little quarrel in that happy family known as the 'ring.'"[48]

Many letters of support were sent to Washington, including those of Methodist ministers Newman and Sonderland, attorneys John Taft Lentz and Frank Tilford (one of the attorneys in the Ann Eliza Young divorce and opposing Maxwell in the John D. Lee trial), and Register of Land Oliver A. Patton. An excerpt from Patton's letter gives the pith of the message:

> You must see how great would be the endeavor to destroy the man who has nearest approached the discovery of the monstrous crimes, and particularly the monsters of the "Mountain Meadows Massacre" (two of the leaders being now in his custody) and the perpetrators of other crimes . . . sufficient in the aggregate to make a history of crime the annals of which would make your blood run cold. . . . [T]he only course to be pursued here in Utah is the earnest, positive and radical policy of General Maxwell. . . . I know him as a war-torn soldier—always courteous, efficient, and certainly earnest in the discharge of duties, many of which but few men would not seek to avoid, but a man of no ordinary spirit, ambitious, possessed of a desire for honorable distinction among men, it is not surprising

---

[47] Brigham Young to George Q. Cannon, December 17, 1875, BYC. Young was mistaken that Maxwell would first submit his financial records to the territorial auditor. He would never have expected fair treatment at the auditor's hands, and in fact he sarcastically said his accounts would be "examined first by the comptroller, second by the auditor, third by the committee on appropriations for the Department of Justice, fourth by the Territorial Legislature, and finally by the honest, starving aspirants [for his position]." "Marshal Maxwell's Reply," *SLT*, December 15, 1875, 4, col. 4.

[48] Brigham Young to Ernest and Arta D. Young, December 13, 1875, BYC.

he should find enemies somewhere to do him injustice. . . . [H]e is one of the pioneers, one of the few, who have dared death in every form—assassinations, in "blood atonement," which happily belongs to the past as the result of that earnest and radical policy pursued by General Maxwell.[49]

On Thanksgiving Day, Maxwell had telegraphed the attorney general asking for a leave of absence to come to Washington, D.C. He did not leave immediately, for the grand jury in Salt Lake City was still in session in December. A diary note by John D. Lee confirms that Maxwell visited him on December 5. By December 31, however, the *Deseret News* noted that General Maxwell was "gone from our gaze": "We are informed that U.S. Marshal Maxwell has gone to Washington, for the purpose of exerting himself with a view to meeting the anticipated pressure against him on account of his alleged official pecuniary defalcations." From the penitentiary, Lee commented on Maxwell's absence from the city and implied that he was pleased that Maxwell remained as the marshal and, even though embattled, was yet trying to help matters in Utah: "Gen. Maxwell has gone to Washington, he left some three weeks ago and we have not heard from him till we read in the *Tribune* where he has asked Congress to appropriate $75,000 to build a penitentiary on Church Island [Antelope Island]. Thus we know that he is still kicking and means business. I want to see my old friend again."[50]

Although securing money for a new penitentiary occupied some of Maxwell's interest while he was in Washington, the salvage of his character and his position as marshal, and the acquisition of reimbursements and funds for the expenses of his office, were far more likely his first concerns. On January 19, 1876, Maxwell addressed a letter to Attorney General Pierrepont, in which he enumerated some of the financial matters:

> March 3, 1875. Congress diverted . . . appropriations made for expenses of the Territorial Legislature and placed it in . . . the Department of Justice, . . . the amount being $23,600. The First Comptroller has apportioned to the Marshal . . . $17,200 to pay for expenses. . . . This amount will not begin to cover the expense of keeping convicts, to say nothing of all other expenses.[51]

---

[49] Oliver A. Patton, Register of Land, to Hon. Edwards Pierrepont, Attorney General of the United States, November 1, 1875, RG 60, Chronological Files, 1871–84.

[50] John D. Lee to his children, January 18, 1876, in Kelly, *Journals of John D. Lee*, 239–40. Maxwell's intent to ask for funds to build on Church Island [now Antelope Island] were described in "Proposed Penitentiary on Church Island," *SLT*, January 14, 1876, 4, col. 5.

[51] Maxwell to Pierrepont, January 19, 1876, RG 60, Chronological Files, 1871–84, box 1017.

After specifying that running the penitentiary cost $1,500 per month, Maxwell noted that prisoners were accumulating, that some of them had unusually long sentences, and that prisoners were being held in Provo, Beaver, and Camp Cameron in addition to the penitentiary. Their trials were to begin in February, and Maxwell anticipated that the trial of John D. Lee alone would cost at least $10,000 and that 150 witnesses were to be subpoenaed. Maxwell then summarized the financial status of the marshal's office. Having "received $13,200 of the $17,200" and used it to pay for court expenses, he emphasized: "Every dollar of the $13,200 has been expended and liabilities have been incurred by me, which must be met." He pointed out that only $4,000 remained "to meet outstanding liabilities" for the first six months of 1876, adding: "It will require at least $30,000 additional . . . to keep the Courts open. It cannot be expected that I should again advance money to pay Court expenses, which . . . I have done to the amount of $30,000." Maxwell closed his letter to the attorney general with a request that "$30,000 be included in the Deficiency Bill" to reimburse him.[52]

On January 24 the comptroller in the Department of Justice reviewed the financial records Maxwell had provided. In a memo sent by request of the chief clerk and signed by Henry Hodges, the comptroller harshly concluded that the marshal was "incompetent to discharge the duties of his office."[53]

In mid-January, George Maxwell had again written to Pierrepont, this time including an exhaustively detailed, twenty-page response to the charges of the Beaver grand jury. The full text of Maxwell's letter to Pierrepont was published in two issues of the *Salt Lake Herald* with an inflammatory heading:

> The Doughty Marshal Spilling Himself in Words
> He Proves His Incompetency to Longer Retain the Office
> Thinness: Thy Name Is George R.[54]

In point-counterpoint fashion, Maxwell answered in his letter the accusations of the witnesses of the grand jury. Maxwell's three deputy marshals who had turned against him in their grand jury testimony in Beaver—Jerome Cross, Arthur Pratt, and H. L. Porter—were men

---

[52] Ibid.   [53] Ibid.
[54] "Maxwell's Defense," *SLH*, February 5, 1876 (article continued on February 6, 1876).

with whom he had long and trusting contact.[55] They had shared dramatic, if not life-threatening, experiences during the Beaver arrests and the John D. Lee trial, and they knew as well as anyone could know the details of Maxwell's expenses across the entire territory and his paltry reimbursement. So their testimony almost certainly came as a surprise, and Maxwell sought for answers to explain their charges. In his letter, he stipulated that the allegations brought by Cross, Pratt, and Porter were attempts to "willfully, knowingly and maliciously" injure him and had been made at the instigation of others, especially Alonzo G. Paddock, whom Maxwell had befriended by giving him a position at the penitentiary and who now sought the marshal's position:

> At the . . . request of my predecessor, [Marshal] M. T. Patrick, I retained Mr. A. G. Paddock in charge of the Penitentiary, although . . . the office was a sinecure, there being no prisoners. . . . [Paddock's] being in very reduced circumstances, his case I regarded as one deserving recognition. My retention of him would save him house rent and fuel. . . . I most emphatically deny that Paddock ever furnished one ration or one pound of coal since I have been Marshal. . . . On the contrary, I have . . . bills from the Rocky Mountain Coal Company, and from Gentile merchants for supplies of every description for both prisoners, guards and *Mr. Paddock and family.*[56]

Maxwell detailed the financial dilemmas that beset him and how monies had been spent. Asserting that Mormon authorities had openly avowed their resolve to defeat the enforcement of the Poland Act by withholding territorial funds provided by the act, Maxwell stated that he had nevertheless been "determined to assume every risk and responsibility and at all hazards not permit that Bill to become a dead letter upon the Statute Books." He related that to keep the courts functioning, he had had to resort to borrowing money from non-Mormon businessmen: "[T]he course I proposed taking [was] contrary to the advice of the then Chief Justice and Governor of the Territory, they giving it as their opinion that I . . . would never be reimbursed. Informing . . . Gentile business

---

[55] Arthur Pratt carried a reputation as an honest and respected lawman. It is in keeping with the remainder of his career that his criticisms of the marshal's office were sincere. Involved lifelong in law enforcement, he participated in the arrest of thirty-six miners at Silver Reef when he was a territorial marshal in southern Utah, was twice the warden of the state penitentiary, and was Salt Lake City police chief. Van Wagoner and Van Wagoner, "Arthur Pratt," 22–35.

[56] RG 60, Chronological Files, 1871–84, box 1017. Emphasis in original.

men of Utah of my determination, they agreed upon my becoming personally responsible to them, to come forward to my relief."[57]

In the letter, Maxwell also defined what he believed was the origin of the matters against him and his office:

> I may be permitted to sum . . . the *animus* which has prompted these cowardly attacks on me[,] . . . upon my sacred honor, upon my most solemn oath. . . . [T]here has been organized a ring, the purpose of which has been to seduce from my side persons to be arrayed against me in the productions of such infamous charges as might result in my removal from the office of Marshal of Utah Territory; and I charge that said ring . . . is incited, prompted, and egged on, . . . supported *by the Mormons of Utah*, my bitterest enemies. . . . A. G. Paddock, Chief of this ring, . . . is the aspirant for the Marshalship of Utah. The other Affiants were, as has been shown, employees and deputies of mine. Paddock proposes . . . to provide for them when he obtains his coveted appointment. . . . [H]is cousin, Senator [Algernon S.] Paddock . . . encourages him in this raid upon me."[58]

In the year preceding Maxwell's dismissal, many letters had been sent to the U.S. attorney general in anticipation of a change in marshalship. Yet the breadth of Maxwell's suspicion regarding the motivations and origins of his accusers is surprisingly narrow. There were other men, far more formidable, more powerful, who had more to gain from his downfall than did Alonzo Paddock. Senator Algernon S. Paddock of Nebraska comes to mind, although Maxwell apparently did not consider the senator to be one of his major enemies. Algernon Paddock was an influential politician who had been offered (but declined) the governorship of Wyoming; had been behind the appointment of his fellow Nebraskan Willett Pottenger to replace Maxwell in the federal land office in Salt Lake City; and would later be appointed to the Utah Commission, created by the provisions of the Edmunds Act. And it was he who had nominated his chronically impecunious cousin, Alonzo, to replace Maxwell as marshal. It is also curious that Maxwell, as an

---

[57] Ibid.

[58] Ibid. Emphasis in original. Cornelia "Nellie" Paddock, the wife of Alonzo G. Paddock, was a Salt Lake City literary lady and one of several female, non-Mormon voices of social conscience. She and her husband were founding members of the First Baptist Church of Salt Lake City. She wrote for and about Utah's women, pleading for their rescue from polygamy. "Tied to the Stake," *slt*, March 21, 1875, 1, col. 2. She was concerned with abused and poor women, and with the plight of Salt Lake's prostitutes. She wrote *The Fate of Madame La Tour*, *In the Toils*, and *A Tale of Salt Lake*. The second printing of *Madame La Tour* ran to one hundred thousand copies, a measure of the public interest in the story of women in polygamy.

antagonist of Mormon leaders at the highest levels, did not name specific adversaries among them. Daniel H. Wells and Hosea Stout were unfailingly his opponents at every step. George Q. Cannon, whose position Maxwell had challenged, had a legion of powerful allies in Washington, D.C. Why General Maxwell did not suspect Timothy O. Howe of Wisconsin, who had been implicated as a major player in Judge McKean's removal and was already nominating a successor to Maxwell as marshal, also remains unanswered.

Maxwell went on to summarize his position his final paragraphs of the letter:

> On my first introduction to Utah . . . my disposition was to . . . execute my duty, . . . without fear, favor of affection, "with malice toward none and charity towards all" but . . . people at once gave evidence that no good will could exist . . . towards me and for the reason only that their attempts to obtain a convert and instrument in me met with a decided rebuff. I became . . . ostracized socially . . . and the target . . . for their most malevolent and deadly shafts. . . . [T]he Gentile community will bear me out in the assertion that the contest on my part [was] unsought by me. When the Government saw fit to change my status . . . by conferring on me the Marshalship—a position neither sought for nor asked for by me—those feelings at once assumed an increased intensity . . . which has finally culminated in this cowardly raid. . . . I ask nothing but fairness and justice.[59]

Maxwell wrote this letter to the attorney general from Washington, D.C., where he was present both to press for the introduction by Senator Christiancy's bill to amend jury law in Utah and to defend himself regarding the allegation of financial misconduct.[60] In the letter, he also reported his need to return to Salt Lake City because his wife was quite ill, and he added that a memorial in his behalf, signed almost unanimously by the members of the Salt Lake City bar, was being sent. Unmentioned by Maxwell was the statement by the entire Michigan congressional delegation, including three Democrats, "that they have known him for years as a citizen and soldier; that he has ever been an upright and honest man, and that they believe the charges preferred were enacted by unworthy purposes of malice and desire to get position."[61]

---

59 Ibid.

60 "Washington—The Utah Marshalship—His Probable Successor," *slt*, January 22, 1876, 4, col. 2; "Senator Christiancy's Bill," January 22, 1876, 2, col. 1.

61 "Washington," by Washington correspondent "Elder B," *slt*, January 21, 1876, 4, col. 2.

Salt Lake Tribune editor Frederic Lockley not only defended the marshal but raised the question of the jurisdiction of those who scrutinized him:

> It has been our belief that the Grand Juries in this District and in Beaver, have transgressed the bounds of their prerogatives and duties, in invading the Marshal's office and examining his accounts. . . . [T]here is a shrewd doubt in our minds whether the books and accounts of the Marshal's office . . . are "public records." These officials [such as marshals] are properly accountable to the several Departments; . . . if they are delinquent in any way, or any person believes that he has been defrauded by any one of them, his recourse is to the head of the Department to whom the offender is responsible and not to the Grand Jury.
>
> The inconvenience and injustice of such an inquisition are conspicuously shown in the clamor raised by the report of the Second District Grand Jury . . . which implicates the Marshal as a fraud. What is this officer to do in such a case? He runs danger of being censured by his superior in office if he divulges all the secrets entrusted to him, and enters into an explanation of every irregularity and every petty delinquency which the Grand Jury suppose they have detected. Clearly he is pleading in a Court which has no jurisdiction over his case.[62]

In the same editorial, Lockley also remarked on the merits of Maxwell's response to the situation and suggested that other matters would perhaps be more deserving of attention from grand juries:

> Question having arisen in the minds of some persons as to the correctness of Marshal Maxwell's accounts, he has, of his own volition, petitioned the Attorney General to send some reliable and competent person to make a thorough search of his books. He can do nothing more, as a public officer, to vindicate his character; and if the Attorney General fails to indulge his request, it may be accepted as evidence that the latter is entirely satisfied of the integrity of his subordinate officer.
>
> For ourselves we have entire confidence in General Maxwell's official integrity, and believe that an examination of his accounts by an expert . . . will result in a complete vindication of his conduct and character.[63]

Lockley concluded that "the personal character of the General, his meritorious war record, and his bold, manly course in Utah . . . should cause all to ask for proof before placing confidence in ex parte affidavits."[64]

On January 4, Congressman George Q. Cannon added his letter to

---

[62] "Marshal Maxwell's Accounts," *slt*, December 24, 1875, 2, col. 1. See also "A Cowardly Attack," *slt*, January 1, 1876, 2, col. 2; "Will Have the Last Word," January 5, 1876, 2, col. 2.
[63] "Marshal Maxwell's Accounts."   [64] Ibid.

those that Attorney General Pierrepont had been receiving for a year. In it he wrote, "I understand there is a probability of there soon being a vacancy in the office of U.S. marshal for Utah." Cannon nominated Edmund Wilkes, a resident of Salt Lake City and the son of Admiral Charles Wilkes. One newspaper stated that Maxwell would retain his position because Michigan senator Zach Chandler and President Grant were "warm, personal friends of General Maxwell" and therefore "considerable showing of corruption will have to be made before the Marshal is decapitated."[65] At a meeting of the Salt Lake City bar, General Maxwell "called [to] the attention of the bar that there were no funds to carry out the criminal business of the Courts and recommended that the bar memorialize Congress for aid."[66] The *Salt Lake Tribune* was also optimistic about Maxwell's future as marshal: "From a private letter from Washington, we learn that General Maxwell has fully vindicated himself from the charges made against him, and is restored to confidence in the Department of Justice. We expect his return to Salt Lake in a few days."[67]

At this time of great personal stress, Maxwell led a delegation to a personal meeting with President Grant on January 28, asking his aid on various serious matters in Utah. With Maxwell was Oliver A. Patton of Utah's land office; Colonel Joseph H. Wickizer, at the time a correspondent of the *Tribune*; former marshal Mathewson Patrick; and "other prominent Gentile citizens of the territory."[68] They petitioned for a way for "the crime of polygamy to be reached in the courts," for the exclusion of polygamists from juries, and for a suffrage matter dealing with Mormon "control of the ballot box."[69] Although the president expressed sympathy for any movement to alleviate the matters in Utah,

---

[65] Photocopy from unnamed newspaper (thought to be the *San Francisco Chronicle*), February 1876, RG 60, AG Papers, Utah Terr.   [66] "A Bar Pow-Wow," *SLT*, March 1, 1876, 4, col. 4.

[67] "City Jottings," *SLT*, January 26, 1876, 4, col. 1.

[68] Patton's wife, Rachel Ellen Tompkins, was the first cousin of Ulysses S. Grant. Oliver Patton had long, dark hair, and the Mormons of the *Salt Lake Herald* called him the "long haired swell cousin of the government," with "raven locks and elegant manners." As might be expected, given the relationship between Grant and Patton, "the interview was more of a semi-social than official nature, and lasted nearly twenty minutes." It is unclear whether former attorney general Williams, who had been engaged to defend Maxwell, attended this meeting. "Washington," by Washington correspondent "Elder B," *SLT*, February 5, 1876, 4, col. 4. Patton was offered the position of U.S. attorney to Utah but declined because of the poor pay. "Washington," *SLT*, February 12, 1876, 4, col. 3. Sumner Howard of Michigan was named to the position.

[69] "Miscellaneous—Maxwell and Patton Visit the President—Utah Gentiles Visit President Grant," *SLT*, January 29, 1876, 1, col. 5.

the *Tribune's* report did not mention Maxwell's making a specific plea to Grant in his own behalf.

No Longer the Marshal

After twelve months of efforts by persons both known and unknown to remove Maxwell from the marshalship, his opponents were finally successful. Late in February 1876, President Ulysses S. Grant conceded that there must be a new U.S. marshal in Utah.[70] Correspondence of William Nelson and George R. Maxwell show that Maxwell's tenure ended between February 28 and March 15, 1876, when Nelson became the successor.[71] President Grant was notorious for his unyielding support of his appointees, best illustrated in the case of Secretary of War William Belknap, whose wife was accused of selling government sutler contracts. However, Grant seems to have uncharacteristically given in when complaints and calls came against Judge McKean and Marshal Maxwell.

Federal regulations called for each U.S. marshal to be covered by a $20,000 bond at the time of his appointment. No record has been found that any of the marshals serving in the territories during this combative period—including Maxwell, Dotson, Patrick, and Nelson, who all experienced severe criticism over their handling of monies—were ever required to surrender their bond.

---

[70] At least seven men were nominated or considered as candidates to replace Maxwell: William Nelson of Wisconsin (nominated on January 7, 1876, by Timothy O. Howe and J. M. Rusk); George E. Whitney (nominated by Senator Sargent of California); Maxwell's former employee Alonzo G. Paddock (nominated by Samuel Augustus Merritt and J. B. Rosborough); Edmund Wilkes, owner of an iron smelting, casting, and milling business in Salt Lake City, and son of Admiral Wilkes (nominated January 4, 1876 by George Q. Cannon and later by Henry Stanbury and later pushed by Solicitor General Phillips); Charles E. Scharlau of Omaha, Nebraska; and James A. Williamson and Thomas H. Bates (both nominated by Senator Roscoe Conkling of New York). Grant submitted William Nelson's name for approval on February 17, 1876. Recall that it was Howe and Stephen J. Field, each Whitney's brother-in-law, who were thought to have been responsible for influencing Grant to remove Judge McKean. It appears that Maxwell did not know of Nelson's nomination by Howe but was incensed at the possibility that Whitney might be his successor, for that would have been a "direct insult" to McKean. "Washington— Gen. Maxwell and the Marshalship," by "Elder B," *SLT*, January 27, 1876, 4, col. 2.

[71] Department of Justice records indicate that Maxwell resigned in February 1876, but they conflict with other official records that give December 13, 1876, as the end date of Maxwell's marshalship. District Attorney of Utah to Attorney General, December 13, 1876, RG 60, AG Papers, Utah Terr., roll 4, part 3, file 5/87.

12

Health, Battles, and Tragedy

I answer the heroic question "Death, where is thy sting?"
with "It is here in my heart and mind and memories."
Maya Angelou

WORD HAD CIRCULATED IN WASHINGTON THAT IF MAXWELL were to be removed as marshal, he would be offered another federal position. When this did not happen, Maxwell briefly formed a law partnership with E. C. Brearley, situating their offices in the Federal Courthouse, room 13.[1] Maxwell appeared in court sporadically and met with members of the bar to discuss a choice for the Republican candidate and the stance that Utah delegates should adopt regarding a third presidential term for Ulysses Grant. Although Maxwell had some reservations because of the treatment he and Judge McKean had received at Grant's hands, he joined with a large number of Republicans who supported a third term.[2] However, the year 1876 brought Maxwell worsening health problems from his war wounds. His pain increased, and the wounds became more serious. Their aggravation added to the personal distress of the recent battles of his marshalship: the stress and worry over debts owed and insufficient money, and coming to terms

---

[1] Their advertisement, in reference to Brearley, read: "Late assistant attorney general, associated with late ex–Attorney General Williams in Washington, D.C." The partnership was later dissolved by mutual consent. "Notice," *SLT*, July 4, 1876, 1, col. 6.
[2] "To the Republican Voters of Utah," *SLT*, February 27, 1876, 1, col. 5.

with the efforts of the unrecognized forces who wanted him negated and unseated.

William Nelson, the newly appointed U.S. marshal, asked Maxwell to verify the inventory and property of the marshal's office and the penitentiary, but Maxwell was confined at home because of illness, so several months passed before he was able to personally attend to Nelson's request. Nelson and Dr. Amos K. Smith visited Maxwell several times in this period and related that he seemed to be in "very critical condition."[3] The gunshot wound of his left forearm had become increasingly painful. In the spring of 1876, Dr. John D. Thompson removed spicules of dead bone and drained a collection of pus, leaving the wound open, unstitched, to heal in slowly from the depths and sides, if nature would allow. *Salt Lake Tribune* editors remarked, "General Maxwell put in an appearance yesterday. He has been convalescent for several days. . . . [He] appears worse for wear." This was the third surgical removal of dead, infected tissues performed on Maxwell in the years 1872 to 1876.[4]

Decoration Day, with the custom of placing flowers on the graves of all those who had died in the country's wars, remained a highly important event in Maxwell's life. Whatever the state of his health at this time, he found strength to participate in the planning of the May celebration and was the orator of the day in 1876.[5]

DEATH OF CUSTER

The days following June 25, 1876, brought news of the deaths of George Armstrong Custer, his brothers Tom and Boston, his nephew Autie Reed, and the 260 men serving with him that day. Lakota and Cheyenne warriors, estimated at three thousand strong, under Chiefs Crazy Horse, Hump, Kills Eagle, Big Road, Crow King, Lame White Man, Brave Bear, No Flesh, Gall, and Red Horse, overran Custer and his five

---

[3] Amos K. Smith had been an assistant surgeon with the First Michigan Cavalry with Maxwell and became a lifelong friend and associate of Maxwell and his family. His function as a medical doctor in Utah was apparently limited.

[4] "Personal," *SLT*, April 12, 1876, 4, col. 1. The operations were probably done at St. Mark's Hospital. Opened in 1873, it was located at Second West and Seventh North streets. Miners and railroad workers were treated there, as well as patients from Salt Lake City, Idaho, Nevada, and Wyoming.

[5] "Decorations," *SLT*, May 28, 1876, 2, col. 4.

companies of the Seventh Cavalry in the Battle of the Little Big Horn in Wyoming Territory. For most of the nation, news of this slaughter was as unexpected and shocking as had been that of the assassination of President Lincoln.

For the recipients of the special Custer Badge, such as George R. Maxwell, the news was more than a surprise; it was deeply and personally disturbing. In addition to his untimely death, Custer was widely judged and criticized, by some segments of the public and by contemporary military men and politicians, as having been rash, imprudent, and injudicious in his leadership in the Big Horn expedition.[6] The more severe of his critics contended that the real Custer incompetence had finally been revealed. He was accused of an overambitious reach for a victory to spark his own run at the presidency. Custer's actions at Little Big Horn and the Indian campaign ongoing in the West immediately were thrust as issues into the politics of the Tilden-Hayes presidential contest.

Maxwell, his former Michigan Cavalry comrades, and the retired soldiers of the time would have been extremely distressed as they read the editorial statement of the *Deseret News* that proclaimed that the nation's sympathy should be felt, not for Custer or for those under his command, but for the Indians: "The Indians are desperate. . . . [They] are fighting for their lives and their lands, their homes and their altars, their wives and their wick-i-ups, their families and their firesides. . . . They must consequently have the sympathy of every just man in the area of the civilized world," wrote the *News* editor. Unable to see the similarity of Mormons taking Indian land throughout the Great Basin, the editors claimed that possession of Black Hills country by whites was of only "doubtful justification."[7]

Criticism of Custer's skill as a military man and battle tactician was unthinkable to those who had served and admired "the Boy General" in Civil War times. Even those who had fought against him respected

---

[6] "Politics Run Mad," *New York Times*, July 8, 1876, 4; "Sturgis on Custer: A Further Expression of His Views—the Slain General Alleged to Have Been Reckless, Tyrannical, Selfish, and Unpopular," *New York Times*, July 21, 1876, 8.

[7] "The Indian War," DN, July 6, 1876, 2. A U.S. government treaty in 1868 had promised the Lakotas that the Black Hills would be exempt from white settlement "forever." Forever lasted only four years, when gold was found. Mormon opinion's siding with the Indians at the Little Big Horn may have arisen from this broken promise.

him highly and were deeply moved by his death. In a telegram sent from Kansas City, Missouri, to President Grant, former Confederate Cavalry general Joseph Orville Shelby was blunt and to the point: "Gen Custer has been killed. We, who once fought [against] him, propose to avenge him. Should you determine to call volunteers, allow Missouri to raise one thousand!"[8] Shelby had been a dashing cavalry officer beloved by his men and was described as the Confederate counterpart to the Union hero Custer.

In Utah, Maxwell and a large group of veterans met in the Federal Courthouse to raise and organize several thousand volunteers to march on the Black Hills Indians in retaliation for the death of Custer and his troops. Judge Strickland said he could raise a company, as did bank owner James H. Nounnan and Col. Cullen Farnham of Brigham City. Judge McKean, Col. William Nelson, and Willis P. McBride added their support, and the plan was made for the volunteers to be led by Gen. Patrick Connor, who was to arrive by train that day. General Maxwell, S. A. McMillan, and Frank J. Humphrey were appointed as a committee to draft a resolution expressing the feelings of those assembled. Their resolution evidenced the unity brought to the Civil War veterans:

> We, the soldiers of the Northern and Southern armies[,] . . . burying all sectional feelings to our deep regret at this loss[,] . . . feel deeply the loss to our country of one so young, so brave and so talented, who, pre-eminent in his soldierly career, would, but for his sudden death, have had this name written by the finger of Fame on her tablets, among the brightest military geniuses of ancient, middle or modern ages.[9]

Comments of condolences and sympathy for the family were included, and copies sent to Custer's wife and father and to the *Monroe Commercial* and the *Monroe Monitor* in Michigan. Gen. Philip H. Sheridan, of the Division of the Missouri, to whom the offer was made, wisely declined it, but the offers of support coming from both former Union and Confederate volunteers constituted a double, irrefutable

―――――――

[8] Telegram from Kansas City, Missouri, to President Grant, July 7, 1876, RG 60, AG Papers, Utah Terr. Joseph Orville Shelby was one of the Confederacy's most effective cavalry leaders. After the War he returned to his business interests in Missouri. O'Flaherty, *General Jo Shelby*, 2000.

[9] "Utah Volunteers," *SLT*, July 8, 1876, 4, col. 3; "The Volunteer Meeting," *SLT*, July 9, 1876, 4, col. 5.

tribute that reflected the esteem in which cavalrymen of both sides, the nonpolitical of them at least, held Custer.[10] Another who had served under Custer, Capt. Jack W. Crawford, also offered to assemble troops willing to march in retaliation. Crawford, best known as "the Poet Scout" of the West, was by this time an associate of William Frederick "Buffalo Bill" Cody. As General Sheridan had done with the others, he politely refused Crawford's offer of troops.[11] Without doubt Generals Maxwell, Shelby, Conner, and Sheridan would have agreed with historian Jeffry Wert's appraisal of Custer: "But the winds that fill the coulees and ravines and lap over the ridges along the Little Big Horn River eventually blow east to Gettysburg, Haw's shop[, and] in those places [in Virginian and Pennsylvania] the measure of George Armstrong Custer must be taken."[12]

THE NATION'S ONE-HUNDREDTH BIRTHDAY

However troubling to Maxwell was the news of Custer's fate, the events of the Little Big Horn were soon eclipsed in the press by the nation's plans that now drew the attention of its war veterans. The one-hundredth anniversary of the nation's independence was, everywhere but in Utah, a major celebration. In all other territories and in the thirty-eight states, "parades, fireworks, and oratory marked the event from Boston to San Francisco." A grand Centennial Exposition in Philadelphia included a July 3 parade by five thousand Grand Army of the Republic veterans. Maxwell longed to attend the July Fourth festivities that featured presidential candidate Rutherford B. Hayes and former Union generals Hooker, Sheridan, and Sherman, as "Southern communities took particular pains to proclaim their loyalty to the ideals of 1776 and 1789."[13]

In Utah this unique opportunity for display of national pride was all but ignored. One train carried a few passengers from Salt Lake City to Ogden, where a small celebration took place. Even smaller was the celebration in Provo. In the capital city of Salt Lake, participation or

---

[10] Varley, *Brigham and the Brigadier*, 270.
[11] Richard White, "Frederick Jackson Turner and Buffalo Bill," in Grossman, *Frontier in American Culture*, 60.
[12] Wert, *Controversial Life of George Armstrong Custer*, 358.
[13] Poll, "Americanism of Utah," 79.

even recognition by Mormon leaders was nil. No hailing the Constitution as a divinely inspired instrument was heard, nor was there praise
for the founding of the nation as an instrument in the Mormon plan for
the Gospel's restoration. Historian Richard Poll asked, "Where in the
accounts of the ceremonial gatherings are the names of Brigham Young
and the other top-echelon L.D.S. authorities—the real leaders of the
people of Utah?"[14] The answer: Mormon president Brigham Young spent
a quiet day at home, senior Mormon apostle Wilford Woodruff went
fishing, and *Deseret News* editor Charles W. Penrose was "indisposed."[15]

Return to Legislative Efforts

Despite his health problems, Maxwell continued his activity in the Liberal Party in 1876 and 1877, giving speeches and, along with his wife,
worked enlisting voters and encouraging the causes of the Liberal
Party. He aimed to have placed on the market more than twenty-four
thousand acres of land in Logan that he claimed Brigham Young had
fraudulently obtained when he "urged" settlers to transfer their titles to
him.[16] Maxwell was still working as a lawyer at this time and, in March
1877, posted a newspaper advertisement announcing his ability to supply
"special attention to land and mining claims.[17]

By the summer of 1877, Maxwell was again working with Michigan's senator Isaac Peckham Christiancy on his jury bill. Mormons
were wary of him: "Judge Christiancy . . . has proposed a new system
of challenges of jurors in polygamy cases which will tend to prevent
the packing of the panel by the 'Saints' and to promote the chances of
securing a fair verdict."[18] Christiancy's actions in the Senate did much
to irritate the Mormon church leadership and earned him these words
from President Young: "He will be cursed if he continues the course he
is taking towards the Latter-day Saints, and when he dies he will be
damned, as have been all who have fought against the Gospel. His end

---

[14] Ibid., 84.
[15] Ibid., 93.
[16] "The Cache Valley Farm," *slt*, March 21, 1877, 4, col. 2.
[17] "The Law," *slt*, March 22, 1877, 1, col. 6, and 4, col. 4. Maxwell is listed as doing business at
   No. 9, Connor's Building.
[18] "A New Departure," *dn*, February 14, 1876, 2, col. 1.

will be shame like all his predecessors in their unholy crusades against truth and righteousness."[19]

With Christiancy's sponsorship, Senate bills were introduced "to provide for challenges to jurors in trials for bigamy and polygamy in the Territory of Utah" and "to regulate elections and the elective franchise in the Territory of Utah." Brigham Young knew the details of Christiancy's planned bills early in 1876 and notified congressman Cannon by letter.[20] Maxwell had also been working on the problem at the local level as well. For example, he watched over the Utah elections in August 1876: "General Maxwell and other Liberals remained at the poles and did effective service in challenging alien concubines. . . . [T]he Danites were highly indignant and threatened to lock General Maxwell in their dungeon."[21] Maxwell's wife, Mary Ann, and her brother Samuel L. Sprague, Jr., were also involved, serving as appointees to a committee that was to prepare a complete list of Liberal Party voters.[22]

DEATH OF THE LION OF THE LORD

Maxwell's legislative labors were under way when the news came that Brigham Young, self-proclaimed as a "first-rate carpenter, painter, glazier," died on August 29, 1877.[23] Young had been the behemoth leader of one hundred thousand people in a commonwealth of three hundred towns and cities founded under his rule. Colonizer, pragmatic organizer, husband of many wives, father of many children, second president and trustee-in-trust of the Church of Jesus Christ of Latter-day Saints, governor of the Territory, and Indian Affairs agent, he had been, with one exception, the undisputed Argus of the Mormons in Utah Territory.[24] His death at age seventy-seven came thirty years after his arrival in the Salt Lake valley,

---

[19] Brigham Young to George Q. Cannon, March 24, 1876, BYC. Though Senator Christiancy represented Michigan, he remained concerned about the matters of plural marriage and theocratic rule in Utah throughout his career. He was the driving force in the appointment of a number of men from Michigan to Utah posts, including that of Philip T. Van Zile as U.S. attorney in 1878.

[20] Brigham Young to George Q. Cannon, January 24, 1876, BYC.

[21] "The Election," *SLT*, August 8, 1876, 4, col. 2.

[22] "The Fifth Precinct," *SLT*, August 25, 1876, 1, col. 2.

[23] When asked how to address letters to him, Brigham Young once answered, "For His Excellency, Brigham Young, Painter and Glazier." Werner, *Brigham Young*, 7.

[24] As an offshoot of the LDS church, the Godbeites, with their New Movement spiritualism and their efforts to override Brigham Young's authoritarian rule and restrictive economic policies, were the one exception.

and exactly twenty-five years to the day after his announcement of the Mormon's practice of plural marriages initiated a maelstrom.[25]

As expected, the reactions were polar, with most Mormons profuse in their praise and most non-Mormons in agreement with a scathing obituary that appeared in the *Salt Lake Tribune*:

> Brigham's rule has been unwise and oppressive, his vicious and criminal course has alienated the affections and destroyed the confidence of a large portion of the Saints. . . . [He] has ruled over the Church with unquestioned sway, evincing a despotism nowhere equaled. . . . Until the day of his death, he was a *de facto* Governor. His habit of mind was singularly illogical, and his public addresses are the greatest farrago . . . of nonsense that ever was put into print. . . . [W]e believe that the most graceful act of his life has been his death. While Brigham lived and exercised his despotic sway there could be no material progress in Israel.[26]

Spoken in behalf of the Mormon majority of Utah Territory's people were the words of tribute that came from the accomplished and respected Mormon leader George Q. Cannon. Cannon gave Brigham Young a eulogy that would be expected from the faithful leaders of the movement Young had guided:

> [Brigham Young was] the brain, the eye, the ear, the mouth and hand for the entire people of the church. . . . Nothing was too small for his mind; nothing was too large. . . . From the greatest details connected with the organization of this Church, down to the smallest minutiae connected with the work, he left upon it the impress of his great mind. . . . [F]rom the construction of Temples, the building of Tabernacles; from the creation of a provisional state government and a territorial government, down to the small matter of directing the shape of these seats upon which we sit this day; upon all these things, as well as upon all the settlements of the Territory, the impress of his genius is apparent.[27]

Tragedy to Be Faced

Anticipating that Salt Lake City would be quiet, with the Saints mourning the death of their president, George R. and Mary Ann ("Mamie")

---

[25] Medical historians now agree on appendicitis as the cause of Young's death. Acute appendicitis can occur in any age group, but its overall incidence falls with increasing age; it is uncommon past age fifty-five.

[26] "Brigham Young as a Ruler," *SLT*, August 30, 1877, 2, col. 1.

[27] Quoted in Nibley, *Brigham Young*, 534, 537.

Maxwell decided to visit family in Monroe, Michigan, on an extended stopover during Maxwell's intended trip to Washington, D.C. Leaving by train in mid-September, they looked forward to seeing Maxwell's sister and her two young children, Emma Louise and Harry Turner.

Maxwell also planned to meet with David Sheldon Barry, his former friend from Monroe who had been selected in 1875 as a senatorial page through the efforts of their common patron Senator Isaac Christiancy. Maxwell knew that Barry, though only eighteen years of age at the time, had become well versed in the practical matters of making contacts and securing an ear among influential senators and congressmen.[28]

Politics and pleasure were tragically interrupted when four-year-old William S. Maxwell, the only child of George R. and Mamie, was taken ill and died on October 11.[29] The cause of the boy's death was said to be typhoid fever. With great reluctance, the parents had their child's remains placed in a temporary vault at Woodland Cemetery in Carleton while Maxwell attended the urgent matters that required him in Washington. He returned to his wife and his dead child's body in Michigan on October 29, and they continued homeward together. The train ride to Salt Lake City was painfully long, endured with the small coffin riding in the baggage compartment. Following a funeral at the home of maternal grandfather Samuel L. Sprague, the boy was quietly buried in the newly opened Mount Olivet Cemetery in Salt Lake City on November 4.[30]

---

[28] Barry, born in Detroit in 1859, had been raised in Monroe, Michigan. As a readily recognized red-headed teen, he soon acquired a reputation for industriousness. At age twelve he was appointed as a messenger in the Michigan state legislature, and at fourteen, a messenger to the president's electoral convention. With the sponsorship of Senator Isaac Christiancy, he was appointed a Senate page at age sixteen, an age at which a page was usually removed from the position. Barry remained a page until age twenty, all the while learning shorthand and becoming increasingly involved as a Senate stenographer. His journalistic talent and contacts with the important men of the Washington scene led to his becoming the Washington correspondent for several large Republican newspapers, including those in Chicago, the *Detroit Post-Tribune* and *Detroit Evening News*, the *New York Sun*, and the *Providence (R.I.) Journal.* Publicity director for the Republican National Committee's 1912 and 1916 presidential campaigns, he became the Senate sergeant at arms in 1919 and remained in that role until 1933. Obituaries, *Monroe (Mich.) Evening News* and *Detroit Evening News*, February 10, 1936. www .senate.gov/artandhistory/history/common/generic/SAA_David_S_Barry.htm. His account of his time in the nation's capital, *Forty Years in Washington*, is primarily a name-dropping compendium and provides little of the inside, unpublished, substantive information to which he may have been privileged.

[29] The child was almost certainly named in honor of Maxwell's younger brother, who died at Harper's Ferry in the Civil War. The middle name was likely "Sprague."

[30] *Monroe Itemizer*, October 15, 1877; "Sad Bereavement," *SLT*, November 4, 1877, 4, col. 3.

Only two exigencies would be sufficient to require Maxwell's presence in Washington at a time when his wife sat weeping at the vault of
their dead son. First was the hearing of the Committee on Expenditures, which was investigating the allegations of financial misconduct
during his tenure as U.S. marshal. The *Salt Lake Herald* claimed that
the congressional committee's failure to censure Maxwell was due to a
bribe—a federal appointment for one of Maxwell's former office clerks
who was a witness at the hearing. Allegedly the witness threw "himself in the way of the committee" and forgot "that he knew anything
important of the wrong-doing in the marshal's office." According to
the *Herald*, Maxwell's "patron," former senator and now secretary of
the interior "Zach" Chandler, intervened behind the scenes to avoid his
own personal embarrassment that would accompany any official action
against Maxwell.[31]

The second matter that could not be delayed, even for his son's death,
was Maxwell's effort to have Congress pass a relief bill that would
reimburse him for the personal funds he had expended and, equally
important, pay the various debts of the office of the marshal that had
remained outstanding for eighteen months. He wished to be able to
pay the bills his office rightly owed to the people of Utah Territory. Up
to this point the Department of Justice and other federal agencies had
been persistently deaf and unresponsive. Mormon opinion was against
this effort, even though it was not only Maxwell but also Mormon
citizens who would benefit from such a bill.[32]

In December 1877 and January 1878, Maxwell and his grieving wife
left Salt Lake City to again return to Washington to work on this special legislation, as well as to work with David Barry and Senator Christiancy on a bill specifically aimed at the guarantee of a secret ballot in
elections. On December 18 a *Salt Lake Tribune* correspondent reported
on the couple's trip to Washington: "General Maxwell and wife have
taken rooms at the National Hotel and the indications are that he has
come to stay, at least for the winter. Since the loss of their child, Mrs.
Maxwell's health has not been as good as usual."[33] A little over a month

---

[31] "Maxwell's Relief Bill," *slh*, January 29, 1878, 2, col. 1.
[32] Ibid.
[33] "Washington," by Washington correspondent "Pablo," *slt*, December 18, 1877, 4, col. 2.

later another Washington correspondent for the *Tribune* wrote: "General Maxwell is still here, though he is keeping quiet and working for passage of his bill to reimburse him for his losses incurred while he was the United States marshal of Utah. He will, in all probability, get his money as the Attorney General has called special attention to the matter in his report, and recommended favorable action thereon."[34]

Even though in Washington, under strain and duress, Maxwell was, as ever, intolerant of those who ridiculed his war injuries. With the House in session, Congressman Beverly Douglas of Virginia became obstreperous and abusive, requiring the call of the sergeant at arms to contain him. Douglas then proceeded to cuff a newspaper correspondent through the cloak halls. Shortly later, Douglas and Maxwell unexpectedly and by chance came face to face in the hallway, and "General Maxwell caned the bibulous Virginian for insulting him when the latter was in his cups, and then tendered the fiery Southerner his weapon when [Douglas] complained he was unarmed."[35]

Frustration continued to dog Maxwell in his quest for reimbursement. In April, Maxwell, his wife, and Robert N. Baskin remained in D.C. "to look after matters of importance in Utah."[36] A week later the *Tribune* reported: "Attorney General Williams and General Maxwell were on hand, fully charged with facts and figures, but unfortunately there was no opportunity to . . . get a full committee together."[37]

In June, Maxwell was again in Washington working on a bill to reform Utah's balloting procedures. On his return to Utah he stopped in Michigan to discuss this with journalist Dave Barry in Monroe. The Mormon practice of using marked ballots was not widely known but received this treatment from the *New York Times*: "The law of Utah, as it now exists, prescribes a marked ballot, which is used . . . as a system of espionage whereby the masses in that Territory are held in complete subjection to the will of the Mormon priesthood."[38] A *Deseret News* editorial retorted that the ballot policy was consistent with the principle of unity, which was integral to the theocratic Kingdom of

---

34 "Washington," by Washington correspondent "Elder B.," *SLT*, January 22, 1878, 4, col. 3.

35 "General Items," *SLT*, March 22, 1878, 2, col. 1.

36 "Washington," *SLT*, April 11, 1878, 3, col. 1.

37 "Washington," *SLT*, April 19, 1878, 3, col. 1. See also "Personal," *SLT*, April 19, 1878, 3, col. 2.

38 "The Utah Social Cancer," *New York Times*, January 23, 1878, 5.

God: "One policy, one ticket, one ballot for all. 'Whatever is more or less than this cometh of evil. One Lord, one faith, one baptism, one hope of their calling,' are accepted principles in spiritual things; and one platform, one party, and one ticket acknowledged fundamentals in political things."[39] The *Deseret News* denied that marked ballots were ever used to ostracize those who failed to vote for Mormon candidates, but went on to virtually admit to the charge: "It cannot be expected that the dissenter will receive as much cordial friendship, countenance and support from his former fellow-partisans as those who remained in accord with them."[40]

Faced with imminent federal intervention, Utah territorial lawmakers quickly passed legislation to abolish the marked ballot. Not to be outdone by the non-Mormon tactics, however, the Mormon lawmakers included provisions that retained several advantages for them: control over elections would remain in the hands of county courts and assessors, and a clause was added requiring proof of "stability of residence."[41] This provision essentially negated the votes of many, if not most, of the miners and non-Mormon laborers whose place of residence lacked the permanence of that of the Mormons. Also countering the votes of the non-Mormons were the votes of Mormon women who were not yet citizens and the votes of the plural wives.[42]

Through the decade of the 1870s, several bills were introduced in Congress for the repeal of women's suffrage in Utah, but support was weak.[43] Maxwell and the non-Mormon women of Utah were later instrumental in the formulation and passage of the 1882 Edmunds Act, whose provisions disfranchised all polygamous women and men. The 1887 Edmunds-Tucker Act disfranchised all women in Utah Territory, avoiding the problem of proving whether a woman was a plural wife.[44]

---

[39] "A Word of Warning," *DN*, February 13, 1878, 7, col. 1.

[40] "The Utah Election Law," *DN*, January 29, 1878, 2.

[41] Salt Lake City lawyers Joseph C. Hemingray and Robert N. Baskin lobbied against the timing associated with the residence stipulation. Dwyer, *Gentile Comes to Utah*, 133.

[42] Bigler, *Forgotten Kingdom*, 313.

[43] From Washington, George Q. Cannon informed Brigham Young by letter, dated January 10, 1874, of six bills pending in Congress relating to Utah, several of which had provisions regarding suffrage. BYC.

[44] C. C. Madsen, *Battle for the Ballot*, 184.

PARTICIPATION IN FRATERNAL ORGANIZATIONS
FOR VETERANS

Formal Grand Army of the Republic (GAR) posts in Utah did not exist until 1878. However, Maxwell and other Civil War veterans had been active in GAR and other fraternal functions for some time before then, including the Improved Order of Red Men and the Veteran Soldiers and Sailors.

The Improved Order of Red Men was begun in Utah Territory on March 4, 1872, when seventy-one charter members, including General Maxwell, formed the Washakie Tribe No. 1 in Salt Lake City.[45] This patriotic fraternity, which descended from the Sons of Liberty, traces back to 1765. Members of the Sons of Liberty concealed their identities and worked underground to help establish freedom in the early Colonies. After the War of 1812 the group's name was changed to the Society of Red Men, and in 1834, to the Improved Order of Red Men. Dedicated to fostering respect and love of flag and country, upholding free democratic government, and linking men in brotherhood and friendship, it became a national fraternal group and exists to the present (though not in Utah).[46] From 1872, General Maxwell was the featured speaker at several of its Utah meetings before the decline of the order in Utah in 1876.[47]

Civil War veterans met at the Liberal Institute on Saturday, September 7, 1872, to elect delegates to the national convention of the Veteran Soldiers and Sailors to be held on September 17 in Pittsburgh.[48] This group was part of a larger group, the Veterans National Committee, which encompassed all "who followed Grant and Farragut over land and sea to victory." Several resolutions were made honoring Grant for

---

[45] Officers in this organization were Charles D. Handy, prophet; Solomon Crown, sachem; William P. Appleby, senior sagamore; Leopold Arnstein, junior sagamore; E. M. Wilson, chief of records; and Samuel Kahn, keeper of wampum. E-mail message from David Lintz, director, Red Men Museum and Library, Waco, Tex., July 15, 2008.

[46] The Washakie Tribe of the Order of Red Men in Utah Territory went defunct in 1876 but was revived in July 1892, and by 1897 there were six active tribes in the state. By 1907 the number of tribes was down to four. Washakie survived until 1911, but all Utah tribes of the order were gone by 1912. Ibid.

[47] "Masonic Notices," *slt*, May 4, 1872, 2, col. 5.

[48] *New York Times*, July 23, 1872. Grant's presidential reelection received strong support from this veterans group.

his service in the war and as president, and speeches were given by Patrick E. Connor, Norman McLeod, General Maxwell, Col. Thomas H. Bates, Judge Dennis J. Toohy, and George A. Black. Maxwell was elected as a delegate to the national meeting, as were Col. William M. Johns, Capt J. H. Bates, Capt. B. B. Zabriskie, and Major Amos K. Smith.[49] The veterans' meeting was adjourned with "three times three" for Grant and endorsement of his reelection.[50]

In May 1873 the *Salt Lake Tribune* reported:

> Members of the G.A.R. assembled at Independence Hall . . . to take into consideration the matter of a proper observance of Decoration Day. . . . Gen Maxwell suggested that the money contributed by Brigham Young and other leaders of the Church of Jesus Christ of Latter-day Saints should be returned to the donors and that the members of the G.A.R. have full charge as to the selection of an orator and poet and that they take their place in the procession.[51]

Maxwell agreed with this course, saying that he "was not prepared to take 'blood money' to decorate the graves of his old comrades who had so faithfully served under him personally."[52]

In August 1878, General Maxwell formed a new law partnership with the former prosecuting attorney of Pioche, Nevada, Judge George Goldthwait, described as the "only successful prosecutor that town ever had."[53] Presumably this gave Maxwell some opportunity to focus on a new task: the formal founding of Grand Army of the Republic units in Utah Territory. It was one of few areas in which he could claim continued public service accomplishment after his marshalship ended.

Founded in Decatur, Illinois, in 1866 by former Union surgeon Benjamin Franklin Stephenson, the GAR limited its membership to honorably discharged veterans of the Union forces who served between April 12, 1861, and April 9, 1865. Stephenson sought to re-create the camaraderie of wartime and envisioned a fraternal organization dedicated to serving veterans. Its public purpose was to serve "those who have borne

---

[49] "City News—The Soldier's Convention," *slt*, September 9, 1872, 3, col. 2.

[50] "Veterans in Council," *Corinne Reporter*, September 9, 1872, 2, col. 1.

[51] "Soldier's Meeting," *slt*, May 27, 1873, 3, col. 3.

[52] Ibid.

[53] "New Law Firm," *slt*, August 1, 1878, 1, col. 5. Judge Goldthwait was a Civil War veteran and a GAR member. He had interests in the Wild Delirium Lode in East Canyon, Summit 6, and the Silver Reef in Washington County, Utah.

the burden, his widows and orphans."[54] It was founded on the three principles of fraternity toward the fellow soldier, charity to the widow and the children, and loyalty to the preserved Union.[55] Walt Whitman, in his *Leaves of Grass*, gave it an unmistakable tribute: "The institution of the dear love of comrades."[56]

The judgment of GAR historian Mary Dearing that "prior to 1883 efforts to give the society a foothold in Utah had failed" is incorrect.[57] The Grand Army of the Republic in Utah commenced on September 18, 1878, when the first post in Utah Territory was organized under special dispensation from the Department of Nebraska. Maxwell was Utah's first GAR commander of the James B. McKean Post 1 of Salt Lake City. A second post in Salt Lake City, named for Maxwell, soon followed, and then a third, named after John A. Dix, in Ogden.[58] It was an uphill struggle for the GAR in Utah Territory, just as it had been a difficult period across the nation for membership in the association.[59] Members focused their efforts on the local level post, the national organization having little to do with actions or makeup of individual posts. At a January 1879 Camp Fire meeting in the Odd Fellows Hall, General Maxwell was asked to respond, for the Union, with a toast to the subject of "Our Fallen Comrades—their Widows and Orphans." Col. Albert Hagan then spoke for the Confederates. Both gave "touching speeches," it was said, "shaking hands, as it were, over the commingling dust of their comrades who sleep on the countless battlefields of the Rebellion."[60] The February meeting was again held at Odd Fellows Hall and drew a large attendance, including Gen. Nathan Kimball, Frederick Salomon, Moses M. Bane, J. M. Moore, and Maxwell. The national vice grand commander, Paul Van DerVoort, was present as

---

[54] McConnell, *Glorious Contentment*, 102, 130–31.

[55] Ibid.

[56] Whitman, "I Hear It Was Charged against Me."

[57] Dearing, *Story of the G.A.R.*, 288. A large part of Maxwell's dedication to the GAR may have had to do with the efforts of the posts to persuade Congress to provide more pension benefits to war veterans, particularly those who were disabled, a prominent theme of GAR stalwarts before and after 1884.

[58] Carter, "Men's Clubs."

[59] The history of the GAR across the nation and the myriad of issues that led to falling membership and participation within the cultural and social changes of the times are extensively described by historian Stuart McConnell. McConnell, *Glorious Contentment*, 20–52.

[60] "G.A.R.," *SLT*, January 19, 1879, 4, col. 4. Colonel Goldthwait, Maxwell's law partner, also responded with a toast.

guest, and his toast to George Washington was followed by a response from General Maxwell.[61]

In April 1879, Maxwell was promoting the founding of GAR chapters in the railroad city of Ogden. The newspaper there reported on the gatherings: "A party of ex-Federal soldiers met last night for the purpose of organizing a Post of the Grand Army of the Republic. . . . An adjournment was made to 7:30 o'clock tomorrow night. . . . General Van DerVoort and Generals Bane and Maxwell of Salt Lake City, will be present. A full representation is requested and all honorably discharged federal soldiers are cordially invited to be present."[62]

The problems of organizing Utah were peculiar, for there had been almost no volunteers for active service from among the territory's men. Maxwell could draw only on those who had immigrated, usually men who had come to join mining or business ventures or who had arrived in Utah as appointed federal officers. Among the men named above who joined Utah's GAR posts were California's Gen. Patrick Connor; Wisconsin's Frederick Salomon, a civil engineer and infantry veteran; and Indiana's Maj. Gen. Nathan Kimball, who had come to Utah as the territory's surveyor general, serving in that post from 1873 to 1877.[63]

Utah GAR posts carried out the celebration of Decoration Day in May 1879. General Maxwell, the post's provisional department commander, and others, addressed a large audience, and a reminder from John C. Robinson, commander in chief of GAR, was read: "Memorial Day is sacred to the memory of our heros [*sic*] dead and is not in any sense a time for pleasure excursions, or merry-making of any kind."[64] Gravesites at Camp Douglas and Mount Olivet Cemetery were decorated.

By October 1883, Maxwell commanded Post 5 in Salt Lake City, which had jurisdiction of the territories of Utah, Idaho, and Montana.[65]

---

[61] "G.A.R.—The Second Campfire of the Veterans in Salt Lake," *SLT*, February 23, 1879, 4, col. 2.

[62] "G.A.R.," *Ogden Junction*, April 26, 1879.

[63] General Kimball, physician, politician, and military officer, served in both the Mexican War and the Civil War, was surveyor general to Utah, and later was appointed postmaster of Ogden, where he served until his death in 1898. Frederick Salomon, born in Prussia, had served in the Ninth Wisconsin Infantry.   [64] "Decoration Day," *SLT*, May 28, 1879, 4, col. 2.

[65] GAR posts of Utah were in the following cities (post namesakes are in parentheses): Salt Lake City, Post 1 (James B. McKean) and Post 5 (George R. Maxwell); Ogden, Post 3 (John A. Dix) and Post 7 (John A. Logan); Park City, Post 4 (W. S. Hancock); Provo, Post 6 (W. T. Sherman); Milford, Post 2 (Mr. Rosseau). Each of the posts, excepting that in Park City, had a Women's Relief Corps bearing the same name. Carter, "Men's Clubs." James B. McKean, along with Frederick Lockley, were instrumental in founding Lincoln Post in Butte, Montana, on July 30, 1883; Maxwell's name does not appear on the record of this formation, however.

By October 1884 the departmental officer for Utah was W. H. Nye of Boise City, Idaho, and the commander in Utah was Elijah Sells. James B. McKean had been the senior vice commander in chief in 1866–67.[66] Long after Maxwell's death, 114 members were still listed on the rolls in Post 5, including four who had been volunteers of the First Michigan Cavalry: Amos K. Smith, Alfred Kent, H. Springstead, and John Deering. The George R. Maxwell Women's Relief Corps of the GAR in Salt Lake City remained organized and active as well.[67] General Maxwell was also honored in Carleton, Michigan, near his family home, when the Women's Relief Corps in that city was named after him.[68] Although the GAR was not prolific in Utah Territory, it thrived elsewhere: "In countless Northern towns, the GAR post became a focus of community activity. Its parades, fireworks, displays, reviews, and receptions became fixtures of small-town life, and under its aegis Memorial Day and the Fourth of July became increasingly martial occasions. . . . [V]eterans organizations in both the North and South often enjoyed a social influence commensurate with that of school and church."[69]

It was not long before the GAR reached beyond its three main purposes, which focused on the war veterans and their families. Soon it evolved into a powerful tool in the hands of politicians. Shortly, its political power made nomination to the Republication ticket almost impossible in most states without an endorsement from the GAR. Behind the public face of service and concern for the veteran, the GAR became a potent voting machine used to further the political ambitions of veterans. In Illinois, where it was founded, the GAR worked to support the election of Gen. John Alexander Logan and Governor Richard Oglesby, both influential Republicans.[70] While Maxwell may have had hopes of using his role in the organization as a base for political advancement, as many of its officers in other parts of the nation had done, he did not run for any elected office after his involvement in the Utah GAR.[71]

---

[66] Past Utah department commanders were George C. Douglass of Deer Lodge, Montana, and H. C. Wardleigh and Ransford Smith, both of Ogden, Utah. W. H. Ward, *Records*, 600–607.

[67] *Roster of the Department of Utah, Grand Army of the Republic, 1908.*

[68] Lester, *Early History of Carleton, Michigan*, 13.

[69] Linderman, *Embattled Courage*, 276.

[70] John Alexander Logan was an important figure in the development of the GAR and became a prominent Republican figure of the times. He was the co-manager of the impeachment attempt of President Andrew Johnson and was the vice presidential candidate on the Republican ticket in 1884. McConnell, *Glorious Contentment*, 26.

[71] Ibid., 25.

The GAR in Utah Territory became an outlet for anti-Mormon rhetoric. By the time of the national Grand Army Tour of 1883, there were eighty thousand subscribers to its newspaper and the GAR was molding the views of veterans on a variety of public issues, among them Mormons and polygamy. When GAR commander in chief Paul Van DerVoort came to Utah Territory on his national tour in 1883, he saw the organization as "a factor on the side of the federal government in the contest waging in Utah against treason." Urging GAR members to "crush Mormonism," he indicated that the GAR's "influence might be needed to preserve the Union against a great conspiracy" and recommended that "Congress enact legislation barring Mormons from holding public office."[72] At the National Encampment for that year, DerVoort's views were endorsed and Congress was asked to "speedily and effectually remove that blot upon the morals and purity of the Nation."[73] When John Alexander Logan was among those considered for the 1885 Republican nomination for U.S. president, he declared that the party must crusade against polygamy just as it had done with slavery.[74] Other GAR speakers used anti-Mormon, anti-polygamy rhetoric as "stock property" in their addresses.[75]

In April 1886 the Utah GAR posts held their annual encampment in Ogden, and General Maxwell was alternate commander of the James B. McKean Post 1.[76] By July of that year, Salt Lake City was filled with thousands of war veterans as many state delegations stopped over on their way, by railroad, to the National Encampment in San Francisco. Addressing the unusually large crowds assembled at the Salt Lake Camp Fire were several national officers from New York City, General Maxwell, and U.S. attorney William H. Dickson. In his speech, Dickson took an anti-Mormon tone with these lines: "The story of Utah's shame, the depths of its infamy, the awful crime for which years has held high carnival here, cannot be told in a day. The Mormon Church is steeped in disloyalty . . . [and] its adherents are steeped in disloyalty. . . . Church leaders regularly preach that the government

[72] Dearing, *Story of the G.A.R.*, 288.   [73] Ibid.
[74] Ibid., 292.   [75] Ibid., 328.
[76] *Proceedings of the Fourth Annual Encampment, Department of Utah, GAR, Ogden, Utah, April 22, 23, 1886*, Utah State History Division, pamphlet 3759.

is the enemy of the Mormon Church."[77] Maxwell, who was asked to chair a subcommittee to host the delegates from Michigan, was also made the concluding speaker of this special Camp Fire evening, but his remarks were appropriate only to the celebration and contained no mention of the Mormons: "[Maxwell] made a speech in his old ringing style of years ago. He told the boys that there has been lighted years ago a campfire which they meant to stand by. When the storm rages the fiercest[,] then the man clings most firmly to the rock. He feels glad that we here have been permitted to stand amid the storm. We will be true to our trust."[78]

TOO FREQUENT A VISITOR

Deaths of friends and family increasingly touched George R. Maxwell. On January 5, 1879, Judge McKean, with whom Maxwell had worked to strengthen the force of federal law in Utah and who had performed Maxwell's wedding to Mary Ann Sprague, died of typhoid. McKean, like Maxwell, had never used his office appointment for self-gain. Several years earlier the *Salt Lake Tribune* had described his penury: "If Judge McKean has made any money in Utah he gives no outward appearance of it. He is apparently as poor as a church mouse. He rents two rooms in a little one story building on a back street, and gets his meals in the Clift House. He wears neat clothes, but exhibits no diamonds. His wife dresses very plainly."[79] A meeting of a large number of the Salt Lake bar met and drafted several tributes to the judge, describing him as "a man of untarnished honor and integrity, a brilliant orator, . . . a man who combined the simplicity of childhood, the gentleness of womanhood, and the bravery of a soldier."[80] Befitting McKean's service as a military officer, his body was accompanied by a military escort from Camp Douglas. With robust attendance of the Salt Lake bar and a long course of citizens, he was buried in Mount Olivet Cemetery, not far from the ground that contained

---

[77] Dearing, *Story of the G.A.R.*, 288
[78] "Last Night's Campfire—General Maxwell," *SLT*, July 28, 1886, 4, col. 5. The forty-third National Encampment of the G.A.R. was held in Salt Lake City in 1909.
[79] "Exposures in Utah," *SLT*, August 30, 1873, 2, col. 3; "Judge McKean and General Maxwell," August 30, 1873, 2, col. 3.
[80] "Death of Judge McKean," *SLT*, January 7, 1879, 2, col. 2.

the Maxwells' firstborn.[81] The list of the pallbearers selected by the family read as a virtual who's who of the anti-Mormon "Utah Ring" to which Brigham Young and other Mormon partisans often alluded.[82]

McKean had been in decline from the moment of his removal from office by President Grant. He had attempted unsuccessfully to appeal Grant's action and recover his judicial status in Utah Territory.[83] He tried to make a living as a lawyer, but clients were frightened by his well-earned reputation as a zealous anti-Mormon jurist on a mission. He had made many enemies, and the public's concern that Mormon jurors would not favor any client of his was well founded. McKean steadily battled poverty and depression. Newspaperman Frederic Lockley said of McKean: "I visited his bedside several times, to hearten a good man in his final suffering, and I felt a sense of relief that his end was near. Suppose he had risen from that sick bed, and gone back to his dusty, deserted law office, enfeebled and impoverished. There was no practice to employ him, and his lot would have been a renewal of his former humiliation and heart sickness."[84] No sorrow troubled the Mormons' reaction to McKean's death, for, to them, God was serving out His measure of retribution and justice. In Old Testament style, LDS apostle Erastus Snow proclaimed, "The outstretched arm of the Almighty is visibly extended to strike down the sacrilegious judge who dared lay his hand on the Lord's anointed."[85]

In October 1879, tragedy again struck the Maxwell family. The second child born to them, Mary Emma Maxwell, died of unknown cause,

---

[81] Judge McKean and all three of the Maxwell children died from infections thought to be associated with contaminated water supply. Robert N. Baskin, in his history of Utah, records that "inhabitants were using water from wells" and that "in their vicinity human excrement had for years been deposited in cesspools and privies." Baskin expresses some pride in his Liberal Party's correcting these public health matters. Baskin, *Reminiscences of Early Utah*, 27.

[82] The pallbearers were Patrick Lannon, Frederic Lockley, J. B. McBride, Henry Simons, Robert N. Baskin, George A. Black, Frank Tilford, and Ovander J. Hollister. "Death of Judge McKean," *SLT*, January 7, 1879, 2, col. 2.

[83] Shortly after McKean's arrival in Salt Lake City, President Grant asked him (through an intermediary, the U.S. marshal to New York, George A. Sharpe) to intervene to ask McKean's brother to drop out of the New York congressional race in which he was running as the third candidate, thus endangering the district for the favored Republican candidate. This may have added to McKean's sense that Grant owed him more consideration than he received. Sharpe, Executive Mansion, Washington, D.C., to McKean, Salt Lake City, Utah Territory, October 6, 1870, RG 60, Chronological Files, 1871–84.

[84] Lockley Papers, 64–65.

[85] Lockley manuscript, 65.

at age two months, nineteen days. She was buried in a grave beside that of her older brother at Mount Olivet Cemetery.[86] Her gravesite remains without a marker or stone. The Maxwell house was very quiet.

WORKING FOR EDMUNDS

Early fall of 1880 found General Maxwell appointed to the Central Territorial Committee to reorganize the Liberal Party. He was sent as a delegate to the county and state meetings of the party, where he contributed to their political efforts.[87]

Maxwell and his good friend William W. Gee, a Salt Lake City lawyer, spent the fall months of 1880 into February of 1881 working in Washington and New York City for passage of Senator George Edmunds's legislation for Utah Territory.[88] The early part of May also found Maxwell in Washington, where a *Salt Lake Tribune* correspondent identified only as "Pablo" had much to say of the former Register of Land and former marshal. According to Pablo, representative Julius C. Burrows from Kalamazoo, who was then chairman of the Committee on Territories, dropped in for a lengthy visit. It was soon remarked that he and Maxwell were old army comrades and intimately acquainted. No one, said Burrows, was better informed or worked harder for Utah than had Maxwell. It was he who kept Michigan senators Chandler, Jacob M. Howard, Christiancy, and Thomas White Ferry and representative Austin Blair in touch with issues in the territory. From 1861 [*sic*] he had kept the Michigan delegation "solid on the Mormon problem." At one point, at Maxwell's instigation, Senator Howard had introduced a bill to appoint "a committee to govern Utah to consist of five judges, they to be the judges of the law and the facts in all cases." On one occasion

---

[86] Mary Emma Maxwell was given her middle name in honor of George R. Maxwell's sister, to whom he remained very close throughout his life.

[87] "The Liberals," *SLT*, August 19, 1880, 4, col. 2; "Liberal Meeting," *SLT*, September 4, 1880, 4, col. 6; "Liberal Convention," *SLT*, September 7, 1880, 4, col. 6.

[88] Gee would later write earnest letters of support for Maxwell's disability claims, and describe his physical limitations in great detail from this time of their sharing rooms while traveling. Following Maxwell's death, Gee was the lawyer who handled his estate probate. Gee also served for Maxwell for a time as a deputy marshal. Gee and his first wife, Phoebe, were living in Salt Lake City in June of 1880. By 1900, he was living with his second wife, Henrietta, who would take up the work of their deceased friend Cornelia "Nellie" Paddock; for a time, they opened their own home for the use of the Woman's Home Association that Cornelia had helped to found. Nichols, *Prostitution, Polygamy and Power*, 110–11, 118–21.

Senator Howard was so interested in Maxwell's report that he "detained a train of cars for some time to take Maxwell on board to talk with him at Monroe, Michigan," and had persuaded Maxwell to accompany him to his home in Detroit to discuss the subject fully. It was reported that Howard showed Maxwell the draft of his commission bill and that had it not been for Howard's untimely death, he would have fulfilled his oath: "We are going to give them Hell!"[89]

In July 1881 the efforts of Maxwell and others working for these congressional bills were given an immense boost by the words published by the Christian churches in Utah. The first was from the Utah Methodist Episcopal Mission Conference, meeting in Ogden, where they issued a scathing condemnation of the affairs in Utah Territory that was sent to the president, members of the cabinet, and every member of Congress, as well as to the *Ogden Herald*, the *Salt Lake Tribune*, and all of the newspapers of the Methodist Church. Included were these comments:

> Neither the death of Brigham Young, the building of railways, the increase of gentile population nor the Supreme Court has checked polygamy and kindred crimes. . . . Mormonism absolutely controls Utah. . . . We believe polygamy is a foul system of licentiousness practiced in the name of religion. . . . Mormonism is hostile to our institutions and disloyal to our government[,] . . . nullifies the laws of the land, controls elections and protects its followers in the commission of the most hienous [*sic*] crimes[,] . . . creates saints and prophets out of thieves and murderers, and clothes with a halo of sanctity, perjury and deeds of villiany [*sic*].[90]

The report ended with a number of suggested resolutions, which included asking Congress to adopt "such statutes as shall secure the extirpation of polygamy and kindred crimes and make the laws of the United States supreme in Utah as elsewhere." This was followed shortly by a similar but multidenominational appeal that contained the same harsh criticisms of polygamy and control by Mormon leaders and urged members of their churches in other parts of the United States to bring

---

[89] "Washington—Utah Interests," by Washington correspondent "Pablo," written on May 4, 1881, published in *SLT*, May 12, 1881, 4, col. 1. Thomas White Ferry served in both houses of the Michigan legislature and in the U.S. House and Senate. Representative Austin Blair never achieved the status of U.S. senator that he sought. Jacob Merritt Howard died on April 7, 1871. Had Howard's commission bill become law, it would have preceded by sixteen years the similar, severe provisions of the Edmunds-Tucker Act.

[90] "Plate-Passers' Palaver," *Ogden Daily Herald (Standard Examiner)*, July 11, 1881, 2, col. 1.

the information "to the attention of the Members of Congress from the various districts in which you live, to the end that they may secure for us . . . such legislation as will at once and forever put a stop to the further spread of polygamy." This message was signed by almost every important denominational representative, including Daniel Tuttle, bishop of Utah; R. M. Kirby, pastor of St. Mark's Episcopal Church; L. Scanlan, vicar-general of the Catholic Church in Utah; Duncan J. McMillin, superintendent of Presbyterian Mission Work in Utah; G. D. B. Miller, headmaster, St. Mark's School; Robert G. McNiece, pastor of First Presbyterian Church; Lewis A. Rudisill, pastor of Methodist Church; D. L. Leonard, superintendent of Congregational Missionary Work in Utah; Theophilus B. Hilton, president of Salt Lake Seminary; and C. M. Armstrong, pastor St. Mark's Episcopal Church.[91]

More Deaths in the Family

In October 1881 a third child was born to George R. and Mary Ann Maxwell. They named their son Robert Mackenzie Maxwell, in honor and recognition of Bvt. Brig. Gen. Ranald Slidell Mackenzie, a Union Cavalry officer who had served in the Michigan Cavalry Brigade and had been engaged, as had Maxwell, in the Battle of Five Forks.[92] The parents' joy in their son's birth was short, as infantile cholera caused his death at ten months of age, in August 1882. Thus it was that all three children of the Maxwells' died in infancy or early childhood. All were buried in the same plot in Mount Olivet Cemetery that would shortly receive the mortal remains of their parents.

---

[91] T. B. Hilton, "Report of the Committee on the State of Affairs in Utah," 58–59.

[92] Mackenzie graduated first in his class at West Point in 1862. He was known for his harsh discipline and was not liked by those under him, but he was respected by his peers and superiors. Mackenzie rose rapidly in rank, was wounded many times, admired Sheridan, and served mostly as a cavalryman throughout the war, all similarities with Maxwell. Unlike Maxwell, he came from a prominent New England family and was educated at West Point. In his memoirs, General Grant described Mackenzie as "the most promising young officer in the Army." After losing fingers at Petersburg, he was called Three Finger Jack by his troopers and Bad Hand by the southwestern Indians. Following the war he remained a regular army officer and served in several important southwestern campaigns. He also led 1,100 troops in the 1876 Sioux and Cheyenne war, attacking the village of Dull Knife in the Big Horn Mountains, and was involved in expelling the White River Utes and Uncompahgres onto reservations. Robinson, *Bad Hand*, 1–40; Korn, *Pursuit to Appomattox*, 137; Hibbard, "Fort Douglas," 177–78; Decker, *"The Utes Must Go!"* 235.

Mary Ann Maxwell continued helping her husband prepare himself to leave the home each morning. Sights, sounds, or demands of young children did not slow their morning absolutions nor interrupt the long afternoons Mary Ann spent alone in their home near the corner of Second South and Third East streets.

General Maxwell was notified by wire of the death of this father, Reuben Maxwell, on the family farm on January 17, 1883. The funeral was delayed in the hope that Maxwell could attend, but the time was too limited. Reuben had been, according to the *Salt Lake Tribune* notation, one of the pioneers of southern Michigan, possessed of considerable wealth, and a man universally respected.[93] Having joined the Methodist Church when he was eleven years old, he had remained dedicated to his church and its service his entire life and was instrumental in organizing the first Methodist group in the northern part of Monroe County, Michigan. His eulogy in the *Monroe Commercial* described him as "always industrious and careful" and noted: "When scarcely of age [he] had bought from his own earnings, a home for his aged parents. [He was] loved and respected as a friend and neighbor, diligent and prosperous in business, exceedingly benevolent and kind to the poor, and one of the best of men."[94] The *Tribune* eulogy proudly proclaimed that his son George was a general and that his will awarded George a twenty-five-dollar remembrance. On this sad day in the Maxwell household, Mary Ann also received news of the death of her favorite aunt.

Edmunds Bill Enacted

The death of General Maxwell's father in 1883 followed on the heels of a year in which Maxwell's strenuous and persistent efforts had helped bring about two monumental events. The first was the passage of a very important piece of legislation, and the second, the refusal by Congress to seat George Q. Cannon.

Having already passed in the Senate, the Edmunds Anti-Polygamy Act was passed in the House on March 14 by a vote of 129 to 42. It embodied several of the important principles of the prior Christiancy

---

[93] "Death of Gen. Maxwell's Father," *slt*, January 18, 1883, 4, col. 3.
[94] *Monroe Commercial*, February 9, 1883.

bills, disfranchised polygamist men, and extended the definition of polygamy as "un-lawful co-habitation," with fines and imprisonment attached.[95] A $50,000 limit on church property was imposed. With this Edmunds Act in effect, anti-polygamy and anti-theocracy efforts in Utah Territory were on the offensive. The number of federal deputy marshals in Utah was increased dramatically, and there followed a very difficult period for Utah's polygamist men and their wives and children. Polygamists were caught in the conundrum between following what they considered God's instructions, in opposition to the unambiguous law imposed on the territory. Many followed the lead of their church president, John Taylor, by going underground, in continual hiding to avoid arrest and imprisonment. President Taylor was never dislodged from his hiding places, but many other Mormon men were found out. Estimates are that more than a thousand men were arrested for violations related to plural marriage or cohabitation.

Also created by the Edmunds Act was a five-man Utah Commission of authorities from outside the territory to take charge of election processes, and voting districts were redrawn.[96] To be registered to vote, men were required to take an oath that they were not polygamists.

The 1880 congressional election pitted George Q. Cannon, looking for a fifth term, against wealthy mining owner Allen G. Campbell of Beaver. Little known outside Beaver, Campbell was felled by the same lopsided loss to Cannon that General Maxwell and Robert N. Baskin had experienced. Accusations were again raised that Cannon was not a citizen and that he lived in defiance of the 1862 Anti-Bigamy Act. On January 8, 1881, Utah governor Eli Houston Murray issued a certificate of election to Campbell on the grounds that Cannon was not a U.S. citizen. The struggle continued, but the stringent Edmunds Act in 1882 doomed Cannon's quest, for the act prohibited a polygamist from holding any public office. In April 1882 the House declared Utah's seat in Congress vacant.

Despite reports of the regulatory Utah Commission that continued to stress the need for changes in the territory, Mormon leaders under-

---

[95] Dwyer, *Gentile Comes to Utah*, 131.

[96] The five members of the commission were Alexander Ramsey of Minnesota, George L. Godfrey of Iowa, Algernon S. Paddock of Nebraska, Ambrose Carlton of Indiana, and James R. Pettigrew of Arkansas.

estimated the significance of the Edmunds and Edmunds-Tucker acts, anticipating that the measures were only transient and would either be set aside by court action on appeal or come to naught by inaction of Congress.[97] Instead, U.S. marshals were set loose on the hunt for polygamist violators. From 1884 to 1889, federal raids were carried out in Salt Lake City and over most of the territory. Terrifying night raids, sudden invasion of the homes and privacy of Mormon families, abusive searches, destruction of furnishings, and tearing into the structures of their homes in search of hiding places were all practiced in the name of the law, hoping to catch polygamists. Mormons complained that these actions violated their most fundamental constitutional rights "to be secure in their persons, houses, papers, and effects, against unreasonable searches and seizures." Even Utah governor Caleb West's 1887 report of the affairs of the territory implied his agreement that abuses of the Mormons' rights had taken place. "It is true . . . ," West wrote, "that a large majority of the people stoutly and stubbornly affirm publicly and privately, that the enforcement of certain laws is destructive of their rights as free men, and assault upon their religion, and an invasion of the sanctity of their homes."[98]

---

[97] "Curbing Mormon Rule: Majority Report of the Utah Commission; Measures Which It Suggests in the Interest of the Territory and Country at Large," *New York Times*, September 29, 1888, 2.

[98] Panek, "Search and Seizure in Utah."

13

A Time of Lengthening Shadows

Soldier, rest! Thy warfare o'er,
Sleep the sleep that knows not breaking;
Dream of battled fields no more.
Sir Walter Scott, *The Lady of the Lake,* Canto First

THE JULY 4, 1885, CELEBRATION WAS TAKEN BY THE MORMONS as an opportunity to protest their treatment under the anti-polygamy sanctions of the Edmunds Act. Daylight revealed the flags on Mormon-owned or Mormon-run buildings, such as the Salt Lake Theater, Zion's Co-operative Mercantile Institution (ZCMI), the *Deseret News,* the Tithing Office, City Hall, and their architectural prize, the Gardo House—all lowered to half-mast. Even the flag at the home of absent-in-hiding Mormon church president John Taylor was lowered. Mormons considered this an entirely appropriate reaction on the national holiday, for they were mourning over lost liberties and rights. Their church president and most of their highest-ranking leaders were hiding from arresting U.S. marshals; families were being broken up as the fathers were on the run. With their homes raided and their women humiliated, they felt that this treatment of the flag was a justified, non-violent protest, an appropriate expression of their suffering and grief.

As with almost all Mormon and non-Mormon disputes of the era, there was virtually no viable middle ground. Non-Mormons, especially members of the Grand Army of the Republic, read the Mormons' action as one of despicable desecration and disrespect of flag, of patriotism, of their wartime sacrifices, and of the nation. During the Civil War, military leaders had not tolerated any abuse of the flag, and the men of the GAR still held that sentiment. Whether the flag was that of the United States or of their own regiment or unit, it was an object of reverence. Flags were not mass-produced by commercial vendors at that time but were usually handmade by the mothers, sisters, and wives of their home city or county. By transference, when they were protecting their flag, they were protecting the home they had left behind.[1] In this war, the importance of advancing one's flag and defending it from capture was accompanied by a devotion far beyond any rational military explanation, and certainly beyond the appreciation of the Mormons:[2] "There was no greater shame than to lose a flag to the enemy, and many color bearers gave their lives trying to protect the unit's banners. Conversely, when Brigadier General Alexander Hays and his aides tied captured rebel flags to their horses' tails and dragged them in the dust . . . they were expressing their deepest contempt."[3] For war veterans the flag carried deep symbolism, almost a religious connotation, that could not be shared or understood by those who had not fought in the war. In a GAR presentation of a national flag to Columbia University in 1896, Admiral Richard Meade's speech included several biblical passages in support of his assertion that "the flag is to us what the cross was to the Christian apostles, what the cross on the hilt of his sword was to the knightly crusader[,] . . . for loyalty to the colors, whether to victory or defeat, whether to life or unto death—these are the marks of the true believer."[4] The GAR placed flags in almost every schoolroom and initiated the practice of addressing the pledge of allegiance to the flag. In 1897, E. W. Tatlock reported to the national GAR encampment that "it was encouraging and inspiring to hear Mormon children, many of whom had never before seen a [U.S.] flag, singing with earnestness and zeal, The Star Spangled Banner."[5]

---

[1] Gerald J. Prokopowicz, "Our Hearts Were Touched with Fire: The Men Who Fought the War," in Sheehan-Dean, *Struggle for a Vast Future*, 81.
[2] Mitchell, *Civil War Soldiers*, 19–20.
[3] Prokopowicz, "Our Hearts Were Touched with Fire," 81.
[4] Ibid.; McConnell, *Glorious Contentment*, 228.
[5] McConnell, *Glorious Contentment*, 228. See also Stuart McConnell, "Reading the Flag: A Reconsideration of the Patriotic Cults of the 1890s," in Bodnar, *Bonds of Affection*, 102–19.

Although the Mormons had lowered their flags in protest on the morning of July 4, 1885, the men of the GAR posts were celebrating the national holiday at Lindsey Gardens, on the north side of the city. Here Maxwell was speaking, saying he "remembered this day as the anniversary of Gettysburg and of Vicksburg." Another speaker alluded both to Maxwell's words and to his apparent aging: "The remarks of our old commander, now nearing the bivouac on the other side of the river, were very touching, and went to the heart of the soldiers present."[6]

It was not surprising that several confrontations with Mormons took place, given that GAR members felt that the flag lowering taking place on *their* holiday was particularly repugnant. One veteran attempted to make a citizen's arrest of Hamilton G. Park, the watchman on duty for the ZCMI building, for allowing its flag to be half-masted.

Seven days of tension followed until the veterans met on the evening of July 11 to decide on a response. Space in the Federal Courthouse filled long before the starting hour with a crowd that overflowed the lobby and poured down the stairs; many were turned away for lack of space. General Maxwell called the meeting to order shortly after eight o'clock. As the first item of business, Parley Lycurgus Williams, a local attorney, was elected chairman, and a committee was appointed to draft a resolution of condemnation of the Mormon action. Next the crowd called for Maxwell, "the battle scarred veteran." During the previous week he had repeatedly sorted through his all-too-vivid memories of the scores of young men he had seen die or suffer mutilation while holding aloft the colors of the United States. He had "heard the shrieks of the dying" far too often.[7] He had been present at Chantilly, when Brig. Gen. Isaac Stevens had five consecutive standard-bearers of his Seventy-ninth New York Highlanders fall, only to be the sixth man to pick up the flag staff and rush across the open field to his own certain death.[8] He recalled the first day at Gettysburg, when the flag of the Twenty-fourth Michigan Infantry was shredded by twenty-three bullets and nine of its color-bearers were killed in succession as they withdrew from the woods atop McPherson Ridge. In the same battle,

---

[6] "The Patriotic Veterans," *SLT*, July 5, 1885, 4, col. 7.

[7] Maxwell's July 4, 1871 oration.

[8] Letter of his son, Capt. Hazard Stevens, cited in C. Clark and Editors, *Voices of the Civil War—Second Manassas*, 154.

thirteen color-bearers of the Twenty-sixth North Carolina Infantry died in as many minutes in their charge against Michigan's Iron Brigade.[9] A young patriot's romantic aspirations to be the color-bearer in this war should have quickly given way to logic, for the recurring reality was that this person became the focus of the most virulent fire the enemy could direct. Tragically, it was passion that more often prevailed. Writers of official war records were careful to include the number of flags taken in any particular battle. Civil War history and Maxwell's experience were replete with instances of soldiers defending the colors, dying, but with their flag in their hand.

Now, as he mulled over the issue of the Mormons' half-mast flags during the courthouse meeting, Maxwell rose and spoke his convictions:

> Last Saturday the American flag was floating at the masthead all over the world. In England, France and Italy it was thrown to the breeze and many a child in those countries had asked the question: "What is that? What is the meaning of those stars and stripes?" They were told that these were the stars of liberty! But here, when the spirit of liberty had gone entirely around the world, here in the very cradle of liberty, behold the flag was hung at half mast! . . . [M]embers of the Grand Army of the Republic had stopped and asked why these things were thus. . . . I have seen that flag wrapped around the body of many a gallant soldier, and I have seen it when men were falling around it thick and fast. Tell me if I ought to LOVE THAT FLAG. Never again, so long as a member of the G.A.R. is alive in Utah will that flag be trailed again![10]

The *Salt Lake Tribune* described what happened next:

> Several Mormon hoodlums on the outskirts of the crowd commenced to hoot the old veteran and interrupt him. Addressing his remarks to them, he said, "I have been forewarned and every speaker here has been forewarned by your paper that you'll make it hot for us. Take that flag (pointing to one of the flags stretched across the street). That's a Butler flag; that flag floated over Baltimore. Some of you try and take down that flag if you dare."[11]

Following Maxwell, Charles S. Varian, General C. H. M. Agramonte, and Col. M. M. Kaughn spoke, each condemning the Mormons'

---

[9] McConnell, "Reading the Flag," 107; Troiani and Pohanka, *Don Troiani's Civil War*, 88.
[10] "Loyal Indignation," *SLT*, July 12, 1885, 4, col. 2.
[11] Ibid. His reference to "a Butler flag" implied his regard for General Butler.

treatment the flag.[12] When the committee returned with its resolution phrasing the condemnation, the vote was unanimous. Gen. Patrick Connor grandly announced that had he yet been the post commander at Fort Douglas, he would have taken decisive military action against those who lowered the flag. The *Springfield Republican*, the *Denver Tribune Republican*, the *Omaha Bee*, the *Rochester (N.Y.) Herald*, the *Butte Intermountain*, and several other newspapers published articles that criticized the Mormon action.

If the Mormons would use the Fourth of July for flag demonstrations, what would their own special holiday of July 24 bring? As usual, this holiday promised to be a far more important event for the Mormons than the national Independence Day, and the story circulated that the U.S. flag would again be placed at half-mast. Whether that was a rumor or a credible threat, GAR units in the surrounding states and territories were alerted by the Salt Lake GAR posts. Told that their presence in Salt Lake City was imperative, they were to come "armed, uniformed, and equipped" for whatever might be necessary. President Grover Cleveland was informed of the potential for violence, and he ordered "all posts of the Western Platte Department [to be kept] in full strength and prepared for any emergency that might arise in Utah in the near future."[13] Serendipity of a sad sort intervened. On July 24, flags in Utah—and across the nation—flew at half-mast with the death of Ulysses S. Grant, whose health had been failing for some time from the ravages of esophageal cancer. Ironically, the death of the former president, whose administrations had sent many federal appointees to Utah to battle with the Mormons, resulted in a peaceful Mormon holiday that passed without untoward incident.

One year later, many of the trains that carried 350,000 people bound for the National Encampment of the GAR in San Francisco made stops in Salt Lake City. Members of the James B. McKean Post made it a point to remind these comrades of the flag incident. The result was that the organization's national Committee on Resolutions adopted the following:

---

[12] The responsibility for the half-mast incident was put on city marshal William G. Phillips. It was also asserted that he had been the perpetrator who showered filth on Mr. and Mrs. T. B. H. Stenhouse at their Arsenal Hill home. Mrs. Stenhouse had torn off the mask of the offender, identifying him as Phillips. Ibid.

[13] Whitney, *History of Utah*, 3:406–407.

Whereas, the Mormon leaders have for years taught, and continue to teach, their people to look upon the Government as an enemy, and continue an organization by and through which the laws are nullified and the flag insulted: Therefore, we, the members of the Grand Army of the Republic, . . . demand that the flag be everywhere respected . . . and do resolve that it is the duty of the American people to require that their Representatives in Congress pass such laws as will effectually release the Territories of the United States from the control of said organization, and will insure to every one the protection of the laws.[14]

To this sentiment, the Women's Relief Corps added: "Liberty is dead in Utah."[15] At a January 1887 Camp Fire in Salt Lake, General Maxwell presented a message of thanks that would be sent to all GAR posts throughout the country, for placing "a statute on the books, that the flag of the country shall never more be dishonored, and that Utah, who is spoken of with scorn will yet rise and take her place second to none in the constellation of States of the Union."[16]

Despite its potential to do so, the incident of the half-mast flags did not prove to be pivotal in worsening Mormon and non-Mormon antipathies. Nevertheless, it illustrates the irreconcilable gap in experience and culture that separated Maxwell and his war veteran peers from the Mormon people, who had no interest in, nor empathy for, those who had experienced the war. It was another near miss of the military might of the U.S. Army's being loosed on the Mormon people for being considered disloyal, treasonous, or in rebellion. The episode continued to work against the Mormons, for in 1887, when Utah's people were again reaching for statehood, the flag incident was referenced by leaders in Washington with comments distinctly unfavorable to the Mormons.[17]

PENSION REQUESTS

At the time of the Grand Review in Washington celebrating the Union victory in May 1865, when the masses of Union survivors had paraded for two days past the reviewing stand on Pennsylvania Avenue, there hung from the Capitol a massive banner that read: "The only national

---

[14] "The Grand Army of Mormonism," *SLT*, August 10, 1886, 4, col. 3.   [15] Ibid.
[16] "Grand Army Campfire," *SLT*, January 15, 1887, 4, col. 2.
[17] On July 4, 1887, John W. Young, one of Brigham Young's sons, wrote to Latter-day Saint leaders saying the flag-lowering incident was still viewed negatively and urged them to "honor the holiday by its celebration in proper form." Lyman, *Political Deliverance*, 70–71.

debt we can never pay is the debt we owe the victorious Union Soldiers."[18] The words were well spun but not long remembered, and generosity was forgotten when thousands of wounded veterans were later denied in their pleadings for additional government funds.

By early 1885, Maxwell's health had so deteriorated that it became the subject of frequent letters of appeal to Washington for an increase in the federal pension allowance that he had received since the time of his medical discharge in 1865. Through 1885, increasingly frequent affidavits were sent by doctors from the medical board in Salt Lake City.[19] All attested to the drastically worsened, impaired state that had come upon Maxwell. In December six appeals were sent in a span of ten days, including an affidavit by Maxwell's hairdresser that he had been unable for at least five years to comb his own hair. Another was a letter from U. S. marshal William Nelson regarding Maxwell's long confinements to his home, and yet another was a testimonial from lawyer William W. Gee, stating that he had traveled and roomed with Maxwell and had seen firsthand his inability to perform the activities of daily living. Gee had assisted Maxwell in dressing and undressing and vouched that when he was not available, the assistance of a servant was required. On July 30, 1885, Mary Ann Maxwell wrote to the pension office that she had been her husband's principal and constant medical attendant for the entire thirteen years of their marriage. She said operations had been done on his left arm at least three times, yet it still drained and was a constant source of pain. "My husband is so helpless from his wounds," she wrote, "that I have to tie his shoes, button his collar, arrange his clothes, and at the table he can help himself but awkwardly where I have to help him with his food." She emphasized that "pain keeps him house and bed-bound much of the time, and his excruciating pain renders him totally helpless." Not able to afford assistants, the Maxwell family was "solely dependant upon the help of neighbors and friends."[20] Her assertions were supported by the affidavit of Dr. Joseph

---

[18] McConnell, *Glorious Contentment*, 10.

[19] The board was made up of Drs. James P. Taggart, A. C. Staudart, and Samuel Potter. Supplementary letters were sent by Drs. John D. Thompson and Joseph Mott Benedict.

[20] NA, Full Pension File for George R. Maxwell. The helping neighbors cited by Mary Ann Maxwell were probably Clarence Merrill and his wife, Bathsheba Smith Merrill, who was the daughter of Mormon leader George A. Smith. Despite Maxwell's widely known anti-Mormon stance, the Mormon couple also kindly provided testimony in support of Mary Ann Maxwell's claims for benefits after her husband's death.

Mott Benedict, who said that the general was in continual suffering from an irritable stump that was the source of unrelenting pain and instability in trying to walk: "His disability is permanent for his hands [are] useless for the ordinary purposes of the day . . . all of which is done by his wife. The cicatricis [*sic*] of his shoulder and groin wounds are inclined to ulcerate[. In short] his condition is one of helplessness."[21]

Even ill health was not sufficient, however, to deter Maxwell from participation in the GAR functions to which he was dedicated. On the Fourth of July 1886 the general spoke briefly to toast the Cavalry of the Army of the Potomac as part of the celebration at Liberty Park in Salt Lake City, and at the March 1887 Camp Fire he was honored with a seat in the band box, alongside other dignitaries on the platform.[22]

Maxwell still functioned as a lawyer in the local courts, but he had a bad day in April 1883, when he was allegedly in a state of "partial inebriation" in the courtroom, and again in July 1886, when he was described as abusive and insulting in his conduct in Police Court. Maxwell was fined and ordered to jail, but he immediately sent the court an "ample apology" and avoided jail. The *Salt Lake Herald* was not subtle in its insinuation that alcohol was the cause of "a string of garrulous and semi-coherent utterances, which were evidently meant for an apology for his disreputable conduct." The newspaper report added that "a few minutes later, the fine having been remitted, he was seen ambling up the street as straight as his befuddled condition would admit of."[23] It is significant that in this case Maxwell was defending a teenage son of Alonzo G. Paddock for burglarizing a store on Second South Street.[24] In so doing, Maxwell was representing the son of the man he had fired as prison warden, who had claimed that Maxwell owed him for prison expenses, who had applied for Maxwell's position, and who had been accused by Maxwell as being prominent among those wishing to unseat him from his marshalship. It is also noteworthy that Paddock had signed as a witness one of Maxwell's pension appeal letters the

---

[21] NA, Full Pension File for George R. Maxwell.

[22] "The GAR Picnic," *SLT*, July 6, 1886, and March 24, 1887, 6, col. 2.

[23] "Maxwell behind Bars," *SLH*, July 20, 1886, 6; *Ogden Standard Examiner*, April 20, 1883.

[24] The two teenage sons of the senior Paddock were Laurence M., age sixteen at the time, and William "Willie" H., age thirteen. Historian Jeffrey Nichols records that the Paddock family was repeatedly in financial difficulty. Nichols, *Prostitution, Polygamy and Power*, 14.

previous year. These events strongly suggest Maxwell and Paddock had resolved their differences and arrived at an amiable relationship. It is highly likely that their accommodation to one another was facilitated by the anti-Mormon, anti-polygamy books, speeches, and activities of Paddock's assertive feminist wife, Cornelia.[25]

Despite extensive documentation and detailed reports, his appeals were turned down. An August 5, 1886, letter informed them: "Mr. Van Mater notes that Maxwell is not entitled to a higher rate as it is not shown that he is permanently disabled and requires an aid and attendance."[26] In a surprising reverse in September, his pension was minimally increased from thirty to thirty-six dollars per month. Frantic, more extensively documented appeals were then sent, including testimony from Civil War veterans living in Utah. Robert W. Crane, who had served in the Pennsylvania Infantry, and Frank Hoffman, a Salt Lake City lawyer and former volunteer in the Thirty-third Ohio Infantry, added their observations of Maxwell's status. Another evaluation was sent by Dr. John P. Taggart in October, reiterating claims made previously and describing Maxwell's left arm as hanging useless at his side.[27] The pension law allowed granting a maximum of one hundred dollars a month for those who were "physical wrecks," unable to wait upon themselves, and required constant assistance of a personal attendant. This amount was never granted to Maxwell.[28]

Despite his physical deterioration, Maxwell gave a speech at a GAR event a few months later. Recently appointed as commander of the Great Plains forces, Maj. Gen. Alfred Howe Terry was the featured guest at the December Grand Army Camp Fire in Salt Lake City, where Maxwell was asked to respond to a toast to the foundation principles of the organization. The *Salt Lake Tribune* reported on his remarks:

---

[25] When asked why concerns about polygamy in Utah were any business of hers, Cornelia Paddock replied: "Because I am a woman, and polygamy degrades my sex below the level of humanity; because I am a wife, and polygamy makes that sacred name a byword; because I am a mother, and polygamy makes maternity a curse, and puts the brand of shame on the innocent foreheads of little children." Paddock, *In the Toils*, 5.

[26] NA, Full Pension File for George R. Maxwell. Mary Ann Maxwell's father, Dr. Samuel Lindsay Sprague, Sr., died on August 16, 1886, but it not known whether his death resulted in a financial benefit to her.

[27] Taggart served a war surgeon from Illinois but was not practicing as a surgeon in Utah. He had been appointed as U.S. tax collector.

[28] Barry, *Forty Years in Washington*, 171.

General Maxwell's speech was short, pithy, and to the point: The Old Soldiers were fraternal, Fraternity bound them indissolubly together. Their Loyalty as soldiers had been proven by their experience, and Charity was the foundation of every Christian nation. Jesus Christ, the most charitable man that ever lived ... [, had] said "Let him that is without sin cast the first stone at her." Many of the audience thought this was the best speech the General had ever made, and were highly pleased with it.[29]

On Christmas Eve 1886, Maxwell's pension was grudgingly increased to fifty dollars per month, backdated to March 1885. The *Tribune* editor was perceptive and offered a loving, poetic tribute to the general on receipt of this Christmas gift: "To him the shadows have turned to the East. It is good to hear that he has been remembered. The path down which he is now descending to the twilight cannot be made too smooth, or bordered with shade too cool, or flowers too sweet. May his evening be as full of calm as the morning was of clouds and thunderbolts."[30]

A Political Success: The Edmunds-Tucker Act

The spring of 1887 brought Maxwell the news of the passage of the most damaging piece of federal legislation yet to be placed against the Mormons. The Edmunds-Tucker Act, passed on March 3; in its provisions, the corporation of the Church of Jesus Christ of Latter-day Saints was dissolved, and all church assets and properties over $50,000 taken by the federal government.[31] The Perpetual Emigrating Fund that the LDS church had formed to aid its members emigrating to Utah was dissolved, and the Nauvoo Legion again outlawed. The act also prohibited the practice of polygamy, levying fines of $500 to $800 and imprisonment of up to five years; required an anti-polygamy oath for prospective voters, jurors, and public officials; annulled Utah territorial law that allowed illegitimate children to inherit; required civil marriage licenses; abrogated the espousal privilege, requiring wives to testify against their husbands; and replaced the powerful local probate court judges with federally appointees.

---

[29] "Grand Army Camp Fire," *SLT*, December 4, 1886, 4, col. 4. Perhaps the mention of Jesus Christ, missing from most of his early speeches, was the feature of his short toast that led to the high praise.

[30] "Gen. Maxwell's Christmas Gift," *SLT*, December 24, 1886, 2, col. 3.

[31] Anticipating the passage of this legislation, the Mormon leadership had transferred ownership of much of its real estate to prominent Mormon men, later to reclaim it.

to apex

Twenty days following the passage of this apical legislation brought against the Latter-day Saints', the James B. McKean Post of the GAR sponsored a "Camp Fire and Ball" at the Walker Opera House to celebrate this culmination of the many years of effort toward ending polygamy and church autocracy. Wanting no interruption of attendees' enjoyment, the gala organizers limited entry to only those holding a printed invitation. The thirty-four-person reception committee for the festivity included many with readily recognized non-Mormon names. Eli Houston Murray was the immediate past governor of the Utah Territory. Pennsylvania born, and a Union veteran, Maj. Gabriel S. Erb was now the manager-proprietor of the Walker House hotel. Among the attendees were Gen. George R. Maxwell and his sister, Emma Maxwell Turner; Maj. Frank Meacham, formerly of Corinne; Elijah Sells, Indian agent to the Southern Utes; and Jennie E. Anderson Froiseth, founder of the Blue Tea Society, founding editor of the *Anti-Polygamy Standard*, and author of *The Women of Mormonism, or the Story of Polygamy*. The total number attending is not known, but Olsen's Band likely continued into the morning hours. For Maxwell, it marked an achievement for which he had worked eighteen years to help bring to fruition. It was fitting that he included his sister, Emma, in his celebration, for she had been his unfailing supporter through the Civil War and the battles he waged to bring federal law to the Utah Territory.[32]

Thy Warfare O'er

In July, General Maxwell was well enough to be elected as a representative of the Liberal Party at the county convention, and he presented a memorial in the Third District Court, honoring another of the federal officers of Utah Territory who came from Michigan, the recently deceased Judge Obed Franklin Strickland.[33] By the end of 1887 and the early part of 1888 his health was becoming increasingly poor. His father had been dead for four years; his three children and many of his friends were dead. His family in Michigan could not ease his loneli-

---

[32] Invitation addressed to George R. Maxwell and his sister Emma Elizabeth Maxwell Turner in possession of Bruce Turner Cunard II. Emma left three sons and a daughter with her husband while attending the Salt Lake City celebration of the passage of the Edmunds-Tucker Bill.

[33] "Liberal Conventions," *SLT*, July 12, 1887, 3, col. 4; "Third District Court," *SLT*, July 17, 1887, 6, col. 3.

ness, for his half-siblings were scarcely known to him: one half-brother had started school to be a dentist and pharmacist, one was a prominent horse breeder, one was working on the railroad in Detroit, one was a farmer in Gratiot County, and one, only eleven years old, was still in school. His sister, Emma, and her husband, Julius Theodore Turner, were prospering with their four children in Fall River, Bristol County, Massachusetts, where Turner now managed a cotton mill.

However, a GAR meeting could still lift up this soldier, and General Maxwell was asked in the February 1888 gathering to formulate an extemporaneous "Toast to the American Soldier." Once again in the company of veterans of the Confederacy, the general said:

> The American Soldier embraces . . . both the Blue and the Gray. The brother's blood belongs to me, mine belongs to them, and the history of both of us belongs to the nation. . . . The ties of liberty have been wound by the best blood of mortal men. . . . If we have filled the measure full, and not poisoned by any semblance of treason, let it be said of us, we have done our level best.[34]

And on Memorial Day that year General Maxwell was one of six selected for special honor of having a place in the four-horse carriage in the procession to the cemetery. Utah commissioners George L. Godfrey and A. B. Carleton, Maj. Gen. Patrick Connor, and Judge Benson and his daughter sat together with Maxwell and enjoyed the ride for the decoration of the graves.[35]

The August GAR meeting at Lake Park attracted an immense crowd, including many veterans brought by train from Ogden. It was the baseball game featuring the general that generated the most excitement and amusement:

> General Maxwell, assuming command as umpire for the veterans[,] wanted some holes bored through the stop boards so he could remain behind with safety to fill the duties of his responsible office. This was not permitted, and the General had to take his position in the midst of the battle. He escaped unhurt, except having received a heavy ball on his wooden limb which was strong enough to withstand the shock.[36]

---

[34] "Grand Army Camp Fire," *slt*, February 23, 1888, 4, col. 2.

[35] "Memorial Observances," *slt*, May 31, 1888, 4, col. 2.

[36] "Grand Army Day at Lake park," *slt*, August 3, 1888, 4, col. 5.

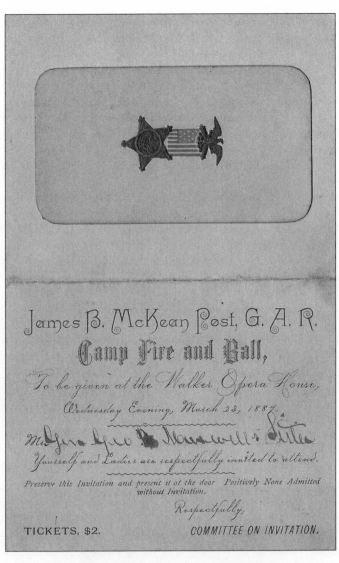

Grand Army of the Republic party invitation,
celebrating passage of the Edmunds-Tucker Act.
Courtesy of Maxwell Fisher Turner,
Elizabeth Jane Cunard Carey, and Bruce Turner Cunard II.

Despite August's brief vigor, by October Maxwell was intermittently housebound and bedfast. On the fourteenth of that month, however, he was able to participate in the county convention of the Liberal Party, held at the Federal Courthouse. Maxwell was assigned to the Committee on Credentials, along with Parley Lycurgus Williams, a young Ohio lawyer named Frank Hoffman, and others.[37] The 1888 winter weather in Utah was fearfully cold, but in January of 1889 the *Salt Lake Tribune* commented, "The General is out again after his recent illness." By February he had regressed, for the newspaper observed that "General Maxwell is very low again."[38] His will, written May 3, 1889, and witnessed by George A. Merrill and William W. Gee, named his wife as executor.[39] Maxwell's signature was halting and irregular.

Death came at ten minutes past midnight, July 2, 1889. Maxwell was forty-six years of age.[40] A brief death note in the *Tribune* affirmed what friends and family had been anticipating: "A man of high calling has fallen out of place, and thousands will mourn."[41] A summary of his service in the war and in Utah, including a poem of tribute, was published the next day.[42] Isaiah White, Maxwell's attending physician, reported the cause of death to the U.S. Pension Office:

> The remote cause [was] a result of suffering from numerous wounds received in battle. . . . [T]here was necrosis of both bones of the forearm at the point of resection with sepsis. . . . [T]here was constant and severe pain both in the arm and the short stump of thigh to such an extent as to induce a gradual wasting and general debility. After many months death [came] from dysentery and exhaustion. No other cause of death can be assigned.[43]

This report makes no mention of the ravages of alcohol abuse that Maxwell's detractors cited.[44] Only two clues survive from which to

---

[37] "The Liberal Convention," *SLT*, October 14, 1888, 4, col. 2.

[38] "Personals," *SLT*, January 3, 1889, 4, col. 3; "Personals," *SLT*, February 6, 1889, 4, col. 6.

[39] George A. Merrill was the twenty-three-year-old son of the Maxwells' neighbors, Clarence and Bathsheba Merrill.

[40] While deaths of General and Mary Ann Maxwell, at ages forty-six and forty-two, respectively, may seem premature, the average life expectancy in the United States at the turn of the nineteenth century was only forty-five to forty-seven years.

[41] "Gen. Maxwell Dead," *SLT*, July 2, 1889, 4, col. 5.

[42] "Death of Gen. Maxwell," *SLT*, July 3, 1889, 4, col. 4.

[43] NA, Full Pension File for George R. Maxwell.

[44] Liver disease, jaundice, muscle wasting, varicose veins forming in the esophagus and producing massive intestinal bleeding episodes, and enlargement of the abdomen from ascitic fluid accumulation were all well-known consequences of alcohol abuse that had been in reports of the medical profession since the time of French physician René Laennec in the early nineteenth century.

judge this question. First, is a note in the *Salt Lake Tribune* in February 1878 that Maxwell, while in Washington, was "wearing a blue ribbon, having been captured by the Murphyites of the capital."[45] Francis Murphy, of the National Christian Temperance Union, had recently been campaigning, and in a New York City rally ten thousand people signed temperance pledges and received a blue ribbon to wear in acknowledgment.[46] Murphy may also have had supporters in Washington, where Maxwell could have heard their abstinence messages; it was at this time that he and Mary Ann were there working with Senator Christiancy on ballot practices in Utah and on legislative relief of debts incurred during the marshalship. The second item of evidence consists of a personal letter written by Mary Ann in which she acknowledges that her husband's alcohol use was, at least in some degree, an issue with her and that he had made several efforts at abstinence to please her. Mary Ann may have held the common, unspoken but widely held perception of the times, that alcohol use was a moral failing, not a mental health matter or addiction or a medical issue. In the letter, which was addressed to Emma Turner, her husband's sister in Michigan, Mary Ann remarked:

> I have some good, good news for you and for father Maxwell. George has at last joined the Reform Club of this city, and I am in hopes forever. I am so glad. This is the fourth time he has taken the Pledge, but I feel great hopes of him. How happy we might be if it will only last.
> He said to me after he had signed, Mamie, I did it *for you*.
> . . . [W]orrying so much [about him] has caused me to be a mere shadow of myself. He could not help seeing it. . . . The best way is to be good and kind, and not to reflect on his past conduct. His temper is not very good at times.[47]

No other personal correspondence has clarified whether Mary Ann Maxwell's worry and weight loss were solely due to concern with her husband's alcohol consumption. Certainly a depressive reaction to the loss of his federal position and their loss of income from a declining law practice would have been ample cause for her worries even if Maxwell's drinking had been unchanged.

[45] "City Jottings," *slt*, February 10, 1878, 4, col. 1.

[46] "The Battle with Alcohol: Murphy's Temperance Work; Close of the Blue Ribbon Advocate's Second Week's Meetings Nearly Five Thousand Pledges Signed," 7.

[47] Letter written from Salt Lake, December 21, probably 1878 or 1879, in possession of Bruce Turner Cunard II. Emphasis in original.

Dr. White's words that death was "a result of suffering from numerous wounds" raises the possibility of addiction to narcotics. Morphine was available for those wounded in the war and was not illegal in any part of the United States at that time; it would have been available in Salt Lake City. Certainly, lesser pain problems than those confronted Maxwell have led others to long-term morphine use. Mormon leaders looking for an issue on which to discredit Maxwell would not have easily let it pass, however, if chronic narcotic use had been apparent. Evidence of morphine addiction in significant numbers of veterans is remarkably absent in the writings early after the war, and students of narcotic use of that time question that addiction occurred, except in small numbers of veterans.[48]

Following the principle of Occam's razor, there are several plausible and probable medical causes of Maxwell's death. Most likely is the progression of osteomyelitis, an infectious and painful disease, in the bones and tissues of the forearm. Bacteria entering the blood, arising from this chronic infection could have resulted in the formation of abscesses in the liver, kidneys, lungs, or brain. Bacteria may have lodged on the heart valves, leading to progressive heart failure. Antibiotics were not available, but alone they would not have been sufficient to obtain a cure. It is unclear why his doctors did not urge amputation of the forearm, for they unequivocally describe it as nearly useless, serving only as a source of pain and infection. Ulceration of the skin, extending even into the bone, from pressure on the amputation stump, or over the coccyx from having to spend long periods in bed, is another possible source of bacterial infection, incurable at that time. Waterborne bacterial infections such as typhoid and cholera (or viral poliomyelitis, which had yet to be recognized) were prevalent and were said to have caused the death of Judge James McKean and Maxwell's children. They could not have been the primary cause of Maxwell's death, however, as the duration and slow progression of his final illness was inconsistent with these more acute infections.

The Mormon *Salt Lake Herald* carried a short note that alluded to his war service and commented that his sister had traveled from Massachusetts for his last days and his funeral:

---

[48] Mandel, "Mythical Roots of U.S. Drug Policy."

At his residence, 276 Second South Street, July 2, 1889. Colonel George R. Maxwell, late First Michigan Cavalry Volunteers, after an almost continuous illness of nine months. He bore his sufferings bravely and peacefully passed to the beyond. He leaves a wife and sister to mourn for him. "*Rest, thy warfare's over.*" Services at First Presbyterian Church and at the grave, conducted by the G.A.R.[49]

A death note in the *Deseret News* was also sparingly informative, recalling Maxwell's military service and his injuries, but it diplomatically avoided comment on his time in Utah, other than that he filled the role of U.S. marshal.[50]

A more complimentary and lengthier death tribute was published in the rival *Salt Lake Tribune*. Maxwell, the editor said, was already a "stricken eagle when he came to Utah":

> He was but a boy when he went to war, he was but a boy when he helped at that bloody angle at Five Forks, but he had made a record which links his name conspicuously and honorably with the heroic men who made their breasts a living wall, between their country and their country's foes, and by their valor and sacrifices preserved us as a nation.
>
> He was a *Custer*, a *Kearny*, a *Murat* by nature.[51] Other men went grandly into battle as a duty, Maxwell went exultantly and all the voices of war were music to his ears. Where men were dying fastest, there Maxwell's trumpets were sounding loudest. Their echoes linger yet about Five Forks . . . [and] at Gettysburg and are heard when the night comes down over all that trail of blood from Washington through the Wilderness to the gates of Richmond.
>
> Once the writer of this asked General Maxwell if he often met men of his command. "Not very often" he replied; then waited a moment, then in a softer voice which ended in a sob, he added, "My boys nearly all died."

---

[49] "Deaths—Maxwell," *SLH*, July 2, 1889, 2, col. 5; *SLH*, "Death of General Maxwell," 3, col. 1. Conduct of the funeral was one of the common services provided by members of the GAR in this period. Depending on the need of the veteran and on the financial circumstances of the local post, the GAR might pay funeral costs and the placement of a gravestone and might give the widow a small stipend. The organization's contribution also depended on the level of commitment and activity of the veteran. Attendees might wear the GAR uniform, giving the ceremony a distinct military flavor rather than a religious one. McConnell, *Glorious Contentment*, 131–33.

[50] "Death of Gen. Maxwell," *DN*, July 6, 1889, 15, col. 3.

[51] Philip Kearny lost his left arm at the Battle of Churubusco in 1847 in Mexico and later served as a general in the Union forces of the New Jersey First Cavalry. On September 1, 1862, he was cut down by Confederate fire at the Battle of Chantilly, Virginia. Werstein, *Kearny the Magnificent*, 235. Murat was a daring cavalry commander under Napoléon.

He was one of Sheridan's thunderbolts! When that impetuous soldier had something desperate to be performed, he was wont to assign MAX-WELL to the task and he never failed him. Love of glory was a passion with him, but above that, love of country was a fiercer incentive and when he, in his decline, ceased to care for glory, that other passion had not abated one jot of its intensity.

Hence, when he came to Utah the system which ruled here came to him like a blow in the face and that he could not be given the task of adjusting it by the direct methods of the soldier, caused him to chafe like a caged lion.

He thought only of his country, its mercies, its blessings, and the opportunities that it offers to all, and when he saw its laws defiled and heard men claiming under the disguise of a religious obligation, the right to be a law to themselves, his fierce heart took fire and burned itself to ashes in his furious breast.[52]

The conclusion of the tribute included the *Tribune*'s perspective of Maxwell's struggles in life after the war:

He has been wasting away for years. Besides the ache of old wounds, there were aches in his heart which he never permitted his lips . . . and [he was] so crippled in body and soul he limped his way. . . . He was a natural soldier, he had within him all the elements to have made one of the world's great commanders. As it was, where thousands of splendid officers were striving to make names, he succeeded in writing his name only below the greatest . . . at 22 years of age.

The ways of peace were a constant friction to his stormy soul, the mysteries of business were enigmas which he could not fathom; he could no more adapt himself to the everyday details of life than could an eagle adapt itself to the routine of a barn-yard fowl. His life since the war has been a failure, but in thinking of him we should keep in mind that his death does not date from yesterday but really from that April day in 1865 when he went down in the storm of battle that swept Five Forks. There he earned the eternal gratitude of his countrymen and so with all tenderness should his wasted and mangled frame be given into the arms of the merciful earth that has opened her breast to receive it.[53]

---

[52] "General Maxwell," *SLT*, July 3, 1889, 2, col. 1. Emphasis in original.

[53] Ibid. Charles C. Goodwin may have been the author of this eulogy. Formerly of the *Nevada Enterprise* in Virginia City, Goodwin joined the *Salt Lake Tribune* editorial staff in 1880, and ownership of the *Tribune* passed from Frederic Lockley and his partners to Goodwin in 1883. During this period Goodwin was strongly anti-Mormon and engaged in skillful verbal combat with Charles W. Penrose, his counterpart at the *Deseret News*. Goodwin, Lockley, and William Nelson all did editorial writing, so all three must be considered as potentially the author. Despite giving up ownership of the *Tribune*, Lockley may have visited Salt Lake City afterward and may have contributed his memories of Maxwell to the editor responsible for the tribute.

Funeral services began with a march of GAR men to the Maxwell residence, where the Sixth Army Band played a dirge. The march continued on to the Presbyterian Church, which was completely filled with friends and prominent businessmen and professionals. Utah governor Arthur Lloyd Thomas, territorial secretary Elijah Sells, Chief Justice Charles S. Zane, Utah commissioners John Alexander McClernand and George L. Godfrey, and large delegations of the GAR and the Women's Relief Corps were present. Rev. Robert G. McNiece spoke of the general's never having swerved from high integrity while serving in public office, and stressed his freedom from hypocrisy: "He did not claim to have virtues he did not." His generosity that was particularly aimed at "any who were soldiers," with whom he would share all that he had, was next in the speaker's praise. "There was no service for his country, that he would not perform, even to laying down his life in affection and love of country." With the truthfulness that Maxwell would have required of him, McNiece pointed out that the general was a Christian who had been neglectful of religion, but McNiece himself had never seen a greater resolution for the better in the final months of a life than Maxwell's acceptance of the salvation awaiting him. At the gravesite, the remarks of Ovander J. Hollister, formerly an Internal Revenue collector for the territory and now part owner of the *Tribune*, were rendered with brevity appropriate to a hot summer day but covered Maxwell's war service, the praise that Custer had given him, his bravery as a soldier, his accomplishments in working against polygamy and theocratic rule in Utah, and the many tributes he had earned in the territory. A salute was fired over the grave by two pieces of artillery from Fort Douglas.[54]

Three months after Maxwell's death the men of the GAR met to find means for a "fitting monument." Veterans and Liberal Party members were asked to remember him, and the *Tribune* called for the hall to be filled because Maxwell had been "among the first to give the Territory lessons in loyalty":

No one was ever permitted for a moment to doubt where he stood, and . . . he was a stalwart to the very close. When other men built grades to cover with long curves a heavy climb, he stalked straight up the height. He did not believe that as between right and wrong there was any such

---

[54] The pallbearers where Fred Solomon, T. M. Bishop, Hugh Anderson, William F. Colfax, Frank Hoffman, C. M. Hammond, E. H. Parson, M. Bryan, S. D. Chase, James F. Bradley, William H. Byrd, and C. M. Brown. "Gen. Maxwell's Funeral," *SLT*, July 4, 1889.

(*above, left*) George R. Maxwell tombstone at
Mount Olivet Cemetery, Salt Lake City.

(*above, right*) Inscriptions of the Custer Medal and
the GAR symbol on the George R. Maxwell tombstone
at Mount Olivet Cemetery, Salt Lake City.
Photographs by John Gary Maxwell.

thing as a fast compromise, and so, resolute, determined, persistent and perfectly honest, he moved on his path with no more variation than has the Polar star.[55]

With the aid of the GAR a modest gray stone obelisk was procured. Now severely eroded, it marks his place of burial in Salt Lake City's Mount Olivet Cemetery. On its sides are two engravings representing the accomplishments to which Maxwell wished his memory to be forever connected. On the west face is a still-recognizable Custer Medal, tying him with his comrades of the Michigan Cavalry Brigade. On the south face are the emblem and ribbon of the Grand Army of the Republic, linking him with his service to his nation during and after the Civil War.[56]

---

[55] "Maxwell Memorial Meeting," *slt*, October 22, 1889, 4, col. 4.
[56] In October 2006 an additional granite marker was placed on Maxwell's grave that recognizes his Civil War rank as a general.

Carving of the Custer Medal on
the Michigan Cavalry Brigade
monument, East Cavalry Field,
Gettysburg National Monument.
Note the sword tips pointed upward.
Photograph by John Gary Maxwell.

Mamie Follows

If Mary Ann Maxwell thought that her troubles with the offices of the U.S. adjutant general were over, she was lamentably mistaken, for she had difficulty in receiving proper benefits after the death of her husband. In May 1890, Brig. Gen. Wesley Merritt, who had also served the Army of the Shenandoah at Five Forks under the cavalry command of Gen. Philip Sheridan, sent a letter to the adjutant general in support of Mary Ann Maxwell's claim for her husband's death benefits. His preface is another instance of Maxwell's commanding officers praising his conduct as a soldier: "I enclose a letter from the widow of a brave soldier who served under me during the War—one of the bravest and best of any command. . . . [W]ill you please let me know what can be done to solve her difficulty?"[57] Widow Maxwell asked the Salt Lake City's Board of Equalization for partial remittance of her taxes because she was "unable to pay." The full amount was remitted.[58]

---

[57] Sheridan, *Personal Memoirs*, 2:136. Merritt, an 1860 West Point graduate, was a cavalry officer; he was at Gettysburg, Todd's Tavern, the Wilderness, Yellow Tavern, Haw's Shop, and Five Forks, all the same engagements in which Maxwell had participated.

[58] "Maxwell's Tax Is Remitted," *SLT*, September 11, 1890, 7, col. 1.

Mary Ann Sprague Maxwell enjoyed visiting intermittently with Otis Adams Critchett, her husband's former law partner from Monroe, during the year he spent in Salt Lake City—1891—as he sought relief from the asthma that had troubled him since childhood.[59] However, Mary Ann, always bird thin, was increasingly aware of her own failing health and made out her will in February 1892, naming her friend Patrick H. Lannan of the *Salt Lake Tribune* as its executor.[60] She bequeathed modest sums to friends and relatives, to the McKean Women's Relief Corps of Salt Lake City, to the Utah Grand Army of the Republic, and to St. Mary's and St. Mark's hospitals. The books of the Maxwell library were to go to Dr. Amos K. Smith. By spring her condition had deteriorated, and on May 16, Dr. White petitioned the court for the appointment of longtime family friend Dr. Amos K. Smith as her guardian, for she was physically weak, confined to her bed, mentally incompetent, unconscious of her surroundings, and incapable of attending to any business.

She died two days later, less than three years after the death of her husband. Her home was assessed at $4,500, with no other assets save a $90 check from the U.S. pension agent that she had not yet cashed.[61] From the sale of her home, Patrick Lannan paid the accumulated claims and bills. Probate of her estate went on for some time, and reimbursement for her dead husband's prosthetic leg was not paid to her estate until August 1894. Recovery suits were filed in 1893 by Dr. Amos K. Smith and Dr. J. M. Benedict against Patrick Lannan as estate executor. The mortgage note on the Maxwell home owed to Hannah Pauline White, the wife of Dr. Isaiah White, was not satisfied until April 1896.[62]

---

[59] Critchett survived George and Mary Ann Maxwell by a short interval. He died in June 1893 in Monroe, Michigan.

[60] By the time of Mary Ann Maxwell's death, Patrick H. Lannan, an Irishman, butcher, businessman, and longtime friend, had risen in community stature to become part owner and an important staff member of the *Salt Lake Tribune*. Her will was contested by her mother, who alleged that her condition in February 1892 was such as to make her will fraudulent. No action is known to have resulted from this contest.

[61] A death note in the *Monroe Democrat*, dated June 12, 1892, inexplicably claimed that she left an estate valued at $16,000.

[62] Hannah Pauline White's holding a note on the home of Mary Ann Maxwell at the time she was being attended in her final illness by Dr. White raises the question of a conflict of interest not addressed in the records that remain.

Mary Ann Sprague Maxwell was buried without a gravestone marker beside her husband and the unmarked graves of her three children. The *Tribune* announced in unadorned words:

Funeral of Mrs. Maxwell

The funeral of the relict of the late General Maxwell took place yesterday from the Presbyterian Church where Dr. McNiece preached the sermon, and the Rev F. L. Arnold spoke very feelingly to the soldiers. The funeral was largely attended. The interment took place at Mt. Olivet Cemetery, where the ceremonies were conducted according to the G.A.R. ritual and were participated in by forty of the McKean and Maxwell Posts and members of the Women's Relief Corps.[63]

In her final illness Mary Ann Sprague Maxwell was attended by the same physician who had attended her late husband. Dr. Isaiah White listed the cause of her death as "paralysis," a term frequently found on death certificates in this era. This lay term is nothing other than a description, however, and does not medically explain the cause of death in this forty-two-year-old woman.

This ended the family, posterity, and property of George R. Maxwell. He had seen not one elephant but two. He had stroked their trunks, bitten their ears, pulled their tails, and earned an honorable rest.

---

[63] *SLT*, May 20, 1892.

14

Stricken Eagle

The storm-bell rings, the trumpet blows;
I know the word and countersign;
Wherever Freedom's vanguard goes,
Where stand or fall her friends or foes,
I know the place that should be mine.
John Greenleaf Whittier, "The Summons"

Show me a hero and I will write you a tragedy.
F. Scott Fitzgerald

THE MAJOR ACHIEVEMENTS OF GEORGE R. MAXWELL'S LIFE
unfolded within two distinct milieus: his military career during the Civil
War and his civil service career in Utah. To determine whether Maxwell
merits hero status, his accomplishments must be judged within both.

As a farm boy and a freshman college student when the Civil War
erupted, Maxwell rose, by leadership and bravery, from enlisted man
to a post of honor and responsibility in command of a thousand-man
cavalry regiment within one of the most respected mounted units of the
war. Never giving up the fight, he was unequivocally a Civil War hero,
although not yet recognized as one. In Utah Territory, however, his
battle and his achievements were more obscure. No longer on the black-
and-white proving ground of war, judged by either defeat or unconditional victory, he sought to impose alignment with American ideals

and moral views, and compliance with federal law, on a population who were separatists and who considered themselves modern saints. The Mormons of Utah met Maxwell's uncompromising demands for change with equally uncompromising defensiveness and moral indignation. Granting George R. Maxwell a hero's status is more complex and controversial in this second milieu than in the first.

UNRECOGNIZED HERO IN MICHIGAN

In the summer of 1861, eighteen-year-old George R. Maxwell abandoned his salad days at Michigan State Normal School to join the Michigan Cavalry. By summer of 1862 the patriotic enthusiasm of the remaining students there led them to organize their own infantry unit, the Normal Company. By the time this Company E of the Seventeenth Michigan Infantry was filled, one-third of its men and all of the officers were former students of the school. At war's end it was estimated that thirty students from the Ypsilanti school had been killed, were missing, or had died of disease. Undoubtedly a number of students, Maxwell among them, were lost to the school's tracking, so the total number is underreported. Maxwell's close friends Edward Bigelow ("Lo") and Cyrus F. Whelan ("Cy") died in the service. Of eighteen surviving student-soldiers gathered at a reunion in 1867 (Maxwell not included), ten bore war wounds and four had survived Confederate prisons.[1]

Among the approximately 120 students at the school in 1860–61, one man, Irwin Shepard, was awarded the Congressional Medal of Honor; twelve men reached the rank of captain; three became majors; three were lieutenant colonels; three were colonels; and one, James H. Kidd of the Sixth Michigan Cavalry, became a brigadier general, according to the school's records.[2] Unknown to the school was that George R. Maxwell was its second student to have been promoted to brevet brigadier general, sharing this honor of highest rank with Kidd. More remarkably, both Kidd and Maxwell were Custer Medal recipients.

---

[1] *Ypsilanti Commercial*, March 2, 1867. The first Normal Company student to fall, Alexander McKinnon, was killed in September 1862 at Fox's Gap on South Mountain, Maryland.

[2] Caleb John Klinger, archivist and graduate student, and Rosina Tammany, archivist, Eastern Michigan University Archives, Ypsilanti, pers. comm., June 2007; Isbell and Disbrow, "The Michigan State Normal School and the Civil War," in Bald, Peckham, and Williams, *Michigan Institutions*, 92–94.

James H. Kidd,
Michigan Normal School student,
Michigan Sixth Cavalry member,
and Custer Medal recipient.
Courtesy Archives of Michigan.

Each of Maxwell's serious wounds offered him the opportunity to retire to home with pride and respect, but he remained, fighting for unconditional victory. Dismissing the advantage that his having only one functional arm gave to his opponents, he fought the last battles with his unit as its leader, on the front line. Add to this record two escapes from Confederate capture, living through the amputation of his leg, and multiple other wounds, and the totality makes for a unique place among his classmates and a highly deserving place among all Michigan volunteers. Among his contemporary cavalry peers, testaments to his hero status are numerous, and the bestowal of the Custer Medal should permanently ensure his place as a legendary war hero.

A Revealing Encounter

Maxwell had been in the Land Office in Utah Territory less than a month—before blatant enmity developed between him and the Mormons—when, in July 1869, the editors of the *Deseret News* published an unusual tribute to him:

Yesterday as our newly appointed register of the land office, Mr. Maxwell, colonel of the 1st Michigan Cavalry during the war was busily engaged in his office, a tall, military looking gentleman walked in, whom he instantly recognized as Mr. Henry E. Lee [Henry Carter Lee], a nephew of General Robert E. Lee, and Col. of the 1st Virginia Cavalry during the rebellion. The recognition was mutual, and called up bitter and painful remonstrances of the events that occurred during the terrible conflict between the armies of the North and the Southern Confederacy.

It appears that during that rebellion, the 1st Virginia and the 1st Michigan Cavalry happened to be arrayed each against the other and the feeling of animosity between the two regiments was as bitter as that entertained towards each other by two single persons who are deadly enemies.

At the famous Battle of Gettysburg, the two regiments fought face to face, each learning to respect and hate the other for blows given and the courage displayed.

Between Colonels Maxwell and [Henry Carter] Lee the leaders of the two regiments, the hate entertained by the respective members of each regiment seemed to concentrate, and when the contending armies were engaged on James River, the two colonels met face to face, and there swore to fight it out in a personal conflict. The resolve was no sooner formed than executed, and a determined and deadly conflict immediately ensued, the two regiments, for the time, being merely spectators. The result was that Maxwell received a sword thrust in the groin, and Lee had his shoulder disabled.

Since that day up to yesterday we suppose that the two men had never met and it may well be supposed the meeting was a strange one and that singular feelings were evoked on the occasion. They both bear the ineffaceable marks of hard service; Col. Maxwell has lost one leg and has sustained other serious physical injuries; while the left arm of Colonel Lee is disabled by the wound received in his conflict with Col. Maxwell.

However, the hatred of the past seems to have no longer a place in their hearts; they have each learned to respect the other . . . and the warm grasp of the hand that followed mutual recognition and the words of kindly greeting that were subsequently exchanged seemed to indicate a friendship more lasting than . . . was their former animosity.[3]

From the famous family of this surname, Lee's father was Commodore Sydney Smith Lee, the brother of the more famous Gen. Robert E. Lee. Henry Carter Lee served first with the Richmond Howitzers, but by the Battle of Gettysburg he was on the staff of his older brother,

---

[3] "A Strange Incident," *DN*, July 14, 1869, 12, col. 3.

cavalry brigadier general Fitzhugh Lee.[4] While the time and place of the described encounter may be an error on the part of the *News*, the report conveys the respect the two officers had for one another during the battle, and its endurance into their meeting long after the war. True cavalrymen, courteous even in deadly combat, they had fought in view of their troops, on horseback with sabers only, until both were seriously injured and unable to compete.

On that summer day in 1869, in the Mormon city beside the Great Salt Lake, nearly a continent away from the battlefields of Gettysburg, far from the Blue Ridge and Massanutten mountains, from the valley of the Shenandoah, far from the Mattaponi, Nottoway, Rappahannock, Pamunkey, and the other beautiful rivers of Virginia with their euphonious, mellifluous, Indian names, George R. Maxwell, the Thunderbolt of Sheridan, was reflective and subdued.

SOME OBSERVATIONS

Mormon polygamist and historian B. H. Roberts; a *Cincinnati Commercial* journalist (probably George Alfred Townsend, also known as "Gath"); a *New York World* correspondent; Utah congressman and widely admired apostle George Q. Cannon; and Scipio Africanus Kenner, Mormon journalist, writer, and wit—each left a brief description of George Maxwell. B. H. Roberts said that as a Civil War veteran "many times wounded while in service," Maxwell was "therefore respected despite his half-insane hatred of 'Mormons' and 'all things Mormon.'"[5] The *World* said he was a "worthless vagabond, whose neglected appearance would in a strange city at once arrest him for vagrancy."[6] The *Cincinnati Commercial* went on to describe Maxwell as a man "with a strong, dissipated face" and looked "as if he had overslept for a week

---

[4] Henry Carter Lee was promoted to captain in the 1865 Appomattox campaign. He married Sally Buchanan Floyd Johnston of Virginia in September 1868. His appearance in Utah Territory may have been a honeymoon trip to the West. To the couple were born four sons and one daughter. Both Maxwell and Lee were forty-seven years of age when they died in 1889, Lee in Richmond, Virginia, and Maxwell in Salt Lake City. Documentation of the battle described in the *Deseret News* has not been found in official war records. However, the distinctly pro-Mormon newspaper would not have invented a fiction complimentary to a newly arrived federal official. Errors of geography, such as the James River being near Gettysburg, give assurance that the account was not written by Maxwell or Lee.

[5] Roberts, *Comprehensive History*, 357n.   [6] *New York World*, November 25, 1871.

and got up mad." The correspondent added that "this, it is not unfair to say, was his habitual appearance."[7] As George Q. Cannon spoke to the gathered Mormons in the Tabernacle in Salt Lake City regarding the happenings in Washington at the time the Poland Bill was being considered, he described Maxwell as a living negative advertisement of the non-Mormon element:

> The presence in Washington of Utah characters like George Maxwell was one of his [Cannon's] strongest weapons. They were talking visual aids. Legislators looked at them and were immediately suspicious of a scheme to despoil the Latter-day Saints. "All I had to do," Cannon said "was to point to these men and ask Senators and members how they would like to have power put in the hands of such persons if they resided in Utah Territory."[8]

Roberts, Cannon, and the *Cincinnati Commercial* and *World* newspapermen either did not know or did not acknowledge in their writing the full extent of Maxwell's chronically painful injuries that interfered with sleep; his draining, malodorous wounds; and his inability to raise either arm to comb his hair, adjust his tie, or carry out the daily grooming maneuvers that, for those not disabled, are automatic. They did not appreciate the ritual of getting into the leather straps that affixed his prosthetic leg to his torso, and the constantly irritated stump. And they either did not know or would not admit that the marshal was using his own salary, and additional personal funds, to pay for judicial and territory expenses, with nothing leftover to use to improve his appearance in the halls of the Congress. Kenner had some additional insight into Maxwell's limitations and personality:

> George, by the bye, was one of the "boys" decidedly, and apparently wanted to make everybody believe that Mormons were his favorite diet three times a day. At heart, he was not half as bad as he tried to make it appear, and generally kept a long way from the methods of deportment which are supposed to characterize the typical Sunday School teacher; but much was overlooked in him because of having fought bravely as a Union soldier through the Civil War and been literally shot to pieces.[9]

---

[7] *Cincinnati Commercial*, cited in Whitney, *History of Utah*, vol. 2, chap. 22, 623.

[8] George Q. Cannon (1875), *Journal of Discourses*, 17:125; Landon, Cannon, and Turley, *Journals of George Q. Cannon*, 1:190.

[9] Kenner, *Utah as It Is*, 88. Kenner had a colorful life as a printer, a telegraph operator, a member of the bar, a city and county attorney, and a state legislator. He helped settlers claim title to their land, and the town of Scipio, in Millard County, honored him by taking his given name as its own.

He was "a man not without his foibles, but true as steel to the cause of right and never one to shirk responsibility," as one *Tribune* editor put it.[10]

A PUBLIC FIGURE WITH A WIDE CIRCLE OF FRIENDS

Maxwell's name and person were highly visible during his time in the land office and the marshal's office in Utah, as hundreds of land and mine notices, bankruptcy notes, and marshal's sales were published in the city's newspapers over his signature. Consequently, he was frequently evaluated openly in the editorial writing of the *Salt Lake Tribune*. In September 1873, for example, the *Tribune* said of him:

> Since Gen. Maxwell's advent here, he has been a consistent, firm, and intelligent advocate and supporter of the views of the administration in its treatment of the alien and rebellious elements comprising the social and political phases of Utah. . . . [H]e intuitively grasped the situation and deeply discerned the fact than an "irrepressible conflict" existed here between theocracy . . . and the government of the United States, between autocracy and American Republicanism.[11]

And as Maxwell was contemplating his run against George Q. Cannon, the *Tribune* published Rev. Norman McLeod's description of the general as a man "made of 'flint stuff,'" and someone who "could not be bought, sold, or intimidated."[12]

One of the ingredients in the disparate mixture of Maxwell's reported personal traits was that, despite his disabilities, he managed an active social life, which also was at times covered in the local papers. For example, a celebration in March 1872 to mark the third anniversary of founding of Corrine was capped with a gala attended by at least 250 guests. Prominently mentioned in the newspaper report of the event was General Maxwell and his partner, Miss M. Sprague, of Salt Lake City. Calling themselves the "Pioneers of 1872," the guests included Governor George L. Woods, Secretary of State George Black, Dr. and Mrs. John P. Taggart, Benjamin Majors and partner Miss Sewell, Oscar G. Sawyer, Anthony Godbe, Cyrus Myron Hawley, Dr. Amos K. Smith, and Mr. Lathrop of the Chicago *Tribune*. Dancing and laughter con-

---

[10] "The Disrupted 'Ring,'" *SLT*, July 26, 1878, 2, col. 2.
[11] "Premonitions," *SLT*, September 14, 1873, 2, col. 1.
[12] "From Ophir City Last Night," *SLT*, August 2, 1872, 2, col. 4.

tinued until five o'clock the next morning, when leave was taken for the returns to Salt Lake City, Ogden, Fort Hall, and Blue Creek.[13]

Maxwell's social circle included many lawyers with whom he came into frequent contact in the course of his jobs as a civil servant, including Robert N. Baskin, William Carey, and Obed Franklin Strickland, all of Salt Lake City, and Dennis J. Toohy from Corrine. Men with military backgrounds were also numbered as friends and acquaintances: Stephen E. Jocelyn, Joseph H. Wickizer, special agent of the U.S. Post Office Department, and Oliver Andrew Patton in the land office.[14] Maxwell is particularly linked with Judges James B. McKean, Philip H. Emerson, and Jacob Smith Boreman and with Henry Andrew Morrow, the commanding officer of Camp Douglas. Morrow was a Civil War veteran, with whom Maxwell shared a special bond. Thirteen years older than Maxwell, he had advantages of circumstance and education that Maxwell did not. Born in Warrenton, Virginia, educated at Rittenhouse Academy in Washington, D.C., Morrow served as a Senate page. He opened a law practice in Detroit and, with the onset of war, served with the Black Hats of the Twenty-fourth Michigan Infantry, the highly regarded Iron Brigade. Both men served from early in the war to its end, both sustained several wounds, both were captured and secured their freedom, both were wounded at Gettysburg, and both were field-promoted to brevet general.[15] At war's end, Morrow resumed his status as a regular army officer and was twice made the commander of Camp Douglas.[16]

---

[13] "Corinne," *Corinne Daily Reporter*, March 26, 1872, 2, col. 3.

[14] The United States Post Office Department was established by an act of Congress on June 28, 1872, www.usps.com/cpim/ftp/pubs/pub100.pdf.

[15] Morrow opened his law practice in Detroit after the Mexican War. He was elected judge of the Recorder's Court in Wayne County and became familiar with several Michigan figures, including Zachariah Chandler. In the Civil War he was acquainted with James H. Kidd and Ranald Mackenzie of the Michigan Cavalry Brigade. Morrow was sent to Camp Douglas in 1871 when it was judged that de Trobriand was not in sympathy with Sherman over enforcing federal laws in Utah. Morrow later commanded Vancouver Barracks in the Washington Territory and died in 1891 serving as Colonel of the 21st U.S. Infantry. Morrow, "To Chancellorsville"; Morrow, "Last of the Iron Brigade"; Boatner, *Civil War Dictionary*, 570; U.S. Federal Census, Washington Territory, Clark County, Vancouver, enumerated June 15, 1880; Hibbard, *Fort Douglas, Utah*, 70.

[16] The command post at Camp Douglas changed several times: de Trobriand from July 15 to October 21, 1870; Morrow from October 22, 1870, to June 30, 1871; de Trobriand from July 1 to October 4, 1871; Morrow from October 5, 1871, to August 27, 1874. Hibbard, *Fort Douglas, Utah*, 233.

Judge Boreman told of a time in the spring of 1873, shortly after his arrival in Salt Lake City, when General Maxwell arrived at the Clift House in a carriage with McKean and Emerson to take the four of them to spend an evening in the company of General Morrow and the other officers of the camp. This friendship between Maxwell, Morrow, and the other judges was to last as long as the men remained in Utah. Boreman included Maxwell in his account of their evening: "All enjoyed the visit, and were especially well pleased with General Morrow's vivacious story telling. He told us one good yarn on General Maxwell, but Maxwell declared it was ficticious [*sic*]. It was about as follows . . ."[17] Although Boreman intended to describe the humorous story, he unfortunately failed to return to his notes to complete it. Elsewhere Boreman described Maxwell as not only "one of the bravest of men and utterly fearless" but also "a man of great big heart, and full of good humor":

> He often repeated a joke I got off him and so I will tell it: We were coming up from Beaver to Salt Lake City in a . . . mail stage drawn by two horses. We were the only passengers and the stage was quite full of baggage. . . . [A]s we came along in the night we both became drowsy—I dropped off to sleep and was aroused by somebody fumbling about my feet. "Is that you Maxwell," I said. "Yes, I was just looking for my package of lunch. I had some eggs and I thought I would eat one—but no matter, I did not want to disturb you." I urged him to look for the eggs until he found them—but no, he would not. In the course of time, I was asleep again, and was awakened again by some one fumbling about my feet. The moon was shining by this time and I saw Maxwell's hand around the neck of a bottle. "Well, well, General, that is the first time in my life when I heard of any body carry[ing] eggs in a bottle." "I give up," he said, and we had a good hearty laugh. He wanted to share the contents of the bottle—but, of course, I did not rob him of his lunch.[18]

Maxwell was well integrated into the fraternity of lawyers of Salt Lake City throughout his years of activity in the land office and as U.S. marshal. An example of their camaraderie is seen in an episode that occurred in November 1875, when Maxwell joined with about twenty other attorneys and judges for an evening of humor arranged in tribute to Judge Boreman. The report of their self-effacing and lighthearted antics to honor Boreman was published in the *Salt Lake Herald*. After all the joking, however, the men resolved that a letter summarizing

---

[17] Arrington, "Crusade against Theocracy," 12–13.　　　　　[18] Ibid., 38–39.

their genuine professional praise for Boreman be drafted and sent to the attorney general and to President Grant.[19]

In addition to their ongoing friendships in Utah, Maxwell and "Mamie" were able to maintain intermittent contact with friends in Michigan. One example can be cited for November 1878, only thirteen months following the death of their son William in Monroe, when they returned to that city. A social note in the *Monroe Itemizer* recorded that they attended the Young People's Literary Society meeting, along with David S. Barry, newspaper correspondent in the Senate, and Miss Emma Reed, daughter of Lydia Ann Kirkpatrick Reed, the half-sister of George Armstrong Custer.[20]

In the Ring with the Heavyweights of Utah

"He would attack the Mormons relentlessly, driving resolute faithful into ever stronger defenses and alienating others willing to compromise." These words, written to describe *Salt Lake Tribune* editor and Maxwell's contemporary and associate Frederic Lockley, are also an apt depiction of Maxwell.[21] Stephen Cresswell emphasizes that underestimating Mormon adversaries was a failing of most of the U.S. attorneys assigned to Utah Territory.[22] And, like the others, Maxwell may have underestimated Mormon leaders, for surely they must have wished him dead or "used up" or "sent across lots" or "salted down" or sent "up the pocket of the Lord" or "nepo," to put outright murder in the peculiar vernacular of the times.[23] Based on his military record, another explanation is more likely: he simply ignored and disregarded the mismatch. Just as he had been in the war, he seemed unmindful of personal injury or consequences in Utah, for he fought almost always as the underdog against a greater power.

Maxwell went up against Brigham Young, called "the Profit" by his critics and "the Lion of the Lord" by his admirers, a man who, with a glance or a flex of his little finger, could command the wayward

---

[19] "Jacob S. Boreman—His Honor Complimented and Honored," *slh*, November 19, 1875.
[20] *Monroe Itemizer*, November 26, 1878.
[21] Charles E. Rankin, "Type and Stereotype," in Ritchie and Hutton, *Frontier and Region*, 69.
[22] Cresswell, *Mormons and Cowboys*.
[23] The code for "open" spelled backward, alluding to the evisceration of body cavities, which were then filled with stones for submersion. MacKinnon, *At Sword's Point*, 55, 303.

Mormon to be "wasted " in blood atonement.[24] Maxwell also engaged the coterie of "Smoothbore" George Q. Cannon, also known as "the Cardinal" or "the British mountain howitzer" (Cannon was born in Canada); Daniel H. Wells, "the One-Eyed Pirate of the Wasatch"; and the multifaceted Hosea Stout. Though ridiculed with these disparaging nicknames coined by their critics in the editorial platforms of the *Salt Lake Tribune*, these were men of extraordinary power and influence in Utah Territory in their time. Historian Gene Sessions describes them as Machiavellian: "The Mormons found ready justification for whatever actions would benefit their purposes. Although it is doubtful that Brigham Young had read Machiavelli, he was often an ardent practitioner of *Prince*-like tactics."[25] Maxwell knew these men were the heavyweights and that he was, by any local, Mormon measure, a minor contender. In a society made up of "nabobs and nobodies" there could be no doubt of who were the nabobs and who was the nobody.[26]

Cannon was a member of the triumvirate of the First Presidency, the first counselor to President Brigham Young. He was intelligent, articulate, prosperous. Editor and publisher of the *Deseret News*, he maintained a ready line of communication to the Mormon populace. He was well known and very connected and influential in Salt Lake City, and after many years in Congress he was equally at ease as one of the power-wielding nabobs in the District of Columbia. He is credited by historian Edward Leo Lyman as the one individual who, more than any other, Mormon or not, delayed or derailed the various anti-polygamy, anti-Mormon legislative acts in Congress.

Daniel H. Wells actively aided the Mormon cause as a member of the ultrasecret Council of Fifty before the band moved west. In Nauvoo he was a justice of the peace, acted as an intermediary between the Mormons and non-Mormons, and earned the title "Defender of Nauvoo." He became second counselor to President Young, and from 1870 to 1876 he was the mayor of Salt Lake City while remaining the shadow

---

[24] Judge Boreman refashioned Brigham Young's statement in this way: "A crook of his little finger would send terror into the hearts of those not inclined to bow to his oppressive power." Arrington, "Crusade against Theocracy," 26. This threat was restated elsewhere too—for example, "the 'crooking of his little finger['] pronounced sentence upon offenders" (Parshall, "'Pursue, Retake and Punish,'" 74–75) and "we try to live so when your finger crooks, we move" (William H. Dame to Brigham Young, in MacKinnon, *At Sword's Point*, 80–81).

[25] Sessions, "Two Utahs," 105.   [26] T. D. Clark and Guice, *Old Southwest*, 183.

commander of the Mormon Militia, despite its official dissolution. His rank as lieutenant general in the militia had been granted to only two other Mormons, Joseph Smith, the first president of the Church of Jesus Christ of Latter-day Saints, and Brigham Young, its second president. It was Wells who focused his one normal, nonwandering eye on the Mormon jury members and orchestrated the Mormon maneuvers during the second trial of John D. Lee.

Hosea Stout was a practicing attorney, the city attorney for St. George, the attorney general for the territory, the former head of the Mormon police in Nauvoo (where he was also a member of the Council of Fifty), and an acknowledged Danite as one of the "Be'hoys," or Brigham's boys.[27] Historian Howard R. Lamar says of his multiple roles: "Hosea Stout . . . was a legislator in the morning, attorney general in the afternoon, and judge advocate of the Nauvoo Legion at night."[28] Appointed by President Abraham Lincoln as the U.S. attorney to Utah Territory, Stout selected a substitute to act in his stead and never defended the interests of the United States in court.[29] He was active in the School of the Prophets and thereby in matters of the land office. His diary records a number of instances in which he was acting either as a representative of the Mormon church or the counsel for a Mormon in litigation over land matters.[30]

Maxwell never made any inroads in the view that the high-echelon Mormon leaders held of him as a blackguard. Speaking to friends in Congress, Cannon sliced Maxwell scathingly when he said that "Mormons took no more notice of Maxwell than they did of a street cur."[31] When a *Washington Post* reporter asked Cannon for his opinion of Maxwell, the response came that "he [Cannon] had fought and beaten him and his gang, and didn't consider them of anymore consequence than flies on a bull's horn."[32]

Maxwell's approach to the imbalance of his task was reminiscent of his past: "The people of Utah must take no backward step. There were those among them who had fought this battle with Theocracy for ten, twelve, fifteen years, knowing well in every encounter they would be

[27] Quinn, "A Culture of Violence," in *Mormon Hierarchy*, 244.

[28] Lamar, "Political Patterns," 378.   [29] Brooks, *On the Mormon Frontier*, 713.

[30] Ibid., 713–40.   [31] Cannon to Young, March 21, 1874, BYC.

[32] "Cannon's Interview," SLT, February 14, 1878, 2, col. 1, reprinted from *Washington Post*, February 8, 1878.

"Enoque's 'Trinity in Unity': Three Souls with but
a Single Thought, Three Heads That Are but One."
Caricatured are (*left to right*) Brigham Young, Daniel H. Wells, and Hosea
Stout. They are wearing homemade wooden shoes in answer to Young's
emphasis on self-sufficiency, with one hand in the pocket where Brigham
Young controlled money as trustee-in-trust for the LDS church. *Published
in Enoch's Advocate, May 18, 1874, reprinted in Bunker and Bitton*, Mormon
Graphic Image, *42*.

beaten. The soldier who goes into battle knowing he will be overpow-
ered, shows the highest qualities of heroism."[33]

RELATIONSHIP WITH A MURDERER

The lone prominent Mormon who expressed any degree of sincere
personal interest in Maxwell was John Doyle Lee. Lee was, for most
of their association, Maxwell's prisoner in circumstances where both
were under immense stress. Despite conditions that were conducive to
prisoner abuse, Maxwell treated Lee with sensitive consideration and
kindness. It can be argued that Maxwell's motive may have been only
to facilitate a plea bargain with Lee, in exchange for evidence about
other participants and planners in the Mountain Meadows massacre.
But Lee surely would have recognized a self-serving motive in Maxwell, for he readily recognized it in others who made the attempt. In his
diary Lee describes Maxwell as "my good friend," and it can seen from
his entries, particularly those from January and February 1876, that a
genuine bond existed between the two.

When Maxwell found Lee, the prisoner under escort, to be the only
person in the party who remained awake on the first night of their
journey from Beaver to the penitentiary in Salt Lake City, the marshal
had reacted with good-natured warmth. Maxwell continued his kindness to Lee long after the prisoner made his final decision to remain
silent about the role of other Mormon men in the massacre. Maxwell
undoubtedly knew of the reputation that Lee had gained among many
of the people of southern Utah as a liar, a swindler, and a brute.[34] The
acrostic poem composed by Lee honoring Maxwell's friend Oliver A.
Patton, in appreciation for the simple act of Patton's arranging delivery
of the newspaper to Lee at the prison, seems to lessen the contention
that Lee was nothing but an insensitive psychopath.

It is a reasonable description that Maxwell and Lee respected one
another as one officer respects another. As officers in their respective
governments, each had followed, from a profoundly held commitment,
the difficult and, certainly in Lee's case, utterly deplorable duty that
fell to them. Both persisted, despite the consequences, in carrying the

---

[33] "City Convention," *SLT*, July 18, 1874, 4, col. 4.
[34] Bagley, *Blood of the Prophets*, 263.

full responsibility of their commitment. Both expected the unwavering support of the authority that sent them, and both experienced the failure of that support when it was most needed. Historian Will Bagley describes Lee as a "troubled, deeply flawed fanatic" but adds that "it is impossible not to recognize his contrary integrity and his unshakable commitment to his beliefs.[35]

Maxwell, like most American Protestants, believed that freedom of religion was characterized, even defined, by separation of church and state. He did not accept the Mormons' opposing view that freedom of religion was defined by the fusion of church and state.[36] Thus Maxwell was not sympathetic to the view, deeply held by many Mormon people of Utah, that polygamy was a complex, profound aspect of their theology, not a simple, easily rectified matter of creed. Like other federal appointees, he did not appreciate the Mormons' profound distrust of government, which stemmed from the treatment they had experienced in Ohio, Missouri, and Illinois, in the 1857 Utah War, and continuing to the time of Maxwell's tenure. Maxwell viewed the Mormon and non-Mormon issues of the times only in binary perspective; he saw them as incompatible, without any middle ground for compromise, as a man more politically aspiring or politically astute might have found.

Despite the improbability of success against an overwhelming Mormon majority, Maxwell may have hosted serious political aspirations. Had he been willing to leave Utah, his military record and his ties with the administration and the Grand Army of the Republic would have granted him important political capital. As in the war, however, the option to leave was never taken; quitting was not in him. Personal gain came second to achieving the republican democracy demanded by the nation and by Utah's non-Mormon merchants and professionals.

In His Own Words

If Maxwell had pursued an elected office, his writing and speaking talents would have lent him a strong advantage over many potential opponents. Records from his own hand, though scarce, provide a window into the

---

[35] Ibid., 317.
[36] Maxwell was associated in Utah with both the Methodist and Presbyterian churches. Both groups were outspoken critics of polygamy and the failure of Mormon leaders to separate church and state.

core of the man. Wartime correspondence with his sister, Emma, gives evidence of an above-average vocabulary, with the correct use of words such as "enigma," "dilatory," "ascertained," "huzza," and "begrimed." He cautioned Emma about holding a high standard for herself and avoiding friends who would endanger that standard. He scolded his family when they failed to write, he was at times jovial about army life, and he was able to see himself the object of camp life humor. Joking to Emma on Frank Hawley's weight gain at Camp Rucker, he ended with a note that he, by himself, individually, naked, without boots or clothing, weighed only 160 pounds.[37]

One surprising letter to his sister survives to tell that this steel-nerved military leader found emotional expression in creating poetry. Following his own brush with death at the Second Battle of Bull Run, and the death of Generals "Kearny the Magnificent" and Isaac Stevens at Chantilly, he paused for a time before leaving Sully plantation on the morning of September 2, 1862. In a poem of eight stanzas, Maxwell lamented the dreadful results of the rebellion of the South that had been hatched in the beautiful buildings of the Southern leaders and proudly memorialized those of the Union who responded to lessen this "mighty shame."

Farewell old Chantilly's halls, farewell
So famed in our nation's story.
Neath this roof there once did dwell
Our country's best and finest glory.

But past is all thy greatness now
Thy name alone, alone remains
The wreath is plucked from off thy brow
Thou art covered now with guilt and shame.

For neath this roof where Washington stood
In days of past and times of yore
Was plotted scenes of death and blood
And a nation's misery was laid in store.

He that dwelt within these walls
Was sheltered by this mossy roof,
He that trod these spacious halls
From his home and friends now stand aloof.

[37] George R. Maxwell to Emma Maxwell, October 2, 1861, letter in possession of Bruce Turner Cunard II.

He sold himself to a traitorous cause
And plotted our nation's misery and woe.
Outraged our noble, sacred and righteous laws
And laid her in dust and ashes low.

But past is all thy greatness now
Chantilly's walls shall lonely stand
A lasting monument of grief and woe
To traitors within our noble land.

Chantilly's pleasant rooms farewell
Thou art better now than when we came.
The past and future we know them well
But we have lessened thy mighty shame.

For Freedom's sons have proudly stood
And on the God of battle and call
Begrimed with thy own owner's blood
Within these ancient and mossy walls.[38]

Formed in iambic tetrameter, this is a surprising creation for a man of sparse formal education, a man not accustomed to sharing his emotion. Noteworthy are the details of the poem's construction that seem more accomplished than expected of a novice. There is the frequent use of end-stopping, in which the end of a line coincides with a punctuation mark or a natural pause, pushing the poem forward in a marching rhythm. Maxwell clearly had an ear for language. Most likely this ability arose from reading a great deal of poetry from books carried in his saddlebags. The meter, the application of stressed and unstressed words and syllables, and the pauses for emphasis may been patterned after works of several poets, notably Whittier, Longfellow, and Tennyson.[39]

Two of the most revealing expressions by which we can judge Maxwell are his centerpiece oration at the celebration on July 4, 1871, and his speech at the delegate nomination convention in Corinne in May 1872, when he ran against George Q. Cannon. Reading the text of the Fourth of July speech permits a view beneath the surface of the farmer, the sailor, the cavalryman, and the federal official. The grandiloquent

---

[38] George R. Maxwell, "Lines Suggested on Leaving Chantilly," September 2, 1862, in letter in possession of Bruce Turner Cunard II. The Sully plantation and slave quarters were built in Chantilly in the late eighteenth century by Richard Bland Lee, the uncle of Robert E. Lee.

[39] I am indebted to my son, Bryan Geoffrey Maxwell, MA, MD, for his analysis and description of the poem's construction.

Victorian tone of his word usage is strange to present-day ears. Some would judge it as mawkish, pompous. However, its structure, subject matter, and language tell us a great deal about the character of the man Maxwell had become in his twenty-nine years. He evidences a better education than many men of his time, especially for one who had spent four years of his life in war service, atop a horse, sleeping on the ground or in a tent, and having little access to the infrastructure and educational opportunities conducive to culture, development of verbal skills, and book learning. In his oration, he quotes from the classical poetry of the time and displays an intellectual bent that is remarkably strong for a mere isolated farm boy.

"Freedom" might well have been the appropriate title of the speech, given that it deals very broadly with the historical context from which America's freedom arose. His was an extraordinarily broad, macroscopic perspective as he spoke of the debt the nation owed, first, to England as its mother country and, second, to France for its aid in freeing America from its maternal ties. His several references to the Civil War emphasize that the freedoms purchased by the war were literally paid in brothers' blood: "No brother stands grimly facing death by a brother's hand. . . . I see my only brother's face, looking at me from the other world." Maxwell rejoices that no involuntary slave's voice mingles in freedom's songs, and he envisions Utah to be standing at the edge of a new freedom that will come when the territory's riches of silver, iron, and copper attract a new population. He sounds a note of softness, of reconciliation, of commonality, with these lines:

> The graves of the late war are now clothed with nature's green, grassy robe. As enemies they fought, as foes they fell, now in silence, as brothers, they lie on the bosom of mother earth, and silently agree in one common grave; thus teaching Americans a lesson that they should cover up the scars and heal the lasting heart wounds as far as possible. [If you] kick over a stone on the earth's surface, it leaves a scar; but nature will not let it remain. Startle not, boy in blue; sleep on, confederate brother; the sounds you hear today are not the sounds that summon you to death, but they are freedom's salutes, fired in commemoration of deeds of valor done. The Nation rejoices that we have a country.[40]

---

[40] Oration delivered by Gen. George R. Maxwell at the Liberal Institute in Salt Lake City on July 4, 1871, full text published as "Oration" in *SLT*, July 7, 1871, 3, col. 3.

Maxwell's vocabulary is remarkably rich and well supplied, his grammatical structures are complex, his use of words is skillful and creative, and the mental images he conveys are vivid and immediately connect with the reader:

—the cheer of France was heard mingling with our huzza.
—the cannon, awkwardly managed on the village green by stalwart farmer's sons.
—young America will . . . sling lightning at the world.
—built steam bridges for the ocean.
—the dogs of war are housed in the dark and silent arsenals.[41]
—the army that has pontooned death's river.
—the sword starting from the scabbard of mother England.
—But dawn now streaks the flowing East.[42]

The man of the Custer Medal, a Thunderbolt of Sheridan, was interpreted by his wartime contemporaries as one lacking fear, but in his oration Maxwell frankly admits to owning the same fears of death and mutilation as others had: "We know what it is to stand where death-shots rattle, and the bravest hold their breath, waiting for their doom. . . . Boys in blue: we have seen that flag where the grim monster, Death, was its bearer, and all that he could reach he gathered to the sepulchre, yet we dressed on center, did we not?" Despite recurring tragedy and disability that dogged him, his unconquerable optimism burns through. He will not submit to depression and defeat: "There is more to life now than there used to be. . . . [W]e go faster and get around quicker. . . . [T]here never was a more propitious time in which to live than now, and in America. There are great works to do, and the world needs heroes now, Utah needs heroes."[43]

The nostalgic and melancholic first line of the concluding paragraph sounds as if it was written by a man who had a clear view that his would not be a long life—"And when we pass off this spot of eternity men call time"—yet he ends in a very uplifting, idealistic conception of freedom whose images appear to have been taken from his sailing days or from Longfellow's "O Ship of State":

---

[41] Maxwell appears to have had exposure to Shakespeare's *Julius Caesar*: "Cry 'Havoc,' and let slip the dogs of war" (act 3, scene 1).
[42] Maxwell oration, July 4, 1871.
[43] Ibid.

May we see the old Ship of State all in repair; may the blood be all washed off its decks, the dents upon its sides all repaired and planked with the laws; her masts fastened with eternal and equal justice; her cordage as strong as the cords that bind human hearts; with the beacon light of Liberty at her mast head, with the Constitution for a rudder and good men at the helm, "Sail on, oh Ship of State."[44]

It deserves the strongest emphasis that on a holiday when the majority and minority groups had segregated themselves from one another, where contention was frequently near flash point between the two, not a single instance of the word "Mormon," nor a criticism or negative comment alluding to the church or its leaders, could be found in his oration.

In his appearances before Congress, Maxwell speech was flowing and articulate, integrating uncommon phrases such as "pliable audacity," "reckless mendacity," "stoma of shame," and "hot furnace of priestly calumny." Maxwell's ability with language made him the featured orator at holiday celebrations, political rallies, meetings of the Liberal Party and the Improved Order of the Red Men. The audience frequently called for him to speak at the Liberal Institute, at meetings of the Territorial Central Committee, and at meetings of the Grand Army of the Republic. In many gatherings he was called by the crowd for an extemporaneous speech befitting the occasion, and he inevitably roused their passions with his words. His oration at the ratification meeting of the Liberal Party, announcing the candidacy of Robert N. Baskin as the opponent of George Q. Cannon in the upcoming 1874 election, illustrates this capability to stir the emotions:

> It is needless to go into the history of Mormonism. Founded in fraud, steeped in iniquity, upheld by fear, cemented with superstition, and colored with blood, its course is paved with broken hearts, crushed hopes and human bones. So fraught with crime as to make all Christians shutter, so tarnished with shame as to make all women blush, so foul with sin and imposture as to make Satan envious! And all this in the name of the LORD![45]

On May 16, 1872, members of the Liberal Party, including Maxwell, gathered in Corinne for a warm-up meeting to garner support for the reelection of President Ulysses S. Grant and Vice President Schuyler Colfax. Maxwell's speech for the occasion was colorfully partisan and

---

[44] Ibid.   [45] "Freedom in Utah," *SLT*, July 29, 1874, 4, col. 2.

gave the Grant administration full credit for any gains that had been made against the fetters imposed by the theocracy of the territory: "For the old Common Law was substituted the Book of Mormon, for statute law was substituted the Doctrine and Covenants, for the jury trial was substituted the will of one man, for the great principle that a man may have his day in court had been substituted the High Council, where, unheard, untried, men are doomed to die."[46] Alluding to the action by Judge McKean against the arrest and indictment of Brigham Young, Maxwell forcefully spelled out that any error in judgment or in the judicial process committed against either Brigham Young or those involved in the Englebrecht case was the responsibility of himself and Judge McKean, for both men were under unequivocal instructions from President Grant that the laws were to be carefully and correctly applied. Grant would not tolerate any illegal shading or shaving of their correct application, Maxwell emphasized.

A Shortened and Tragic Life

Maxwell's personal life could easily be viewed as a series of tragedies. His mother died when he was seven. His father's remarriage brought a stepmother who did not fill the role of a committed parent, and this marriage ended in an acrimonious divorce. Maxwell then found himself with a second stepmother only twelve years older than he. Too old to be mothered by Emeline and too young to be totally independent, Maxwell became the outsider in a family that would grow to include nine children.

After taking up arms in the Civil War, he was fired in the crucible of adversity for almost the entire duration of his service and acquired the psychological baggage of having seen the violent deaths of most of the young men he had commanded. He heard of the deaths of his fellow schoolmates at the Michigan State Normal School, Bigelow and Whelan. Maxwell's chronically agonizing physical wounds and exhausting disabilities denied him the inheritance privileges of the family land traditionally afforded to the firstborn son. Prosthetic replacements for amputated limbs, especially at the level of Maxwell's amputation, were

---

[46] Speech of Gen. George R. Maxwell, in "Grant and Colfax," *Corinne Reporter*, May 17, 1872, 2, col. 1.

expensive, primitive, cumbersome, ill fitting, and painful. When criticism was leveled that he had not paid his taxes, he replied on several occasions that he paid them daily with every step he took.[47]

To these burdens were added the death of his younger brother at Harper's Ferry within months of joining the same cavalry unit and within days of becoming an officer. Next was the sudden, inexplicable death of first wife in Michigan, just months after their wedding. His three children all died in infancy. Matthew Burgher, a friend and fellow soldier of the Michigan Cavalry with whom he had shared the experience of being a prisoner of the Confederates, and whom he had placed in the penumbra of danger by appointing him warden of the U.S. Territorial Penitentiary, was bludgeoned to death by penitentiary escapees only months before his pending wedding to a beautiful and accomplished young lady from Philadelphia.[48] Then came the inglorious death and the mutilation of the body and honor of his role model and respected commander, George Armstrong Custer, and the various indignities to Custer's memory that followed. His close friend Judge McKean died impoverished, depressed, extremely lonely, and unappreciated by many.

Near his own death, Maxwell would surely have questioned whether he had made an acceptable mark, as some of his former supporters vacillated or remained silent. Despite accusations of fraud and corruption for financial gain that began as early as his time in the land office, he was, at death, in penury. He was unable to pay for any home health care and had to rely on what care his wife could provide. The only item of monetary value declared in his will was a reimbursement bill wherein the federal government owed him ninety dollars for his purchase of a prosthesis for his stump. Were the gold Custer Medal, the Grand Army of the Republic pin, and the gold Joslin and Park watch, a gift of respect from fellow lawyers, sold to meet expenses?[49] Did he pawn his saber, his Colt revolver, his other personal Civil War memorabilia? At the last he was reduced to virtually begging the federal government for an increase in his Civil War disability pension.

Despite these burdens, several of Maxwell's contemporaries commented on his humor, his good heart, his willingness to be the subject

---

[47] Some states made Civil War veterans, especially disabled ones, exempt from taxes. Utah Territory did not.

[48] "Death of Capt. Bergher [sic]," *slt*, March 17, 1876, 4, col. 3.

[49] Joslin and Park was a Salt Lake City jewelry firm.

of a joking or ribald story, and his ability to laugh at his own behavior. It was said that he was a man who wanted to appear ferocious and formidable, but in fact he was far more mild. Even John D. Lee, as he was transported from the Beaver prison to the Utah penitentiary as Maxwell's prisoner, commented that Maxwell was in his "usual frivolity" and joking with the carriage driver. In his time of highest stress over the charges of financial malfeasance Maxwell was able to summon a humorous comment on his treatment. He said if he were to be removed as marshal, he would "urge the appointment of 'Guerilla' Mosby to be his successor, as he had long cherished a hatred for this man," and that if he could "succeed in getting him in the marshal's office, he [would] be fully revenged."[50]

A Hero in Utah?

Depending on whether he is viewed from the perspective of the dedicated Mormons or from that the non-Mormon men and women of Utah, distinctly different portraits of George R. Maxwell can be painted. Mormons saw in him a Wolverine, propelled in a mindless charge against their fundamental beliefs in theocratic rule and plural marriage. Thought to be a major figure in a secret ring, in a plan originated by eastern federal leaders against Utah's people, he was seen as self-serving, of marginal competence, a myrmidon in the forces of evil assailing God's appointed people. To the non-Mormons of Utah he was a person of more than average gifts, who attempted under extremely trying circumstances and life-altering disabilities, to sincerely perform his duty as it was framed for him by his president and as he viewed it from his own patriotic perspective. Having vanquished the Confederates and slavery, the first of the Republican Party's "the twin relics," he arrived in the Salt Lake valley, to contend with polygamy, its second relic. In Utah he was frustrated by anemic administrative support in the land office. As marshal he was callously deprived of the money needed to meet his professional obligations. His best efforts to move Congress to enact the laws needed for carrying out the mandates given him in both positions were slow to bear fruit. In the military he had been surrounded by like-minded men;

---

[50] "Washington," *SLT*, January 26, 1876, 4, col. 2.

but in the West, he was in a minuscule, unwelcome minority, at times abandoned by those who had promised support. Yet he persisted in seeking federal laws to bring solutions for the issues in which he could not permit compromise. In Utah his allegiance to men who had served the Union and his respect for those of the Confederacy were constant. He fully supported GAR veterans, and he earned admiration from members of the business community and from his fellow government appointees, forging enduring bonds with many. He held an inspirational, uplifting vision of Utah's future that transcended the conflict between Mormons and non-Mormons that had enveloped him, and he predicted that Utah would become a beautiful addition among the galaxy of statehood stars.

If he were to return to the state and people of Utah in the present day, he would undoubtedly know "the place that should be mine." In life he was unappreciated, even vilified, by the very people whose rights and freedoms under statehood he fought to attain. Maxwell might find sufficient reward if he were able to observe Utah's present-day society, not one with features dangerously close to a totalitarian state structured by Mormon stalwarts Brigham Young, Daniel H. Wells, George Q. Cannon, and Hosea Stout, but one that has acquired most of the attributes of freedom that he and many of his non-Mormon contemporaries devoted their lives to bring to pass. Writer David Bigler would include Maxwell among those whose contribution to Utah is "as profound as it is largely unknown . . . found mainly in the freedoms that Utahns of all faiths now often take for granted," freedoms that include "the right to live where one wishes, to own property, to equal protection under the law, to vote in secret, to come and go as one chooses, to make economic choices that decide the quality of life, to [have] normal family relationships, and to worship as one wishes."[51]

"In the quest for western heroes, there is good reason now to look in unexpected, less explored places," historian Patricia Nelson Limerick suggests.[52] Recognized for his accomplishments, respected for his admirable qualities, and loved for his faults, George R. Maxwell was a hero.

---

[51] David L. Bigler, "More Than a Beacon," unpublished 2005 article on Utah Lighthouse Ministry, which honors the contributions of the many non-Mormon, Christian missionaries who brought public education to the people of the Utah.

[52] Limerick, *Something in the Soil,* 315.

15

Lance of Iron, Wings of Stone

He shakes his lance of iron and he claps his wings of stone.
G. K. Chesterton, "Lepanto"

GEORGE R. MAXWELL SPENT FOUR YEARS OF HIS ADULT LIFE
AS a soldier, living with death and violence. Through self-study during
and after the war, he followed a different path. He became a lawyer and
advantageously used this and his Michigan and Civil War associations
to help bring about the changes in Utah Territory that leaders in the
federal government and society sought. He lobbied Congress for the legislation needed to neutralize the power of the Mormon theocracy, while
he worked to bring the Mormon populace into compliance with existing
law. His "prime, only, and everlasting instruction" from his superiors was
to "compel obedience to the laws."[1] He claimed that he began his professional duties in Utah with "malice toward none and charity towards all."
If he arrived without bias, as he claimed, his transformation into a critic
was very rapid, for he had become outspoken by the time of the Fourth
of July festivities in Corinne less than a month later. Several experiences
awaited him, as well as other federal appointees in the territory, that
could readily fuel nascent ill will against the Mormon leadership.

---

[1] "Brigham Young's Janissary," *New York World*, November 25, 1871. Judge Jacob S. Boreman is
recorded as having said almost the same words: "The only way to peaceably settle . . . the
'Mormon problem['] is simply to enforce the laws. . . . A rigid but just enforcement of the
laws is the most terrible process to which the priestly criminals who rule in the Territory can
be subjected." Arrington, "Crusade against Theocracy," 45.

Two Worlds That Did Not Meet

Immediate adjustment to social isolation and antagonism was the first task that confronted the arriving non-Mormons. They had no place in an isolated society that was closed to all but those of the same religious allegiance. U.S. marshals and attorneys and other federal appointees were viewed as aliens, as intruders. Brigham Young thought that contact between Mormons and non-Mormons, especially government appointees, would only "create a kind of . . . Babylon" in their midst.[2] Historian Charles S. Peterson relates the words of the Mormon stalwart George Q. Cannon about the presence of non-Mormons: "It is because they are in Salt Lake City, that I am opposed to them. [Cannon wanted] 'no power to be brought into our midst as the wooden horse was in to Troy.'"[3] Apostle John Taylor, later the third president of the Mormon church, advised his Saints in 1871 to treat outsiders as unclean:

> Do not mingle with those abominations that have been imported into your midst; keep away from them and let them alone, and let the wicked and corrupt wallow in their wickedness and corruption. Have nothing to do with it. Don't go to their balls, assemblies, or associations; keep apart from them and let them alone, they are not worthy of your association. We live in a purer atmosphere, we breathe a purer air, we worship another God, we have another religion, one that is very willing and liberal enough to extend to all, the rights that all men want; but we will not associate with them in their corruptions and infamy. . . . Be not timid . . . for God is on the side of right, and he will protect his people; and let their enemies look out.[4]

This separation of worlds had many practical manifestations. For nearly every marshal in Utah Territory there is on file in the Department of Justice a collection of letters alleging some combination of incompetence, intemperance, fraud, and corruption. Alongside this is a similar set of letters counterbalancing with words of praise and defense. The duties of the marshal, by their very nature, were conducive to his becoming an outcast. The office controlled the expenditure of substantial amounts of money, and a marshal could readily make enemies by failing to patronize certain vendors or important figures in

---

[2] Brigham Young (October 6, 1863), *Journal of Discourses*, 12:306.

[3] C. S. Peterson, *Utah*, 46. Cannon's words are taken from his sermon October 7, 1863, *Journal of Discourses*, 12:296.

[4] Discourse by John Taylor, Salt Lake Tabernacle, presented December 15, 1871, published in *DN*, December 17, 1871.

the community. Other enemies came from people who were arrested, from persons served warrants to appear as unwilling witnesses, and from associates or underlings who wished to ascend politically to the marshal's office. In Utah there was a unique divide, between Mormons and non-Mormons.

Not only were the male federal officers ostracized from the tight-knit Mormon society, but isolation also extended to their wives and families. Women responded by forming Gentile-only groups such as the Blue Tea Society for social interaction and intellectual stimulation.[5] George R. Maxwell and Mary Ann Sprague were married in Salt Lake City in the home of her physician father, who had been a well-respected Mormon of many years standing. Yet the newlyweds chose the non-Mormon town of Corinne in which to celebrate their marriage. This was the one and only city in the territory where there were almost no Mormons, where non-Mormons could find acceptance and an active, inclusive social life.

Maxwell carried out his responsibilities with grudgingly given, if any, support from the people of the territory. When first appointed U.S. marshal, he found there were no offices for occupation and use by the federal courts, there were no jails for incarceration of federal prisoners, and no records had been maintained.[6] All of these services had to be provided without funds advanced for the purpose. For a year and a half, the officials of the Third District Court (which, at times, also functioned as the territorial Supreme Court) found that the only quarters non-Mormon owners would rent for federal court use was a hayloft over the Faust and Houtz livery stable on Second South between Main and State streets. It was here that crowds gathered when Ann Eliza Webb Young sued Brigham Young for divorce in 1871. For many years the federal courtrooms at Salt Lake were located near malodorous privies, and for a time they were located below a second-floor brothel. Maxwell's experience was not unlike the June 1859 episode when Judge Charles E. Sinclair, unable to rent appropriate space, tried unsuccessfully to use the small office of the secretary of state. When he was offered a large tent by a circus passing through, Governor Alfred Cumming finally intervened and compelled the Mormons to provide space for court functions.[7]

---

[5] P. L. Scott, "Jennie Anderson Froiseth."
[6] Cresswell, "U.S. Department of Justice," 214.
[7] Ibid.

MORMON HYPERBOLE AND INVECTIVE

The forty-year rancorous relationship between the Mormons and the federal representatives in Utah was not entirely the fault of the criticisms and demands for change leveled by the non-Mormons. The very words of Brigham Young and other Mormon leaders contributed significantly to the tensions of the times. Eugene E. Campbell describes Young's rhetoric as very often being inflammatory, excessive, full of hyperbole, sarcasm, and rough farm talk and frontier humor. The result was that "many federal appointees came expressing good will toward Mormons, only to be disillusioned by the anti-government sentiment pronounced in public gatherings."[8] Many influential Mormons followed Young's lead "in alienating almost every territorial officer who came to Utah between 1850 and 1877" and contributed to antagonizing "every president from Zachary Taylor to Ulysses S. Grant."[9] David Bigler describes "a deep sense of Mormon resentment toward the federal government and its leaders, conveyed in language at the highest level that often offended other Americans."[10] Young frequently behaved as though he was convinced that federal officials were in conspiracy to destroy the Mormon community. He told his faithful Saints in a Fourth of July oration that only selfish goals, only greed and hatred of the Mormons, would motivate non-Mormons to live and serve in Utah: "No person comes here because he prefers this country. None but sinister or pecuniary motives can prompt those who are not of us to abide in our midst. This country suits us merely because no other well informed people can covet its possession."[11]

The faithful Mormon listener may have appreciated this style, for strong, colorful, and shocking words could push sleep away in the long summer sermons in the heat under the Bowery. However, the non-Mormons who heard him or later read his published sermons often considered him a dangerous, irresponsible demagogue. A sample taken from Young's sermons illustrates his inflammatory language, which was far removed from being carefully chosen or even minimally diplomatic: "If these officers are like many who have previously been sent here . . .

---

[8] Campbell, *Essential Brigham Young*, xxi, xxii.
[9] Ibid.
[10] Bigler, "Theocracy versus Republic."
[11] Brigham Young, July Fourth oration, in *DN*, July 9, 1856.

they are poor, miserable blacklegs, broken down political hacks, robbers, and whoremongers—men that are not fit for civilized society."[12] Young's close associates Heber C. Kimball and George A. Smith followed suit, with use of strong language. Jedediah Morgan Grant (who described himself as Mormon Thunder) and Daniel H. Wells were also among those of the upper echelons of the Mormon hierarchy who often used Young's style. On this evidence, many non-Mormons concluded that the Mormon leaders, and hence the Mormon people, were profoundly disloyal and in opposition to the federal government.[13] Campbell concludes that Brigham Young's spoken and written words were, like the man, complicated and difficult to unravel and interpret. Although he was a very able organizer and an effective colonizer, his "attitude towards the federal government may be described as ambivalent to paranoid, resulting in almost constant difficulties with federal officials. [Young] . . . fostered an attitude of antagonism toward the federal government which led to hardship and almost resulted in the destruction of the [Mormon] church."[14]

In his treatment of the events leading to the 1857 Utah War, William P. MacKinnon credits the 1854–55 actions of Bvt. Lt. Col. Edward Jenner Steptoe and his men as generating in Brigham Young a permanent distrust of federal presence. Steptoe's mission had been, in part, to investigate the murder of Capt. John W. Gunnison and his party. Through the fall, winter, and spring the presence of Steptoe's 325 soldiers and an unknown but large number of camp followers, residing in the Salt Lake valley, resulted in an unwelcome mixture of eligible Gentile men with Utah's pristine young women. On their departure in the spring, Steptoe and his men took with them "as many as one hundred single and married Mormon women seeking an exit from the LDS church under the protection of a military escort to California." Brigham Young vowed "never again to allow federal troops into Utah and in proximity to its women."[15] However, most federal appointees arriving in Utah had been soldiers and were undoubtedly painted by Young and Mormon leaders with the same brush of mistrust. As Young

---

[12] Brigham Young, *Journal of Discourses*, 5:232.
[13] Campbell, *Essential Brigham Young*, xxii.
[14] Ibid.
[15] MacKinnon, *At Sword's Point*, 49–50; MacKinnon, "Sex, Subalterns, and Steptoe."

put it: "Such dogs and skunks as Drummond, Burr, Hurt and others of a similar stripe [have been] sent here by the authority of the Government to rule over men as far above them, as they are above the low and vicious animals they so faithfully represent."[16]

Author Wallace Stegner takes the view that the Mormons intentionally courted public discord for its advantages to a people for whom unity and solidarity in their isolation were critical:

> Brother Brigham and Heber C. Kimball . . . were always offering to send their enemies to hell across lots, or give them a dose that would puke them worse than lobelia. . . . Persecution and hardship are an exceedingly effective trying ground. . . . Throughout his career Brigham kept that firmly in mind; he fanned the hatred of the Gentiles, he fostered the sense of being surrounded and persecuted.[17]

THREATS FOR MORMON BLOOD

Historian William P. MacKinnon writes of the threats by the enemies of the Mormons to repeal the organic law that had brought Utah Territory into existence, and of the decades-long paring down of the geographical boundaries originally claimed by Brigham Young. This near obliteration of Utah as a geopolitical entity arose from widely held public perceptions that Mormons were immoral, un-American, disloyal, theocratic, and anti-mining.[18]

Without the efforts of truculent, abrasive, disliked, and persistent men such as Maxwell working within the law for legislative solutions, the threats of another type of violence against the Mormons, that of U.S. military forces, particularly targeting Mormon leadership, might have become reality. At the time of the impending 1857 Utah War, the *New York Times* editorial urged President Buchanan to strike a decisive blow that "may require much bloodshed." Buchanan's advisers suggested that attacking the Mormons would transfer the nation's focus from the problems of slavery to polygamy. In April 1857, while the talk was of sending troops from Fort Leavenworth, *Harper's Weekly* commented: "The matter has, in fact, passed beyond the line of argument,

---

[16] MacKinnon, *At Sword's Point*, 67.
[17] W. Stegner, *Mormon Country*, 61, 143–44.
[18] MacKinnon, "Like Splitting a Man,'" 103.

and it is time . . . for the Government of the United States to interpose. We do not call for fire or slaughter. No Highland clan sort of operation—no Glencoe massacre. But, *at whatever cost*, the United States must declare and vindicate its supremacy."[19] In July 1864, Gen. Patrick Connor, contending that the Mormons were refusing to recognize the federal "greenback" currency, sent a contingent of troops to occupy quarters on South Temple Street very near to the Mormon Tabernacle. Connor's reports described Brigham Young as a traitor and told his military commanders that he was prepared to defeat any military effort launched by the Mormon militia. Only on the command of his superior officers from San Francisco did Connor withdraw the provost guard; San Francisco military commanders further cautioned that war with the Mormons at the time would require numbers that would weaken the Union forces needed elsewhere.[20]

In 1866 testimony before James M. Ashley's Committee on Territories, General Connor and other witnesses made two pointed assertions: the Utah militia was vastly overrated, and with five thousand troops Connor could "sweep the Utah Territory as with a broom."[21] In March 1867, two years after the Civil War ended, Gen. William Tecumseh Sherman, who had obliterated much of the South on his campaign, made it known that "any action against them [Mormons] would call for troops much needed on the plains."[22] Shortly after the start of the first trial of John D. Lee for the murders in Mountain Meadows, the *San Francisco Post* editor called for extermination of the Mormons: "No Mormon should be left in the United States."[23] In 1880, Rev. Thomas Dewitt Talmage, a nationally known Protestant minister in Brooklyn, New York, called for the physical destruction of the Mormons: "I tell you that Mormonism will never be destroyed until it is destroyed by the guns of the United States government. It would not be war. I hate war.

---

[19] *Harper's Weekly*, April 25, 1857. Emphasis added.

[20] Colton, *Civil War*, 190.

[21] T. B. H. Stenhouse, Washington, D.C., to Brigham Young, June 19, 1866, BYC. In this meeting of the Committee on Territories, Connor also made four serious accusations about the Mormons that greatly angered Brigham Young: one-third of the adult population practiced polygamy in violation of the 1862 law that made it illegal; Mormons taught disloyalty and treason against the government; Mormons engaged in justified homicide through their Danite bands; and Mormons opposed the development of mining in Utah. B. D. Madsen, *Glory Hunter*, 161.

[22] Atherton, *William Tecumseh Sherman*, 107.

[23] Reprinted in an editorial in *DN*, July 31, 1875.

It would be national police duty, executing the law against polygamy."[24] Charles Carroll Goodwin, *Salt Lake Tribune* editor, took the extremist pessimistic view that another civil war, this time over polygamy, would take place:

> There will come a time, if this monster in Utah [polygamy] is left to grow, when there will be another call for volunteers and for money; and as before, tens of thousands of brave young men will go away, never to return; as before, there will be an enormous debt incurred; as before, the country will be hillocked with graves, and the whole land will be moistened by the rain of women's tears.[25]

Preachers, politicians, and editors called for extermination of the Mormons. However, evidence that ranking military officers—those who would carry out such military actions—subscribed or encouraged such a view is less readily documented. Only in response to violent rebellion did the military have authority to execute a civilian. In the opinion of Wilford Hill LeCheminant, had Gen. William Selby Harney not been diverted to troubled Kansas and replaced by the less volatile Col. Albert Sidney Johnston, the conduct of the 1857 Utah War might have been extraordinarily violent, with open civil war ensuing. Harney allegedly forewarned that "he would capture Brigham Young and the twelve apostles and execute them in a summary manner and winter in the temple of the Latter-day Saints."[26] The accuracy of this statement predicting his actions in Utah is seriously questioned by other historians, who have found no contemporary evidence that Harney publically engaged in such irresponsible talk. Indeed, Harney's letter that was carried to Brigham Young by Lt. Stewart Van Vliet in the spring of 1858, was professional in language and moderate in tone.[27] Yet William MacKinnon admits that Harney "had self control and emotional problems so severe that by the spring of 1857, the army had courtmartialed him four times and a civilian court in Saint Louis had tried [him] for torturing and bludgeoning to death a female slave."[28] Harney furthermore had suggested that he be made both the civil and military

---

[24] Quinn, *Mormon Hierarchy*, 778.
[25] Goodwin, "Mormon Situation," 758.
[26] LeCheminant, "Crisis Averted?" 30.
[27] Reavis, *General William Selby Harney*.
[28] MacKinnon, "And the War Came," 36–37.

governor of Utah and be given the power to invoke martial law with its attendant, unfettered powers.[29]

Violence originating from Mormons must also be addressed as a possibility. Following the Edmunds Act, U.S. marshals conducted raids on Mormon men thought to be polygamists, with invasion of homes and brutal violations of privacy. The uncivil and dangerous treatment to which their wives and children were subjected brought the Mormon populace to near-violent rebellion. George Q. Cannon wrote to President Grover Cleveland in 1885 that it required great effort on the part of ranking Mormon leaders to "prevent violent resistance to the acts considered so outrageous."[30]

Brigham Young and his contemporaries frequently accused federal appointees of trying to precipitate armed invasion for a military solution to the peculiar differences with the Mormons. In his January 1857 memorial to President Buchanan, Young charged that federal officials, "whenever checked in their mad career, threaten us with death and destruction by the United States troops, which they seem to consider are ready to march against us at their foul and false instigations."[31] However, the records of Maxwell and other marshals and attorneys serving after the war, speak most powerfully of their efforts to work within legislative solutions to the "Mormon problem."

AGAINST OVERWHELMING ODDS

Both Maxwell and his Mormon adversaries would find it ironic that he and other federal officials were indirectly responsible for the transformation of the LDS church. From a parochial object of scorn and criticism by the northeastern public, and ridicule by voices of organized religion and the secular press, Mormons gradually moved to a position of acceptance far beyond their small, isolated colonies in western America. Though Congress never enacted the Browning, Wade, Voorhees, Logan, McKee, Ashley, Cragin, Christiancy, Frelinghuysen, and Cullom bills, their formulations had cumulative impact. Eventually these efforts resulted in the passage of the pivotal 1874 Poland Act, the drastic Edmunds Act

---

[29] MacKinnon, *At Sword's Point*, 154.
[30] Lyman, *Political Deliverance*, 27.
[31] Cited in MacKinnon, *At Sword's Point*, 70.

in 1882, and finally the draconian Edmunds-Tucker Bill of 1887. Mormon president Wilford Woodruff's manifesto denouncing the practice of polygamy in 1890 resulted largely from the accumulated consequences of these three legislative decrees on the Mormon people.

Edward Leo Lyman and Henry J. Wolfinger dispel the common belief that the manifesto was a sudden, dramatic turning point by the Mormon leadership regarding plural marriage. They describe the three- to four-year protracted period before 1890, when the Mormons attempted to remove the public focus on polygamy by adding the Scott Amendment to the Tucker Bill, which would have delayed by six months the provisions of Edmunds-Tucker after its enactment into law. Lyman and Wolfinger view these negotiations as highly political in a time of national stress in order to achieve a superficial, rather than substantive, penitent settlement of the issue. A provision to forbid the practice of polygamy was placed in the state constitution then being formulated for Utah's next attempt at statehood. However, Mormons felt that once statehood was achieved, federal interference could be minimized and Mormon appointees would loosely enforce the statute; thus the abandonment of polygamy could have been more in appearance than by profound, sincere change.[32]

The issuance of the manifesto may be viewed, as Mormon believers do, as a revelation from God, or as nonbelievers do, as a pragmatic social, economic, and political accommodation to remove the practice from public scrutiny and to protect the endangered Mormon temples and other real estate from government seizure. In either case or both, profound change followed, and the contribution made by the federal outcasts who labored for their government "on the picket line of civilization . . . against overwhelming odds" deserves telling and recognition.[33]

---

[32] Lyman, *Political Deliverance*, 69–95; Wolfinger, "Reexamination of the Woodruff Manifesto," 328–49. Historian Michael Quinn describes Woodruff's publication of the manifesto without the full knowledge or consent of the Quorum of the Twelve. The majority of apostles were on out-of-town assignments; he consulted only four who were present. Afterward the quorum members met and said they would not have voted for its publication, just as they had not voted for it when proposed in 1888. Quinn, *Mormon Hierarchy*, 48–49. The manifesto does not deny the principle of polygamy; rather, it denies only its practice as it conflicts with enacted law. It is distinctive as it begins "To Whom It May Concern" rather than other Mormon revelations that begin "Thus saith the Lord." There is incontrovertible evidence that the performance of plural marriages did not end in 1890 but continued in secret at least to 1910. Not until 1914 was the Woodruff Manifesto added as a declaration to the *Doctrine and Covenants*. Quinn, *Mormon Hierarchy*, 791.

[33] Philip T. Van Zile, *Memorial of the Non-Mormon People of Utah*, October 7, 1882, printed copy (n.d.), NA, Department of the Interior, Utah file, 1–4.

In his analysis of Utah's political deliverance, Lyman emphasizes that plural marriage was the foremost obstacle preventing statehood, and had it not been for external and internal efforts for its eradication, polygamy would have persisted for at least another generation, especially among the ecclesiastical elite and prosperous men of Mormon society.[34] Had polygamy died more slowly, Utah would have struggled beyond 1896 to achieve statehood. The shockingly difficult, painful, and disruptive experiences suffered by the women and children of plural marriages such as those narrated by Annie Clark Tanner were the outcome of the Edmunds and Edmunds-Tucker acts imposed on the unyielding Mormon position.[35] For many, the principle of "celestial marriage" remained both the basic foundation stone and the very capstone of their religion. Living "the principle" determined their position and progression in the afterlife.[36] The violation of the civil rights of many Mormon men and their families resulted from the abusive enforcement of the two federal acts in the period after 1882.

These tragic casualties notwithstanding, the legislation that George R. Maxwell and many others helped bring into existence had the salubrious effect of gradually moving the Mormon people and their religion toward the political and societal mainstream of the United States. The practice of polygamy died slowly, however, and continued secret plural marriages attracted the scrutiny of a Senate investigation from 1904 to 1907. Although instigated by the seating of a monogamous Utah senator, Reed Smoot, the investigation probed deeply into whether Mormon people had complied with their 1890 promises to end polygamy and follow federal law. Historian Kathleen Flake credits President Joseph Fielding Smith with saving the LDS church by shifting public attention from a focus on polygamy to the celebration of the significance of Joseph Smith's first vision.[37] He was able to lead those in and outside the church to forget the fundamental place that plural marriage

---

[34] Lyman, *Political Deliverance*, 2–4.

[35] Cooley et al., *Mormon Mother.*

[36] The Fundamentalist Church of Jesus Christ of Latter-day Saints, a splinter group of the larger body, insists that the principle of plural marriage remains a fundamental tenet and that its practice should never have been altered. A conservative estimate of about six thousand members who defy the law are living in Hildale, Utah; Colorado City, Arizona; Eldorado, Texas; and Pringle, South Dakota. Gwen Florio and Brian Passey, "Some Members of Polygamy Sect Fleeing as Law Closes In," *USA Today*, April 13, 2006, 3A.

[37] K. Flake, *Politics of American Religious Identity*, 109–36.

had occupied in Joseph Smith's restoration of Christ's one and only true church and in Brigham Young's continuance of that basic premise.

Mormonism's appeal has since expanded to an international scale, to the universality and world-mindedness described by Mormon philosopher Sterling McMurrin. Gene A. Sessions characterizes the Mormons as being in a state of "placid Christianity and social conservatism," with the "twentieth-century Mormon leader in his business suit, expounding the ideals of passive Americanism—the good life filled with material comforts and middle class elitism."[38] With emphasis that it is no longer the Mormon church, nor the LDS church, but the Church of Jesus Christ of Latter-day Saints, with distinct emphasis on Jesus Christ, accommodations in their practices have made them and their culture less radical, less peculiar, less of a fringe cult.[39] No longer heard are the peculiar fundamentalist views of blood atonement, imminent arrival of the millennium, communal living, and the need for a physical gathering of all Latter-day Saints in Missouri or Salt Lake City. Out-migration and assimilation into the national and international societal fabric have resulted from this transformation.[40] The change of doctrine, or policy, in the 1978 declaration that granted African Americans and other people of color full membership privileges had the identical effect: enhancing worldwide acceptance of Mormons and their church.[41] Mormonism has moved, as Flake has observed, from a polygamous family structure, a communal economy, and a rebellious theocracy to idealization of the nuclear family, unapologetic capitalism, and patriotic republicanism.[42] Maxwell was one among a number of scorned and ridiculed men who helped move Utah Mormons from "an absolute monarchy" under "Brigham Young is King" into a democratic "institution embodying everything it originally sought to destroy."[43]

Following the apparent abandonment of polygamy and the acceptance of Americanization, Latter-day Saints membership increased

---

[38] Sessions, review of *A Winter with the Mormons*; Sessions, *Mormon Thunder*, xi.

[39] Shipps, *Sojourner in the Promised Land*, 7, 36.

[40] Johnson and Johnson, "Twentieth-Century Mormon Outmigration," 64.

[41] Social historian Armand Mauss observes that more recently there has been a reaction among Mormons against their successful assimilation, with some efforts to reacquire their former "cultural tension and special identity." Mauss, *Angel and the Beehive*, x.

[42] K. Flake, *Politics of American Religious Identity*, 1.

[43] Will Bagley, "Conan Doyle Was Right: Danites, Avenging Angels and Holy Murder in the Mormon West," in Klinger, *Tangled Skein*, 4, 20.

from about five hundred thousand members in 1890 to 13.5 million members in 2008.[44] As historian D. Michael Quinn has stressed, the greatest growth has taken place outside the United States. A new cohort of "pioneers" in developing countries are seeking a greater spiritual and secular life and, ironically, desire to become Americanized.[45]

HERO, NOT FAILURE

Maxwell's meritorious record in the massive intramural hemorrhage of the Civil War would have been ample for most men to have earned hero's laurels for service to country. His second life in Utah after the war was not "a failure," as an unidentified *Salt Lake Tribune* editor contended in his eulogy of Maxwell.[46] George R. Maxwell deserves remembrance as an important contributor to the events of Utah history, one of a relatively small group of "Davids" sent by the federal government who served out of a motivation that cannot be fully identified and who did individual battle with the "Goliaths" among the Mormons over polygamy and Mormon theocracy.

Maxwell was instrumental in the formation of the first political party to oppose the Mormon majority, and he contributed to the development of Corinne, the first non-Mormon city of the territory. By contesting the congressional seat of two imposingly powerful Mormon candidates, he attempted to represent the non-Mormon interests of Utah and to attract the nation's attention to irregular voting practices. While

---

[44] LDS church statistical report 2008, http://tinyurl.com/m8fcky. The unqualified statement that the Church of Jesus Christ of Latter-day Saints has grown to more than 13 million members does not address several important questions implicit in the definition of membership: the distinction between children born into membership (baptized or not) by virtue of their parents' membership, and those who convert as adults without prior church affiliation or those who come from another denomination. Should those totally inactive for many years continue to be counted as members? Are the dead removed from the counts? Some sources cite statistics that 50 to 80 percent of new converts to Mormonism do not remain active. Only about 4 million of the 13 million are classed as active members—that is, attending church services regularly. Approximately 6.5 million members are now found outside the United States in developing countries, and 5.5 million reside within the States; the percentage of Mormons within the Utah population is falling. The Church of Jesus Christ of Latter-day Saints claims to be the fastest-growing Christian denomination, a claim vigorously disputed by others.

[45] Wright, "Lives of the Saints," 57.

[46] "General Maxwell," *SLT*, July 3, 1889, 2, col. 1; "Death of Gen. Maxwell," *SLT*, July 3, 1889, 4, col. 4.

in the land office, he attempted to provide fairly, to both Mormons and non-Mormons, the long-delayed land ownership rights provided them by federal homesteading statutes. He lobbied in Washington, D.C., for laws to deal fairly with all contenders in the decisions of land distribution. His efforts in the divorce of Ann Eliza Webb Young helped reveal that only the first polygamist wife had legal standing, whereas the others were outside the benefits of territorial and federal law, and that women's lives as plural wives were often tragically difficult. Maxwell's encouragement of Ann Eliza Webb Young inaugurated what became a ten-year, public relations sweep of national scope whose message, heard by uncountable thousands, was that polygamy still flourished and that federal law in Utah needed strengthening. While treating his charge with sensitive consideration, Maxwell had a significant, professionally well-conducted role in the arrest, imprisonment, and prosecution of John D. Lee, the only man ever tried or convicted of the murders of more than 120 people at the Mountain Meadows. In Lee's first trial, it was under Maxwell's leadership that a jury was, for the first time in Utah, professionally controlled and protected, despite the trial's having been set in a severely stressful and hostile environment. Maxwell aided in identifying and serving papers to scores of men thought to be guilty of participating or witnessing the despicable massacre. He contributed to the first successful conviction for polygamy that went on to be a precedent-setting Supreme Court case. He was instrumental in the formation and activities of the Grand Army of the Republic in Utah. He labored in Utah and lobbied in Washington for the numerous bills—authored by Cullom (1870) Frelinghuysen (1873), Poland (1874), Christiancy (1876, 1877), and Edmunds (1882)—whose purpose in common was to ensure that federal laws were operative in Utah.

From all these considerations, the historian has the ingredients for a portrait that should not be painted with a single brush. Maxwell's portrait should be much like those of his adversaries, Brigham Young, George Q. Cannon, and Daniel H. Wells, men whose colorful, complicated personalities reflected a mix of laudable and lamentable, rash and considered, wise and foolish. Maxwell can be criticized for wearing blinders that limited his peripheral vision. He was immune to an appreciation of the earnestly held views of his adversaries. Scholars would allow that similar blinders and immunity afflicted high-level Mormon leaders. Both Maxwell and many Mormon leaders were frequently intemperate and abrasive in their rhetoric. He was, like his contemporary non-Mormon attorney peer Robert N. Baskin, "brash, outspoken, combative, and absolutely fearless."[47]

A better example than General Maxwell cannot be found to graphically illustrate a major issue never yet adequately addressed by historians: the unbridgeable chasm that separated the Mormons from the Civil War veterans, whether Union men or former Confederates, sent to Utah as agents of the federal government. A unique bond was forged among the men who had lived together, fought together, foraged together, and survived. None would ever forget the smell of burnt black powder, the smoke that hung over the gore of battlefields, the flags that were carried, the tears shed for their dead comrades. With his quintessential record in the war, having survived many wounds, having seen hundreds perish from combat and illness, this man was as much an enigma to the Mormons as the Mormons were to him. Death and suffering on an unprecedented scale had been inflicted on millions in a consuming struggle for union and against slavery. One-fourth of the fighting force on both the Union and Confederate side was lost. For its entire course, Maxwell had willingly served and was a firsthand witness. Yet for Mormons the Civil War was a foreign, distant experience; they were not involved except to savor the destruction they felt America had earned from God for having spilled the blood of their prophet, for rejecting God's millennial warnings, for depriving them of their blessings in Ohio, Missouri, and Illinois.[48] Mormons offered nothing to either the Union or the Confederacy. The unique experiences of each side made it incomprehensible to the other. This unbridgeable chasm to understanding and communication was added to the estrangement already present from their differences regarding theology, polygamy, and theocratic rule.

Recognition and deserved praise have yet to be granted to George R. Maxwell. Wings of flight are overdue him. His self-image, his world,

---

[47] Bigler, review of *Reminiscences of Early Utah*, 191.

[48] In 1861 the *Millennial Star* promised its faithful they would be "in the bosom of a vast continent, far removed from the scene of strife, and encompassed by lofty mountains and interminable deserts and plains, the country they inhabit will be but little affected by the battles and dissensions of the outer world." "Civil War in America—Its Importance as a Warning to the Saints," *Millennial Star* (May 11, 1861): 297–300.

was defined by duty, courage, honor, and selfless service to country. Totally committed by his unusual patriotism, he put his life at stake and his limbs to sacrifice for the preservation of the Southern states as part of the Union and the abolition of the practice of slavery. His career in Utah repeated the same offers of life and limb in order to unify Utah into the Union and to bring about the abandonment of polygamy and of theocratic oligarchy. Maxwell was correct: Utah needed heroes. He survived through a difficult era of two irreconcilable, irrepressible conflicts, in a time when a single individual's actions could indeed affect an entire issue. He became one of those heroes needed by the people of the United States and of Utah Territory.

Bibliography

ARCHIVAL COLLECTIONS

Christiancy, Henry Clay. Diary, 1862–64. Accession no. 10070. Albert and Shirley Small Special Collections Library, University of Virginia, Charlottesville.

Christiancy, Isaac Peckham. Papers, 1830–74. Michigan Historical Collection, Bentley Historical Library, University of Michigan, Ann Arbor.

Civil War Unit Histories. Microfiche holdings. Detroit Public Library, Detroit, Mich.

Journal History of the Church. Microfilm collection of a wide variety of documents, typescripts from diaries, letters, reports, office journals, and newspaper clippings pertaining to church history. Chronologically ordered but not indexed microfilms are available for on-site use in the Family History Library and a partially indexed collection is available for on-site use in the newly constructed LDS Church History Library in Salt Lake City.

Lockley, Frederic. Fred Lockley manuscript. Department of Rare Books and Special Collections, Princeton University Library, Princeton, N.J.

Lockley, Frederic E. Papers. Henry E. Huntington Library, San Marino, Calif.

Moorman, Donald R. Papers. Stewart Library, Weber State University, Ogden, Utah.

National Archives. General Records of the Department of Justice, RG 60, Chronological Files, 1871–84. Washington, D.C.

Reed, George W. Papers. Marriott Library, Special Collections, University of Utah.

Rockwood, Albert Perry. "A Report . . . and a concise history of Utah penitentiary, its inmates and officers, from the year 1855 to 1878." Manuscript. Salt Lake City: compiled for H. H. Bancroft, 1878. BANC MSS P-F 85. Hubert Howe Bancroft Collection, University of California, Berkeley.

Utah Territorial Papers, 1850–96. Utah State Archives, ser. 241.

Wood, Thomas Fanning. "Wood's Recollections." Manuscript. Papers, 1765–1924, 2nd 37:E, box 1. Special Collections Library, Duke University, Durham, N.C.

Young, Brigham. Collection. Outgoing and incoming correspondence of President Brigham Young found in the LDS Family History Library and the LDS Church History Library in Salt Lake City.

Published Works

Alexander, Robert. *Five Forks: Waterloo of the Confederacy.* East Lansing: Michigan State University Press, 2003.

Alexander, Thomas G. *Brigham Young, the Quorum of the Twelve, and the Latter-day Saint Investigation of the Mountain Meadows Massacre.* Leonard J. Arrington Mormon History Lecture Series, no. 12. Logan: Utah State University Press, 2007.

———. "Charles S. Zane, Apostle of the New Era." *Utah Historical Quarterly* 34 (Fall 1966): 300–302.

———. *A Clash of Interests: Interior Department and Mountain West, 1863–96.* Provo, Utah: Brigham Young University Press, 1977.

———. "An Experiment in Progressive Legislation: The Granting of Woman Suffrage in Utah in 1870." *Utah Historical Quarterly* 38 (Winter 1970): 20.

———. "Federal Authority versus Polygamic Theocracy, James B. McKean and the Mormons, 1870–1875." *Dialogue: A Journal of Mormon Thought* 1, no. 99 (1966): 85–100.

———. "Relativism and Interest in the New Mormon History." *Weber Studies* 13 (Winter 1996): 133–41.

———. *Utah: The Right Place.* Salt Lake City: Gibbs Smith, 2003.

Alexander, Thomas G., and James B. Allen. *Mormons and Gentiles: A History of Salt Lake City.* Boulder, Colo.: Pruett, 1984.

Allen, James B. "The Unusual Jurisdiction of County Probate Courts in the Territory of Utah." *Utah Historical Quarterly* 36 (Spring 1968): 135.

Allen, James B., and Glen Milton Leonard. *The Story of the Latter-day Saints.* Salt Lake City: Deseret Book Co., 1992.

Allen, James B., Ronald W. Walker, and David J. Whittaker. *Studies in Mormon History, 1830–1997.* Urbana: University of Illinois Press, 2000.

Alter, J. Cecil. *Utah, the Storied Domain.* Chicago: American Historical Society, 1932.

Anderson, Bernice Gibbs. "The Gentile City of Corinne." *Utah Historical Quarterly* 9 (July–October 1941): 154.

Arrington, Leonard J., ed. "Crusade against Theocracy: The Reminiscences of

Judge Jacob Smith Boreman of Utah, 1872–1877." *Huntington Library Quarterly* 24 (November 1960): 1–45.

———. *Great Basin Kingdom: An Economic History of the Latter-day Saints, 1830–1900*. Salt Lake City: University of Utah Press and Tanner Trust Fund, 1993.

———. "Taxable Income in Utah, 1862–1872." *Utah Historical Quarterly* 24 (January 1956): 29.

Arrington, Leonard J., and Davis Bitton. *The Mormon Experience: A History of the Latter-day Saints*. New York: Alfred Knopf, 1979.

Arrington, Leonard J., Feramorz Y. Fox, and Dean L. May. *Building the City of God*. Urbana and Chicago: University of Chicago Press, 1992.

"Artificial Limbs and How to Make Them." *Confederate States Medical and Surgical Journal* 1 (April 1864): 59.

Atherton, Robert G. *William Tecumseh Sherman and the Settlement of the West*. Norman: University of Oklahoma Press, 1956.

Backus, Anna Jean. *Mountain Meadows Witness: The Life and Times of Bishop Philip Klingensmith*. Spokane, Wash.: Arthur H. Clark, 1995.

Bagley, Will. *Blood of the Prophets: Brigham Young and the Massacre at Mountain Meadows*. Norman: University of Oklahoma Press, 2002.

———. "'One Long Funeral March': A Revisionist's View of the Mormon Handcart Disasters." *Journal of Mormon History* (Winter 2009): 50–116.

Bailey, David T. *Shadow on the Church: Southwestern Evangelical Religion and the Issue of Slavery, 1783–1860*. Ithaca, N.Y.: Cornel University Press, 1985.

Bak, Richard. *A Distant Thunder: Michigan in the Civil War*. Ann Arbor, Mich.: Huron River Press, 2004.

Bald, F. Clever, Howard H. Peckham, and Frederick D. Williams, Publication Committee. *Michigan Institutions of Higher Education in the Civil War*. Lansing: Michigan Civil War Centennial Observance Commission, 1964.

Ball, Larry D. *The United States Marshals of the New Mexico and Arizona Territories, 1846–1912*. Albuquerque: University of New Mexico Press, 1978.

Bancroft, Frederic. *Calhoun and the South Carolina Nullification Movement*. Gloucester, Mass.: Peter Smith, 1966.

Bancroft, Hubert Howe. *History of Utah, 1540–1887*. San Francisco: History Co., 1889.

Barnes, Joseph K., George A. Otis, and D. L. Huntington. *The Medical and Surgical History of the War of the Rebellion*. 12 vols. Washington, D.C.: Government Printing Office, 1870–83; reprint, Wilmington, N.C.: Broadfoot, 1990–91.

Barry, David S. *Forty Years in Washington*. New York: Beekman, 1924.

Baskin, Robert N. *Reminiscences of Early Utah*. Salt Lake City: private printing, 1914.

Beadle, John Hanson. *Life in Utah; or, Mysteries and Crimes of Mormonism.* Philadelphia: National Publishing Co., 1870.

Bearss, Ed, and Chris Calkins. *Battle of Five Forks.* Lynchburg, Va.: H. E. Howard, 1985.

Beckendorf, John Peter. "Maj. Wallece's Custer Medal." *North-South Trader's Civil War Magazine* 31 (2005): 22–27.

Berlin, Ira. "American Slavery in History and Memory and the Search for Social Justice." *Journal of American History* 90 (March 2004): 1257–60.

Bigler, David L. "The Aiken Party Executions and the Utah War, 1857–1858." *Western Historical Quarterly* 38 (Winter 2007): 459.

———. *Forgotten Kingdom: The Mormon Theocracy in the American West, 1847–1896.* Logan: Utah State University Press, 1998.

———. *Fort Limhi: The Mormon Adventure in Oregon Territory, 1855–1858.* Spokane, Wash.: Arthur H. Clark, 2003.

———. Review of *Reminiscences of Early Utah,* by Robert N. Baskin (1914; reprint, 2006). *Journal of Mormon History* 33 (Fall 2007).

———. "Terror on the Trail." Paper presented at the twenty-third National Convention of the Oregon-California Trails Association, Salt Lake City, August 19, 2005.

———. "Theocracy versus Republic: An 'Irrepressible Conflict.'" Paper presented at the meeting of the Mormon History Association, Casper, Wyo., May 26, 2006.

———, ed. *A Winter with the Mormons: The 1852 Letters of Jotham Goodell.* Salt Lake City: Tanner Trust Fund and J. Willard Marriott Library, University of Utah, 2001.

Bigler, David L., and Will Bagley. *Army of Israel: Mormon Battalion Narratives.* Logan: Utah State University Press, 2000.

———. *Innocent Blood: Essential Narratives of the Mountain Meadows Massacre.* Norman, Okla.: Arthur H. Clark, 2008.

Bitton, Davis. *The Ritualization of Mormon History.* Urbana: University of Illinois Press, 1994.

Blanthorn, Ouida. *A History of Tooele County.* Utah Centennial County History Series. Salt Lake City: Utah Historical Society, 1998.

Blight, David W. *Beyond the Battlefield: Race, Memory and the American Civil War.* Amherst: University of Massachusetts Press, 2002.

Bliss, Jonathan. *Merchants and Miners in Utah: The Walker Brothers and Their Bank.* Salt Lake City: Western Epics, 1983.

Boatner, Mark Mayo. *The Civil War Dictionary.* New York: Vintage Books, 1987.

Bodnar, John. *Bonds of Affection: Americans Define Their Patriotism.* Princeton, N.J.: Princeton University Press, 1996.

Bollett, Alfred Jay, M.D. *Civil War Medicine: Challenges and Triumphs.* Tucson: Galen Press, 2001.

Bonner, Robert E. "Buffalo Bill Cody and Wyoming Water Politics." *Western Historical Quarterly* 33 (Winter 2002): 432–51.

Bordewich, Fergus M. *Bound for Canaan: The Underground Railroad and the War for the Soul of America.* New York City: Harper Collins, 2005.

Bourne, Russell. *Floating West: The Erie and Other American Canals.* New York: W. W. Norton and Co., 1992.

Bringhurst, Newell G. *Brigham Young and the Expanding American Frontier.* Boston: Little, Brown, 1986.

Brodie, Fawn McKay. *No Man Knows My History: The Life of Joseph Smith, the Mormon Prophet.* New York: Knopf, 1975.

Brooke, John L. *The Refiner's Fire.* New York: Cambridge University Press, 1994.

Brooks, Juanita. *The History of Jews in Utah and Idaho.* Salt Lake City: Western Epics, 1973.

———. *John Doyle Lee: Zealot, Pioneer Builder, Scapegoat.* Logan: Utah State University Press, 1992.

———, ed. *Journal of the Southern Indian Mission: Diary of Thomas D. Brown.* Logan: Utah State University Press, 1972.

———. *The Mountain Meadows Massacre.* Board of Trustees of Leland Stanford Junior University, 1950; new ed., Norman: University of Oklahoma Press, 1970.

———, ed. *Not by Bread Alone: The Journal of Martha Spence Heywood.* Salt Lake City: Utah State Historical Society, 1978.

———, ed. *On the Mormon Frontier: The Diary of Hosea Stout, 1844–1861.* 2 vols. Salt Lake City: University of Utah Press and Utah State Historical Society, 1930.

Brown, Vernal A. "The United States Marshals in Utah Territory to 1896." MS thesis, Utah State University, Logan, 1970.

Bulkley, John McClelland. "Biography of James Edward Keegan." In *History of Monroe County, Michigan,* vol. 1, 789–92. Chicago: Lewis Publishing Co., 1913.

Bunker, Gary L., and Davis Bitton. *The Mormon Graphic Image.* Salt Lake City: University of Utah Press, 1983.

Busey, John W., and David G. Martin. *Regimental Strengths and Losses at Gettysburg.* Hightstown, N.J.: Longstreet House, 1994.

Bush, Lester E., Jr. "Brigham Young in Life and Death: A Medical Overview." *Journal of Mormon History* 5 (1978): 90–91.

———. "Mormonism's Negro Doctrine: An Historical Overview." *Dialogue: A Journal of Mormon Thought* 8 (Spring 1973): 23.

Bush, Lester E., and Armand L. Mauss, eds. *Neither White or Black: Mormon Scholars Confront the Race Issue in a Universal Church.* Midvale, Utah: Signature Books, 1984.

Bushman, Richard L. *Joseph Smith and the Beginnings of Mormonism.* Urbana: University of Illinois Press, 1988.

Bushman, Richard Lyman. *Joseph Smith: Rough Stone Rolling.* New York: Vintage Books of Random House, 2007.

Butler, Wendy. "The Iwakura Mission and Its Stay in Salt Lake City." *Utah Historical Quarterly* 66 (Winter 1998): 31.

Cady, Edwin H. *John Woolman.* New York: Twayne, 1965.

Calhoun, Frederick S. *The Lawmen: United States Marshals and Their Deputies, 1789–1989.* New York: Viking Penguin, 1991.

Calkins, Chris. "The Battle of Five Forks: Final Push for the South Side." *Blue and Gray Magazine,* April 1992, 105–106.

———. "History and Tour Guide of the Battle of Five Forks." *Blue and Gray Magazine,* August 1990, 101.

Campbell, Eugene E. *The Essential Brigham Young.* Salt Lake City: Signature Books, 1992.

———. *Establishing Zion: The Mormon Church and the American West, 1847–1869.* Salt Lake City: Signature Books, 1988.

Cannon, Kenneth L., II. "'Mountain Common Law': The Extralegal Punishment of Seducers in Early Utah." *Utah Historical Quarterly* 51 (Fall 1983): 308–27.

Carleton, James Henry. *The Mountain Meadows Massacre: A Special Report.* Spokane, Wash.: Arthur H. Clark, 1995.

Carmack, Noel A. "Running the Line: James Henry Martineau's Surveys in Northern Utah, 1860–1882." *Utah Historical Quarterly* 68 (2000): 292–312.

Carmer, Carl. *The Farm Boy and the Angel.* Garden City, N.Y.: Doubleday, 1940.

Carroll, John M., ed. *Custer in the Civil War: His Unfinished Memoirs.* San Rafael, Calif.: Presidio Press, 1977.

Carter, Kate B. *Heart Throbs of the West.* 12 vols. Salt Lake City: Daughters of the Utah Pioneers, 1940.

———, ed. "Men's Clubs in Salt Lake City: Grand Army of the Republic." In *Heart Throbs of the West,* 11:233–34. Salt Lake City: Daughters of the Utah Pioneers.

Case, Victoria, and Robert Ormond Case. *We Called It Culture: The Story of Chautauqua.* Garden City, N.Y.: Doubleday and Co., 1948.

Catton, Bruce. *Michigan: A History.* New York: W. W. Norton, 1976.

Cavanaugh, Michael A., comp. *Military Essays and Recollections of the Pennsylvania Commandery of the Loyal Legion of the United States,* vol. 2: *February 10, 1904–May 10, 1933.* Wilmington, N.C.: Broadfoot, 1995.

Chamberlain, Joshua Lawrence. *The Passing of the Armies: An Account of the Final Campaign of the Army of the Potomac.* Lincoln: University of Nebraska Press, 1998.

Chisholm, Clive Scott. *Following the Wrong God Home: Footloose in an American Dream.* Norman: University of Oklahoma Press, 2003.

Clancy, Susan A. *Abducted: How People Come to Believe They Were Kidnapped by Aliens.* Cambridge, Mass.: Harvard University Press, 2005.

Clark, Champ, and Editors of Time-Life Books. *The Civil War: Gettysburg; The Confederate High Tide.* Alexandria, Va.: Time-Life Books, 1985.

———. Record of Private Frank Wilkeson, 11th Battery, New York Light Artillery. In *Voices of the Civil War—The Wilderness.* Alexandria, Va.: Time-Life Books, 1985.

———. *Voices of the Civil War—Second Manassas.* Richmond, Va.: Time Life Books, 1995.

Clark, James R. "The Kingdom of God, the Council of Fifty, and the State of Deseret." *Utah Historical Quarterly* 26 (April 1958): 133.

———. *Messages of the First Presidency of the Church of Jesus Christ of Latter-day Saints, 1833–1964.* Salt Lake City: Bookcraft, 1965.

Clark, Thomas D., and John D. W. Guice. *The Old Southwest, 1795–1830: Frontiers in Conflict.* Norman: University of Oklahoma Press, 1989.

Cleland, Robert Glass, and Juanita Brooks. *A Mormon Chronicle: The Diaries of John D. Lee, 1848–1876.* 2 vols. San Marino, Calif.: Huntington Library, 1955.

Clements, Louis J., ed. *Fred T. Dubois' "The Making of a State."* Rexburg: Eastern Idaho Publishing Co., 1971.

Coddington, Edwin B. *The Gettysburg Campaign, A Study in Command.* New York: Touchstone, 1997.

Coffin, Charles C. "Late Scenes in Richmond." *Atlantic Monthly* 15 (June 1865): 744–55.

Colburn, Harvey C. *The Story of Ypsilanti.* Ypsilanti, Mich.: Ypsilanti Committee on History, 1921.

Colton, Ray Charles. *The Civil War in the Western Territories.* Norman: University of Oklahoma Press, 1959.

Cooley, Everett L. "Carpetbag Rule—Territorial Government in Utah." *Utah Historical Quarterly* 26 (April 1958): 116.

Cooley, Everett L., Brigham D. Madsen, S. Lyman Tyler, and Margery W. Ward, eds. *A Mormon Mother: An Autobiography by Annie Clark Tanner.* Salt Lake City: Tanner Trust Fund and University of Utah Library, 1983.

Coyner, John McCutchen. *Handbook on Mormonism.* Salt Lake City: Handbook Publishing, 1882.

Cresswell, Stephen. *Mormons and Cowboys, Moonshiners and Klansmen.* Tuscaloosa: University of Alabama Press, 1991.

———. "The U.S. Department of Justice in the Utah Territory," 1870–90. *Utah Historical Quarterly* 53 (Summer 1985): 207.

Cummings, Homer, and Carl McFarland. *Federal Justice*. New York: MacMillan, 1937.

Cunningham, Frank. *General Stand Watie's Confederate Indians*. Norman: University of Oklahoma Press, 1998.

Cushman, Stephen. *Bloody Promenade: Reflections on a Civil War Battle*. Charlottesville: University Press of Virginia, 1999.

Daughters of the Utah Pioneers. *Journal of Alma Elizabeth Mineer Felt*. Vol. 7 of *An Enduring Legacy*. Salt Lake City: Daughters of the Utah Pioneers, 1984.

Davis, David Brion. *Inhuman Bondage: The Rise and Fall of Slavery in the New World*. Oxford: Oxford University Press, 2006.

Day, Robert O. *The Enoch Train Pioneers: Trek of the First Two Handcart Companies—1856*. Oviedo, Fla.: Day to Day Enterprises, 2003.

Daynes, Kathryn M. *More Wives Than One: Transformation of the Mormon Marriage System, 1840–1910*. Urbana: University of Illinois Press, 2001.

Dearing, Mary R. *The Story of the G.A.R.* Baton Rouge: Louisiana State University Press, 1952.

Decker, Peter R. *"The Utes Must Go!" American Expansion and the Removal of a People*. Golden, Colo.: Fulcrum, 2004.

DePillis, Mario S. "Bearding Leone and Others in the Heartland of Mormon Historiography." *Journal of Mormon History* 8 (1981): 79.

Deverell, William. "Thoughts from the Farther West: Mormons, California, and the Civil War." *Journal of Mormon History* 34, no. 2 (2008): 1–19.

DeVoto, Bernard. *The Year of Decision, 1846*. New York: St. Martin's Griffin, Truman Talley Books, 2000.

Duffy, John-Charles. "Can Deconstruction Save the Day? 'Faithful Scholarship' and the Uses of Postmodernism." *Dialogue: A Journal of Mormon Thought* 41, no. 1 (Spring 2008): x–xi.

Dwyer, Robert J. "The Irish in the Building of the Intermountain West." *Utah Historical Quarterly* 25 (January 1957): 224.

Dwyer, Robert Joseph. *The Gentile Comes to Utah: A Study in Religious and Social Conflict (1862–1890)*. Salt Lake City: Western Epics, 1971.

Eddins, Boyd L. "The Mormons and the Civil War." MA thesis, Utah State University, Logan, 1966.

Edwards, Paul M. "The Irony of Mormon History." *Utah Historical Quarterly* 41 (Fall 1973): 409.

Ellis, Catherine H. "A Common Soldier at Camp Douglas, 1866–1868." *Utah Historical Quarterly* 65 (Winter 1997): 55.

England, Eugene. *Brother Brigham*. Salt Lake City: Bookcraft, 1980.

Fahs, Alice, and Waugh, Joan, eds. *The Memory of the Civil War in American Culture*. Chapel Hill: University of North Carolina Press, 2004.

Farrand, Max. *The Legislation of Congress for the Government of the Organized Territories of the United States, 1879–1895*. Newark, N.J.: William. A. Baker, 1896.

Faust, Drew Gilpin. *This Republic of Suffering*. New York: Alfred A. Knopf, 2008.

Fielding, Robert Kent, and Dorothy S. Fielding, eds. *The Tribune Reports of the Trials of John D. Lee for the Massacre at Mountain Meadows, November 1874–April 1877*, Higganum, Conn.: Kent's Books, 2000.

Firmage, Edwin Brown, and Richard Collin Mangrum. *Zion in the Courts: A Legal History of the Church of Jesus Christ of Latter-day Saints, 1830–1900*. Urbana: University of Illinois Press, 1988.

Fisher, Margaret May Merrill, C. N. Lund, and Nephi Jensen, eds. *Utah and the Civil War*. Salt Lake City: Deseret Book Co., 1929.

Flake, Chad J. *A Mormon Bibliography*. Salt Lake City: University of Utah Press, 1978.

Flake, Kathleen. *The Politics of American Religious Identity: The Seating of Senator Reed Smoot, Mormon Apostle*. Chapel Hill: University of North Carolina Press, 2004.

Foote, Shelby. *The Civil War: A Narrative*. Vol. 1, *Fort Sumter to Perryville* (1958); vol. 2, *Fredericksburg to Meridian* (1963); vol. 3, *Red River to Appomattox* (1974). New York: Random House.

———. *The Civil War: A Narrative; Five Forks to Appomattox: Victory and Defeat*. New York: Random House, 2005.

Ford, Thomas, and Milo Milton Quaife, eds. *A History of Illinois from Its Commencement as a State in 1818 to 1847*. Chicago: S. C. Griggs and Co., 1854; Lakeside Classics edition, 2 vols., Chicago: Lakeside Press, 1954.

Fraser, George MacDonald. *The Steel Bonnets: The Story of the Anglo-Scottish Border Reivers*. Hammersmith, London: Harper Collins, 1989.

Freehling, William W. *The Nullification Era: A Documentary Record*. New York: Oxford University Press, 1965.

Frost, Lawrence A. *General Custer's Libbie*. Seattle: Superior Publishing Co., 1976.

Fry, Eleanor. *Peter K. Dotson, Federal Marshal–Rancher, 1823–1898*. Pueblo, Colo.: Pueblo County Historical Society, 2004.

Furniss, Norman. *The Mormon Conflict, 1850–1859*. New Haven, Conn.: Yale University Press, 1960.

Gallay, Alan, ed. *Voices of the Old South: Eyewitness Accounts, 1528–1861*. Athens: University of Georgia Press, 1994.

Gallman, J. Matthew. *America's Joan of Arc: The Life of Anna Elizabeth Dickinson*. Oxford: Oxford University Press, 2006.

Gates, Paul W. *Agriculture and the Civil War.* New York: Alfred A. Knopf, 1965.

Goodwin, Charles Carroll. "The Mormon Situation." *Harper's New Monthly Magazine,* October 1881, 758.

Gordon, Sarah Barringer. *The Mormon Question: Polygamy and Constitutional Conflict in Nineteenth Century America.* Chapel Hill: University of North Carolina Press, 2002.

————. "The Mormon Question: Polygamy and Constitutional Conflict in Nineteenth Century America." *Journal of Supreme Court History* 28 (March 2003): 16.

Grandstaff, Mark R. "General Regis de Trobriand, the Mormons, and the U.S. Army at Camp Douglas, 1870–1871." *Utah Historical Quarterly* 64 (Summer 1996): 204–23.

Greiner, James M., Janet L. Coryell, and James R. Smither, eds. *A Surgeon's Civil War: The Letters and Diary of Daniel M. Holt, M.D.* Kent, Ohio: Kent State University Press, 1994.

Grossman, James R., ed. *The Frontier in American Culture.* Berkeley: University of California Press, 1994.

Hafen, LeRoy R., and Ann W. Hafen, eds. *Mormon Resistance: A Documentary Account of the Utah Expedition, 1857–1858.* Lincoln: University of Nebraska Press, 2005.

Hafen, LeRoy R., and Francis Marion Young. *Fort Laramie and the Pageant of the West, 1854–1890.* Glendale, Calif.: Arthur H. Clark, 1938.

Hansen, Jennifer Moulton, ed. *Letters of Catharine Cottam Romney, Plural Wife.* Urbana: University of Illinois Press, 1992.

Hansen, Klaus J. *Quest for Empire: The Political Kingdom of God and the Council of Fifty in Mormon History.* East Lansing: Michigan State University Press, 1970.

Hardy, B. Carmon, ed. *Doing the Works of Abraham: Mormon Polygamy; Its Origin, Practice, and Demise.* Norman: Arthur H. Clark, 2007.

————. *Solemn Covenant: The Mormon Polygamous Passage.* Urbana: University of Illinois Press, 1992.

Heffner, Loretta L. "Amasa Mason Lyman, the Spiritualist." *Journal of Mormon History* 6:75–76.

Hesseltine, William B. *Ulysses S. Grant, Politician.* New York: Frederick Ungar, 1935; reprint, 1957.

Hewett, Janet B., ed. *The Roster of Union Soldiers, 1861–1865.* 31 vols. Wilmington, N.C.: Broadfoot, 2000.

————, ed. *Supplement to the Official Records of the Union and Confederate Armies.* Wilmington, N.C.: Broadfoot, 2001.

Hibbard, Charles Gustin. "Fort Douglas, 1862–1916: Pivotal Link on the Western Frontier." PhD diss., University of Utah, Salt Lake City, 1980.

————. *Fort Douglas, Utah, 1862–1991: A Frontier Fort; The Civil War to Desert Storm*. Fort Collins, Colo.: Vestige Press, 1998.

Hilton, Hope A. *"Wild Bill" Hickman and the Mormon Frontier*. Salt Lake City: Signature Books, 1988.

Hilton, Theophilus B. "Report of the Committee on the State of Affairs in Utah and the Action Thereon by the Utah Methodist Episcopal Mission Conference at Ogden, Utah, July 9, 1881." *Utah Review* 1, no. 2 (August 1881): 58–59. Also signed by L. A. Rudisill, George E. Jayne, and I. W. Wiley, Presiding Bishop.

Hinckley, Bryant S. *Daniel H. Wells and Events of His Time*. Salt Lake City: President Heber J. Grant and the Deseret News Press, 1942.

Hirshon, Stanley P. *The White Tecumseh: A Biography of General William T. Sherman*. New York: John Wiley and Son, 1997.

Holland, Edwin Clifford. *A Refutation of the Calumnies Circulated against the Southern and Western States*. Charleston, S.C.: A. E. Miller, 1822.

Homer, Michael W. *On the Way to Somewhere Else: European Sojourners in the Mormon West, 1834–1930*. Spokane, Wash.: Arthur H. Clark, 2006.

Hoogenboom, Ari. *Rutherford B. Hayes, "One of the Good Colonels."* Abilene, Tex.: McWhiney Foundation, McMurry University Press, 1999.

Huchel, Frederick M. *A History of Box Elder County*. Utah Centennial County History Series. Salt Lake City: Utah State Historical Society and Box Elder County Commission, 1999.

Hulse, James W. "C. C. Goodwin and the Taming of the Tribune." *Utah Historical Quarterly* 61 (Spring 1993): 164–81.

Humphreys, Andrew Addison. *The Virginia Campaign of '64–'65: The Army of the Potomac and the Army of the James*. New York: Charles Scribner's Sons, 1883.

Hutchinson, Craig E., and Kimberly A. Hutchinson. *Monroe: The Early Years*. Images of America Series. Charleston, S.C.: Arcadia, 2004.

Isbell, Egbert R. *A History of Eastern Michigan University, 1849–1965*. Ypsilanti: Eastern Michigan University Press, 1971.

Ivins, Stanley S. "A Constitution for Utah." *Utah Historical Quarterly* 25 (April 1957): 103–105.

————. Review of *The Twenty-seventh Wife*, by Irving Wallace. *Utah Historical Quarterly* 29 (1961): 377–78.

Johnson, G. Wesley, and Marian Ashby Johnson. "On the Trail of the Twentieth-Century Mormon Outmigration." *BYU Studies* 46 (2007): 41–83.

Josephy, Alvin M., Jr. *The Civil War in the American West*. New York: Alfred A. Knopf, 1991.

Kammen, Michael. *Mystic Chords of Memory: The Transformation of Tradition in American Culture*. New York: Alfred A. Knopf, 1991.

Keller, Charles L. *The Lady in the Ore Bucket*. Salt Lake City: University of Utah Press, 2001.

Kelly, Charles, ed. *Journals of John D. Lee, 1846–1847 and 1859*. Salt Lake City: Western Printing Co., 1938; reprint, Salt Lake City: University of Utah Press, 1984.

Kenner, Scipio Africanus. *Utah as It Is*. Salt Lake City: Deseret Book Co., 1904.

Kenney, Scott G., ed. *Wilford Woodruff's Journal*. 10 vols. Midvale, Utah: Signature Books, 1983.

Kidd, James Harvey. "The Michigan Cavalry Brigade in the Wilderness." In *Military Order of the Loyal Legion of the United States*. Detroit: Winn and Hammond Publishers and Binders, 1889; reprint, Wilmington, N.C.: Broadfoot, 1993.

———. *Personal Recollections of a Cavalryman with Custer's Michigan Cavalry Brigade in the Civil War*. Ionia, Mich., 1908.

———. *Riding with Custer: Recollections of a Cavalryman in the Civil War*. Lincoln: University of Nebraska Press, 1997.

Kirby, Robert. *End of Watch: Utah's Murdered Police Officers, 1858–2003*. Salt Lake City: University of Utah Press, 2004.

Klinger, Leslie S., ed. *A Tangled Skein*. New York: Baker Street Irregulars, 2008.

Koonce, Donald B., ed. *Doctor to the Front: The Recollections of Confederate Surgeon Thomas Fanning Wood, 1861–1865*. Knoxville: University of Tennessee Press, 2000.

Korn, Jerry. *Pursuit to Appomattox: The Last Battles*. Civil War Series. Alexandria, Va.: Time-Life Books, 1987.

Krenkel, John H., ed. *The Life and Times of Joseph Fish, Mormon Pioneer*. Danville, Ill.: Interstate Printers and Publishers, 1970.

Ladd, David L., and Audrey J. Ladd. *The Bachelder Papers: Gettysburg in Their Own Words*. Dayton, Ohio: Morningside Press, 1994.

Lamar, Howard R. "Political Patterns in New Mexico and Utah Territories, 1850–1900." *Utah Historical Quarterly* 28 (October 1960): 363–87.

Landon, Michael N., Adrian W. Cannon, and Richard E. Turley, Jr., eds. *Journals of George Q. Cannon*. Vol. 1, *To California in '49*. Salt Lake City: Deseret Book Co., 1999.

Larson, Gustave O. *The Americanization of Utah for Statehood*. San Marino, Calif.: Huntington Library, 1971.

———. "Land Contest in Early Utah." *Utah Historical Quarterly* 29 (October 1961): 309–25.

———. "Utah and the Civil War." *Utah Historical Quarterly* 33 (Winter 1965): 56.

Larson, T. A. "Women Suffrage in Western America." *Utah Historical Quarterly* 38 (Winter 1970): 14.

Leale, Charles Augustus. "Intermediary Haemorrhage, Parenchymatous in Character, following Secondary Amputation of Thigh; Recovery." *United States Sanitary Commission Memoirs: Surgical* 1 (1870): 176.

LeCheminant, Wilford Hill. "Crisis Averted? General Harney and the Change in Command of the Utah Expedition." *Utah Historical Quarterly* 51 (Winter 1983): 30.

Leckie, Shirley A. *Elizabeth Bacon Custer and the Making of a Myth.* Norman: University of Oklahoma Press, 1993.

Lee, John D. *Mormonism Unveiled: Life and Confessions of John D. Lee.* Albuquerque: Fierra Blanca, 2001.

Lee, Lawrence B. "The Homestead Act—Vision and Reality." *Utah Historical Quarterly* 30 (July 1962): 215–34.

———. "Homesteading in Zion." *Utah Historical Quarterly* 28 (January 1960): 29–38.

Lester, Ireta E. *The Early History of Carleton, Michigan.* Carleton, Mich.: I. E. Lester, 1989.

Limerick, Patricia Nelson. *Something in the Soil: Legacies and Reckonings in the New West.* New York: W. W. Norton and Co., 200.

Linderman, Gerald F. *Embattled Courage: The Experience of Combat in the American Civil War.* New York: Macmillan, Free Press, 1987.

Linford, Lawrence L. "Establishing and Maintaining Land Ownership in Utah Prior to 1869." *Utah Historical Quarterly* 42 (1974): 126–43.

Linn, William Alexander. *The Story of the Mormons: From the Date of Their Origin to the Year 1901.* New York: Macmillan, 1902.

Lockley, Frederic E. *The Lee Trial! An Expose of the Mountain Meadows Massacre.* Salt Lake City: Tribune Printing Co., 1875.

Long, E. B. *The Saints and the Union: Utah Territory during the Civil War.* Urbana: Illinois Press, 1981.

Longacre, Edward G. *The Cavalry at Gettysburg.* London and Toronto: Fairleigh Dickinson University Press, 1986.

———. *Custer and His Wolverines: The Michigan Cavalry Brigade, 1861–1865.* Conshohocken, Pa.: Combined Publishing, 1997.

Lyman, Edward Leo. "The Mormon Quest for Utah Statehood." PhD. diss., University of California, Riverside, 1981.

———. *Political Deliverance: The Mormon Quest for Utah Statehood.* Urbana: University of Illinois Press, 1986.

———. "Statehood, Political Allegiance, and Utah's First U.S. Senate Seats: Prizes for the National Parties and Local Factions." *Utah Historical Quarterly* 63 (Fall 1995): 341.

Lythgoe, Dennis L. "Negro Slavery in Utah." *Utah Historical Quarterly* 39 (Winter 1971): 40–54.

MacKinnon, William P. "And the War Came: James Buchanan, The Utah Expedition, and the Decision to Intervene." *Utah Historical Quarterly* 76 (2008): 22–37.

———. *At Sword's Point.* Part 1: *A Documented History of the Utah War to 1858.* Norman, Okla.: Arthur H. Clark, 2008.

———. "The Buchanan Spoils System and the Utah Expedition: Careers of W. M. F. Magraw and John M. Hockaday." *Utah Historical Quarterly* 31 (Spring 1963): 128.

———. "'Like Splitting a Man up His Backbone': The Territorial Dismemberment of Utah, 1850–1896." *Utah Historical Quarterly* 71 (Spring 2003): 103.

———. "'Lonely Bones': Leadership and Utah War Violence." *Journal of Mormon History* 33, no. 1 (Spring 2007): 158

———. Review of *Camp Floyd and the Mormons,* by Donald R. Moorman, with Gene A. Sessions. *Journal of Mormon History* 32, no. 3 (2006): 224–32.

———. Review of *Glory Hunter: A Biography of Patrick Edward Connor,* by Brigham Madsen. *Utah Historical Quarterly* 61 (Winter 1993): 97.

———. "Sex, Subalterns, and Steptoe: Army Behavior, Mormon Rage, and Utah War Anxieties." *Utah Historical Quarterly* 76 (2008): 227–46.

Madsen, Brigham D. *Corinne: The Gentile Capital of Utah.* Salt Lake City: Utah State Historical Society, 1980.

———. *Exploring the Great Salt Lake: The Stansbury Expedition of 1849–50.* Salt Lake City: University of Utah Press, 1989.

———. *Glory Hunter: A Biography of Patrick Edward Connor.* Salt Lake City: University of Utah Press, 1990.

Madsen, Brigham D., and Betty M. Madsen. "Corinne, the Fair: Gateway to the Montana Mines." *Utah Historical Quarterly* 37 (Winter 1969): 102–23.

Madsen, Carol Cornwall, ed. *Battle for the Ballot: Essays on Woman Suffrage in Utah, 1870–1896.* Logan: Utah State University Press, 1997.

Mahon, John K. *History of the Militia and the National Guard.* New York: Macmillan, 1969.

Malmquist, O. N. *The First 100 Years: A History of the Salt Lake Tribune, 1871–1971.* Salt Lake City: Utah State Historical Society, 1971.

———. *The Alta Club, Salt Lake City, 1883–1974.* Salt Lake City: Alta Club, 1974.

Mandel, Jerry. "The Mythical Roots of U.S. Drug Policy: Soldier's Disease and Addiction in the Civil War." Schaffer Library of Drug Policy, www.druglibrary.org/schaffer/History/soldis.htm.

Mason, Patrick Q. "The Prohibition of Interracial Marriage in Utah, 1888–1963." *Utah Historical Quarterly* 76 (2008): 116.

Mauss, Armand. *The Angel and the Beehive: The Mormon Struggle with Assimilation.* Urbana and Chicago: University of Illinois Press, 1994.

McAlexander, Ulysses Grant. *History of the Thirteenth United States Infantry.* Fort McDowell, Calif.: Regimental Press, 1905.

McConnell, Stuart. *Glorious Contentment: The Grand Army of the Republic, 1865–1900.* Chapel Hill: University of North Carolina Press, 1992.

McCormick, John S. "Hornets in the Hive: Socialists in Early Twentieth-Century Utah." *Utah Historical Quarterly* 50 (Summer 1982): 237.

McPherson, James W. *Battle Cry of Freedom: The Civil War Era.* New York: Oxford University Press, 1988.

Merington, Marguerite. *The Custer Story: The Life and Intimate Letters of General George A. Custer and His Wife Elizabeth.* New York: Devin-Adair, 1950.

Merkley, Arid G., ed. *Monuments of Courage: A History of Beaver County.* Beaver, Utah: Milford News.

Metcalf, Brandon J. "The Nauvoo Legion and the Prevention of the Utah War." *Utah Historical Quarterly* 72 (Fall 2004): 305–306.

Miller, Rod. *Massacre at Bear River: First, Worst, Forgotten.* Caldwell, Idaho: Caxton Press, 2008.

Minor, James M. "Report on Artificial Limbs." *Bulletin of the New York Academy of Medicine* 1 (1861): 165.

Mitchell, Reid. *Civil War Soldiers.* New York: Viking Press, 1988.

Monaghan, Jay. *Custer: The Life of General George Armstrong Custer.* Boston and Toronto: Little, Brown, 1959.

Moorman, Donald R., with Gene A. Sessions. *Camp Floyd and the Mormons: The Utah War.* Salt Lake City: University of Utah Press, 1992.

Morgan, Dale L., ed. "The State of Deseret." *Utah Historical Quarterly* 8 (April–October 1940): 67–155.

———. *The State of Deseret.* Logan: Utah State University Press and Utah Historical Society, 1987.

Morris, Roy, Jr. *Sheridan: The Life and Wars of General Phil Sheridan.* New York: Crown, 1992.

Morrow, Col. Henry A. "The Last of the Iron Brigade." In "The H. A. Morrow Diary," *Civil War Times, Illustrated* 14 (February 1976): 10–21.

———. "To Chancellorsville with the Iron Brigade" In "The Diary of Colonel Henry A. Morrow," *Civil War Times, Illustrated* 14 (January 19, 1976): 19–22.

Neff, Andrew Love. *History of Utah, 1847 to 1869.* Salt Lake City: Deseret News Press, 1940.

Nelson, Lowry. *The Mormon Village: A Pattern and Technique of Land Settlement.* Salt Lake City: University of Utah Press, 1952.

Nelson, Pearl Udall. *Arizona Pioneer Mormon: David King Udall; His Story and His Family, 1851–1938.* Tucson: Arizona Silhouettes, 1959.

Nibley, Preston. *Brigham Young: The Man and His Work.* 4th ed. Salt Lake City: Deseret Book Co., 1960.

Nichols, Jeffrey. *Prostitution, Polygamy and Power: Salt Lake City, 1847–1918.* Urbana and Chicago: University of Illinois Press, 2002.

Nolan, Alan T. *The Iron Brigade: A Military History.* Bloomington and Indianapolis: Indiana University Press, 1961.

Novak, Shannon A. *House of Mourning: A Biocultural History of the Mountain Meadows Massacre.* Salt Lake City: University of Utah Press, 2008.

O'Connor, Richard. *Sheridan, the Inevitable.* Indianapolis: Bobbs-Merrill, 1953.

O'Dea, Thomas F. *The Mormons.* Chicago and London: University of Chicago Press, 1957.

O'Donovan, Connell. "The Life and Murder of Thomas Coleman, a Mormon Slave." Paper presented at the Mormon History Association conference, Sacramento, Calif., May 23, 2008.

O'Flaherty, Daniel. *General Jo Shelby: Undefeated Rebel.* Chapel Hill: University of North Carolina Press, 2000.

Ogden, Annegret S., ed. *Frontier Reminiscences of Eveline Brooks Auerbach.* Berkeley: Friends of the Bancroft Library, University of California, Berkeley, 1994.

Orton, Chad M., and William W. Slaughter. *Joseph Smith's America: His Life and Times.* Salt Lake City: Deseret Book Co., 2005.

Otis, George Alexander. *Histories of Two Hundred and Ninety Six Surgical Photographs Prepared at the Army Medical Museum.* Washington, D.C. : Surgeon General's Office, 1865–72.

Owens, Kenneth N. *Gold Rush Saints: California Mormons and Great Rush for Riches.* Spokane, Wash.: Arthur H. Clark, 2004.

Paddock, Mrs. A. G. *In the Toils.* Chicago: Shepard, Tobias and Co., 1879.

Panek, Tracey E. "Search and Seizure in Utah: Recounting the Antipolygamy Raids." *Utah Historical Quarterly* 62 (Fall 1994): 316–34.

Papanikolas, Helen Z. *The Peoples of Utah.* Salt Lake City: Utah State Historical Society, 1976.

Parshall, Ardis E. "'Pursue, Retake and Punish': The 1857 Santa Clara Ambush." *Utah Historical Quarterly* 73 (Winter 2005): 74–75.

Pederson, Lyman C., Jr. "The Daily Union Vedette—A Military Voice on the Mormon Frontier." *Utah Historical Quarterly* 42 (Winter 1974): 39–48.

Peterson, Charles S. *Utah: A Bicentennial History.* New York: W. W. Norton and Co., 1977.

Peterson, Thomas Virgil. *Ham and Japheth: The Mythic World of Whites in the Antebellum South.* Metuchen, N.J.: Scarecrow Press, 1978.

Phipps, Michael. *"Come On, You Wolverines!" Custer at Gettysburg.* Gettysburg, Pa.: Farnsworth House Military Impressions, 1996.

Poll, Richard D. "The Americanization of Utah." *Utah Historical Quarterly* 44 (Winter 1976): 76–93.

———. "The Mormon Question Enters National Politics." *Utah Historical Quarterly* 25 (April 1957): 117–31.

———. "The Political Reconstruction of Utah Territory, 1866–1890." *Pacific Historical Review* 27 (May 1958): 111–26.

Poll, Richard D., general ed., and Thomas G. Alexander, Eugene E. Campbell, and David E. Miller, associate eds. *Utah's History*. Logan: Utah State University Press, 1989.

Pratt, Orson, ed. "Celestial Marriage." *Seer* 1 (January 1853); 2 (August 1854). Republished, Salt Lake City: Eugene Walker, n.d. Cited in Hardy, *Doing the Works of Abraham*.

Prince, Gregory A., and William Robert Wright. *David O. McKay and the Rise of Modern Mormonism*. Salt Lake City: University of Utah Press, 2005.

Proceedings of the Fourth Annual Encampment, Department of Utah, GAR, Ogden, Utah, April 22, 23, 1886. Pamphlet 3759. Utah State History Division.

Putnam, Daniel. *A History of the Michigan State Normal School at Ypsilanti, 1849–1899*. Ypsilanti, Mich., 1899.

Quinn, D. Michael. *Early Mormonism and the Magic World View*. Salt Lake City: Signature Books, 1998.

———. *The Mormon Hierarchy: Extensions of Power*. Salt Lake City: Signature Books and Smith Research Associates, 1997.

Rankin, Charles E., ed. *Legacy: New Perspectives on the Battle of the Little Bighorn*. Helena: Montana Historical Society Press, 1996.

———. "Sweet Delusion: The Life and Times of Frederic E. Lockley, Western Journalist." PhD diss., University of New Mexico, Albuquerque, 1994.

Rawick, George P., Jan Hillegas, and Ken Lawrence, eds. *The American Slave: A Composite Autobiography*. Westport, Conn.: Greenwood, 1978.

Reavis, L. U. *Life and Military Services of General William Selby Harney*. St. Louis: Bryan, Brand, and Co., 1878.

Reid, John Philip. *Policing the Elephant: Crime, Punishment, and Social Behavior on the Overland Trail*. San Marino, Calif.: Huntington Library, 1997.

"Revolutionary Pensioners on the Roll of Michigan under the law of March 18th, 1818, from the passage thereof to this day with the Rank they served and the Lines in which they served." In *The Pension List of 1820* (Washington, D.C.: Gales and Seaton; LOC 91-73094)

Reynolds, Arlene. *The Civil War Memories of Elizabeth Bacon Custer*. Austin: University of Texas Press, 1994.

Rhodes-Jones, Carolyn. "Transcontinental Travelers' Excursions to Salt Lake City and Ogden: A Photographic Essay." *Utah Historical Quarterly* 47 (1979): 273–90.

Ritchie, Robert C., and Paul Andrew Hutton. *Frontier and Region: Essays in Honor of Malcolm Ridge.* San Marino, Calif.: Huntington Library Press; Albuquerque: University of New Mexico Press, 1997.

Roberts, B. H. *A Comprehensive History of the Church of Jesus Christ of Latter-day Saints.* Vol. 5. Salt Lake City: Deseret News Press, 1930.

Roberts, David. *Devil's Gate: Brigham Young and the Great Mormon Handcart Tragedy.* New York: Simon and Schuster, 2008.

Robertson, James I., Jr. Introduction to *The Medical and Surgical History of the Civil War,* vol. 1. Wilmington, N.C.: Barefoot Publishing Co., 1992.

Robinson, Charles M., III. *Bad Hand: A Biography of General Ranald S. Mackenzie.* Austin, Tex.: State House Press, 1993.

Rose, Blanch C. "Early Utah Medical Practice." *Utah Historical Quarterly* 10 (January–October 1942): 14–33.

Roster of the Department of Utah, Grand Army of the Republic, 1908. Pamphlet PAM 22617. Utah State History Division.

Sadler, Richard W. "The Impact of Mining on Salt Lake City." *Utah Historical Quarterly* 47 (Summer 1979): 243–44.

———. "The Spence-Pike Affair." *Utah Historical Quarterly* 76 (Winter 2008): 79–93.

Schindler, Harold. *Orrin Porter Rockwell: Man of God, Son of Thunder.* Salt Lake City: University of Utah Press, 1966.

Scott, Patricia Lyn. "Jennie Anderson Froiseth and the Blue Tea." *Utah Historical Quarterly* 71 (2003): 20–35.

———. "The Widow and the Lion of the Lord: Sarah Ann Cooke vs. Brigham Young." *Journal of Mormon History* (Spring 2004): 189–212.

Scott, Robert Nicholson, and Henry Martyn Lazelle. *The War of the Rebellion: A Compilation of the Official Records of the Union and Confederate Armies.* 4 ser., 70 vols. Washington, D.C.: Government Printing Office, 1880–1901.

Sculley, Bradley, and Harold W. Blodgett, eds. *Leaves of Grass: Authoritative Texts, Prefaces, Whitman on His Art, Criticism.* New York: W. W. Norton and Co., 1973.

Seifrit, William C., ed. "'To Get U[tah] in U[nion]': Diary of a Failed Mission." *Utah Historical Quarterly* 51 (Fall 1983): 378–81.

Sessions, Gene A. *Mormon Thunder: A Documentary History of Jedediah Morgan Grant.* Urbana: University of Illinois Press, 1982.

———. Review of *A Winter with the Mormons: The 1852 Letters of Jotham Goodell,* ed. David L. Bigler. *Utah Historical Quarterly* 71 (2003): 77–79.

———. "Two Utahs: A Centennial Retrospective." *Weber Studies: An Interdisciplinary Humanities Journal* 13 (Winter 1996): 103–12.

Shaara, Michael. *The Killer Angels.* New York: Ballantine, 1974.

Sharpe, William D. *Confederate States Medical and Surgical Journal.* Metuchen, N.J.: Scarecrow Press, 1976.

Shaw, Ronald E. *Erie Water West: A History of the Erie Canal, 1792–1854.* Lexington: University of Kentucky Press, 1966.

Sheehan-Dean, Aaron C., ed. *Struggle for a Vast Future: The American Civil War.* New York: Osprey Publishing, 2006.

Sheridan, Philip H. *Personal Memoirs of P. H. Sheridan, General United States Army.* 2 vols. New York: Charles L. Webster and Co., 1888, 1891.

Shipps, Jan. *Sojourner in the Promised Land.* Urbana and Chicago: University of Illinois Press, 2000.

Simon, John Y. *The Papers of Ulysses S. Grant.* Vol. 24. Carbondale and Edwardsville: Southern Illinois University Press, 1998.

———. *The Personal Memoirs of Julia Dent Grant (Mrs. Ulysses S. Grant).* New York: G. P. Putnam's Sons, 1975.

Smart, Donna Toland, ed. *Mormon Midwife: The 1846–1888 Diaries of Patty Bartlett Sessions.* Logan: Utah State University Press, 1997.

Smith, George D. *Nauvoo Polygamy: "But We Call It Celestial Marriage."* Salt Lake City: Signature Books, 2008.

Smith, George Winston, and Charles Judah. *Life in the North during the Civil War.* Albuquerque: University of New Mexico Press, 1966.

Soderlund, Jean R. *Quakers and Slavery: A Divided Spirit.* Princeton, N.J.: Princeton University Press, 1985.

Staker, Steven L. *"Mark Twain v. John Caine, et al.:* A Utah Territorial Case of Copyright Enforcement." *Utah Historical Quarterly* 71 (2003): 348–61.

Staker, Susan. *Waiting for World's End: The Diaries of Wilford Woodruff.* Salt Lake City: Signature Books, 1993.

Stansbury, Howard. *Exploration and Survey of the Valley of the Great Salt Lake.* Washington, D.C., and London: Smithsonian Institution Press, 1988.

Starr, Stephen Z. *The Union Cavalry in the Civil War.* Vol. 1. Baton Rouge: Louisiana State University Press, 1979.

Stegner, Page, ed. "At Home in the Fields of the Lord." In *Marking the Sparrow's Fall: The Making of the American West.* New York: Henry Holt and Co., 1998.

Stegner, Wallace. *The Gathering of Zion: The Story of the Mormon Trail.* Lincoln and London: University of Nebraska Press, 1992.

———. *Mormon Country.* Lincoln and London: University of Nebraska Press, 1981.

———. *Recapitulation.* New York: Penguin Books, 1979.

Stenhouse, Thomas B. H. *The Rocky Mountain States: A Full and Complete History of the Mormons, from the First Vision of Joseph Smith to the Last Courtship of Brigham Young.* New York: D. Appleton and Co., 1873.

Stewart, George R. *Pickett's Charge: A Microhistory of the Final Attack at Gettysburg.* Boston: Houghton Mifflin, 1959.

Sillitoe, Linda. *The History of Salt Lake County.* Utah Centennial County History Series, Salt Lake City: Utah State Historical Society; Salt Lake County Commission, 1996.

Stone, Irving. *Men to Match My Mountains.* Garden City, N.Y.: Doubleday, 1956.

Swanson, Glenwood J. *G. A. Custer: His Life and Times.* Agua Dulce, Calif.: Swanson Productions, 2004.

Taggart, Stephen G. *Mormonism's Negro Policy: Social and Historical Origins.* Salt Lake City: University of Utah Press, 1970.

Takaki, Ronald T. *A Pro-Slavery Crusade: The Agitation to Reopen the African Slave Trade.* New York: Free Press, 1971.

Tanner, Obert C. *One Man's Journey in Search of Freedom.* Salt Lake City: Humanities Center at the University of Utah, 1994.

Tapia, John E. *Circuit Chautauqua: From Rural Education to Popular Entertainment in Early Twentieth Century America.* Jefferson, N.C.: McFarland and Co., 1997.

Taylor, Samuel W. *The Kingdom or Nothing: The Life of John Taylor, Militant Mormon.* New York: Macmillan; New York and London: Collier Macmillan, 1976.

Thomason, John W., Jr. *JEB Stuart.* New York: Charles Scribner's Sons, 1930.

Troiani, Don, and Brian C. Pohanka. *Don Troiani's Civil War.* Southbury, Conn.: Stackpole Books, 1995.

Trowbridge, L. S. "The Operation of the Cavalry in the Gettysburg Campaign." *War Papers, Being Papers Read before the Commandery of the State of Michigan, October 6, 1886.* Reprint, Wilmington, N.C.: Broadfoot, 1993.

Tullidge, Edward W. *History of Salt Lake City.* Salt Lake City: Star Printing, 1886.

The Union Army: New Jersey, Indiana, Illinois, and Michigan. Vol. 3. Wilmington, N.C.: Barefoot, 1998.

Urwin, Gregory J. W. *Custer Victorious: The Civil War Battles of General George Armstrong Custer.* London: Fairleigh Dickinson University Press, 1983.

Utah Genealogical Association, Golden Spike Chapter, comp. *Historical and Genealogical Register of Indexes to Corinne, Utah Newspapers, 1869–1875.* Brigham City, Utah: Genealogical Association, Golden Spike Chapter, 1975.

Van Wagoner, Richard S. *Mormon Polygamy: A History.* Salt Lake City: Signature Books, 1989.

Van Wagoner, Richard S., and Mary Van Wagoner. "Arthur Pratt, Utah Lawman." *Utah Historical Quarterly* 55 (Winter 1987): 24.

Varley, James V. *Brigham and the Brigadier: General Patrick Connor and His California Volunteers in Utah and along the Overland Trail.* Tucson, Ariz.: Westernlore Press, 1989.

Verdoia, Ken, and Richard Firmage. *Utah: The Struggle for Statehood.* Salt Lake City: University of Utah Press, 1996.

Waite, C. V. *The Mormon Prophet and His Harem.* Chicago: J. S. Goodman and Co.; Cincinnati: C. F. Vent and Co., 1868.

Walker, John Philip, ed. *Dale Morgan on Early Mormonism: Correspondence and a New History.* Salt Lake City: Signature Books, 1986.

Walker, Newell R. "They Walked 1,300 Miles." *Ensign* (July 2000): 44–49.

Walker, Ronald W., Richard E. Turley, Jr., and Glen M. Leonard. *Massacre at Mountain Meadows.* New York: Oxford University Press, 2008.

Walker, Ronald Warren. "The Commencement of the Godbeite Protest: Another View." *Utah Historical Quarterly* 42 (Summer 1974): 216–44.

———. "The Godbeite Protest in the Making of Modern Utah." PhD diss., University of Utah, 1977.

———. "The Liberal Institute: A Case Study in National Assimilation." *Dialogue: A Journal of Mormon Thought* 10 (1977): 74–85.

———. *Wayward Saints: The Godbeites and Brigham Young.* Urbana: University of Illinois Press, 1995.

———. "When the Spirits Did Abound: 19th Century Utah's Encounter with Free-Thought Radicalism." *Utah Historical Quarterly* 50 (Fall 1982): 304–332.

Wallace, Irving. *The Twenty-seventh Wife.* New York: Simon and Schuster, 1961.

Ward, Geoffrey C., and Dayton Duncan. *The West.* Boston: Little, Brown, Back Bay Books, 1996.

Ward, William H. *Records of the Members of the Grand Army of the Republic.* San Francisco: H. S. Crocker and Co., 1886.

Wegner, Ansley Herring. *Phantom Pain: North Carolina's Artificial-Limbs Program for Confederate Veterans.* Raleigh: Office of Archives and History, North Carolina Department of Cultural Resources, 2004.

Werner, M. R. *Brigham Young.* New York: Harcourt, Brace and Co., 1925.

Werstein, Irving. *Kearny the Magnificent: The Story of General Philip Kearny, 1815–1862.* New York: John Day, 1962.

Wert, Jeffry D. *The Controversial Life of George Armstrong Custer.* New York: Simon and Schuster, 1996.

———. *From Winchester to Cedar Creek: The Shenandoah Campaign of 1864.* New York: Simon and Schuster, 1989.

Whitman, Walt. "I Hear It Was Charged against Me." In *Leaves of Grass: Authoritative Texts, Prefaces, Whitman on His Art, Criticism,* ed. Bradley Sculley and Harold W. Blodgett, 128. New York: W. W. Norton and Co., 1973.

———. "A Night Battle, over a Week Since." In "Specimen Days," *Prose Works.* Philadelphia: David McKay, 1892.

————. "The Real War Will Never Get in the Books." In *Specimen Days and Collect*. 1882–1883; reprint, New York: Dover Publications, 1995.

————. *Specimen Days in America*. London, 1887.

————. *Walt Whitman: Civil War Poetry and Prose*. New York: Dover, 1995.

Whitney, Orson Ferguson. *History of Utah*. 4 vols. Salt Lake City: George Q. Cannon and Sons, 1904.

Williams, Charles R. *The Life of Rutherford Birchard Hayes, 19th President of the United States*. 2 vols. New York: Da Capo Press, 1971.

Wing, Talcott E., ed. *Monroe County, Michigan*. New York: Munsell and Co., 1890.

Wittenberg, Eric J., ed., and Karla Jean Husby, comp. *Under Custer's Command: The Civil War Journal of James Henry Avery*. Washington, D.C.: Brassey's, 2000.

Wolfinger, Henry J. "A Reexamination of the Woodruff Manifesto in the Light of Utah Constitutional History" *Utah Historical Quarterly* 39 (1971): 328–49.

Wood, Paul M. "The Irony of Mormon History." *Utah Historical Quarterly* 41 (Fall 1973): 393–409.

Woods, Fred E. "East to West through North and South: Mormon Immigration during the Civil War." *BYU Studies* 39, no. 1 (2000): 6–29.

Wright, Lawrence. "Lives of the Saints." *New Yorker*, January 21, 2002, 57.

Wyl, Dr. Wilhelm [Dr. Wilhelm Ritter von Wymetal]. *Mormon Portraits: Joseph Smith the Prophet, His Family, and His Friends*. Salt Lake City: Tribune Printing and Publishing Co., 1886.

Young, Ann Eliza. *Wife No. 19, or The Story of a Life in Bondage*. Salt Lake City: private printing, 1875.

Index

References to illustrations appear in italics.

Adair, George Washington, Jr.229, 210
Agramonte, Gen. C. H. M., 286
Allsop, "Elder," 136
Alta, Utah Terr., 19, 183
Anthony, Susan B., 156
Arkansas emigrants, 171; death at
  Mountain Meadows, 208–209, 208n3
Armory Square Hospital, Washington,
  D.C., 76, 77n17, *78*
Armstrong, C. M., 279,
Ashley bill (anti-polygamy), 339
Ashley, Rep. James Monroe, 339;
  Committee on Territories, 106; on
  Sherman's troops coming to Utah
  Terr., 106
Axtell, Gov. Samuel B., 129; aligned
  with Mormons, 182n37; and certificate
  of election for Cannon, 181; epithet of
  "Bishop," 182n37

Backman, Benjamin, 215
Bacon, Daniel (father of Elizabeth), 41
Bacon, Elizabeth "Libbie" (Mrs.
  George Armstrong Custer), 41
Baker, John T. "Jack" (trail captain),
  208–209

Barry, David Sheldon, 267, 316;
  description of career, 265n28;
  Washington connections, 265
Barton, J. A., 215, 229
Baskin, Robert Newton, 160, 163,
  164, 171, 190, 231, 281, 268n41, 314,
  326, 345; prosecutor in trial of John
  D. Lee, 218; author of Cullom Bill,
  158; case of illegal marching, 154;
  closing arguments in Lee trial, 220;
  confession of William Hickman, 160;
  congressional contest with Cannon,
  202; desire to prosecute murderers of
  Mountain Meadows, 218n36; lobbyist
  for Christiancy bills, 193; prosecutes
  Thomas Hawkins for adultery, 145–
  46; prosecutor in Robinson murder
  trial, 144; in Reynolds trial, 199; with
  Maxwell in Washington, 267
Bates, George Caesar, 167n74, 212,
  235; defense team for Lee, 218n37; on
  penitentiary conditions, 212; Maxwell
  accused of fraud 140; removed as U.S.
  attorney 167
Battle of the Little Big Horn, 258–59
Battles of Civil War: Antietam, 91;

Battles of Civil War (*continued*)
Brandy Station, 57; Brentsville, 56; Buckland Mills 84; Bull Run, first, 49; Bull Run, second, 55, 322; Chancellorsville, 57; Cold Harbor, 91; Five Forks, 23, 75; Gettysburg, 23, 58, 62–63, 310; Haw's Shop, 66; Kelly's Ford, 57; Salem Church, 66; Shiloh, 91; South Mountain, 50; Stone's River, 56n20; Yellow Tavern, 66

Bayonet Rule, 202–204. *See also* Force Act

Bell, Alonzo (sec. of interior), 136

Benedict, Dr. Joseph Mott, 304; on Maxwell's debility, 289–90; claims against estate of Mrs. Maxwell, 304

Bigelow, Edward, 39, 50, 308

Benson, Ezra T., 104, 137

Bingham, John A., 165

Bishop, William W., 206, 218n37

Black, George A.: Utah territorial sec. and gov., 212, 270, 313; transfer of federal funds, 234

Blacks: full LDS privileges "forever" denied, 95; penalty for intermarriage, 95; LDS position on blacks changed in 1978, 95n26; place in Mormon theology, 93–95, 95n26

Blaine, Rep. James Gillespie, 180, 180n31; Committee on Territories, 166; Speaker of the house, 166; rumors of bribery, 166

Blair, Austen: gov. of Mich., 43; informed by Maxwell of Utah issues, 277, 278n89

Bliss, D. W. (surgeon), 77, 77n19

Blood atonement: Cannon admits existence, 170; signaled by crook of finger, 316–17, 317n24

Blythe, Maria M., 192

Book of Mormon, 33, 94, 111; and reviews in N.Y. newspapers, 34

Boreman, Judge Jacob Smith, 206, 216; brief history of, 193n14; business ties with Calif. railroads defeat Frelinghuysen Bill, 166; on enforcing

law, 331n1; grand jury call in Beaver, 245; grand jury call in Salt Lake City, 243; inherits court action on Brigham Young, 240; no verdict in first trial of John D. Lee, 220; order for Brigham Young and George A. Smith to testify, 214; order to Maxwell to warn crowd at Lee trial, 218; story of Maxwell and liquor bottle, 315; unfinished humorous story on Maxwell, 315; warrants for arrest of Beaver witnesses, 219; women voting, 193; Young ordered to appear, 240

Brazier, John, 144–45

Brearley, E. C., 257

Brown, Capt. Albert, 122, *122*

Brown, B. F., 215

Browning Bill, 339

Buchanan, Pres. James, 339; Brigham Young replaced as governor, 207; Mormons in rebellion, 207

Buford, Brig. Gen. John, 59

Burgher, Capt. Matthew, 56, 230n83, *238*, 328; beating sustained during jailbreak, 229–30; burial at Camp Douglas 230; death of, 230; marriage pending when he died, 328; military service record, 56n20; praise from grand jury, 243–44; prison accommodations for Lee, 228; tended by Lee, 230; warden of prison in Salt Lake City, 227; warning to Brigham Young over prison violence, 238–39

Burr, David Auguste (brother of David Hugh), 120

Burr, David Hugh, 336; relationship with Brigham Young and Mormons, 120–21; federal surveyor, 120; influence on Buchanan to send troops to Utah, 121; letter of Mormons in rebellion, 121

Burr, Frederick H. (son of David Hugh), 120

Burrows, Rep. Julius C., 277; chairman, Committee on Territories, 277;

longtime association with Maxwell, 277

Burt, Andrew H. (chief of police): marching episode, 153; destroyed Englebrecht liquor store, 161; election riot, 204; city police officer, 144, 161; named in murder of Dr. Robinson, 144–45

Burton, Robert T.: indicted for treason, 102; Morris rebellion, 192n13; in 1857 guerrilla forces, 102; register of voters for Salt Lake County, 192; sabotage of army train, 192n13; service in Civil War, 102

Butler, Gen. Benjamin F.: Butler Medal, 83; in Civil War, 166n70; rumors of bribery to oppose Frelinghuysen Bill, 166

Camp Douglas, Utah Terr., 44n34, 87, 93, 143, 151, 154, 163, 196, 198, 204, 215, 230, 272; contaminated water, 187; de Trobriand in command, 314n16; Morrow in command, 314n16. *See also* Fort Douglas

Camp Lyon, 51

Camp Rucker, Va., 51

Camp Russell, Va., 69

Campbell, Allen G., 282

Campbell, Gov. John A., 128, 128n38

Campus Martius Square, 51, 53

Cannon, George Q., 162, 163, 169, 192, 263, 326, 330, 344; address at Mormon July celebration, 156; appeal of appropriations, 234n3, 235; and blood atonement, 170; bribery rumors, 171–72; caricature, 319; Civil War as retribution 96; comments on Maxwell, 312; congressional seat open, 281; contest with Baskin, 202; decries non-Mormon presence, 332; defeat of Maxwell in 1872, 168; denies Maxwell's allegations, 169; denies his plural wives, 169; 1870 election, 151; eulogy honoring Brigham Young,

264; opposed by Allen Campbell, 281; petition of Mormon women, 162; positions of power, 317; Reynolds polygamy conviction, 201–202; scathing description of Maxwell, 318; seat in Forty-third Congress, 180; seeks fifth term, 281

Carbines: Burnside, Sharps, Spencer, 82, 82n28

Carey, William, 189, 205, 231, 314; appointed as U.S. attorney, 167; and bank failure, 234; and Cannon seating in Congress, 172; childhood friend of Ulysses Grant, 167n75; dispute of riot authority, 204; efforts to prevent Cannon seating, 181; inquiry over Mormons denied jury seating, 235; Lockley opinion of, 218n36; prosecutor in Lee trial, 218; prosecutor in Reynolds trial, 199, 201; travels with Maxwell to Washington, 140

Carleton, Maj. James Henry, 209; First U.S. Dragoons, 209; Mountain Meadows site investigated, 209

Carpenter, Sen. Matthew, 165

Carrot eaters (insult to Mormons by veterans), 216–17

Cavalry: carbines, 52n13; changing role in warfare, 54; fighting dismounted, 67n53; functions, 54; hardships, 53; mounts, 53, 72; rifles, 52n13; special skills, 54; weapons, 51, 52n13

Cavalry commanders (Confederate): Hampton, 36,56, 60; W. H. F. Lee, 57, 71; Stuart, 54, 58, 59

Cavalry commanders (Union): Kearny, 45, 54; Kilpatrick, 45, 54; Pleasonton, 45, 54, 57; Sheridan, 45, 54, 80, 81

Centennial Exposition: GAR veterans attend, 261; ignored in Utah Terr., 261–62; in Philadelphia, 261; Southern support strong, 261

Chandler, Zachariah, 41, 255, 266; informed by Maxwell of Utah issues, 277

Chautauqua Circuit, 26, 178–84, 179n27;
    influence on Poland Act, 173
Chicago Times, 180
Chiliasm, 101
Christiancy bills, 148, 339; in 1876 and
    1877, 344
Christiancy, Henry Clay (son of Isaac),
    42–43
Christiancy, Isaac Peckham, 89, 193,
    253, 258, 265, 297; ambassador to Peru,
    193n17; bills to restrict polygamy, 193,
    263; career of, 42–43, 193n17; cursed
    by Brigham Young, 262; force behind
    many Utah appointees, 263n19;
    informed by Maxwell of Utah issues,
    277; with Maxwell on legislation, 262;
    Mormon opinion of, 193; patriotic
    speech, 49
Christiancy, James Isaac (son of Isaac),
    89; Medal of Honor recipient, 43n31;
    wounded, 67
Church of Jesus Christ of Latter-
    day Saints, 34, 101, 318; change of
    emphasis from Joseph Smith to
    Jesus, 342; dissolved as corporation,
    292; enhanced acceptance from
    change in belief and practice, 342;
    full membership for people of color,
    342; growth claims disputed, 343n44;
    growth outside United States, 343;
    history inseparable from history of
    Utah, 109; idealization of the family,
    342; move toward mainstream, 342;
    number of members, 342–43, 343n44;
    out-migration and assimilation, 342;
    preparations for millennium, 25; on
    slavery as moral issue, 95; unapologetic
    capitalism, 342. *See also* Mormons
Civil disobedience, 26n13
Civil rights, 282
Civil War, 22–27; as "harvest of
    death," 91; costs to the South, 92–93;
    ideological views of Mormons
    concerning, 96–102; Mormon
    prophecy regarding, 97–100;

Mormons' view of conflict, 96–102;
    Mormons disconnected from war,
    103–104; Mormons who did not serve,
    102; number who served, 91, 91n12;
    numbers of wounded and dead, 91–92;
    unique perspective of Mormons, 24;
    as Second American Revolution, 92;
    on widows flocking to polygamist
    men in Utah Terr., 98; veterans
    volunteer to avenge Custer's death,
    260–61. *See also* War of Rebellion;
    War of Northern Aggression
Civil War veterans, 345
Clagett, William Horace, 190, 165
Clarke, John A., 125
Clawson, Hyrum B., 177–78, 178n19
Clayton, William, 140
Cleveland, Pres. Grover, 287, 339
Clements, Courtland C.: accused of
    land jumping, 125n31; co-investor in
    Rollins mine, 216; register of land for
    Utah Terr., 125
Clinton, Jeter: ballot box tampering
    alleged, 203; Englebrecht liquor
    store destroyed, 161; Salt Lake police
    officer, 161
Colbert, William, 92
Coleman, Thomas (also Thomas
    Colbourn): imprisoned for
    manslaughter, 124n27; murdered and
    castrated, 124; possible witness to Dr.
    Robinson's murder, 124
Colfax, Vice Pres. Schuyler, 41, 326
Committee on the Conduct of the War,
    127, 127n36
Committee on Territories, 106, 159, 166,
    277, 337, 337n21
Compromise of 1850, 94; failure to give
    territory land allocation powers, 118;
    failure to include Preemption Act of
    1841, 118
Congressional anti-polygamy bills:
    Edmunds Act, 339; Edmunds-
    Tucker Bill, 340; many introduced
    but not passed, 339; Poland Act, 339.

See also Ashley bill; Browning bill; Christiancy bill; Cragin bill; Cullom bill; Frelinghuysen bill; Logan bill; McKee bill; Voorhees bill; Wade bill

Conkling, Sen. Roscoe: judiciary committee on Frelinghuysen Bill, 165; N.Y. sen., 128; visits Utah in 1869, 128

Connor, Brig. Gen. Patrick Edward, 270, 272; arrival in Utah Terr., 103; chairman of Liberal party, 151; commander of Powder River campaign, 87, 87n1; on leading volunteer's march on Black Hills to avenge Custer, 260; mineral exploration and mining, 122, 194; regarding Mormons at Committee on Territories, 337, 337n21; relationship with James Kidd, 151n15; threat of military action at flag lowering, 287

Cooke, Col. Philip St. George, 102–103

Corinne, Utah Terr., 331, 343; polygamy outlawed, 149n10; support for Maxwell in, 164

Corinne Daily Reporter, 139

Cradlebaugh, Judge John, 209

Cragin bill, 339; anti-polygamy bill by Abram H. Cragin of N.H., 158; withdrawn for Cullom bill, 158

Craig, Brig. Gen. James, 102

Crawford, Capt. Jack W., 261

Critchett, Otis Adams, 88–89, 90; death of, 304n59; education at Lodi Academy, 88; law degree at University of Mich., 88; law partner and teacher of Maxwell, 88–89; recurring asthma, 88, 88n6; trustee of Albion College, 89; visit to Salt Lake City, 304

Cross, Jerome B., 250; deputy marshal at Beaver, 218–19, fraud by Maxwell alleged, 246; pursuit of Klingensmith, 218–19

Cullom bill (anti-polygamy), 148, 158, 159, 339, 344

Custer, Gen. George Armstrong, 23, 26, 54, 60–62, 66–67, 72–75, 80, 316;

accusations over his actions in Big Horn expedition, 259; attends West Point, 41; birth, 41; death, 44, 258–59; death politicizes western Indian campaign, 259; at Five Forks, 73–74; at Gettysburg, 60–62; indignities after death, 328; marriage to Elizabeth Bacon, 41; saber, 61n34; veterans volunteer to avenge death, 260–61; Washita massacre, 44, 128n40. *See also* Custer Medal

Custer, Elizabeth "Libbie" Bacon (Mrs. George A. Custer), 67

Custer Medal, 23, *84*, 259, 308, 325, 328; awarded for bravery, 82–84; created by Tiffany, 82; controversy about, 83n33; engraved on Maxwell's gravestone, 302, *302*; Maxwell wearing, *81*. *See also* Kidd, James Harvey; Wallace, Lt. Robert C.

Dame, William Horne: arrest for Mountain Meadows killings, 210, 212; fellowship with Mormon church, 231n90; removed to U.S. Penitentiary, 212; return to Beaver prison, 215

Dame, William M., 119

Deaver, John, 122

Dee, Ann Eliza Webb (wife of Brigham Young), 174

Deering, John: GAR member from First Mich. Cav., 273

Delano, Columbus, 139, 142

Denver Tribune, 182

Deseret News: account of personal battle of Maxwell and Henry Carter Lee, 309–10; celebration instructions, 20; cites Maxwell for embezzlement, 247; condemns arrests of Saints for marching, 154, criticism of Maxwell in land office, 139; disparages Judge Hawley, 128; marked ballots defended, 267–68; on Mormon sympathy with Indians at Custer massacre, 259; report of Maxwell in land office, 131–32; report of Maxwell seeking funds, 249; report of Robinson trial, 145

Desert Land Act (1877), 134n57
De Trobriand, Col. P. Regis: commander of Camp Douglas, 157, 157n32, 314n16; orders against illegal marching, 157–58
Devin, Brig. Gen. Thomas C., 69, 72, 74
Dickinson, Anna E., 129
Dickinson, Rev. J. (brother of Anna E.), 129
Dickson, William H. (U.S. attorney), 274–75
Dotson, Peter Kessler (U.S. marshal), 191, 210
Douglas, Beverly, 267
Drummond, Willis, 139; federal land commissioner, 135; rules on plural wife land filings, 135
Duncan, B. L. "Pony," 213
Dupraix, John, 216

Edmunds Act (1883), 280, 281–82, 339, 341, 344
Edmunds-Tucker Act (1887), 340, 341; provisions, 292–93; violence to Mormons arising from, 341
Eighth Wisc. Infantry, 210
Eldredge, Horace S.: Utah territorial marshal, 26n14
Elections in Utah Terr.: election control, 193n16; marked ballots eliminated, 268, residency requirements added, 268; results directed by Mormons, 193n16
Eleventh Mich. Infantry, 48
Eleventh Miss. Infantry (University Grays), 63
Emancipation Proclamation, 97
Emerson, Judge, Philip H., 44n34, 177, 177n18, 192, 314
Emerson, J. C., 122
Emery, Gov. George W., 224
Emma Mine (Alta, Utah Terr.), 21, 21n6
Endowment House, 174, 186
Englebrecht v. Clinton, 161, 162, 327;

effect on Utah cases, 145; and Paul Englebrecht, 161, 204
Erb, Maj. Gabriel S., 293, 293
Erie Canal, 32–33, 35
Evans, David, 212, 210

Fancher, Alexander, 208–209
Farnham, Col. Cullen, 260
Federal appointees: denied office space, 333; meet with isolation and antagonism, 31; ostracized from Mormon society, 331
Ferry, Thomas White, 277, 278n89
Ficklin, Benjamin Franklin, 26n14
Field, Stephen J., 256n70
First Mass. Cavalry, 56
First Mich. Cavalry, 48, 50, 52, 80, 66; at Five Forks, 71–77; at Gettysburg, 60, 61, 62; mustered into service, 51; reputation for bravery, 51
First Mich. Veteran Cavalry: mustered out in Salt Lake City, 87; in Powder River campaign, 87, 87n2
First National Bank of Utah, 233, 234
First N.J. Cavalry, 61
First U.S. Dragoons, 209
First Va. Cavalry, 60
Fish, Franklin R., 210, 229
Fitch, Rep. Thomas (Nev.), 159
Five Forks, 132; casualties, 75n14; strategic importance, 72, 72n5
Flag lowering by Mormons: crisis averted with death of Ulysses Grant, 287; GAR units activated and armed, 287; newspapers critical of Mormon action, 287; protest for lost liberties under Edmunds, 283–88, 287n12
Flags in Civil War: handmade, 284; object of reverence, 284; protecting the colors beyond rational explanation, 284; symbolism and religious connotation, 284
Foote, Prof. Ezra Mead, 49
Force Act, 202–203. *See also* Bayonet Rule
Fort Cameron, 212, 221, 222

Fort Crittenden, Utah Terr., 102–103
Fort Douglas, 301. *See also* Camp Douglas
Fort Laramie, Nebr. Terr., 87, 102, 208
Fort Leavenworth, Kans. Terr., 87, 207
Fort Russell, Wyo. Terr., 179
Fort Sumter, S.C., 49
Forty-third Congress: Maxwell contests Cannon seating, 169–70; Maxwell escorts Ann Eliza Webb Young to House of Representatives, 180
Fourteenth U.S. Infantry, 230
Fourth of July, 331; lack of Mormon celebration, 19; non-Mormon celebration, 19; tone and content of Maxwell's orations, 323–24
Fox, Jesse W., 119
Fox, Samuel R., 121
Frazer, Alexander, 195
Frelinghuysen bill, 148, 339, 344; provisions of, 164–65, Maxwell lobbies for, 164; bribe of James Gillespie Blaine, 166
Frelinghuysen, Sen. Frederick Theodore (N.J.), 164n65
Froiseth, Jennie E. Anderson: author of *Women of Mormonism; or, The Story of Polygamy*, 293; and celebration ball, 293; founder of the Blue Tea Society, 293; founding editor of the *Anti-Polygamy Standard*, 293
Front Royal, Va., 55

Garden of Eden, 96, 111
"Gath," 146, 311. *See also* Townsend, George Alfred
Gee, Lysander, 195
Gee, William W.: accompanies Maxwell to Washington, 277; attests to Maxwell's debility, 289; attorney colleague of Maxwell, 277; brief biography, 277n88; contributions to women's welfare, 277n88; support of Maxwell's disability claims, 277n88; as witness to Maxwell's will, 296

Gentile League of Utah (GLU), 164, Maxwell prominent in, 162–64; quasi-secret non-Mormon society, 162–64
Gilson, Samuel, 145
Godbe, William Samuel, 148, 155, 155n27, 171; address at July 4th celebration, 156; esteemed by President Grant, 149n6; excommunicated from LDS church, 149; octagonal home, 155; and spiritualism, 149; supports mining efforts, 149
Godbeites, 148–50
Godfrey, George L.: Utah Commission member, 294, 301; honorary carriage ride, 294; at Maxwell's funeral, 301
Goldthwait, Judge George: brief biography of, 270n53; mining interests of, 270n53, partnership with Maxwell, 270; prosecuting attorney of Pioche, Nev., 270
Goodwin, Charles Carroll, 300n53, 338,
Grand Army of the Republic (GAR), 132, 326, 328, 344; beginnings in Utah, 269, 271; campfire and ball celebrating Edmunds-Tucker Act, 293; confrontations with Mormons over flag lowering, 285; delegations stop in Utah, 274; emblem engraved on Maxwell's gravestone, 302, *302*; fraternity, charity, and loyalty, 271; history of, 270–71; Maxwell's role of founding in Utah, 271–75; members decorate grave sites, 230; members incensed at flag lowering, 283–84; National Encampment of 1886, 274; Ogden beginnings, 272; outlet for anti-Mormon rhetoric, 274; purpose of, 270–71; resolution demanding respect for flag, 288; significance of flag to war veterans, 284; takes on political role, 273; units outside Utah activated with threat of July 24 flag lowering, 287; units passing through Utah are informed of flag lowering, 287–88

Grandin, Egbert B., 34

Grand jury in Beaver, 245–47

Grand jury in Salt Lake City: notes
  Maxwell's financial records correctly
  kept, 244; praise for replacements
  of prison items stolen by A. P.
  Rockwood, 243; praise for warden
  Matthew Burgher, 243–44; report of
  notes prison guards not paid, 244; visit
  to lunatic asylum, county prison, and
  city jail, 243; visit to penitentiary, 243

Grand Review, 79, 288

Grant, Jedediah Morgan, 186, 335

Grant, Pres. Ulysses, 23, 71, 80, 90,
  139, 152, 154, 159, 162, 181, 197, 221, 255,
  256, 260, 269, 287, 326, 334; at Cold
  Harbor, 91–92; death, 287; personally
  known to Maxwell, 132; presses for
  passage of Frelinghuysen Bill, 165;
  removes George Caesar Bates as U.S.
  district attorney, 167

Gravelly Run Methodist Episcopal
  Church, 76

Gunnison, John W. (1st Lt. and Capt.),
  335; first federal surveys, 119; killed in
  Utah, 119n7

Hagan, Col. Albert, 271; attorney for
  Ann Eliza Young in divorce from
  Brigham Young, 175; retainer and
  contingency fee, 175n11; shares parade
  stand with Maxwell, 230

Haight, Isaac Chauncey:
  excommunicated from LDS church,
  231n90; excommunication reversed
  and blessings restored, 231n90;
  indictment for murders at Mountain
  Meadows, 210

Hampton, Gen. Wade, 56, 60. *See also*
  Cavalry commanders

Hampton, Brigham Y., 144; and
  election riot, 204; Salt Lake
  policeman, 144–45, suspect in murder
  of Dr. Robinson, 145; prostitution
  sting scheme, 204n51

Harding, Stephen S., 100–101

Harney, Brig. Gen. William Selby:
  emotional instability, 338; initially
  assigned command of 1857 troops to
  Utah, 207n1; requested powers of
  martial law in Utah Terr., 339; and
  rumors of violence against Mormons,
  338

Harper's Ferry: and death of William
  B. Maxwell, 70, 328

Harrison, Elias Lacy Thomas, 148;
  address at July 4th celebration, 156;
  excommunicated from LDS church, 149;
  Godbeite and advanced spiritualism,
  149; supported mining efforts, 149

Harrison, Mary E., 37

Hawkins, Thomas, 145–47

Hawley, Cyrus Myron, 313; arrives in
  Salt Lake City, 128; associate justice to
  Utah Terr., 128; Cannon seating, 172;
  considers illegal marching a serious
  offense, 154; efforts to prevent Cannon
  seating, 181; as justice, 154

Hawley, Emeline (wife of Reuben
  Maxwell), 38

Hawley, Francis "Frank" (brother of
  Emeline), 38, 39, 50, 76, 107; at Camp
  Douglas, 93; life after Civil War,
  51n10; Powder River campaign, 87

Hayes, Lucy (wife of Rutherford B.),
  183–84

Hayes, Pres. Rutherford B., 183; attends
  centennial celebration, 261, Cannon's
  letter to, 202; regarding Mormon
  theocracy and polygamy, 184

Hayne, Robert Y. (S.C. governor), 99–100

Hempstead, Maj. Charles H., 156, 161

Healington, Alfred, 217

Heritage, Mary Elizabeth (wife of
  Reuben Maxwell), 36–37

Heritage, Reuben Lewis (cousin), 48

Heywood, Joseph Leland, 26n15;
  financial difficulties led to dismissal,
  26n15; Mormon U.S. marshal, 26;
  polygamist, 26

Hickman, William Adams "Bill": admitted to murder of Richard Yates, 160, 224; among visitors to Lee in prison, 231; attorney general nomination, 224; baptized by John D. Lee, 224; cash delivery for Brigham Young, 224; as guard in Lee transfer, 222–24; leader of the Danites, 224; member of Joseph Smith's bodyguard, 224; posthumous rebaptism, 224n66; spiritual son of Brigham Young, 224; status with Mormon leaders, 224n63

Higbee, John Mount, 210

Hilton, Theophilus B., 279

Hoffman, Frank: lawyer from Ohio, 296; and Liberal Party, 296; and Maxwell's disability appeal, 291

Hoge, Enos Dougherty, 206, 218n37, 227

Holbrook, Chandler, 119

Hollister, Col. Ovander J., 90n11; address at Maxwell's grave site, 301; Internal Revenue collector, 159; shares parade stand with Maxwell, 230

Homestead Act (1862), 120n11, 134

Hooper, Samuel, 129

Hooper, William H.: congressional delegate from Utah Terr., 125; election of 1867, 152n17; election of 1870, 151; given 30,000 acres of land by legislature, 138–39; land ownership legislation for Utah Terr., 125; reports failure of Frelinghuysen bill, 165

Horrocks, James, 200–201

Houghton, Capt. Charles H., 81

Howard, Jacob M.: bill to form governance committee for Utah, 277, 278n89; informed by Maxwell of Utah issues, 277; Maxwell in his home to discuss legislation, 278

Howard, Sumner, 44n34, 230

Howath, John, 124–25

Howe, Timothy O., 253, 256n70

Humphrey, Frank J., 260

Humphreys, Gen. Andrew Atkinson, 42, 74

Humphreys, Lt. W. H., 81

Hunter, Judge John A., 192

Hyde, Orson, 95, 191

Improved Order of Red Men, 326; officers of, 269n45; Society of Red Men, 269; Sons of Liberty, 269; Washakie Tribe, 269, 269n46

Iwakura Mission, 143

Jack, James: conflict of interest, 205; payment of Brigham Young's legal fees in divorce, 238; surplus of $35,000, 205; treasurer of the Utah Terr., 205

Jackson, Pres. Andrew, 99–100

Jackson County, Mo., 110, 111

James, William F., 202

Jencks, James, 152

Jewkes, Samuel, 210

Jocelyn, Col. Stephen E., 314; address at July 4th celebration, 156; claim regarding murder of Dr. Robinson, 123

Johnston, Col. Albert Sidney, 207n1, 338

Julian, George Washington (Ind. congressman), 129

Kaughn, Col. M. M., 286

Kearny Cross, 83

Keegan, James Edward, 37

Kelsey, Eli Brazee, 148, 150; and advance of spiritualism, 149; excommunicated from LDS church, 149; supports mining efforts, 149

Kent, Alfred, 273

Kenner, Scipio Africanus, 312, 312n9

Kidd, James Harvey, 39, 51, 65, 309, 309; Custer Medal recipient, 83–84, 83n33, 308; Powder River campaign, 87; praise of First Mich. Cavalry, 51

Kimball, Brig. Gen., 55

Kimball, Anna Marian (wife of Samuel L. Sprague, Jr.), 225

Kimball, Gen. Nathan, 272; at GAR meeting, 271; brief biography of, 272n63

Kimball, Heber C., 335
Kimball, William Henry, 225, 160
Kingdom of God, 25, 149; as defined by
   Mormons, 112; rebuilding in the west,
   112; unity required, 267–68
Kingsley, J. H., 195
Kirby, A. Jack, 215; as guard in Lee
   transfer, 222; assistant deputy and
   subpoenas served in Beaver, 215
Kirby, R. M., 279
Kirkpatrick, Lydia Ann (half-sister
   of George Armstrong Custer, Mrs.
   David Reed), 41
Klingensmith, Philip, 246; appearance
   at trial, 219; confession to Mountain
   Meadows killing, 211; and fate after
   Lee trial, 219n43; flight to Nevada,
   218–19; indictment, 210; Maxwell
   moves him to safety of marshal's
   quarters, 219; Mormon bishop, 211;
   Mormon militiaman, 211; testimony at
   first trial, 219; witness for prosecution,
   210

Lakota Indians, 44; chiefs at Little Big
   Horn, 258; treaty of 1868 broken by
   whites, 259n7
Land surveys (Utah, 1847), 117
Land office, disputes in, 133–40
Land ownership: federal requirements,
   119; top-down distribution by LDS
   leaders, 118; in Utah Terr., 118–22;
   wives transfer land to husbands,
   135–36
Lannan, Patrick H., 304, 304n60
Lawrence, Henry W., 148, 171;
   candidate for mayor of Salt Lake City,
   150
Leale, Assistant Surgeon Charles
   Augustus, 77; case report of
   Maxwell's hospital course, 77; with
   Pres. Lincoln at Ford's theater, 77,
   77n18; report of operation, 77
Leonard, D. L., 279, 279
Lee, Henry Carter: brief biography of,

311n4; cavalry duel with Maxwell,
   309–11; chance encounter with
   Maxwell in Utah Terr., 310–11
Lee, John Doyle, 206, 240, 318, 344;
   acrostic poem for Patton, 229; arrest
   and trial, 148; arrest of, 211, 251;
   arrival at Nephi, 226; Brigham Young
   trusted with cash, 225; colonizer of
   southern Utah, 225; and death of
   Warden Burgher, 229–30; descriptions
   of prison life, 229; escape attempt
   foiled, 220; excommunicated from
   LDS church, 231n90; excommunication
   reversed 231n90; execution at
   Mountain Meadows, 231; on favors
   given by Maxwell and Burgher,
   228; first trial, 213, 217–22; formerly
   active Mason, 226; guard to Joseph
   Smith, 225; guilty verdict, 231;
   humorous episode with Maxwell, 223;
   indictment for Mountain Meadows
   murders, 210; journalistic skill, 225;
   journey from Beaver to Salt Lake
   City, 222–29; on Maxwell's frivolity,
   329; member of Council of Fifty,
   225; mistrial declared, 220; placed in
   irons, 226; refusal to reveal names of
   men of massacre, 231, 212; protects
   Maxwell from threats, 223; remarks
   confirm Maxwell's needs for money
   for prisoners, 229; second prosecution
   team, 231; spiritual son of Brigham
   Young, 225; and testimony of Daniel
   H. Wells, 231
Lee, Rachel (wife of John D. Lee), 228,
   213
Lee, Gen. Robert E., 47, 57, 310; at
   Five Forks, 72; and surrender at
   Appomattox, 104
Lee, Commodore Sydney Smith (father
   of Henry Carter Lee), 310
Lee, Brig. Gen. William H. Fitzhugh
   "Rooney," 71, 57. See also Cavalry
   commanders
LeFevre, Thomas, 210

Lemon, William M., 119
Liberal Institute, 143, 144, 149, 155, 155n27, 269, 326
Liberal Party, 194, 262, 293, 326; aligned with Republican Party, 150; first non-Mormon party, 148; formation of, 148–51; Maxwell at county convention, 296; Maxwell's role, 148; official organized, 150; plans for campaign of Maxwell against Cannon, 162–63; platform, 151
Lincoln, Pres. Abraham, 58; appoints Hosea Stout attorney general for Utah, 318; assassination of, 105; Emancipation Proclamation, 97; lamented magnitude of war deaths, 92; Mormon response to assassination, 105
Lincoln Mining and Smelting Company, 189n1; Maxwell part owner, 247; Lincoln mining area, 216–17. *See also* Rollins mine
Lion House, 213
Little Cottonwood Canyon, 19
Little, Feramorz: and land claim at Sandy Station, 136
Little, J. C. (Mormon bishop), 150
Little Swan Creek, 36, 46, 48
Little's Run, 60
Livingston, J., 204
Lockley, Sr., Frederic E., 21, 177n18, 203, 300n53, 316; brief biography of, 22n9; on Carey as ineffective lawyer, 218n36; claim of McKean lacking political skills, 239n17; comments on Wells flag lowering, 200, 200n36; crowds surrounding penitentiary, 239; editor of *Salt Lake Tribune*, 21; election riot, 204; empathy for John D. Lee, 222; on jurisdiction of Maxwell's critics, 254; with Maxwell in Tooele Republic dispute, 195; on McKean's final days, 276; praise for Maxwell as fire eater, 200n36; praise for Maxwell at election riot, 204n47; reaction to

mistrial of Lee, 220; release of eagle, 21; tribute at Lincoln's death, 105
Lodi Academy, 88
Logan, John Alexander, 273, 273n70
Logan bill, 339
Long, John Varah, 224
Lowenstein, Lt. Moretz, *81*
Lyman, Amasa Mason, 156, 156n29
Lyon v. Stevens (U.S. Supreme Court), 136

Mackenzie, Brig. Gen. Ranald Slidell, 314n15; Battle of Five Forks, 279; brief history and military career, 279n92, Maxwell's son named for, 279; and Mich. Cavalry Brigade, 279
Manifesto: added to *Doctrine and Covenants*, 340n32; details of origin and publication, 340n32. *See also* Woodruff, Wilford
Marshal's bond, 256
Martineau, James Henry (surveyor), 119
Masons: in Ill., 112; symbols expropriated, 113; lodges in Ill., 113
Maxwell, Charles E. (half brother), 38, 88
Maxwell, Cyrus (uncle), 32
Maxwell, Cyrus Wesley (cousin), 32, 48
Maxwell, Daniel (half brother), 38
Maxwell, Edwin Clark (half brother), 38, 88
Maxwell, Emma Belle Turner (first wife): portrait, *89*; death, 90, 90n10; burial, 90
Maxwell, Emma Elizabeth (sister), 37, *40*, 293
Maxwell, Frank Elmer (half brother), 38, 88
Maxwell, Horton Jerome "Auty" (half brother), 38
Maxwell, George (grandfather), 32
Maxwell, George R., 2, 22–23, *81*, 109, *127*, *206*, 230; accompanied to Utah Terr. by Frank Raleigh, 126; addressed as "General," 132; admits to fear, 325;

Maxwell, George R. (*continued*)
alcohol use, 296–98; Algernon
Paddock efforts for removal
overlooked, 251; Alonzo G. Paddock
blamed for his removal, 251; Alta
celebration, 21–22; altercation over
subpoena to Brigham Young, 213–14;
amiable relationship with Paddock
and wife, 290–91; ancestors trace to
Revolutionary War, 22; and author
of his newspaper eulogy, 300n53;
Ann Eliza Webb Young's divorce,
173–78; answer to criticism of prisoner
escapes, 244–45; appearance in land
office, 140; appearance at enlistment,
49–50; appointment as U.S. marshal,
167; arguments for contesting Cannon
seating, 168–69; Arizona appointment
as Indian affairs commissioner
changed, 90n11; arrest and trial of
John D. Lee, 148; arrival in Nephi
with prisoner Lee, 227; arrival with
Lee in Salt Lake City, 126; language
skills, 321–27; assigned as Register
of Land in Utah Terr., 90; assists
with trial of Thomas Hawkins, 145;
attempts for his removal from land
office, 139–40; becomes a Mason, 57;
birth, 36; broken line at Five Forks
closed, 74; burial, 301; candidates
nominated to succeed, 256n70; capable
of broad perspective, 324; care of
chronic wounds, 130–31; cause of
death, 296; celebration of passage
of Edmunds-Tucker, 293; censures
Brigham Young for nonparticipation
in Civil War, 150; chance encounter
with Henry Carter Lee in Utah Terr.,
309–11; cited at rank of general by
Confederate surgeon, 133; complaint
of prison expense never paid by
legislature, 244–45; contests seating
of Hooper, 148; contest for Hooper's
seat not successful, 152; contributions
in Utah Terr., 343–46; control of

crowd at Lee trial, 218; critical of
excessive land claims for cities, 137;
criticisms confirmed truth of his
pleas for money, 246–50; Custer's
praise of, 68; death of, 296; decides
on second run against Cannon, 162;
defines heroism, 319–20; delegation
from Utah meeting with Pres. Grant,
255; described as aging, 285; desperate
need for money, 233; dichotomous
evaluations by Mormons, non-
Mormons, 115–16; difficulties serving
warrants, 215; difficulties of daily
living, 130–31; difficulty ambulating,
131; drawing depicting amputation, 79;
editorial eulogy, 299–300; efforts for
relief bill, 265–66; efforts to influence
Lee's confession, 227; efforts to
obtain federal monies, 235–37; efforts
to reclaim land taken by Brigham
Young, 262; election volunteer, 263;
encounter with Sen. Beverly Douglas,
267; enforcing unpopular law, 212;
enlistment papers signed by Prof.
Welch, 49; envisions Utah's future
after polygamy, 324; expenses of
Ricks trial, 237; extensive newspaper
coverage of his financial crisis, 247,
247n46; failure to suspect Timothy
O. Howe, 253; featured speaker at
Decoration Day, 215; fights against
voting practices, 148; financial crisis,
196–98, 236–37; first commander of
the McKean Post of GAR, 271; forces
seeking his removal as marshal, 233;
as former active Mason, 226; founding
and sustaining of GAR in Utah, 344;
frequent appeals for increase in
disability allowance, 289–90; friend
of many federal appointees, 313–14;
friendship with John D. Lee, 320–21;
funeral service, 301; GAR expansion
beyond Utah Terr., 272–73; gift of
gold watch and chain by lawyers of
Salt Lake City, 245; gunshot wound

to left knee, 76; hero laurels in Civil War, 309; home in Salt Lake City burgled, 189; honorary carriage ride on Memorial Day, 294; humorous episode with John D. Lee, 223; humorous story of eggs in liquor bottle, 315; illegal marching, 154; inability to house prisoners, 196–98; infection complications leading to death, 298; innuendo of alcohol abuse, 235; instructed to act on illegal timer cutting, 138; intolerant of ridicule of war injuries, 267; investment in Rollins mine, 216, 216n34; involvement in Gentile League, 148; joins lawyers of Salt Lake to honor Judge Boreman, 315–16; July 4th oration in Corinne, Utah Terr., 126; kindnesses to Lee, 227; language conveys mental images, 325; law partnership with Brearley, 257, 257n1; law partnership with Goldthwait, 270; law practice in Salt Lake City, 262; length of service in Civil War, 47; lenient with Lee, 213; letter to Pierrepont anticipates expense of Lee trial, 249–50; Liberal Party representative at county convention, 293; lives two different lives, 307; lives in Washington to work on Edmunds Bill, 277; living in Washington, 266; lobbying in Congress for legislation, 148; lobbyist for Poland at own expense, 190; lodges with Sprague family, 187–88; mandamus for removal of women voters, 192; marriage in Salt Lake City and/or Corinne, 333; marriage to Emma Belle Turner, 88; marriage to Mary Ann Sprague, 185, 186n47; meeting Ann Eliza Young in Washington, 180; memorial to Congress against Utah statehood, 144; merits hero recognition, 346; in Michigan en route to Washington, 265; Mich. State Normal School,

38–40; mining legislation, 189; mining ventures, 189n1; Monroe register of deeds, 89; move of Klingensmith to personal quarters, 219; multiple wounds, 80; "next best friend" of Ann Eliza Young, 176–77; newspaper death notices, 299; no evidence of financial gain, 247; no middle ground on Mormon against non-Mormon issues, 321; nominated as candidate of Liberal Party for congressional seat, 151; old antagonisms with policemen of election riot, 204; opportunities missed in land office, 131; opposes bail for Brigham Young, 160; opposing evaluations of Mormons and non-Mormons, 329–30; orations that stir emotions, 326; orator for July 24, 1869, celebration in Corinne, 150; other Utah delegates meet with Pres. Grant, 255; pallbearers at funeral, 301n54; penniless at death, 328; pension increased slightly, 292; phantom pain in missing leg, 130; pistol serenade at Fort Cameron, 221; possible narcotic use, 298; pretrial duties in Beaver, 215; preparations for battle, 72–73; promotion despite disability, 69; prosecutes Brigham Young for lascivious cohabitation, 148; prosecution of George Reynolds, 148; qualified in law, 89; reasons for enlistment, 48; recovery from amputation, 78–79; recurring tragedies, 327–29; Reform Club, 297; as Register of Land, 23; rejects Mormon money for Decoration Day, 270; release from post as marshal, 256, 256n71; renewed efforts with Christiancy, 262–63; reorganizes Liberal Party, 277; replaced by William Nelson, 231; report of attempts to bribe newspapers, 182; request for $75,000 to build penitentiary on Antelope Island, 249;

Maxwell, George R. (*continued*)
request for deficiency bill of $30,000,
250; request for investigation of his
finances, 242; resolution honoring
Custer, 260–61; retainer and
contingency fee in case of Ann Eliza
Young, 175–76; return to Monroe
after discharge, 88; Reynolds trial not
intended as test case, 200–202; role
in divorce of Ann Eliza Webb Dee
Young, 148; role in first non-Mormon
political party, 148; role in GAR in
Ogden, 272; runs for congressional
seat, 148; sailor on Lake Erie, 46;
schooling, 37; seating of Cannon
contested, 148; self-deprecating,
322, 329; social life, 313; speaks at
Lindsay Gardens, 285; speaks for
Ann Eliza Young at Walker House
reception, 182; speaks to GAR groups
en route to National Encampment,
275; starts campaign against Cannon,
162; storms flaming bridge, 55;
street appearance, 131; support by
Michigan congressional delegation,
253; surveying conflicts inherited,
121; taken prisoner, 55; thanks GAR
for action on flag resolution, 288;
temperance pledge, 297; "Thunderbolt
of Sheridan," 23; toast to the Cavalry
of the Army of the Potomac, 290;
toast to Confederate and Union
veterans, 294; total disability
discharge, 80; transfer of Lee to
Warden Burgher, 227; transfer to
Cavalry Corps Hospital at City Point,
Va., 76; trip to Washington to obtain
money, 249; umpire for veterans
baseball game, 294; unwilling to give
up and leave Utah Terr., 321; urgent
visit to Monroe, 238; warnings in
court over lack of funds in Lee trial,
246; Wells, Stout, and Cannon not
suspected in removal, 253; wife's
concerns about alcohol use, 297;

willing object of humor, 322, 329;
with wife Mary Ann when injured
in carriage crash, 167; works for
reimbursement, 267; writes will, 296
Maxwell, Mary Ann Sprague (wife),
185, 225–26; burial, 305; death
of, 304, 305; describes husband's
limitation in activities of daily living,
289–90; funeral, 305; letter regarding
husband's alcohol use, 297; probate
of estate, 304, 304n61; problems
receiving husband's death benefits,
303; relationship with Ellen Kay
Robinson, 225n68; remittance of tax
bill, 303; unable to afford assistance
caring for husband, 289; works for
Liberal Party, 263; writes will, 304
Maxwell, Mary Emma (daughter),
276–77
Maxwell, Reuben D. (cousin), 48
Maxwell, Reuben R. (father), 32; and
move to Michigan, 35–36; death, 280
Maxwell, Robert Mackenzie (son), 279
Maxwell, Sarah Rosetta (half sister), 37
Maxwell, Thompson (great-
grandfather), 31–32, 32n3, 35; birth,
31; death and burial, 32; French and
Indian War, Revolutionary War, War
of 1812, 31–32; government pension of,
32n3; land on Raisin River, 32, 32n2;
marriages of, 31n1
Maxwell, Wallace "Willis" Grant (half
brother), 38, 88
Maxwell, William B. (brother), 42, 48;
birth, 37; death, 70, 328
Maxwell, William S. (son), 265
McAllister, John D. T.: destroys
Englebrecht liquor store, 161; disrupts
meeting of non-Mormons, 150; as Salt
Lake police officer, 161; territorial
marshal, 150
McAusland, William (deputy marshal),
205
McBride, John R., 192, 231
McBride, Willis P., 260

McClernand, John Alexander: Utah commissioner, 301; at Maxwell's funeral, 301; and adding John McFarlane to Lee defense team, 218n37

McGrorty, William H., 152n17

McKean, Judge James Bedell, 160, 161, 177, 182, 230, 253, 257, 260, 273, 298, 314, 327, 328; appointed by Grant, 159; arrest of Brigham Young for lascivious cohabitation, 160–61; arrest of Brigham Young for murder of Richard Yates, 160–61; brief biography of, 159n45; Cannon's criticism of, 171; capable of reasoned analysis, 239n17; censure of George E. Whitney as cause of removal, 239n17; charges Brigham Young with contempt of court, 238; death of, 275, 276n81; debt owed him by Pres. Grant, 276n83; decline after removal from bench, 276; depression described by Lockley, 276; dynamics behind removal by Grant, 239n17; final days described, 276; GAR post named for him, 293; judge in the Robinson murder trial, 144; letters pleading for interview with Grant, 239n17; mandamus for release of Tooele records, 194; Mormons hail his death, 276; prison ordered for Brigham Young, 238; telegram from Pres. Grant releasing him from office, 239; tributes, 275–76; wedding of Maxwell and Mary Ann Sprague, 275; warns Maxwell to adjourn courts, 236

McKee bill, 339

McLeod, Rev. Norman, 270; comments on Maxwell, 313; lobbies for Frelinghuysen Bill, 164

McMillin, Duncan J., 279

McMillan, S. A., 260

McNiece, Rev. Robert G.: address at Maxwell's funeral, 301; at Mary Ann Maxwell's funeral, 305; condemnation of polygamy, 279; corroborates account of James Horrocks, 202; pastor of First Presbyterian Church, 279

Meacham, Maj. Frank, 293

Meade, Maj. Gen. George G., 23, 65; takes command at Gettysburg, 58

Medal of Honor awards: Christiancy, 43n31, Miller, 61n32, Shepard, 308

Merriam, Clinton Levi, 169; resolution to investigate seating of Cannon, 181; resolution contesting Cannon's seat, 169

Merritt, Samuel Augustus, 190, 192; works for passage of Frelinghuysen Bill, 165

Merritt, Brig. Gen. Wesley, 303

Mich. Cavalry Brigade, 23, 40, 79, 302; at Gettysburg, 60–62; casualties experienced, 80; mounts color-matched, 82; reputation for bravery, 82; units making up, 80

Mich. State Normal School, 38–40, 49, 88, 308, 308n1, 309

Mich. Veteran Cavalry, 51, 51n10; Powder River campaign, 51

Military action against Mormons: annihilation calls from Calif., 337; calls for violence from Protestant pulpits, 338; Connor threatens battle with Mormon militia, 337; Connor's threats before Committee on Territories, 337, 337n21; *Harper's Weekly* calls for military solution, 337; rumors of violence by General Harney, 338; Sherman cautions over movement of troops to Utah, 337; urged by Rev. Talmage of N.Y., 337; in Utah War of 1857, 336–37

Millennial Star, 152

Miller, G. D. B., 279

Miller, Capt. William E., 61, 61n32

Missouri-Mormon war of 1838, 96

Monroe Commercial, 42; resolution honoring Custer, 260; eulogy for Reuben Maxwell, 280

Monroe, Pres. James, 36

Monroe County, Mich., 48n4

Moore, John M., 216, 271

Mormon: beliefs summarized, 111–12; block voting, 113; church, 25; irreconcilable polarization, 114–15; polygamists and flight from marshals after Edmunds bill, 281–82; scriptures, 34n5. *See also Book of Mormon*

Mormons: converts from British Isles and Scandinavia, 114; disengagement from the Civil War, 24; longest campaign of overt civil disobedience in American history, 26, 26n13; persecution courted, 114, 336; three civil wars invoked, 114; unique perceptions of the Civil War, 345; uninvolved in Civil War, 345; violated federal mail, 114

Mormon "Richelieu," 163, 163n58. *See also* Cannon, George Q.

Morrill Anti-bigamy Act of 1862, 158; not enforced, 103; provisions of, 103n58

Morrill, Justin S. (sen. from Vt.), 129

Morris, Elias, 213

Morrow, Gen. Henry Andrew, 154; brief biography of, 314n15; commander of Camp Douglas, 314n16; housing of prisoners, 196; military career, 157n32; war service similar to Maxwell's, 314; wounded at Gettysburg, 196n25

Mount Olivet Cemetery, 265, 272, 277, 279, 301, 302

Mountain Meadows massacre: emigrants attacked, 208; Calif. volunteers to exterminate Mormons, 209n5; emigrants surrender, 208; grand jury investigation, 210; number killed not known, 208, 208n3; seventeen children spared, 209; warrants issued, 210

Murray, Eli Houston: certificate of election to Allen Campbell, 281; at celebration ball, 293; Utah Terr. governor, 281

Murphy, Francis, 297

"Next best friend" (legal term), 176–77

National Christian Temperance Union, 297

National Republican, 182

Nauvoo, Ill., 110, 113–14

Navarre, Francois, 32

Negley, John Scott, 190

Nelson, William, 260, 300n53; appointment as U.S. marshal, 256; attests to Maxwell's debility, 289; editor of *Tribune*, 300n53; financial problems, 191; in second trial of Lee, 231; nominated by Howe and Rusk to succeed Maxwell, 256n70; request of office inventory from Maxwell, 258

New York Evening Post, 124

New York Times, 267

New Jerusalem: advantages, 133–34; model of community, 133–34; settlement of, 125. *See also* City of Zion

New Movement, 148. *See also* Godbeites; Godbe, William Samuel

Newman, John Philip: chaplain of the Senate, 143; debates Orson Pratt, 143; Methodist minister, 143; pastor of Metropolitan Methodist Church in Washington, D.C., 143, 143n91

Ninth Mich. Infantry, 48

Nobel, David A., 89

Non-Mormon(s): beliefs summarized, 113–14; interface with Mormons defined by conflict, 109; irreconcilable polarization, 114–15; request for Utah statehood to be withheld, 143

Nounnan, James H., 260

Nye, Sen. James (Nev.), 159

Nye, W. H., 273

Oakden, Charles, 125

"Off to see the elephant," 47–48, 47n1

Ogden Junction, 202

Oglesby, Richard, 273

Oquirrh mountain range, 122, 194

Orr, James Milton: confrontation with Mayor Wells, 203; as deputy marshal in congressional election riot, 203; lawyer, 142; unsuccessful filing for land, 142

Ottinger, George M., 153

"Pablo" (Washington correspondent), 277, 278n89

Paddock, Algernon S., 167, 241

Paddock, Alonzo G.: appointment a sinecure granted out of pity, 251; Maxwell dismisses as prison warden, 241; nominated by Merritt and Rosborough to succeed Maxwell, 256n70; nomination for marshal position, 241

Paddock, Cornelia "Nellie" (wife of Alonzo): and abuse, poverty of women in Utah Terr., 252n58; author of books about women in polygamy, 252n58; and mandamus regarding suffrage, 192; non-Mormon voice of social conscience, 252n58; opinion of polygamy, 291n25

Palmyra, N.Y., 22, 33, 110

Panguitch, Utah Terr., 211

Patrick, Mathewson T., 176, 196, 233, 251; arrest warrant for Brigham Young, 160; delegate with Maxwell to meet Pres. Grant, 255; financial problems, 191; U.S. marshal who preceded Maxwell, 141, 160

Patton, Oliver Andrew, 314; and acrostic poem by John D. Lee, 320; among many visitors to Lee in prison, 231; Civil War activities, 228n78; meeting Pres. Grant, 255; gift of newspaper to Lee, 228; letter praising Maxwell, 248; on visits to Lee in prison, 228; wife as cousin to Pres. Grant, 255n68

Pottenger, Willett, 228

Penrose, Charles W., 262, 300n53

People's Party (Mormon), 151, 194

Perris, Frederick Thomas, 162

Phelps, William W., 118–19

Phillips, S. F.: appointment as acting attorney general, 242; continued criticism of Maxwell, 243; incorrect accusations, 242; support of Edmund Wilkes as Maxwell's replacement, 242; unreceptive to Maxwell's pleas, 242

Phillips, William G., 204, 287n12

Pickett, Maj. Gen. George Edward, 63, 71–72, 71n2, 75

Pierce, Pres. Franklin, 26n15

Pierrepont, Atty. Gen. Edwards: low opinion of Mormons, 243; Maxwell's letter anticipating expenses of Lee trial, 249–50; successor to Williams as atty. gen., 242

Pike, Sgt. Ralph, 186, 224

Pleasonton, Maj. Gen. Alfred, 54, 57

Poland Act, 148, 168, 173, 182, 198, 207, 242, 251, 332, 344, 339; arrests for Mountain Meadows massacre authorized, 210; contains provisions of the Frelinghuysen Bill, 167; credit for passage due Ann Eliza Young, 182–83; federal funding of law enforcement, 205; new grand jury indictments for Mountain Meadows murders, 210; passes, 190; provisions, 190; seeds of financial disaster for Maxwell, 190–91

Polygamy, 192; begun in Ill., 109, 109n1; beneficent neglect during Civil War, 103; as cause of Mormon–non-Mormon conflict, 109; initially denied by leaders, 113; and Joseph Smith, 112;

Pond, James Burton, 178, 178n23, 179; rumors of liaison with Ann Eliza Young, 180–81

Pool, Sen. John:,165

Porter, C. P., 81

Porter, H. L., 250; criticism of Maxwell, 247; denial of criticisms of Maxwell, 247; father doubted son's accusations, 247

Porter, Samuel, 125

Pottenger, Willett, 167, 252

Powder River Expedition, 87, 87n1, 93

Pratt, Arthur (deputy marshal), 250; account of events of Reynolds trial for polygamy, 201–202; career of, 251n55;

Pratt, Arthur (deputy marshal) (*continued*) excommunication for anti-polygamy stance, 214n25; James Horrocks with indictment of Reynolds, 201–202; opinion that Amos K. Smith to blame for financial matters, 246; role in Reynolds conviction for polygamy, 201–202; son of Orson Pratt, 214n25; subpoena to Brigham Young, 213; trial of second wife of Reynolds, 201–202

Pratt, Orson, 99, 117

Pratt, Sarah M. Bates (first wife of Orson Pratt), 214n25

Preemption Act of 1841, 118, 134

Prescott, George F., 183

Quinn, Michael D., 340n32, 343

Raisin River, 36

Raleigh, Frank, 89; accompanies Maxwell to Utah, 126; admitted atheist, 126; aids Maxwell in study of law, 89; assists Maxwell with medical leave requests, 126; death of, 126n34

Redpath, James C., 179

Redpath Lyceum Bureau, 179, 179n24

Reed, Emma (daughter of Lydia Ann), 316

Reed, Lydia Ann Kirkpatrick, 41; attends social meeting with Maxwell and wife, 316; half sister of George Armstrong Custer, 316

Reynolds, Maj. Gen. John F., 59, 59n25

Reynolds, George, 142; allegations of a trial case, 199n34, 199–200; conviction appealed to U.S. Supreme Court, 200; first successful prosecution in Utah Terr. for polygamy, 199–202; freedom of religion claim, 200; secretary to Brigham Young, 199; trial not intentionally instigated, 200–202; witnesses refuse facts to prove second marriage, 201

Ricks, Thomas E., 237

Riddle, Isaac, 125

Rights to timber and water, 136–39

Ringwood, Charles, 204

Robertson, Reuben Howard: as Salt Lake attorney, 158; co-authors Cullom bill, 158; toast at gathering to fete Maxwell, 245

Robinson, Ellen "Nellie" Kay, 225

Robinson, John C., 272

Robinson, Dr. John King, 154, 187, 204, 224; brief history of, 123n19; grave decorated, 230; land claim, 122–23; murder of, 123

Rochester Daily Advertiser, 34

Rockwood, Albert Perry, 141–42; author of history of Utah penitentiary, 141n84; files on land of prison site, 141; history as Mormon convert, 141n84; salary as prison warden, 142n87; territorial prison warden, 141

Rogers, Samuel S., 210

Rollins mine, 189n1, 216–17. *See also* Lincoln Mining and Smelting Company

Rucker, Gen. David Henry, 127–28

Rudisill, Lewis A., 279

Rush Valley, Utah Terr., 186, 194

Sabotage: of U.S. Army supply trains in 1857, 192n13; charges of treason against Wells, Smith, and Burton, 102, 102n55

Salisbury, Joseph, 162

Salt Lake City, 119, 174, 119; land claim exceeded legal limits, 121; water supply contaminated, 276n81

Salt Lake Herald: account alleging intervention in hearings of Maxwell, 266; cites Maxwell for fraud, 247; full account of Maxwell's letter to Pierrepont, 250; Maxwell defends of son of Alonzo G. Paddock, 290; Maxwell's claims against Cannon, 168–69; provisions of Frelinghuysen Bill, 165; report of Maxwell inebriated in court room, 290

Salt Lake Tribune, 100; account of threats against Maxwell and deputies in Beaver, 220; account of Rollins mine altercation, 217; advice about land ownership, 134; altercation at serving Brigham Young's subpoena, 213–14; city records, 244; correspondent "Pablo," 277, 278n89; description of Mormon influence on elections, 163; editorial predicting civil war over continued polygamy, 338; and Klingensmith arrest, 210; Lee's risk of assassination, 212; *Lyon v. Stevens* ruling on land filing by plural wives, 136; Maxwell's appearance, 258; Maxwell's grasp of affairs in Utah Terr., 313; Maxwell's testimony against Cannon in Congress, 170–71; need for night travel in Lee's transfer, 222; notices for sale of illegal lumber, 138; obituary note on Brigham Young, 264; plural wives filing on land claims, 135; praise for Maxwell and deputies at Lee trial, 221–22; praise for Maxwell and Merritt, 190; publication of Maxwell's imperiled financial status, 242; questions jurisdiction of Maxwell's critics, 254; report of election riot, 203; report of Maxwell's oration over Mormon flag lowering, 286; report of "Pablo" of Maxwell's ties with Mich. statesmen, 277–78; report of seating of Cannon, 182; report on accusations of sexual liaison between Ann Eliza Young and Pond, 180; tribute to an aging Maxwell, 292n30; tribute to Ann Eliza Webb Dee Young, 182–83; on women voting, 192

Sawyer, Oscar G., 313; allegations of publishing anonymous editorials by Judge McKean, 240n19; on attempts to remove Maxwell from land office, 139; editor of *Salt Lake Tribune*, 139, 240n19

Scanlan, L., 279

Schaeffer, Chief Justice Michael, 230; and award of menial wages, 241; on

ruling marriage of Ann Eliza Webb to Brigham Young not valid, 241

Schofield, Amelia Jane (second wife of George Reynolds), 201, 202

School of the Prophets, 126, 163

Scott Amendment to Edmunds-Tucker bill, 340

Second Pa. Cavalry, 56

Segregated holiday celebrations, 154

Selectman's Ford (Occoquan River), 56

Sells, Elijah: and celebration ball, 293; GAR commander, 273; Indian agent to the Southern Utes, 293; at Maxwell's funeral, 301; territorial secretary, 301

Seventh Mich. Cavalry, 43, 66, 68, 259; at Gettysburg, 60

Seventeenth Mich. Infantry, 308

Seventy-ninth N.Y. Highlanders, 285

Seward, Sec. of State William H., 100

Shaffer, Gen. John Wilson (gov. of Utah Terr.), 153, 159

Shaw, Joseph, 213

Shearman, William H., 148

Shelby, Joseph Orville, 260

Shepard, Irwin, 308

Sheridan, Gen. Philip Henry, 26, 54, 71, 80; at Centennial, 261; at Five Forks, 72; offers to avenge Custer refused, 260; visit to Utah in 1869, 127

Sherman, Gen. William Tecumseh, 71, 337; attends Centennial, 261; and total war on civilians, 92

Sherwood, Henry G., 117, 119

Sixth Mich. Cavalry, 39, 66. *See* Kidd, James Harvey

Skeen, Elisha David, 237

Slavery, in Utah Terr., 94, 94n24

Smith, Amos K. (deputy marshal): assists Maxwell with move to marshal's office, 167; as doctor, 44n34, 167, 205, 258, 258n3; elected as delegate to national veterans meeting, 270; GAR member from First Mich. Cav., 273; given books from Maxwell library, 304; Lockley praise for, 246n43; service of

Smith, Amos K. (deputy marshal)
(*continued*)
  contempt orders to Brigham Young, 238
Smith, Apostle George A., 106; claim
  of ill health, 214; death from heart
  failure, 215; deposition taken, 214;
  given timber west of Jordan river,
  137; greets federal dignitaries on
  arrival in Salt Lake City, 128; use
  of inflammatory rhetoric, 335; visits
  Maxwell on arrival in Utah, 128
Smith, F. M., 175, 175n11
Smith, Hyrum, 112
Smith, Joseph, Jr., 33–35, 110, 111, 318,
  342; candidate for U.S. presidency,
  113, Civil War prophecy not fulfilled,
  106–107; claims location of Garden
  of Eden, 96; killed, 112; as king, 113;
  multiple marriages, 112; negative
  judgments by non-Mormons, 113; and
  New Jerusalem city model, 133–34
Smith, Joseph, Sr., 33
Smith, Lot, 102, 102n55
Smoot, Reed, 341
South Carolina, 99
Spears, Benjamin A. (assistant deputy),
  212, 213, 213n23
Spencer, Howard Orson, 186
Sprague, Mary Ann (daughter), 185, *185*;
  among those moving Lee to Salt Lake
  City, 225–26; disclaimer of respect for
  Maxwell, 188; marriage, 333
Sprague, Samuel Lindsay, Jr., 225;
  among Lee's visitors in prison, 231;
  court bailiff, 225; deputy on Lee's
  move to Salt Lake City, 225; sometime
  deputy marshal, 225; volunteers for
  Liberal Party, 263
Sprague, Samuel Lindsey, Sr.: among
  those moving Lee to Salt Lake
  City, 225; attends Jedediah Morgan
  Grant, 186; on contaminated water
  from Fort Douglas, 187; and Deseret
  Agricultural and Manufacturing
  Society, 187; disclaimer of respect
  for Maxwell, 188; Eastern States

mission, 187; election riot, 204;
  first doctor in Salt Lake valley, 186;
  Flower Committee, 187; Horticultural
  Society, 187; interview by Brigham
  Young, 187–88; ministers to many, 186;
  officiates in Endowment House, 186;
  personal doctor to Brigham Young,
  186; spiritual son of Brigham Young,
  186, 225; in territorial legislature, 187;
  treats Howard Orson Spencer, 186
Springstead, H., 273
Stephenson, Benjamin Franklin, 270
St. Louis Republican, 166
Stagg, Brig. Gen. Peter, 71, 72
Stambaugh, Samuel C., 121
Stansbury, Capt. Howard, 119
Stanton, Elizabeth Cady, 156
State of Deseret, 191n7
Stenhouse, Fannie (wife of Thomas B.
  H.), 164
Stenhouse, Thomas B. H., 153, 164
Steptoe, Bvt. Lt. Col. Edward Jenner,
  335–36
Stevens, Brig. Gen. Isaac, 285, *285*
Stewart, William Cameron, 210
Stokes, William, 227; among many
  visitors to Lee in prison, 231; attempt
  to arrest Haight, Higbee, Stewart,
  and Willden, 229; background, 210,
  Civil War veteran, 210; duties in
  Beaver, lenient with Lee, 213; and
  pistol serenade at Fort Cameron, 221;
  restraint in arrest of Lee, 211
Stout, Hosea, 330; broad legal skills
  serve Mormons, 317–18; caricature,
  319; charged with murder of Richard
  Yates, 160; Mormon heavyweight, 318
Stratton, C. C., 182; adviser to Ann
  Eliza Webb Dee Young, 175–76;
  claim of blackmail 176; as Methodist
  minister, 175
Strickland, Obed Franklin, 44n34, 164,
  314; promise of volunteer company to
  avenge Custer, 260
Stringham, George A., 224n65, 231
Stuart, James Ewell Brown (J. E. B.),

54; as Confederate general, 23; at Gettysburg, 59–62. *See also* Cavalry commanders

Sully plantation (Chantilly, Va.), 323n38

Sutherland, Jabez Gridley, 192, 227; attorney for William Dame, 212; and Brigham Young's contempt charges, 240; complaints on penitentiary conditions, 212; and defense team for Lee, 218n37

Taggart, James P.: as doctor, 313; and Maxwell's disability appeal, 291; represents Rev. Newman on trip to debate polygamy, 143; war surgeon, not practicing in Utah, 291n27

Talmage, Rev. Thomas Dewitt, 337

Taylor, Apostle John, 106; on avoiding contact with non-Mormons, 332; City of Zion plan, 134; goes into hiding, 281; Mormons have no concerns with Civil War, 99; views of Civil War, 99; visits Maxwell on arrival in Utah, 128

Taylor, Pres. Zachary, 334

Terry, Maj. Gen. Alfred Howe, 291

Third Battle of Winchester, 68n60

Third Mich. Cavalry, 42

Third N.J. Cavalry, 74

Third Pa. Cavalry, 61

Thirty-eighth N.C. Infantry, 63

Thomas, Gov. Arthur Lloyd, 301

Thompson, John D.: as doctor, 132; operation on Maxwell to remove dead bone, 258; support for increase in federal pension allowance, 289n19

Thurman, Sen. Allen Granberry (Ohio), 129; on Mormons denied seating on juries, 235; judiciary committee considering Frelinghuysen Bill, 165; opponent of Mormons, 129; visits Salt Lake City, 129

Tiffany and Company, 82

Tilford, Judge Frank, 20; attorney for Ann Eliza Young in divorce, 175; brief biography of, 175n11; retainer and contingency fee, 175n11

Tompkins, Rachel Ellen (wife of Oliver Andrew Patton), 228, 255n68; connection to Jacob Smith Boreman, 228n79; cousin to Ulysses S. Grant, 228, 255n68

Toms, James, 144–45

Tooele Republic, 194–95

Toohy, Judge Dennis J., 270, 314; judge in Corinne, 156; address at July 4 celebration, 156

Townsend, George Alfred, 146; correspondent for *Cincinnati Commercial*, 311; description of Maxwell, 311–12; opposes conviction of Thomas Hawkins, 146; pseudonym of "Gath," 311. *See also* "Gath"

Trowbridge, Gen. Luther S., 60, 62

Trumbull, Sen. Lyman (Ill.), 129

Tulledge, Edward William, 144, 148, 154, 160, 162, 164; economic sanctions by "Z. C. M. I." used to defeat Frelinghuysen Bill, 166

Turk, Lt. J. G., 81

Turner, Emma Belle, 88, 89

Turner, Emma Louise (daughter of Julius), 265

Turner, Harry (son of Julius), 265

Turner, James Lawrence (father of Emma Belle Turner), 88

Turner, Julius Theodore, 294

Twelfth Va. Cavalry, 69

Twentieth Maine Infantry, 59

Twenty-fifth N.Y. Cavalry, 68

Twenty-fourth Mich. Infantry, 285

Twenty-sixth N.C. Infantry, 63, 286

United States v. Reynolds, 200

United States Penitentiary, Utah, 212, 237; costs paid from U.S. marshal's salary, 141; jailbreak and beating of Warden Burgher, 229–30

U.S. Army Corps of Topographical Engineers: first survey, 119

U.S. flag, 200

U.S. House of Representatives, 182. *See also* Committee on Territories

Utah Commission, 281, 281n96

Utah Magazine (later *Salt Lake Tribune*), 149, 149n9

Utah Methodist Episcopal Mission Conference: condemns polygamy in Utah, 278–79; congregations to seek legislation against polygamy, 278–79; report sent to Congress, newspapers, and churches, 278–79

Utah Terr., 22, 23, 44n34, 115, 207, 208, 307; atmosphere of conflict in, 24–25; considered in rebellion, 207; officers from Mich., 44n34; unequal, divisive camps of Mormons and non-Mormons, 24

Utah Territorial Penitentiary, 141. *See also* United States Penitentiary, Utah

Utah War (1857–58), 24, 208, 338; subject of intense research, many publications, 208, 209n8

Van Cott, John (terr. marshal), 26n14

Van DerVoort, Paul, 271, 274

Van Vliet, Lt. Stewart, 338

Van Zile, Philip Taylor, 44n34

Varian, Charles S., 286

Vaughn, Vernon H. (terr. gov.), 153

Veterans National Committee, 269

Veteran Soldiers and Sailors, 269

Violence arising from Mormons: from marshals pursuing polygamists, 339; intrusions into privacy, sanctity of homes, 339; violations of Mormons' constitutional rights by marshals, 339; Young's allegations that government wanted war, 339

Voorhees bill, 339

Wade, Sen. Benjamin Franklin (Ohio), 127, 158

Wade bill, 158, 339

Walker, Ronald W., 149n7, 155

Walker House Hotel, 164, 175; brief history, 182; description, 182n39

Wallace, Lt. Robert C., 83, 83n33

Wallaceville Cemetery, 32

War of Northern Aggression, 25. *See also* Civil War

War of Rebellion, 25. *See also* Civil War

Warm Springs, 122

Warren, Maj. Gen. Gouverneur K., 74n8; infantry at Five Forks, 73–74; relieved of command at Five Forks, 73n7

Warren, Lt. Robert P., 230

Wasatch Mountains, 20, 122, 222

Washington, D.C., 164, 180, 249

Washington Capital, 139

Webb, Chauncey G. (father of Ann Eliza): building of 1856 handcarts, 174; excommunicated, later restored, 174n4; Joseph Smith's grammar instructor, 173–74; opposed late start of handcart companies, 174; skilled wagonwright, 174

Webb, Ann Eliza, 173, 174

Weeks, Lt. W. C., *81*

Welch, Rev. Josiah, 20

Welch, Prof. Adonijah Strong, 38, 38n22, 49

Wells, Daniel H., 344; accused of Robinson murder, 123; caricature, *319*; challenges Deputy Orr, 203; charged with murder of Richard Yates, 160; cites Maxwell for pro bono work, 142; clothing torn in election riot, 203; commands Mormon militia, 153; commander of Nauvoo Legion, 102; "Defender of Nauvoo," 317; and guards at Lion House, 213; held in contempt, 200; hires extra police for congressional election, 203; indicted for treason, 102; inflammatory rhetoric, 335; influence on elections, 163, leader with many powers, 317; led Mormon guerrilla forces in 1857 war, 102; Mormon Militia at parade, 157; multifaceted skills, 317–18; procession on release from penitentiary, 200; sentenced to penitentiary, 200;

subpoena of Brigham Young accepted, 214; testimony in Reynolds trial, 199–200; timber- and lumber-cutting dispute, 138; and timber, lumber, grass, and water of Emigration Canyon, 137; witness at second trial of John D. Lee, 231, 317

Wells, Emmeline B. (wife of Daniel H. Wells), 183–84, 192

Wells, Spicer, 218n37, 206

Whaley, Capt. Edward A., *81*

Whedon, D. P., 215n33

Whelan, Cyrus F., 39, 50, 308

White, Hannah Pauline, 304, 304n62

White, Isaiah (doctor), 296–97, 304, 305

White, Justice Alexander, 240, 241

White, Joel, 219

Whitney, George E., 256n70

Whitney, Orson F., 147

Wickizer, Col. Joseph H., 182; with Maxwell in meeting with Pres. Grant, 255; special agent of the U.S. Post Office Department, 314

Wiem, Tom, 222

Wilkins, James R., 216, 246

Willden, Ellott, 210

Williams, U.S. Atty. Gen. George Henry, 142, 189, 205, 212, 265; allegations of misuse of funds, 196–98; criticism of Maxwell, 197; criticism over deposit of funds, 233; delay in federal money, 241; and financial panic of 1873, 197; inaction on requests for money for Utah Terr., 236; Maxwell's letter regarding arrests, financial crisis, 196–97, 198; Maxwell's pleas for money, 198; resignation of, 197; support of Maxwell's effort for reimbursement, 267; urgent pleas for money, 196–98; and voluntary retirement under duress, 242

Williams, Parley Lycurgus, 296, 285

Williams, Zina, 183–84

Williamson, Jonathan M., 122

Williamson, James A.: commissioner of the land office, 241; land agent for the Union Pacific Railroad, 241; nomination for marshalship by George Q. Cannon, 241; rule on land holding by plural wives, 136

Winn, Thomas: assistant deputy in Beaver, 210; capture of George Adair, 229

Women's Relief Corps of GAR, 273

Women's suffrage: abolished in Edmunds-Tucker Act, 268; Brigham Young endorses, 191; Congress suggests for Utah Terr., 191; provisions of, 191; Utah legislators approve, 191

Wood, Thomas Fanning, 133

Wooden Gun Marching Episode, 153–54, 204

Woodruff, Apostle Wilford: Civil War deaths avenge Joseph and Hyrum Smith, 96–97; fishing on Centennial Day, 262; late observations on Civil War, 107; manifesto of 1890, 340, 340n32; polygamy practice denounced, 340. *See also* Manifesto

Woods, Gov. George Lemuel, 313; attests to Maxwell's sobriety at election riot, 204; crowd at election riot disbursed, 204; denies Mormons funds for constitutional convention, 161; difficulties obtaining appropriations, 236; governor of Utah Terr., 161, 181; letter to Grant regarding *Englebrecht*, 161; refusal to issue election certificate to Cannon, 181–82

Wooster, S. R., 67n55

Wright, Sen. George C., 165

Young, Ann Eliza Webb Dee, 173, 344; Brigham Young abandons, 174–75; castigates Pres. Grant for mistrial, 221; claim of bribery by Mormon lawyer George Cesar Bates, 180n28; credit for Poland Act passage, 182; divorce from Brigham Young,

Young, Ann Eliza Webb Dee
(*continued*)
174–78; divorce settlement, 237–41; last
speech, 184; letter to Lucy Hayes, 183;
marriage to Moses R. Deming, 184;
opinion of Utah women voters, 192;
penniless from fighting rumors, 183;
reaction to Lee mistrial, 221; return to
Salt Lake City welcome, 182; visit to
House of Representatives, 180
Young, Brigham, 153, 166, 170, 172,
173, 178, 185, 327,330, 338, 344;
apology to Maxwell, 214; argument
over bail, 160; assigns motives to
federal appointees, 335; caricature,
319; Centennial not celebrated, 262;
characterized by non-Mormons, 114;
charges dismissed by *Englebrecht*, 161;
Civil War as prelude to millennium,
101–102; Civil War prophecies not
fulfilled, 106–107; claim of invalidism,
214, 215n30; confrontation with de
Trobriand, 157–58; contempt charges,
238; crooks finger to order killing,
316–17, 317n24; curse on Christiancy,
262–63; death of, 263–64; deposition
taken, 214; divorce advice to Ann
Eliza Webb Dee, 174; divorce
settlement, 237–41; first knowledge
of *Book of Mormon*, 34; influence
on elections, 163; insults to civil
servants, 335; land claim at Sandy

Station, 136; Machiavellian tactics,
317; meeting with Granberry and
Morrill, 129; monarchical ruler, 342;
most powerful man in Utah Terr., 177;
non-Mormon's response to his death,
264; papers for divorce served, 176;
polygamy affirmed as doctrine, 112;
prayer cited by editor Goodwin, 100;
predictions about Civil War, 99–100;
prediction of Civil War involving
Great Britain, 104; prison sentence
one day, 238; professed loyalty to
United States, 100; profits by closure
of Fort Crittenden, 103, 103n56; reign
of Satan, 101; rhetoric inflammatory,
334–36; on Robinson and his murder,
123–24; self-interest motivates federal
officers, 147; to southern Utah to
avoid arrest, 160; subpoena for
testimony in Beaver, 213; summons
Samuel Sprague and daughter Mary
Ann, 187–88; suspicious of surveyors,
119–20; teachings about blacks, 95;
threat of expulsion of federal officers,
129; timber, minerals, and water of
City Creek Canyon, 137; troops of
de Trobriand threatened, 157; troops
to Utah seen as persecution, 207;
vow regarding soldiers contact with
Mormon women, 335

Zane, Chief Justice Charles S., 301